Reparations by Non-State Armed Groups under International Law

This book examines whether and how non-state armed groups might be required to provide reparations for the harm caused by their violations of international law committed during situations of non-international armed conflict.

Most of today's armed conflicts are waged between states and non-state armed groups or between such groups. Societies ravaged by these conflicts endure extensive harm resulting from violations of international humanitarian law and international human rights law. This reality prompts a series of pressing questions. Akin to states, should non-state armed groups be held responsible for making reparation when violating international law? And if so, what measures can these groups take to repair the harm they have caused? The book begins by clarifying if there exists, in contemporary international law, a duty for armed groups to provide reparation. It considers whether non-state armed groups have primary international obligations as distinct duty bearers, and whether reparation can be one of the legal consequences when violating these obligations. Subsequently, the book sheds new light on how non-state armed groups' duty of reparation can be operationalised in international law. This involves elucidating both the conceptualisation and practical application of this duty. Combining this legal analysis with practical perspectives, the book unveils important insights for international law, drawn from an in-depth analysis of Colombia's experiences with reparations by armed groups in the context of transitional justice.

This book will be of interest to scholars and practitioners working in the fields of international law related to armed conflict, accountability and redress, and transitional justice more broadly.

Olivia Herman is a practitioner and researcher in the fields of international law and transitional justice. She holds a PhD in International Law from the KU Leuven and has worked across civil society, academia, and international organisations.

Transitional Justice

Series editor
Kieran McEvoy, *Queen's University Belfast, UK*

for information about the series and details of previous and forthcoming titles, see https://www.routledge.com/Transitional-Justice/book-series/TRANJ

A GlassHouse book

Reparations by Non-State Armed Groups under International Law

From Conflict to Repair in Colombia and Beyond

Olivia Herman

Routledge
Taylor & Francis Group
LONDON AND NEW YORK

First published 2025
by Routledge
4 Park Square, Milton Park, Abingdon, Oxon OX14 4RN

and by Routledge
605 Third Avenue, New York, NY 10158

Routledge is an imprint of the Taylor & Francis Group, an informa business

a GlassHouse book

British Library Cataloguing-in-Publication Data
A catalogue record for this book is available from the British Library

Library of Congress Cataloging-in-Publication Data
Names: Herman, Olivia, 1991- author.
Title: Reparations by non-state armed groups under international law : from conflict to repair in Colombia and beyond / Olivia Herman.
Description: Abingdon, Oxon [UK] ; New York, NY : Routledge, 2024. | Series: Transitional justice | Includes bibliographical references and index.
Identifiers: LCCN 2023056740 (print) | LCCN 2023056741 (ebook) | ISBN 9781032512389 (hardback) | ISBN 9781032512396 (paperback) | ISBN 9781003401292 (ebook)
Subjects: LCSH: Reparation (Criminal justice)--Colombia. | Liability for human rights violations--Colombia. | Non-state actors (International relations)--Colombia. | War (International law) | Reparation (Criminal justice) | Liability for human rights violations. | Non-state actors (International relations) | Victims of crimes--Legal status, laws, etc. | Criminal justice, Administration of.
Classification: LCC KHH1011 .H47 2024 (print) | LCC KHH1011 (ebook) | DDC 341.6/6--dc23/eng/20231214
LC record available at https://lccn.loc.gov/2023056740
LC ebook record available at https://lccn.loc.gov/2023056741

ISBN: 978-1-032-51238-9 (hbk)
ISBN: 978-1-032-51239-6 (pbk)
ISBN: 978-1-003-40129-2 (ebk)

DOI: 10.4324/9781003401292

Typeset in Sabon
by Taylor & Francis Books

Contents

Acknowledgements xi
List of Abbreviations xiii

Introduction 1

I.1 Setting the scene 1
I.2 Definition of the key concepts 8
I.2.1 Non-state armed group 8
I.2.2 Responsibility 10
I.2.3 Reparation 12
I.3 Scope of the book 13
I.4 Design and structure of the book 15

PART I
Duty of non-state armed groups to provide reparation under current international law 19

1 Non-state armed groups as distinct entities under international law 21

1.1 Introduction 21
1.2 International legal personality of non-state actors 22
1.3 International humanitarian law 27
1.3.1 Situating the discussion 27
1.3.2 The application of Common Article 3 and Additional Protocol II to non-state armed group 28
1.3.3 Theories on how international humanitarian law binds non-state armed groups 33
1.3.4 The scope of the international legal personality of non-state armed groups 37

1.4 International human rights law 40
1.4.1 The application of human rights law beyond the state 40
1.4.2 Non-state armed groups as duty bearers 42
1.4.3 A context-dependent approach to the application of human rights law 44
1.5 Conclusions 49

2 Existing international law frameworks, approaches and building blocks for reparations by non-state armed groups 52

2.1 Introduction 52
2.2 International responsibility of non-state armed groups and their duty to repair: a preliminary assessment 52
2.2.1 Reparation for wrongful acts as a fundamental principle of international law 52
2.2.2 International humanitarian law 55
2.2.3 International human rights law 60
2.2.4 International criminal law 61
2.2.5 Contemporary responses to violations committed by non-state armed groups 63
2.2.6 A responsibility gap in current international law regulating armed conflict 67
2.3 Recognition that non-state armed groups should provide reparation 69
2.3.1 Historical precedent in the laws of insurgency and belligerency 70
2.3.1.1 The general legal frameworks of insurgency and belligerency 70
2.3.1.2 Reparations by non-state armed groups in situations of belligerency and insurgency 71
2.3.2 Contemporary evidence in domestic jurisdictions and state practice 79
2.3.2.1 United States of America 79
2.3.2.2 Northern Ireland and Colombia 82
2.3.2.3 Agreements concluded between states and non-state armed groups 83
2.3.3 UN Basic Principles and Guidelines 86
2.3.4 UN practice 91
2.3.5 The practice of truth commissions 97
2.3.6 International expert documents 99
2.4 Conclusions 102

PART 2
Establishing a duty for non-state armed groups to provide reparation 105

3 Character of an international responsibility regime for non-state armed groups 107

3.1 Introduction 107
3.2 The law of state responsibility 108
3.2.1 Non-state armed groups in the ILC Articles on the Responsibility of States for Internationally Wrongful Acts 108
3.2.1.1 State responsibility in the case of government or state formation 110
3.2.2 Taking the law of state responsibility as a baseline 114
3.3 Individual criminal responsibility 117
3.3.1 The criminal responsibility of group members and its limitations 117
3.3.2 The collective criminal responsibility of non-state armed groups 122
3.3.2.1 An appraisal 122
3.3.2.2 An evaluation of the law and practice of international criminal courts and tribunals 124
3.4 A proposal for a new sui generis *regime of international responsibility for non-state armed groups 130*
3.5 Conclusions 134

4 Operationalising a duty for non-state armed groups to provide reparation 135

4.1 Introduction 135
4.2 Feasibility of obtaining reparations from non-state armed groups 135
4.3 Cascading regime of responsibility for reparation 138
4.4 Conceptualising a duty of non-state armed groups to provide reparation 143
4.4.1 Actor-specific approach 143
4.4.2 Principle of full reparation 147
4.4.3 Forms of reparations 149
4.4.3.1 Restitution 150
4.4.3.2 Compensation 150

4.4.3.3 Rehabilitation 151
4.4.3.4 Satisfaction 152
4.4.3.5 Guarantees of non-repetition 154
4.5 Reparations by non-state armed groups during and after armed conflict 154
4.5.1 Engagement on reparations during and at the end of an armed conflict 155
4.5.2 Post-conflict reparations 160
4.5.2.1 Asset tracing and recovery for reparations purposes 161
4.5.2.2 Representation order in civil proceedings 162
4.5.2.3 Actors with representative authority 165
4.6 Conclusions 175

PART 3
Insights from the operationalisation of reparations by non-state armed groups in Colombia 177

5 Reparations by the AUC under the Justice and Peace Law 179

5.1 Introduction 179
5.2 An overview of the Justice and Peace Law 181
5.3 The raison d'être *of the Justice and Peace Law 185*
5.4 Scope of application 186
5.4.1 Organised armed groups at the margins of the law 186
5.4.2 The AUC under the Justice and Peace Law 188
5.4.3 Concluding insights on non-state armed groups as responsible actors 191
5.5 Monetary compensation 191
5.5.1 The collective duty to hand over illegally obtained goods 191
5.5.2 Ruling C-370/06: introducing a cascading responsibility scheme 194
5.5.2.1 Solidarity civil responsibility of non-state armed groups 196
5.5.3 Anonymous harm 198
5.5.4 Fund for the Reparation of the Victims: order of affection 200
5.5.5 Concluding insights for non-state armed groups under international law 202

5.5.5.1 Operationalising the obligation to provide monetary compensation 202
5.5.5.2 Rearranged cascading regime of responsibility for monetary compensation 203
5.5.5.3 Special criminal proceedings as a forum for reparations 204
5.6 *Other forms of reparations 205*
5.6.1 Satisfaction 205
5.6.1.1 Apology and recognition of responsibility 205
5.6.1.2 The building of a monument 206
5.6.1.3 The rebuilding of a health centre 206
5.6.2 Guarantees of non-repetition 208
5.6.3 Concluding insights on engagement in satisfaction and guarantees of non-repetition 209
5.7 *Conclusions 209*

6 Reparations by the FARC-EP under the Comprehensive System for Truth, Justice, Reparation and Non-Repetition 211

6.1 *Introduction 211*
6.2 *Comprehensive transitional justice system with a reparations component 212*
6.3 *Responsibility and reparation 215*
6.3.1 Recognition of the FARC-EP's responsibility and duty to contribute to reparation 215
6.3.2 Concluding insights on non-state armed groups' international responsibility and their duty to repair 220
6.4 *Understanding the FARC-EP as a responsible actor 221*
6.4.1 During and before the end of the armed conflict 221
6.4.2 Post armed conflict 225
6.4.2.1 Political transformation of the FARC-EP 225
6.4.2.2 Representative authority of the political party and former high-level commanders 228
6.4.2.3 Nature of the successor entity's responsibility 230
6.4.3 Concluding insights on non-state armed groups as responsible actors 232
6.5 *Engagement of the FARC-EP in the comprehensive reparations measures for peacebuilding 234*
6.5.1 Introductory remarks 234

6.5.2 Early acts of acknowledgement of collective responsibility 234
6.5.3 Concrete actions of contribution to reparations 236
6.5.3.1 General framework 236
6.5.3.2 Humanitarian demining 239
6.5.3.3 Search for the disappeared 241
6.5.3.4 Some challenges 243
6.5.4 Collective goods and assets for material reparations 244
6.5.5 Concluding insights on non-state armed group's engagement regarding reparations 246
6.6 *Conclusions* 248

Conclusion 250

C.1 *The duty of non-state armed groups to provide reparation at an incipient stage in international law* 250
C.2 *A multifaceted proposal for operationalising a duty of non-state armed groups to provide reparation under international law* 254
C.3 *Concluding insights from reparations by non-state armed groups in Colombia* 258
C.4 *Final remarks* 263

Annex 1 List of Interviews 265
Index 267

Acknowledgements

I received invaluable support, guidance and generosity from many persons while writing this book. Although I cannot list all of them here, I take this opportunity to acknowledge at least some of those who have left an important mark on this journey.

I want to start by sincerely thanking my PhD supervisors Prof. Jan Wouters and Prof. Stephan Parmentier at the KU Leuven, Belgium. Their guidance, support and trust were instrumental during the various stages of completing my PhD dissertation, on which this book is based. I also greatly benefitted from the support and feedback provided by the members of my PhD Supervisory Committee: Prof. Felipe Gómez Isa and Prof. Cedric Ryngaert. I feel honoured that, along with my supervisors, Prof. Felipe Gómez Isa, Prof. Katharine Fortin and Prof. Letizia Paoli evaluated this research as members of the PhD Examination Committee. I would like to express my gratitude for their thorough and generous feedback. I also thank Prof. Jacques Herbots for chairing this Committee with a great sense of humour. A special note of appreciation goes to Prof. Katharine Fortin and Prof. Kieran McEvoy, whose encouragement was the necessary push to turn my dissertation into this book.

Over the years, I was fortunate to receive stimulating feedback on different parts and aspects of the research from researchers, practitioners, colleagues and friends. These persons include, among many others, Prof. Juana Acosta, Prof. Katharine Fortin, Lene Guercke, Laura Íñigo Álvarez, Fin-Jasper Langmack, Prof. Luke Moffett, Nina Pineau, Prof. Nelson Camilo Sánchez León, Prof. Camilo Umaña, Thomas van Poecke and Nele Verlinden. I also received valuable comments from other researchers during my research stay at the University of Vienna. I thank Prof. Stephan Wittich for being so welcoming and for his encouragements. My thanks also go to the anonymous reviewer at Routledge whose suggestions and comments helped improve the manuscript of the book.

For my research on Colombia, I extend sincere thanks to Prof. Felipe Gómez Isa for hosting me at the University of Deusto. His support greatly contributed to the design of the case studies and the organisation of the field research. During this time, I benefitted strongly from insightful conversations with other researchers working on Colombia, particularly Liliana Zambrano Quintero, Maria del Pilar Bernal-Gómez and Pablo Cortés Ferrández, as well as with

María Clara Calle. I also thank Director Gorka Urrutia Asua for welcoming me at the Pedro Arrupe Human Rights Institute.

I am deeply grateful for the hospitality and support I experienced during my field research in Colombia. I start by expressing my heartfelt gratitude to the persons who shared their experiences and views with me. I thank Prof. Manuel E. Salamanca for hosting and welcoming me at the Pontificia Universidad Javeriana, in Bogotá. At the Instituto de Estudios Interculturales, in Cali, I received invaluable support from Grace Boffey, for which I am extremely grateful. I further thank Gaia Pagano and other researchers at the Institute for their assistance and participation in my research. Other persons have supported my field research in important and various ways, including Prof. Camilo Umaña, Prof. Susan Brewer-Osorio, Prof. Pedro Valenzuela, Mariana Casij Peña and Daniel Marín. I am particularly indebted to Manuel Alejandro Albarracín Pinzón, for his hospitality, friendship and support. I owe thanks to Emerita, Fernando and Paola for their generosity and assistance. I also extend my gratitude to Laura Baron-Mendoza for her help, prior to my stay in Colombia. The same holds for Isabella Bueno, who kindly shared her insightful research on Colombia with me.

I am grateful for the generous PhD fellowship awarded by the Research Foundation – Flanders (FWO), which allowed me to carry out this research project. I would also like to thank the FWO for their support in funding the fieldwork underpinning the research on Colombia. I am indebted to the KU Leuven, which offered me invaluable opportunities for professional and personal growth as a student and later as a researcher.

Parts of the analysis in this book are based on a previous publication: Olivia Herman, 'Beyond the State of Play: Establishing a Duty of Non-State Armed Groups to Provide Reparations' (2020) 102 International Review of the Red Cross 1033–1056.[1] They have been adapted and reprinted with permission.

Finally, and above all, I owe incredibly much to Christoph, my partner, who has carried me through the past years with patience, love and humour. Thank you for encouraging me to always follow my dreams, wherever they lead me. I would not be where I am today without the unconditional support and trust of my family, especially my parents Monica and Marc. Your curiosity in life has been a constant source of inspiration to learn, explore and expand my horizons. I dedicate this work to them.

List of Abbreviations

ANC	African National Congress
ARIO	Articles on the Responsibility of International Organizations
ARS	Articles on the Responsibility of States for Internationally Wrongful Acts
ATCA	Alien Tort Claims Act
ATS	Alien Tort Statute
AUC	*Autodefensas Unidas de Colombia*/United Self-Defence Forces of Colombia
CEDAW	Committee on the Elimination of Discrimination against Women
CESCR	Committee on Economic, Social and Cultural Rights
CSIVI	Commission for Monitoring, Promoting and Verifying the Implementation of the Final Agreement
DDR	Demobilisation, disarmament and reintegration
ECtHR	European Court of Human Rights
ELN	National Liberation Army
EPL	Popular Liberation Army
ETCR	Territorial areas for training and reincorporation
FALINTIL	Armed Forces for the National Liberation of East Timor
FARC	*Fuerza Alternativa Revolucionaria del Común*
FARC-EP	*Fuerzas Armadas Revolucionarias de Colombia – Ejército del Pueblo*/Revolutionary Armed Forces of Colombia – People's Army
FIS	Islamic Salvation Front
FMLN	*Frente Farabundo Martí para la Liberación Nacional*
FPA	Final Peace Agreement (Colombia)
FPLC	*Forces Patriotiques pour la Libération du Congo*
FWO	Research Foundation – Flanders
HR Committee	United Nations Human Rights Committee
IACHR	Inter-American Commission on Human Rights
IACtHR	Inter-American Court of Human Rights
ICC	International Criminal Court

ICCPR	International Covenant on Civil and Political Rights
ICESCR	International Covenant on Economic, Social and Cultural Rights
ICJ	International Court of Justice
ICL	International criminal law
ICRC	International Committee of the Red Cross
ICTR	International Criminal Tribunal for Rwanda
ICTY	International Criminal Tribunal for the former Yugoslavia
IHL	International humanitarian law
IHRL	International human rights law
ILA	International Law Association
ILC	International Law Commission
IRA	Irish Republican Army
IMT	International Military Tribunal
IRA	Irish Republican Army
KLA	Kosovo Liberation Army
LRA	Lord's Resistance Army
LTTE	Liberation Tigers of Tamil Eelam
MILF	Moro Islamic Liberation Front
MRM	Monitoring and Reporting Mechanism
NGO	Non-governmental organisation
NIAC	Non-international armed conflict
NPA	New People's Army
NPFL	National Patriotic Front of Liberia
NSAG	Non-state armed group
PCIJ	Permanent Court of International Justice
PLO	Palestinian Liberation Organization
RUF	Revolutionary United Front
SCSL	Special Court for Sierra Leone
TOAR	Works, actions and activities with reparative-restorative content
TVPA	Torture Victims Protection Act
UN	United Nations
UNAMA	United Nations Assistance Mission in Afghanistan
UNCHR	United Nations Commission on Human Rights
UNGA	United Nations General Assembly
UNHRC	United Nations Human Rights Council
UNOHCHR	United Nations Office of the High Commissioner for Human Rights
UNSC	United Nations Security Council
UNSG	United Nations Secretary-General
URNG	Guatemalan National Revolutionary Unity
US	United States of America
USSR	Union of Soviet Socialist Republics
VCLT	Vienna Convention on the Law of Treaties

Introduction

I.1 Setting the scene

The purpose of this book is to clarify whether and how non-state armed groups (NSAG) might be required to provide reparations for the damages, or harm, caused by their violations of international law committed during situations of non-international armed conflict (NIAC). In examining this complex issue, the book responds to the predominance of this type of armed conflict in contemporary warfare. NSAGs, alongside states, are the main protagonists in these situations of armed violence, which continue to have a devastating impact on societies around the world. Despite this reality, the possibility of holding an NSAG collectively responsible for violations of international law remains a thorny issue. As a responsible state is required to make reparation for the loss or injury caused, this situation raises the question of whether an NSAG should bear a similar duty to the victims affected by its wrongs under international law.[1]

Although armed conflicts involving NSAGs are not a new phenomenon, their prevalence and characteristics have shifted considerably. The majority of contemporary conflicts are no longer international armed conflicts between states, but rather NIACs involving NSAGs. In the post-Cold War era, NSAGs have gained increased influence and power to the detriment of states.[2] The International Committee of the Red Cross (ICRC) recently estimated that more than 100 NSAGs worldwide have the capacity to cause violence of humanitarian concern within the context of NIACs, with around 60–80 million civilians living under the state-like governance of armed actors including NSAGs.[3] Armed

1 Laura Íñigo Álvarez, 'The Obligation to Provide Reparations by Armed Groups: A Norm under Customary International Law?' (2020) 67 Netherlands International Law Review 427, 428.

2 ILA Committee on Non-State Actors, 'Johannesburg Conference Non State Actors' (2016) para 10; ICRC, 'The Roots of Restraint in War' (2018) 13; ICRC, 'International Humanitarian Law and the Challenges of Contemporary Armed Conflicts' (2019) 50.

3 Bruno Demeyere, 'Editorial' (2020) 102 International Review of the Red Cross 979; ICRC, 'ICRC Engagement with Non-State Armed Groups: Why, How, For What Purpose, and Other Salient Issues' (2021) 2.

DOI: 10.4324/9781003401292-1

conflicts involving NSAGs in countries such as Sudan, Syria, Yemen and Colombia concretely show how severely civilian populations suffer from armed violence resulting in deaths, physical and psychological harm, massive displacement and property damage.[4] In response to these developments, NSAGs have been firmly placed on the international peace and security agenda.

Reparations for victims fulfil a fundamental role in acknowledging and repairing the harmful consequences they have suffered because of atrocities committed during situations of armed conflict. Under international law, reparations were traditionally granted through inter-state mechanisms that broadly followed from the classical state-centric nature of the international legal system. However, the right of individual victims to claim reparation for violations of international law has become increasingly accepted and particularly well-established in human rights law.[5] In addition, besides states, certain non-state actors, including individuals and international organisations, have been required to provide reparation under contemporary international law.[6]

Some further significant advances have been made in the quest for reparations, with prominent examples including the 1989 landmark ruling *Velásquez Rodríguez v. Honduras* of the Inter-American Court of Human Rights, which set the beginning of the Court's progressive body of case law on reparations; the adoption, by the United Nations (UN) General Assembly in 2005, of the UN Basic Principles and Guidelines on the Right to a Remedy and Reparation for Victims of Gross Violations of International Human Rights Law and Serious Violations of International Humanitarian Law (UN Basic Principles and Guidelines); and, the first cases dealing with reparations for international crimes before the International Criminal Court.[7] Furthermore, the demand for

4 Amnesty International, '"Nowhere Is Safe for Us": Unlawful Attacks and Mass Displacement in North-West Syria' (2020); Mwatana for Human Rights 'A Country Falling Apart: Human Rights Situation in Yemen 2021' (2022); Truth Commission of Colombia, 'Informe Final: Hasta La Guerra Tiene Límites' (2022): Amnesty International, '"Death Came to Our Home": War Crimes and Civilian Suffering in Sudan' (2023).

5 Emanuela-Chiara Gillard, 'Reparation for Violations of International Humanitarian Law' (2003) 85 International Review of the Red Cross 529; Elizabeth Salmón and Juan-Pablo Pérez-León-Acevedo, 'Reparation for Victims of Serious Violations of International Humanitarian Law: New Developments' (2022) 104 International Review of the Red Cross 1315, 1318–1322.

6 Art 75 Rome Statute of the International Criminal Court (1998) 2187 UNTS 38544 (ICC Statute); Art 31 ILC, Articles on the Responsibility of International Organizations with Commentaries, Yearbook of the International Law Commission (2011) Vol II Part Two (ARIO).

7 *Case of Velásquez Rodríguez v Honduras* IACtHR (Judgment Reparations and Costs) Series C No 7 (21 July 1989); UNGA, Basic Principles and Guidelines on the Right to a Remedy and Reparation for Victims of Gross Violations of International Human Rights Law and Serious Violations of International Humanitarian Law adopted by UNGA Res 60/147 on 16 December 2005 (21 March 2006) UN Doc A/RES/60/147 (UN Basic Principles and Guidelines). At the International Criminal

reparations in conflict and post-conflict situations is recognised as an essential component of transitional justice, particularly for the delivery of justice to victims.[8]

These developments have sparked a discussion on the possibility of holding NSAGs responsible, as distinct entities, for their wrongful conduct under international law, in turn possibly resulting in a legal duty for NSAGs to make reparation. Such an evolution could directly benefit the victims of present-day armed conflicts.[9] Yet, this delicate question remains unsettled in international law. Although it is commonly accepted that NSAGs bear primary obligations under at least international humanitarian law (IHL) during situations of NIAC, it remains controversial whether such groups can be held legally responsible when violating these obligations. It is particularly unclear whether this determination of responsibility would result into a duty to provide reparation as a legal consequence thereof.[10] Currently, there is no treaty law or forum that offers the substantive and institutional frameworks to hold NSAGs legally responsible for violating their primary obligations under international law. Within this context, international law scholars have evaluated, in different instances, the possibility of holding NSAGs responsible and to a duty of reparation as "a doctrine in *statu nascendi*", "a question of progressive development of the law", or "*de lege ferenda* rather than *de lege lata*".[11] This state

Court, four cases have at the time of writing reached the reparation stage, namely in the *Lubanga*, *Katanga*, *Al Mahdi* and *Ntaganda* cases.

8 UNSC, 'The Rule of Law and Transitional Justice in Conflict and Post-Conflict Societies – Report of the Secretary-General' (23 August 2004) UN Doc S/2004/616 paras 8, 55.

9 Laura Iñigo Álvarez, *Towards a Regime of Responsibility of Armed Groups in International Law* (Intersentia 2020) 8, 59–61.

10 Jean-Marie Henckaerts and Louise Doswald-Beck (eds), *Customary International Humanitarian Law*, vol I: Rules (Cambridge University Press 2005) 536; Veronika Bílková, 'Establishing Direct Responsibility of Armed Opposition Groups for Violations of International Humanitarian Law?' in Noemi Gal-Or, Cedric Ryngaert and Math Noortmann (eds), *Responsibilities of the Non-State Actor in Armed Conflict and the Market Place* (Brill Nijhof 2015) 263–264; Ezequiel Heffes and Brian Frenkel, 'The International Responsibility of Non-State Armed Groups: In Search of the Applicable Rules' (2017) 8 Goettingen Journal of International Law 39; Luke Moffett, 'Violence and Repair: The Practice and Challenges of Non-State Armed Groups Engaging in Reparations' (2020) 102 International Review of the Red Cross 1057, 1062.

11 ILA Committee on Non-State Actors, 'Washington Conference Non State Actors' (2014) 11; Luke Moffett, 'Beyond Attribution: Responsibility of Armed Non-State Actors for Reparations in Northern Ireland, Colombia and Uganda' in Noemi Gal-Or, Cedric Ryngaert and Math Noortmann (eds), *Responsibilities of the Non-State Actor in Armed Conflict and the Market Place* (Brill Nijhof 2015) 346; Paloma Blázquez Rodríguez, 'Does an Armed Group Have an Obligation to Provide Reparations to Its Victims? Construing an Obligation to Provide Reparations for Violations of International Humanitarian Law' in James Summers and Alex Gough (eds), *Non-State Actors and International Obligations* (Brill Nijhof 2018) 427; Iñigo Álvarez (n 9) 195; Salmón and Pérez-León-Acevedo (n 5) 1325.

of play suggests that a disconnect exists between the international legal system, which seeks to hold on to its traditional state-centric nature, and the prevalence of modern armed conflicts, which have pushed NSAGs onto the international political scene.[12]

For a long time, the development of a regime of responsibility for NSAGs was not deemed practically and legally relevant. It was assumed that an NSAG would either win by establishing a new government or state, which would result in the absorption of its international responsibility into that of the state, or would be defeated, rendering its responsibility irrelevant due to the disappearance of the group.[13] However, the reality of modern armed conflicts has largely debunked these assumptions by displaying that NSAGs may continue to exist for a considerable period of time.[14] Moreover, not all groups necessarily strive to replace the existing state structures. Nevertheless, the temporary existence of NSAGs under international law does pose a significant challenge in the quest to apportion responsibility to such actors. This challenge differs for states, due to their status as rather stable entities.[15]

Although legal scholars have addressed the possible international responsibility of NSAGs, this scholarship remains considerably less in comparison to the significant body of work which considers their primary obligations under international law. The questions as to whether and how responsible NSAGs should provide reparations to victims of armed conflict have gained some attention in recent legal scholarship and international practice. However, a comprehensive international legal study on this topic is lacking. This situation conveys a sense of urgency when considering, in the words of the UN Special Rapporteur on extrajudicial, summary or arbitrary executions, the "unacceptably large deficits with regard to access to justice, remedies, and reparations" in the accountability framework regarding NSAGs.[16] A study of this nature is not only relevant for international law, but also for the broader field

12 Liesbeth Zegveld, *The Accountability of Armed Opposition Groups* (Cambridge University Press 2002) 224; Marco Sassòli, 'Taking Armed Groups Seriously: Ways to Improve Their Compliance with International Humanitarian Law' (2010) 1 Journal of International Humanitarian Legal Studies 5, 9–10.

13 Éric David, *Principes de Droit Des Conflits Armés* (6th edn, Bruylant 2019) 899.

14 Bílková (n 10) 275–276; Sten Verhoeven, 'International Responsibility of Armed Opposition Groups: Lessons from State Responsibility for Actions of Armed Opposition Groups' in Noemi Gal-Or, Cedric Ryngaert and Math Noortmann (eds), *Responsibilities of the Non-State Actor in Armed Conflict and the Market Place* (Brill Nijhof 2015) 296.

15 'Fourth Report on State Responsibility, by Mr Roberto Ago, Special Rapporteur' Yearbook of the International Law Commission (1972) Vol II UN Doc A/CN.4/264 and Add.1 para 154.

16 UNHRC, 'Report of the Special Rapporteur on Extrajudicial, Summary or Arbitrary Executions on Armed Non-State Actors: The Protection of the Right to Life' (5 June 2018) UN Doc A/HRC/38/44 para 21.

of transitional justice, which has paid insufficient attention to the role that NSAGs could play within processes dealing with the past.[17]

At least three observations can explain the underdeveloped state of the field. First, several authors have noted that there is little practice on the issue.[18] These observers have concluded on distinct occasions that instances of NSAGs being held responsible for international law violations very much constitute "a textbook case", reparations claims against NSAGs remain largely "theoretical", or reparations are "rarely asked" from NSAGs and "rarely awarded" to their victims.[19] However, as pointed out by Moffett, NSAGs have provided reparations in conflict and post-conflict societies.[20] For example, practice has recently emerged in Colombia. The peace agreement signed in 2016 between the Colombian government and the Revolutionary Armed Forces of Colombia – People's Army (FARC-EP) recognises that the NSAG must contribute to reparations.[21] In this regard, Capone concludes that the "FARC's engagement to satisfy victims' rights and award reparations, both material and symbolic, as a non-State entity represents a significant achievement".[22] This process builds on a pre-existing transitional justice initiative governed by the Justice and Peace Law of 2005.[23] The latter initiative has been noted for its recognition of "the ability of armed groups to be held responsible for reparations on the basis of violating human rights law [...] by the organisation as a whole".[24]

Second, Zegveld concluded in her seminal monograph of 2002 that the "international accountability of armed opposition groups is primitive and the prospects for further development are limited".[25] More than a decade later,

17 Ita Connolly and Colm Campbell, 'The Sharp End: Armed Opposition Movement, Transitional Truth Processes and the Rechtsstaat' (2012) 6 International Journal of Transitional Justice 11, 11–12; Ron Dudai and Kieran McEvoy, 'Thinking Critically about Armed Groups and Human Rights Praxis' (2012) 4 Journal of Human Rights Practice 1, 18. However, see Annyssa Bellal, 'Non-State Armed Groups in Transitional Justice Processes: Adapting to New Realities of Conflict' in Roger Duthie and Paul Seils (eds), *Justice Mosaics: How Context Shapes Transitional Justice in Fractured Societies* (ICTJ 2017).

18 Gillard (n 5) 534–535.

19 Jann K Kleffner, 'The Collective Accountability of Organized Armed Groups for System Crimes' in Andre Nollkaemper and Harmen Gijsbrecht van der Wilt (eds), *System Criminality in International Law* (Cambridge University Press 2009) 255; Sassòli (n 12) 47; ILA Committee on Non-State Actors (n 11) 11.

20 Moffett (n 10) 1058.

21 Acuerdo Final para la Terminación del Conflicto y la Construcción de una Paz Estable y Duradera (Government of Colombia – FARC-EP) (24 November 2016) (Final Peace Agreement or FPA).

22 Francesca Capone, 'From the Justice and Peace Law to the Revised Peace Agreement between the Colombian Government and the FARC: Will Victims' Rights Be Satisfied at Last?' (2017) 77 Heidelberg Journal of International Law 125, 159.

23 Law No 975 of 2005 (Justice and Peace Law) (Colombia).

24 Moffett (n 11) 343.

25 Zegveld (n 12) 229. Zegveld defines the concept of accountability as including both the substantive obligations of NSAGs and responsibility for breaches of these obligations. Ibid. 5.

Mastorodimos argued that the first part of this conclusion remains largely true, while simultaneously emphasising that increasing debate on the topic has subsequently taken place.[26]

The second observation feeds into the final one, namely that discussions regarding the international responsibility of NSAGs, and specifically their duty of reparation as a potential legal consequence thereof, have been confronted by several legal, practical and political dilemmas and challenges. This complexity could lead one to conclude that the question of reparation is simply not relevant for NSAGs. The first of these challenges is that the international legal personality of NSAGs as distinct legal entities must be determined, before any questions relating to responsibility can be addressed. As will be discussed further, this process forms a necessary precondition in the traditional law of international responsibility.[27] Moving beyond this preliminary issue, it remains unclear what the character of a future regime of responsibility for such entities should be. Such a regime could, for instance, be construed by analogy with the responsibility of states, or individual criminal responsibility, or even as a new type of international responsibility altogether. There is also a need to clarify the regime's relation to the responsibility of other subjects of international law.[28] Moreover, from a procedural perspective, the forum in which reparations could possibly be claimed from a responsible NSAG remains to be determined.[29]

A further practical challenge consists in the fact that NSAGs may not have the capacity or resources to provide reparations. It may also be the case that their organisational structure has dissolved or fragmented, preventing structured engagement in providing redress.[30] Indeed, an NSAG may simply cease to exist in the aftermath of an armed conflict. Ultimately, this may render reparations from such groups infeasible. This is reinforced by the possibility that NSAGs may lack the political willingness to provide or at least contribute to such measures.[31]

NSAGs are also characterised by their structural disparity. Such groups may "range from those that are highly centralized (with a strong hierarchy, effective chain of command, communication capabilities, etc.) to those that are decentralized (with semi-autonomous or splinter factions operating under an ill-defined leadership structure)".[32] This may render the development of a legal

26 Konstantinos Mastorodimos, *Armed Non-State Actors in International Humanitarian and Human Rights Law: Foundation and Framework of Obligations, and Rules on Accountability* (Ashgate 2016) 135–136.

27 Íñigo Álvarez (n 9) 66.

28 Bílková (n 10) 278–279, 281–282.

29 Ibid. 282; Íñigo Álvarez (n 9) 158.

30 ILA Committee on Non-State Actors (n 11) 9–10; Moffett (n 11) 334.

31 Ron Dudai, 'Closing the Gap: Symbolic Reparations and Armed Groups' (2011) 93 International Review of the Red Cross 783, 785–786; Íñigo Álvarez (n 9) 158.

32 Michelle Mack, 'Increasing Respect for International Humanitarian Law in Non-International Armed Conflicts' (ICRC 2008) 11.

regime that uniformly regulates their potential international responsibility more difficult.[33] In this respect, Íñigo Álvarez argues that there is a need to take account of such structural differences for any potential regime to be realistic.[34]

Perhaps the main political hurdle obstructing the development of a regime of international responsibility for NSAGs remains the general reluctance of states, as primary international law subjects, to recognise the legal existence, or rather personality, of such groups in international law. The concern of states is that any form of recognition could confer some sort of legitimacy upon NSAGs.[35] Instead, states prefer to address the responsibility of the individuals making up the NSAG, rather than the group itself.[36] According to Dudai, such an attitude could be even more pronounced with regard to reparation since it could be viewed as a measure reserved for states.[37] Any analysis of the position of NSAGs in international law needs to take into account that such groups are not ordinary non-state actors. Their defiant nature towards states makes them into one of the most controversial non-state actors on the international stage. As Daboné puts it: "armed groups are not desired or wanted [...] their existence is not usual in international law. Armed groups are born to disturb order, in the physical and legal sense".[38]

Despite these unresolved issues, scholars have advanced specific advantages or reasons why NSAGs should provide reparations. McEvoy, Lawther and Moffett argue, based on empirical work, that the engagement of NSAGs in reparations can contribute to meeting the needs of victims.[39] On their part, Mastorodimos and Íñigo Álvarez both contend that the possibility of obtaining reparations increases if the respondent is a collectivity rather than an individual.[40] Bellal notes in this regard that the person who committed the violation with the support of the group might be deceased. This could hamper the possibility of obtaining reparations in an individualised trial. In addition, the group

33 Annyssa Bellal, 'Establishing the Direct Responsibility of Non-State Armed Groups for Violations of International Norms: Issues of Attribution' in Noemi Gal-Or, Cedric Ryngaert and Math Noortmann (eds), *Responsibility of the Non-State Actor in Armed Conflict and the Market Place* (Brill Nijhof 2015) 307.
34 Íñigo Álvarez (n 9) 67.
35 Mastorodimos (n 26) 136.
36 Zegveld (n 12) 223.
37 Dudai (n 31) 793; UNHRC, 'Report of the Special Rapporteur on the Promotion of Truth, Justice, Reparation and Guarantees of Non-Recurrence: Role and Responsibilities of Non-State Actors in Transitional Justice Processes' (12 July 2022) UN Doc A/HRC/51/34 para 80.
38 Zakaria Daboné, 'International Law: Armed Groups in a State-Centric System' (2011) 93 International Review of the Red Cross 395, 424.
39 Kieran McEvoy, Cheryl Lawther and Luke Moffett, 'Changing the Script: Non-State Armed Groups, Restorative Justice and Reparations' (2022) 14 Journal of Human Rights Practice 454, 463–464.
40 Mastorodimos (n 26) 3; Laura Íñigo Álvarez, 'La Responsabilidad Internacional de Los Grupos Armados: ¿Responsabilidad Individual o Colectiva?' (2018) XVIII Anuario Mexicano de Derecho Internacional 481, 503.

might have significant assets that could be seized if and where responsibility has been established.[41] In her contribution to the debate, Blázquez Rodríguez points to the disparity in legal status between the victims of abuses committed by states and NSAGs. She considers this unsatisfactory from a justice perspective.[42] Furthermore, Moffett explains that attaching responsibility for reparation to perpetrators, whether individual or organisational, provides for an important psychological function for victims in appropriately directing blame and relieving their guilt. From the perspective of the responsible NSAG, taking responsibility for reparation can help symbolise the group's commitment to remedying the past.[43] More generally, the argument has been made that reparations could ensure better compliance with international law, by taking an important part in enforcement and deterrence of future violations.[44]

I.2 Definition of the key concepts

Before discussing the specific research focus and design of this book, it is necessary to define certain key concepts to set out the conceptual framework applied in the present study.

I.2.1 Non-state armed group

Despite the significant body of legal scholarship on armed groups, a uniform term or definition of such actors is lacking in scholarly writings and international law more broadly.[45] Instead, a variety of terms are used, such as organised armed group,[46] armed opposition group,[47] rebel group,[48] insurrectional

41 Bellal (n 33) 305–306; Verhoeven (n 14) 286.
42 Blázquez Rodríguez (n 11) 406.
43 Moffett (n 11) 324–325.
44 Gillard (n 5) 530; ILA Committee on Compensation for Victims of War, 'Compensation for Victims of War (Background Report)' (2004) 7; Íñigo Álvarez (n 9) 5–6; Moffett (n 10) 1059.
45 The UN Security Council has, for instance, used over fifteen different terms to refer to armed groups, while not expressly defining many of these terms in its resolutions. Jessica S Burniske, Naz K Modirzadeh and Dustin A Lewis, 'Armed Non-State Actors and International Human Rights Law: An Analysis of the Practice of the U.N. Security Council and U.N. General Assembly – Briefing Report with Annexes' (Harvard Law School Program on International Law and Armed Conflict 2017) 8–9.
46 For instance, Art 3 common to the Geneva Conventions of 1949 broadly refers to "Parties to the conflict", whereas Art 1 of Additional Protocol II of 1977 uses the term "organized armed groups". However, no general definition is provided. Geneva Conventions (1949) 75 UNTS 31, 85, 135, 287; Protocol Additional to the Geneva Conventions of 12 August 1949, and relating to the Protection of Victims of Non-International Armed Conflicts (Additional Protocol II) (1977) 1125 UNTS 609.
47 See, e.g., Zegveld (n 12) 1.
48 Schneckener refers to rebel or guerrilla groups as those that seek the liberation of a social class or a nation, whilst fighting to overthrow a government, secede from a

movement,[49] paramilitary group or terrorist organisation. The choice to employ certain terminology can depend on the context or type of group one is dealing with.[50] For instance, states may label an armed group that opposes them as terrorists, which may serve a political motivation to justify the use of force over dialogue.[51] Another example is the term paramilitary group, which has been used to identify "irregular combat units that usually act on behalf of, or are at least tolerated by, a given regime".[52] This state of play can, in part, be understood as a consequence of their heterogeneous nature. Even though armed groups are characterised by their common use of armed violence as *modus operandi* and their denomination as outlaws under national law, they are, at the same time, marked by their diversity in terms of a wide array of features, such as origins, motivations, organisational structures and tactics.[53] Some armed groups are small, or have shaky organisational structures, whilst others resemble the armed forces of a state, or even exercise effective control over territory and the populations living there.[54] Such control can, of itself, take distinct forms and go as far as substituting the state in the provision of particular services and competences, such as health care, education, tax collection and the administration of justice.[55] Hence, such armed groups appropriate certain state-like characteristics.[56]

For the purpose of this study, the neutral term 'non-state armed group', or in short NSAG, is preferred and is defined as encompassing any NSAG that is a party to a NIAC against a state, several states and/or rival NSAG(s), in order to

region or end an occupational or colonial regime. Ulrich Schneckener, 'Fragile Statehood, Armed Non-State Actors and Security Governance' in Alan Bryman and Marina Caparini (eds), *Private Actors and Security Governance* (LIT & DCAF 2006) 25.

49 See, e.g., Art 10 ILC, Articles on the Responsibility of States for Internationally Wrongful Acts with Commentaries, Yearbook of the International Law Commission (2001) Vol II Part Two (ARS).

50 Jo notes, for instance, that the definition of a rebel group is based on the group's goal of opposing the national government, whereas the denomination of terrorist organisation derives from the group's tactics to create fear and intimidation. However, both may also overlap. Hyeran Jo, 'Compliance with International Humanitarian Law by Non-State Armed Groups: How Can It Be Improved?', *Yearbook of International Humanitarian Law*, vol 19 (Asser Press 2016) 67–68.

51 Nicolas Florquin and Elisabeth Decrey Warner, 'Engaging Non-State Armed Groups or Listing Terrorists? Implications for the Arms Control Community' (2008) 1 Disarmament Forum 17, 18; Bellal (n 17) 247–248.

52 Bellal (n 17) 237.

53 DCAF and Geneva Call, 'Armed Non-State Actors: Current Trends & Future Challenges' (2015) 7–8.

54 Mack (n 32) 11; Vincent Bernard, 'Editorial: Understanding Armed Groups and the Law' (2011) 93 International Review of the Red Cross 261, 261–262.

55 See, for instance, Daragh Murray, *Human Rights Obligations of Non-State Armed Groups* (Hart Publishing 2016) ch 8; Geneva Call, 'Administration of Justice by Armed Non-State Actors' (2018).

56 UNHRC (n 16) 3–4; ICRC, 'International Humanitarian Law and the Challenges of Contemporary Armed Conflicts' (n 2) 52.

reach certain objectives of, for instance, a political, social or economic nature. In accordance with the threshold requirements set by IHL regarding the existence of such armed conflicts, an NSAG needs to have a sufficient level of organisation, regardless of whether or not it exercises control over a territory, and must be engaged in armed hostilities of a certain intensity.[57] Therefore, this study focuses on NSAGs which trigger at least the application of IHL. Only NSAGs that are distinct and operate on an independent basis from states fall within the scope of this study, hence the inclusion of 'non-state' in the adopted term. As a result, this broadly excludes NSAGs that carry out conduct under the direction, control, support or authority of one or more states.

I.2.2 Responsibility

The concept of responsibility takes different meanings within international law. Amongst other utilisations, the word 'responsibility' has been used as a synonym for a legal obligation; to refer to political or moral principles; to hold individuals liable in international criminal law (ICL); and, to deal with international wrongs committed by states.[58] This study concerns itself with the responsibility of an NSAG, as a distinct entity, for a particular act that gives rise to a duty or obligation to provide reparation. The concept of collective responsibility concerning NSAGs remains unclear under international law. Therefore, the manner in which the international responsibility of states is formulated and defined is used as the initial conceptual framework for analysis of the responsibility of NSAGs.[59] This is justified by the character of state responsibility as "the paradigm form of responsibility" in international law, which logically follows from the historical supremacy of states in this body of law.[60] Indeed, this understanding of responsibility has become "a central structuring principle of the international legal system" in and of itself.[61] The majority of legal scholars working on issues relating to NSAGs' international responsibility have followed a similar approach.[62] Nevertheless, this

57 *Prosecutor v Tadić* ICTY (Decision on the Defence Motion for Interlocutory Appeal on Jurisdiction) IT-94–1-AR72 (2 October 1995) para 70.

58 André Nollkaemper, 'Responsibility' (2017) ACIL Research Paper No 2017–03.

59 See the ARS; James Crawford and Jeremy Watkins, 'International Responsibility' in John Tasioulas and Samantha Besson (eds), *The Philosophy of International Law* (Oxford University Press 2010).

60 James Crawford and Simon Olleson, 'The Character and Forms of International Responsibility' in Malcolm Evans (ed), *International Law* (4th edn, Oxford University Press 2014) 444.

61 Nollkaemper (n 58) 2. See also Alain Pellet, 'The Definition of Responsibility in International Law' in James Crawford, Alain Pellet and Simon Olleson (eds), *The Law of International Responsibility* (Oxford University Press 2010).

62 See, e.g., Verhoeven (n 14) 287; Heffes and Frenkel (n 10); Agata Kleczkowska, 'Filling the Gap: The New Regime of Responsibility for Armed Non-State Actors' (2018) 25 Australian International Law Journal 137, 138; Tilman Rodenhäuser, *Organizing Rebellion: Non-State Armed Groups under International Humanitarian*

should not be understood as implying that the study considers this conceptualisation as being set in stone. Instead, the distinct nature of NSAGs in comparison to states and relating practice may eventually result in a tailor-made approach to responsibility and reparation.

Thus, the starting point for this study is the conceptualisation of responsibility as the general conditions under international law for an NSAG to be considered responsible for internationally wrongful actions or omissions, and the resulting legal consequences.[63] The latter constitutes the so-called content or substance of international responsibility.[64] More specifically, an internationally wrongful act gives rise to a new legal relationship which places on the responsible actor a duty to make reparation for the harmful consequences flowing from the international wrongful act itself.[65] In other words, responsibility concerns itself with a process of determining the international wrongfulness of a particular act and the legal consequences arising from it for the wrongdoer, which involves a duty of reparation.

Furthermore, responsibility is tied to the concept of accountability. Holding an entity that has committed a violation of international law responsible ensures that the wrongdoer accounts for its acts. The idea of responsibility requires a response, *respondere*, or account about the act to another actor.[66] In this sense, international responsibility can be understood as an element of the broader concept of accountability, which encompasses a variety of processes that seek to monitor and scrutinize behaviour, regardless of whether or not these acts can be qualified as violations of international law, and may potentially lead to some sort of sanction.[67]

Law, Human Rights Law, and International Criminal Law (Oxford University Press 2018) 307; Iñigo Álvarez (n 9) 90–91.

63 By analogy with the ILC Commentary to the ARS 31 para 1. By analogy with the law of state responsibility, an 'internationally wrongful act' consists of an action or omission that is attributable to an NSAG under international law and constitutes a breach of an international obligation of that group. See Art 2 ARS.

64 By analogy with the ILC Commentary to the ARS 86 para 1.

65 By analogy with the ILC Commentary to the ARS 86–87 para 2; Arts 28 and 31 ARS.

66 *Prosecutor v Thomas Lubanga Dyilo* ICC (Amended Order for Reparations) ICC-01/04–01/06–3129-AnxA (3 March 2015) para 2; Mark Bovens, *The Quest for Responsibility* (Cambridge University Press 1998) 23; George P Fletcher, 'The Storrs Lectures: Liberals and Romantics at War: The Problem of Collective Guilt' (2002) 111 Yale Law Journal 1499, 1555; Moffett (n 11) 324.

67 Deirdre Curtin and André Nollkaemper, 'Conceptualizing Accountability in International and European Law' (2005) XXXVI Netherlands Yearbook of International Law 3, 8; Kleffner (n 19) 240; Jean d'Aspremont and others, 'Sharing Responsibility Between Non-State Actors and States in International Law: Introduction' (2015) 62 Netherlands International Law Review 49, 52; Bílková (n 10) 265; Katharine Fortin, 'Armed Groups and Procedural Accountability: A Roadmap for Further Thought', *Yearbook of International Humanitarian Law*, vol 19 (TMC Asser Press 2016) 164–165; Nollkaemper (n 58) 1.

I.2.3 Reparation

A final concept requiring further clarification is that of reparation. The previous discussion has made clear that a close relationship exists between responsibility and reparation. More specifically, the duty to provide reparation is one of the legal consequences which arises from the attribution of responsibility to a wrongdoer.[68] As stated by the Permanent Court of International Justice, it is "a principle of international law, and even a general conception of law, that any breach of an engagement involves an obligation to make reparation".[69]

In this study, the duty of reparation is defined as encompassing individual and collective measures that are provided by a responsible actor to acknowledge and redress the various types of damage or harm that victims have suffered as a result of violations of international law.[70] Accordingly, reparation takes an important role in recognising the suffering and dignity of the victims and in providing a measure of redress.[71] The concept of reparation can be understood as involving a dual dimension: the duty to provide redress or relief to the victims (the substantive dimension) and the process before a court, an administrative body or another competent mechanism through which arguable claims are decided and substantive redress is afforded (the procedural dimension, which is subsumed in the notion of remedy).[72] Regarding the former dimension, the plural term 'reparations' is used to refer to the different measures or forms of redress, while 'reparation' is applied with reference to the right or duty in that regard. The duty to make reparation aims to restore, through various forms of redress, the situation that existed prior to the wrong.[73] According to the UN Basic Principles and Guidelines, these forms may include restitution, compensation, rehabilitation, satisfaction and guarantees of non-repetition.[74]

68 Art 31 ARS; *Prosecutor v Thomas Lubanga Dyilo* (n 66) para 2; Liesbeth Zegveld, 'Victims' Reparation Claims and International Criminal Courts: Incompatible Values?' (2010) 8 Journal of International Criminal Justice 79, 81; Dinah Shelton, *Remedies in International Human Rights Law* (3rd edn, Oxford University Press 2015) 13, 31; Íñigo Álvarez (n 9) 159.

69 *Case concerning the Factory at Chorzów (Germany v Poland)* PCIJ (Merits) [1928] PCIJ Rep Series A No 17 29; Naomi Roht-Arriaza, 'Reparations Decisions and Dilemmas' (2004) 27 Hastings International and Comparative Law Review 157, 157.

70 Pablo de Greiff, 'Justice and Reparations' in Pablo de Greiff (ed), *The Handbook of Reparations* (Oxford University Press 2006) 452.

71 Moffett (n 11) 324–325.

72 UNOHCHR, 'Rule-of-Law Tools for Post-Conflict States: Reparation Programmes' (2008) 6; Shelton (n 68) 16; International Commission of Jurists, 'The Right to a Remedy and to Reparations for Gross Human Rights Violations' (2018) xiii.

73 Arts 31, 34 ARS; UN Basic Principles and Guidelines principle 18; *Factory at Chorzów Case (Merits)* (n 69) 47; *Case of Velásquez Rodríguez v Honduras* (n 7) para 26; *Papamichalopoulos v Greece (Article 50)* ECtHR (Judgment) Series A No 330-B (31 October 1995) paras 34, 36; Henckaerts and Doswald-Beck (n 10) Rule 150; Shelton (n 68) 19.

74 UN Basic Principles and Guidelines principles 18–23.

The instrument further recognises that reparation should be "adequate, effective and prompt" as well as "proportionate to the gravity of the violations and the harm suffered".[75] Nonetheless, full reparation may not be feasible in some instances, due to, for instance, the nature of the violation or the large number of victims.[76] Although reparations generally provide a means for dealing with the past, they may also fulfil a forward-looking function by contributing to victims' reintegration into society or by providing a step towards a common future, among other possibilities.[77]

Last, reparation intends to promote and afford justice to the victims.[78] It has also been understood as a means to ensure that wrongdoers account for their acts.[79] Reparation is recognised as one of the main pillars of transitional justice alongside efforts which seek to provide truth, criminal justice and guarantees of non-repetition.[80] Reparations measures stand out as an effort that is intentionally designed to directly and primarily benefit the victims of violations. They acknowledge their suffering and needs and aim to redress the harm suffered. Thus, they extend beyond the confined scope of criminal prosecutions.[81]

1.3 Scope of the book

The responsibility of NSAGs, as such, constitutes "a grey area in international law": one marked by uncertainty and a clear need for further enquiry.[82] The aim of this book is to bring clarity to one of the possible legal consequences which may arise from violations of international law committed by NSAGs during situations of NIAC. This consequence concerns a possible duty to

75 UN Basic Principles and Guidelines principles 11(b), 15.

76 Carla Ferstman, *International Organizations and the Fight for Accountability: The Remedies and Reparations Gap* (Oxford University Press 2017) 92; ICTJ, 'Getting to Full Restitution' (2017) 2–3.

77 Naomi Roht-Arriaza, 'Reparations in the Aftermath of Repression and Mass Violence' in Eric Stover and Harvey M Weinstein (eds), *My Neighbor, My Enemy: Justice and Community in the Aftermath of Mass Atrocity* (Cambridge University Press 2004) 122.

78 UN Basic Principles and Guidelines principle 15; Shelton (n 68) 19.

79 *Prosecutor v Thomas Lubanga Dyilo* (n 66) para 2; Moffett (n 11) 324.

80 UNHRC, 'Report of the Special Rapporteur on the Promotion of Truth, Justice, Reparation and Guarantees of Non-Recurrence' (9 August 2012) UN Doc A/HRC/21/46.

81 Pablo de Greiff, 'Repairing the Past: Compensation for Victims of Human Rights Violations' in Pablo de Greiff (ed), *The Handbook of Reparations* (Oxford University Press 2006) 2; Lisa Magarrell, 'Reparations in Theory and Practice' (ICTJ 2007) 2; Jemima García-Godos, 'Victim Reparations in the Peruvian Truth Commission and the Challenge of Historical Interpretation' (2008) 2 International Journal of Transitional Justice 63, 65; Dudai (n 31) 787; UNGA, 'Promotion of Truth, Justice, Reparation and Guarantees of Non-Recurrence – Note by the Secretary-General' (14 October 2014) UN Doc A/69/518 para 10.

82 Zegveld (n 12) 220.

provide reparation for any injury caused by these violations. Clarifying the applicable legal and conceptual framework is significant not only for international law, but also for the field of transitional justice and justice efforts more broadly. This exercise seeks to strengthen the accountability framework applicable to NSAGs and to address the shortcomings in victims' access to justice, remedies, and reparation therein.[83]

The book's overall aim translates itself into three interrelated research objectives. The first objective is to examine whether and, if so, to what extent NSAGs which are party to a NIAC are recognised as subjects within the international legal system. Under traditional international law, responsibility is considered to be "the consequence of international legal personality" or rather one of its "main practical manifestations".[84] As a result, it is a necessary precondition to determine whether NSAGs have international legal personality, before considering any questions relating to their potential responsibility under international law. This requires an examination into whether NSAGs bear certain primary international obligations, as direct and distinct duty bearers. This discussion provides the basis to subsequently analyse whether breaches of these international obligations could lead to the responsibility of NSAGs and, particularly, to a resulting duty to provide reparation for harmful consequences.

The second objective is to analyse whether a duty to provide reparation might constitute one of the legal consequences which arises for NSAGs when they commit violations of international law. Under international law, a duty of reparation is understood to stem from the holding of an entity as responsible. As a result, the study is required, in the first instance, to examine whether NSAGs can incur international responsibility for wrongful acts. To this end, a comprehensive analysis must be carried out regarding NSAGs' place in the current international legal framework governing questions relating to responsibility and reparation for wrongs committed during situations of armed conflict.

The final objective is to explore how a possible duty of NSAGs to provide reparation could be operationalised under international law. This process involves examining how such a duty could be conceptualised and put into practice. Indeed, the discussion in Section I.1 has revealed some of the legal, but also practical and political, dilemmas and challenges that need to be addressed as part of this examination. In this respect, it is necessary to obtain an understanding of how the role of NSAGs in reparations has been addressed in international practice and in other relevant sources. Moreover, an examination needs to be carried out as to whether the existing legal principles and rules concerning reparation in international law could be applied to NSAGs. It follows that this examination will have to reflect on whether particularities specific to these NSAGs need to be considered. Last, as previously indicated, important practice has emerged in Colombia, where NSAGs have been required to provide

83 UNHRC (n 16) para 21.
84 Pellet (n 61) 6; Nollkaemper (n 58); Kleczkowska (n 62) 139; Íñigo Álvarez (n 9) 66.

reparations, since 2005, as part of two distinct transitional justice processes. Consequently, the Colombian case may hold considerable insights that could further inform the international legal debate.

The scope of this study is limited in a number of ways. As was discussed previously, the focus of the book is on NSAGs which operate independently from states and are party to a NIAC. Thus, the research does not consider armed actors that are involved in other situations of violence, such as riots or civil unrest. Moreover, although Chapter 5 deals with paramilitary groups operating in Colombia, this study does not consider legal issues that may arise from potential cases of collusion with the state. Yet, this should not be interpreted as any sort of dismissal of the state's responsibility. Furthermore, this study focuses on the duty to repair as a legal consequence of international responsibility. Other aspects of a possible responsibility regime for NSAGs, such as the rules of attribution, are not or only indirectly addressed. In addition, the study does not concern itself with the other side of the responsibility coin, namely whether victims have an enforceable right to reparation with respect to responsible NSAGs under international law. The question as to which victimised persons or other actors NSAGs might owe obligations in respect of their responsibility also falls beyond the scope of this study. Victims of violations perpetrated by such groups could broadly include civilians, the territorial state, third states and even other NSAGs. These possibilities are not strictly defined within this study. As a final note, this study considers the practice of NSAGs which is akin to reparations as conceptualised in international law. This practice can, for example, significantly inform how the operationalisation of the duty to repair could take place and, therefore, assist in solving theoretical and practical challenges.[85] Such an exercise could help ensure that obligations are realistic. This study recognises that there are strong arguments to consider NSAGs' practice for the purpose of determining the existence of customary norms applicable in NIACs. However, it does not aim to solve the complex question as to *how* this practice could contribute to the process of international law-making.[86]

I.4 Design and structure of the book

The book is divided into three parts, followed by a concluding chapter that presents the main findings of this study. Part 1 examines the current international legal framework governing a possible duty of NSAGs to provide reparation to victims of armed conflict. Chapter 1 begins by analysing whether NSAGs have distinct legal personality under international law. This sets the starting point to consider questions related to NSAGs' international responsibility and, particularly, their duty of reparation. The chapter first deals with the concepts of international legal

85 Heffes and Frenkel (n 10) 69.
86 Íñigo Álvarez (n 1) 444–449; Marco Sassòli, 'How Will International Humanitarian Law Develop in the Future?' (2022) 104 International Review of the Red Cross 2052, 2072–2076.

personality and subject of international law, with a particular focus on the position of non-state actors within the framework of international law. The chapter continues by determining the international legal personality of NSAGs, as distinct legal entities, with certain primary obligations under IHL and possibly international human rights law (IHRL). Building on the findings of this analysis, Chapter 2 subsequently scrutinises whether NSAGs hold a duty, under contemporary international law, to provide reparation for violations of these obligations committed during NIACs. This involves determining whether these groups can be held internationally responsible, as a duty of reparation would potentially follow from such responsibility. The chapter concludes that a duty of NSAGs to provide reparation under international law constitutes primarily a question of *lex ferenda.* Simultaneously, some legal precedent and recognition for such a duty is identified. The chapter sheds light on how this duty of reparation has been conceptualised and put into practice when recognised, which informs the analysis in the subsequent chapters.

Part 2 of this book explores the establishment of a possible duty for NSAGs under international law to provide reparation for internationally wrongful acts. Moving beyond present international law, the overall analysis is conducted from a *de lege ferenda* perspective. This endeavour is driven by the understanding of reparation as an important measure of justice and accountability for victims. Given the current reality of armed conflict, this should not exempt NSAGs from redressing the harm caused by their internationally wrongful conduct. As a first step, Chapter 3 seeks to determine what the character of a future regime of international responsibility of NSAGs should be. This examination considers whether NSAGs' responsibility could be likened to, or integrated with, the existing frameworks of state responsibility or individual criminal responsibility, respectively. An alternative is to develop a distinct and independent form of responsibility. Based on this exercise, the chapter proposes the establishment of a new *sui generis* regime of international responsibility tailored to NSAGs. This conclusion sets the baseline to explore in Chapter 4 how the content of this future responsibility regime could be operationalised in international law. More specifically, the aim of this chapter is to analyse how a potential duty of reparation for NSAGs could be conceptualised and practically applied under international law. Within this scope, the chapter also reflects on when an NSAG could be called upon to provide reparations. This discussion addresses the important, but underexplored, questions of whether and how a responsible NSAG could fulfil its duty of reparation after the end of an armed conflict, when it ceases to exist as a legal entity. The international legal analysis in this chapter also draws from NSAGs' practice and social science scholarship. An innovative, multifaceted proposal for operationalising a duty of NSAGs to provide reparation under international law is presented.

Part 3 examines how the duty of NSAGs to provide reparation has been operationalised within the framework of two successive transitional justice processes established in Colombia. These processes concern the Justice and Peace Law of 2005, with a focus on the United Self-Defence Forces of Colombia (AUC), discussed in Chapter 5 and the Comprehensive System for Truth, Justice, Reparation and Non-Repetition, which was established based on the 2016 Final Peace Agreement with the FARC-EP, in Chapter 6. Both processes have sought to address the harm caused by serious violations of international law committed within a context of prolonged armed violence in the country. The Colombian conflict can be understood as a set of non-international armed conflicts, which have involved a range of armed actors, including NSAGs, since the 1960s. The overall aim of these case studies is to obtain insights that can inform, as possible lessons and approaches, the international legal debate on how NSAGs' duty of reparation could be conceptualised and put into practice under international law. In this sense, the purpose of these insights is not to necessarily formulate normative claims. While the two Colombian processes are addressed to the extent necessary in the preceding parts of the book, a comprehensive analysis is reserved for this third part. Nevertheless, the previous chapters provide the broader international legal framework against which the case-based insights are considered. This approach allows previously posited theories to be scrutinised and refined, while also pinpointing new perspectives and areas of contention. Several reasons justify the selection of the two case studies. Despite little practice on the subject of this book, Colombia has obtained considerable experience over the years in requiring NSAGs to provide reparations to victims of armed conflict. This has been implemented within the frameworks of the aforementioned processes. Yet, both processes remain underexplored in international legal scholarship from the perspective of a possible duty to repair on the part of NSAGs as distinct entities.[87] In addition, the differences between the NSAGs involved and the processes in which their duty to repair is operationalised enrich the analysis. The case studies are based on desk-based research complemented by field research conducted in Colombia in 2019. In addition to informal interviews, a total of 23 semi-structured interviews were conducted with magistrates appointed in the Justice and Peace Law process; officials of other transitional justice and government institutions; former FARC-EP members; representatives of the FARC-EP's successor political party; representatives of victims and their organisations; civil society actors; and, the UN.[88] Most interviews were conducted in-person in Colombia, and a few online or by phone. One of the primary objectives of these interviews was to gain insights into the interviewees' opinions, perceptions and experiences concerning reparations and NSAGs within the framework of these transitional justice processes. Additionally, they aimed to gather broader perspectives on topics encompassing NSAGs, collective responsibility and reparations for victims of armed conflict.

87 However, see Moffett (n 11) 340–343; Capone (n 22) 159–160; Íñigo Álvarez (n 9) 185–186.
88 See Annex 1 for an overview of the interviews.

Part I

Duty of non-state armed groups to provide reparation under current international law

Chapter 1

Non-state armed groups as distinct entities under international law

1.1 Introduction

Before analysing the responsibility of NSAGs under international law, it is necessary to determine whether and, if so, to what extent such groups are recognised as subjects within the international legal system. The law of international responsibility requires that an NSAG has international legal personality as a precondition to any consideration about the responsibility of such a collective entity under international law.[1] This necessitates that an NSAG is "a legal entity distinct from its members".[2] Or, as put similarly by Schmalenbach, an NSAG's "responsibility requires an entity which is – de facto or *de iure* – distinguishable from its individual members".[3] It follows that the objective of this chapter is to determine whether an NSAG has distinct international legal personality. This necessitates an examination as to whether an NSAG bears, in its own right, certain primary obligations under international law. Such analysis provides the basis to subsequently examine whether possible international responsibility and a duty of reparation could be assigned to an NSAG when it has violated these primary obligations.[4]

1 Alain Pellet, 'The Definition of Responsibility in International Law' in James Crawford, Alain Pellet and Simon Olleson (eds), *The Law of International Responsibility* (Oxford University Press 2010) 6; Agata Kleczkowska, 'Filling the Gap: The New Regime of Responsibility for Armed Non-State Actors' (2018) 25 Australian International Law Journal 137, 139; Laura Íñigo Álvarez, *Towards a Regime of Responsibility of Armed Groups in International Law* (Intersentia 2020) 66.

2 *Advisory Opinion on Western Sahara* ICJ [1975] ICJ Rep 12 para 148. By analogy, "The legal personality of an organization, which is a precondition of the international responsibility of that organization, needs to be 'distinct from that of its member States'". See ILC, Articles on the Responsibility of International Organizations with Commentaries, Yearbook of the International Law Commission (2011) Vol II Part Two (ARIO) Art 2, 50 para 10.

3 Kirsten Schmalenbach, 'International Responsibility for Humanitarian Law Violations by Armed Groups' in Heike Krieger (ed), *Inducing Compliance with International Humanitarian Law: Lessons from the African Great Lakes Region* (Cambridge University Press 2015) 499.

4 This understanding follows the traditional conceptualisation of international responsibility, as provided for in the law of state responsibility, see Arts 1–2 ILC,

DOI: 10.4324/9781003401292-3

The chapter starts with laying the groundwork for this examination by considering more broadly the concepts of international legal personality and subject of international law, while reflecting on the legal position of non-state actors within international law. This is followed by an enquiry into the international legal personality of NSAGs under IHL and IHRL. Aside from acting as a means to identify whether NSAGs are legal subjects under these bodies of international law, the analysis provides a deeper understanding of the scope of their international legal personality. In the final part of the chapter, several key findings will be drawn from the overall analysis. These will be relevant for the further analysis of the international responsibility of NSAGs and their duty to repair in the subsequent chapters.

1.2 International legal personality of non-state actors

Traditional public international law was construed as a state-centric system, aimed at regulating state behaviour in an increasingly global and interconnected society. A consent-based system developed for and by states and based on the principles of non-interference, sovereignty and equality, amongst others. As a result, states were recognised as the primary and exclusive subjects of international law having international legal personality, while non-state actors were regarded as subjects falling under the exclusive domestic jurisdiction of states. However, as will be shown, the international legal system has gradually opened its door to such actors and has consequently acquired a more heterogeneous nature.[5]

The concepts of 'international legal personality' and 'subject of international law' take prominent places in public international law.[6] The primary reason being that these concepts distinguish those actors which are recognised as participants within the international legal system and those which are excluded.[7] Hence, an actor lacking legal personality, or the quality of subject, simply does

Articles on the Responsibility of States for Internationally Wrongful Acts with Commentaries, Yearbook of the International Law Commission (2001) Vol II Part Two (ARS); James Crawford and Simon Olleson, 'The Character and Forms of International Responsibility' in Malcolm Evans (ed), *International Law* (4th edn, Oxford University Press 2014) 444.

5 Hersch Lauterpacht, *International Law: Being the Collected Papers of Hersch Lauterpacht*, vol 1: The General Works (Elihu Lauterpacht ed, Cambridge University Press 1970) 136–150; Jan Klabbers, '(I Can't Get No) Recognition: Subjects Doctrine and the Emergence of Non-State Actors' in Jarna Petman and Jan Klabbers (eds), *Nordic Cosmopolitanism: Essays in International Law for Martti Koskenniemi* (Martinus Nijhoff 2003).

6 For an in-depth discussion, see Janne Elisabeth Nijman, *The Concept of International Legal Personality: An Inquiry into the History and Theory of International Law* (TMC Asser Press 2004); Roland Portmann, *Legal Personality in International Law* (Cambridge University Press 2010).

7 Portmann (n 6) 5.

not legally exist from an international law perspective. Accordingly, the concepts constitute important analytical tools when studying the international legal order. This observation notwithstanding, there is no "centralized law of persons" in international law that regulates the acquisition, content and consequences of international legal personality.[8] Even within legal doctrine, there is no general consensus about its conceptualisation, and a codified definition remains absent. Consequently, the concept is open to diverse interpretations.

It is generally understood that when an actor has international legal personality, it is a bearer of rights and obligations derived from international law.[9] Such personality has been defined to include the ability to exercise specific capacities, such as the ability to participate in the creation of international law, to seek redress for alleged violations and to participate in international organisations.[10] However, the extent to which an actor should be capable of exercising these various capacities – in order to be considered as having international personality – remains unclear.[11] Notably, the aforementioned examples correspond to the common legal capacities of states. Yet, when actors are required to fulfil such state-based capacities, some may be excluded simply due to their non-state nature. On the other hand, subjects of international law, or international legal persons, can be described as those actors which possess international personality. Hence, they are actors which independently bear direct rights and obligations under international law.[12] Accordingly, these entities constitute the active participants of the international legal order.[13] It is, however, debatable whether all bearers of rights and obligations can be regarded as subjects.[14]

The lack of clarity concerning the concepts of international legal personality and subject of international law has led many authors to treat them as

8 Ibid. 9.
9 Dapo Akande, 'International Organizations' in Malcolm Evans (ed), *International Law* (2nd edn, Oxford University Press 2006) 281; Malcolm N Shaw, *International Law* (8th edn, Cambridge University Press 2017) 155.
10 Michèle Olivier, 'Exploring Approaches to Accommodating Non-State Actors within Traditional International Law' (2010) 4 Human Rights & International Legal Discourse 15, 26; Daragh Murray, *Human Rights Obligations of Non-State Armed Groups* (Hart Publishing 2016) 46–47; Rebecca MM Wallace and others, *International Law* (8th edn, Sweet and Maxwell 2016) 63; William Thomas Worster, 'Relative International Legal Personality of Non-State Actors' (2016) 42 Brooklyn Journal of International Law 207, 210–211.
11 Portmann (n 6) 8–9. See also *Advisory Opinion on Reparation for Injuries Suffered in the Service of the United Nations* ICJ [1949] ICJ Rep 174.
12 Lauterpacht (n 5) 136; Jan Klabbers, *An Introduction to International Institutional Law* (Cambridge University Press 2002) 42.
13 Karsten Nowrot, 'Legal Consequences of Globalization: The Status of Non-Governmental Organizations under International Law' (1999) 6 Indiana Journal of Global Legal Studies 579, 621.
14 Klabbers (n 5) 352.

synonyms, or even to reject the notion of the subjects doctrine.[15] One may even speak of a general trend in modern international law to treat both concepts as one and the same.[16] As argued by Klabbers: "there is nothing particularly wrong with treating them as such in a pragmatic fashion".[17] For the purposes of this book, this pragmatic and modern approach will be followed. Thus, although both concepts are, strictly speaking, distinct, they will be treated as synonyms. This means that all actors that have international legal personality are considered as subjects of international law and conversely all subjects are considered as having international legal personality. Nonetheless, as will be discussed, the degree of international legal personality may differ across international subjects.

Gradual attempts have been made to bridge the traditional dichotomy between state and non-state actors in international law. The 1949 Advisory Opinion on *Reparation for Injuries Suffered in the Service of the United Nations* of the International Court of Justice, which deals with the legal personality of the UN as an international organisation, marks an important moment in this development.[18] Notably, it has paved the way to also consider other non-state actors, while revealing more about the general nature of their legal personality in international law.[19] The Court held that:

> The subjects of law in any legal system are *not necessarily identical in their nature or in the extent of their rights*, and their nature depends upon the *needs of the community*. Throughout its history, the development of international law has been influenced by the *requirements of international life*, and the progressive increase in collective activities of States has already given rise to instances of action upon the international plane by *certain entities which are not States*.[20]

15 Rosalyn Higgins, *Problems and Process: International Law and How We Use It* (Clarendon Press 1994) 49; Andrew Clapham, *Human Rights Obligations of Non-State Actors* (Oxford University Press 2006) 59–63; Murray (n 10) 25.

16 Portmann (n 6) 1.

17 Klabbers (n 12) 43.

18 *Advisory Opinion on Reparation* (n 11); Gus Waschefort, 'The Pseudo Legal Personality of Non-State Armed Groups in International Law' (2011) 36 South African Yearbook of International Law 226, 226. The logic of the Reparation Advisory Opinion was extended to include all other international organisations, see *Advisory Opinion on the Legality of the Use by a State of Nuclear Weapons in Armed Conflict* ICJ [1996] ICJ Rep 66 para 27. For similar reasoning, which was presented in 1920 in relation to the League of Nations, see Lassa Oppenheim, *International Law: A Treatise*, vol 1 (Ronald F Roxburgh ed, 3rd edn, Longmans 1920).

19 Robert McCorquodale, 'The Individual and The International Legal System' in Malcolm D Evans (ed), *International Law* (2nd edn, Oxford University Press 2006) 309; Olivier (n 10) 26; Portmann (n 6) 100.

20 *Advisory Opinion on Reparation* (n 11) 178 [emphasis added].

The International Court of Justice's Advisory Opinion clarifies that there can be international subjects other than states. In particular, the precise content of the rights and obligations conferred upon such subjects may differ and, accordingly, they may vary amongst themselves.[21] This is a reflection of a more general tendency to reconceptualise international personality as a matter of degree rather than the traditional binary distinction between subjects and non-subjects of international law.[22] Klabbers has held in this regard that "personality is flexible, rather than an all-or-nothing concept: one can have personality in various graduations".[23] Or as Shaw puts it, international legal personality is "a relative phenomenon varying with the circumstances".[24] However, this interpretation is not universally accepted. D'Aspremont, for instance, finds the possible acceptance of degrees of legal personality by the International Court of Justice to be "a bewildering argument" and instead speaks of "variations in the *capacities that accompany such a personality*".[25] The Advisory Opinion further clarifies that the concept of legal subject is dynamic in nature and may change with "the needs of the community" and more broadly with "the requirements of international life", however, still conditioned upon the will of states.[26] The International Court of Justice further held that:

> Whereas a State possesses the totality of international rights and duties recognized by international law, the rights and duties of an entity such as the Organization [UN] must *depend upon its purposes and functions* as specified or implied in its constituent documents and developed in practice.[27]

Accordingly, a functional approach is taken in which international personality is based upon the specific purposes and functions of the actor in question.[28]

A final relevant element of the Advisory Opinion reads that the UN "is a subject of international law and *capable of possessing international rights and duties*".[29]

21 McCorquodale (n 19) 309.

22 Klabbers (n 12) 44; Veronika Bílková, 'Treat Them as They Deserve!? Three Approaches to Armed Opposition Groups under Current International Law' (2010) 4 Human Rights & International Legal Discourse 111, 115; Worster (n 10) 211.

23 Jan Klabbers, 'The Concept of Legal Personality' (2005) II Ius Gentium 35, 47.

24 Shaw (n 9) 156.

25 Jean d'Aspremont, 'Conclusion: Inclusive Law Making and Law-Enforcement Processes for an Exclusive International System' in Jean d'Aspremont (ed), *Participants in the International Legal System: Multiple Perspectives on Non-State Actors in International Law* (Routledge 2011) 433.

26 *Advisory Opinion on Reparation* (n 11) 178; McCorquodale (n 19) 309–310; Bílková (n 22) 115; Portmann (n 6) 106–107; Wallace and others (n 10) 63–64.

27 *Advisory Opinion on Reparation* (n 11) 180 [emphasis added].

28 Confirmed in the subsequent *Advisory Opinion on the Legality of the Use by a State of Nuclear Weapons in Armed Conflict* (n 18) para 25. See also Murray (n 10) 28–29.

29 *Advisory Opinion on Reparation* (n 11) 179 [emphasis added].

Scholars have also recognised the central role of the criterion of capacity to possess international rights and obligations in the acquisition of an actor's international legal personality.[30] As argued by Clapham, "We need to admit that international rights and duties depend on the capacity of the entity to enjoy those rights and bear those obligations; such rights and obligations do not depend on the mysteries of subjectivity."[31] In this regard, Green draws the attention to an entity's factual capacity by considering that "if an entity is to possess international rights and duties, it must have the factual capacity to possess those rights and duties".[32] Accordingly, legal capacity should be rooted in factual circumstances and the characteristics of the entity itself.[33] It ultimately ensures that international law is effective.[34] Similarly, Lauterpacht adds:

> whether a person or a body is a subject of international law must be answered in a pragmatic manner by reference to actual experience and to the reason of the law as distinguished from a pre-conceived notion as to who can be subjects of international law.[35]

Four broad conclusions can be drawn from the discussion and form the starting point to consider the legal personality of NSAGs, as non-state actors, under international law: first, non-state actors may have international legal personality alongside states and therefore may constitute subjects of international law; second, legal subjects may vary in terms of their nature as well as in the extent of their rights and obligations; third, the concept of subject of law is a dynamic one, but states maintain the upper hand; and, lastly, international legal personality should not be determined *in abstracto*, but instead depends on the capacity of the actor to bear certain rights and obligations, the particular context in which the actor operates and the relevant field of law.[36]

30 Note that the capacity to possess rights and obligations is not considered sufficient for an entity to attain international legal personality. It is rather a prerequisite to becoming a subject of international law. Anna Meijknecht, *Towards International Personality: The Position of Minorities and Indigenous Peoples in International Law* (Intersentia 2001) 34, 45; Akande (n 9) 281; Worster (n 10) 210–211.

31 Clapham (n 15) 68–69. Clapham gives some examples concerning the rights of states under international law to illustrate this argument, e.g. a state as a fictional legal person could not claim to be subjected to torture under IHRL or that it had been denied the right to marry.

32 Fergus Green, 'Fragmentation in Two Dimensions: The ICJ's Flawed Approach to Non-State Actors and International Legal Personality' (2008) 9 Melbourne Journal of International Law 47, 72.

33 Meijknecht (n 30) 35.

34 Hans Kelsen, *Principles of International Law* (Rinehart & Company 1952) 414; Murray (n 10) 43–44, 49.

35 Hersch Lauterpacht, 'The Subjects of the Law of Nations' (1947) 63 Law Quarterly Review 438, 444.

36 In this respect the approach of Rodenhäuser is followed, see Tilman Rodenhäuser, *Organizing Rebellion: Non-State Armed Groups under International Humanitarian*

1.3 International humanitarian law

1.3.1 Situating the discussion

NIACs are regulated by Article 3 common to the four Geneva Conventions of 1949 (Common Article 3), customary IHL and Additional Protocol II to the Geneva Conventions of 1949 (Additional Protocol II). This international legal framework imposes a range of obligations on the parties to such armed conflicts, including NSAGs. In this regard, it is necessary to establish whether and, if so, to what extent an NSAG that is party to a NIAC bears these international obligations itself, or whether it derives its subjectivity indirectly from its individual members, who are bound by IHL at least through their criminal responsibility for war crimes.[37] The latter entails that an NSAG would be bound through those individuals' international obligations, but not in its own right. It is also possible that both the group and its constituent members have separate international legal personality and are therefore distinct from each other.[38] An analysis of the *travaux préparatoires* concerning Common Article 3 and Additional Protocol II does not provide a definite answer to these questions.[39]

Law, Human Rights Law, and International Criminal Law (Oxford University Press 2018) 11.

37 Jann K Kleffner, 'The Applicability of International Humanitarian Law to Organized Armed Groups' (2011) 93 International Committee of the Red Cross 443, 449; Andrew Clapham, 'Focusing on Armed Non-State Actors' in Andrew Clapham and Paola Gaeta (eds), *The Oxford Handbook of International Law in Armed Conflict* (Oxford University Press 2014) 769–770; Marco Sassòli, *International Humanitarian Law: Rules, Controversies, and Solutions to Problems Arising in Warfare* (Edward Elgar Publishing Limited 2019) para 6.72.

38 Marko Milanovic, 'Is the Rome Statute Binding on Individuals? (And Why We Should Care)' (2011) 9 Journal of International Criminal Justice 25, 42; Sassòli (n 37) 196–199.

39 For instance, concerning Common Art 3, see the statements of the delegations of the United Kingdom, Australia and Greece in 'Final Record of the Diplomatic Conference of Geneva of 1949' Vol II (B) 47, 94. In relation to Additional Protocol II, see the statements made by the representatives of Belgium, Zaire (currently known as the Democratic Republic of the Congo) and Italy in 'Official Records of the Diplomatic Conference on the Reaffirmation and Development of International Humanitarian Law Applicable in Armed Conflicts (Geneva 1974–1977)' Vol VII 76, 104, 122; see also the statements of the representatives of the United Kingdom and the ICRC in 'Official Records of the Diplomatic Conference on the Reaffirmation and Development of International Humanitarian Law Applicable in Armed Conflicts (Geneva 1974–1977)' Vol VIII 203 (para 13), 236 (para 37), 239 (para 55); see further the statement made by the delegation of the USSR in 'Official Records of the Diplomatic Conference on the Reaffirmation and Development of International Humanitarian Law Applicable in Armed Conflicts (Geneva 1974–1977)' Vol XIV 314. See also Astrid Kjeldgaard-Pedersen, 'A Ghost in the Ivory Tower: Positivism and International Legal Regulation of Armed Opposition Groups' (2017) 7 Journal of International Humanitarian Legal Studies 32, 48, 52.

Such an examination forms an essential step since the international legal personality of an NSAG needs to be "distinct from its members" as a precondition for the possible international responsibility of that group.[40] Consequently, the examination has direct implications for how the responsibility of NSAGs could be conceptualised in international law. For instance, if an NSAG were distinguishable in its international legal personality, this would entail that a particular internationally wrongful act could result in a duality of responsibility of both an individual member and the group he or she is part of. In contrast, if an NSAG lacks a distinct legal existence, this would put into question whether such groups could be held internationally responsible.[41]

1.3.2 The application of Common Article 3 and Additional Protocol II to non-state armed groups

The treaty text of Common Article 3 provides: "[i]n the case of armed conflict not of an international character occurring in the territory of one of the High Contracting Parties, *each Party* to the conflict shall be bound to apply, as a minimum, the following provisions" [emphasis added]. The wording of the provision, which differentiates between High Contracting Parties and Parties to the conflict, clearly suggests that it directly binds NSAGs as collective legal entities following from their status as parties to a given NIAC.

Such an interpretation is in accordance with the traditional understanding that the concepts of war, or armed conflict, require at least two collective entities that are engaged in armed hostilities with each other, rather than taking place between individuals.[42] As asserted by Rodenhäuser, being a collective entity is one of the fundamental criteria for qualifying as a party to an armed conflict.[43] This is demonstrated in the authoritative definition of a NIAC provided by the Appeals Chamber of the International Criminal Tribunal for the former Yugoslavia (ICTY) in the *Tadić* case: "whenever there is [...] protracted armed violence between government authorities and organized armed groups or between such groups within a State".[44] The definition indicates that it is the organisation of a group of individuals and this group's engagement in intense violence of a collective nature that raises a given situation to an armed conflict. This two-fold legal test, involving requirements of organisation and intensity, is a means to distinguish armed conflicts from internal tensions and disturbances.[45] The requirement that an

40 *Advisory Opinion on Western Sahara* (n 2) para 148.

41 Marek St Korowicz, 'The Problem of the International Personality of Individuals' (1956) 50 The American Journal of International Law 533, 535; Murray (n 10) 42.

42 See Rodenhäuser (n 36) 20–22, 39–40, 72.

43 Ibid. 87, 314–315.

44 *Prosecutor v Tadić* ICTY (Decision on the Defence Motion for Interlocutory Appeal on Jurisdiction) IT-94–1-AR72 (2 October 1995) para 70.

45 Art 1(2) Additional Protocol II; *Prosecutor v Tadić* ICTY (Trial Judgment) IT-94–1-T (7 May 1997) para 562.

NSAG be organised for it to be considered a party to a NIAC makes a further distinction between violence carried out by isolated or random individuals and violence conducted on the part of a group.[46]

Moreover, the application of Common Article 3 to an NSAG, as a party to an armed conflict, requires that such a group is an identifiable and distinct legal entity.[47] Such an entity will have to be in "such a position that it possesses, in regard to its Members, rights which it is entitled to ask them to respect".[48] As noted by the International Court of Justice, this expresses "the essential test where a group, whether composed of States, of tribes or of individuals, is claimed to be a legal entity distinct from its members".[49] When applying this logic to NSAGs, scholars have argued that one of the main functions of the organisation requirement, which underpins the existence of a NIAC, is to determine whether an NSAG has achieved a sufficient level of organisation to be treated as a legal entity separate from its constituent members. Sufficient organisation should provide the group with the capacity to ensure its members' compliance with obligations under IHL.[50] From this perspective, the groups of indicative factors identified in international case law to assess the requisite level of an NSAG's organisation can be understood as allowing for such an evaluation.[51] The factors signalling, for instance, the ability of an NSAG to implement the basic obligations of Common Article 3 (e.g. the existence of disciplinary rules and internal regulations), the ability of a group to speak with one voice (e.g. its capacity to represent its members in political negotiations, its ability to negotiate and conclude agreements) and the presence of a command structure (e.g. the

46 *Prosecutor v Tadić* ICTY (Appeals Judgment) IT-94–1-A (15 July 1999) para 120; *Prosecutor v Ramush Haradinaj Idriz Balaj Lahi Brahimaj* ICTY (Trial Judgment) IT-04–84-T (3 April 2008) para 60; Kleffner (n 37) 450; Yoram Dinstein, 'Concluding Remarks on Non-International Armed Conflicts' (2012) 88 International Law Studies 399, 400–401; Sandesh Sivakumaran, *The Law of Non-International Armed Conflict* (Oxford University Press 2012) 177; ICRC, 'Commentary on the Third Geneva Convention: Convention (III) Relative to the Treatment of Prisoners of War' (2020) para 463.

47 Meijknecht (n 30) 41–42; Green (n 32) 72.

48 *Advisory Opinion on Reparation* (n 11) 178.

49 *Advisory Opinion on Western Sahara* (n 2) para 148 see also 149.

50 *Advisory Opinion on Reparation* (n 11) 178; Murray (n 10) 44.

51 Michael N Schmitt, 'The Status of Opposition Fighters in a Non-International Armed Conflict' (2012) 88 International Law Studies 119, 129–131; Rogier Bartels and Katharine Fortin, 'Law, Justice and a Potential Security Gap: The "Organization" Requirement in International Humanitarian Law and International Criminal Law' (2016) 21 Journal of Conflict & Security Law 29, 38. Similarly, see Murray (n 10) 75. See *Prosecutor v Boškoski and Tarčulovski* ICTY (Trial Judgment) IT-04–82-T (10 July 2008) paras 199–203; *Prosecutor v Vlastimir Dordević* ICTY (Trial Judgment) IT-05–87/1-T (23 February 2011) para 1526; *Prosecutor v Thomas Lubanga Dyilo* ICC (Trial Judgment) ICC-01/04–01/06–2842 (14 March 2012) para 537.

establishment of a high command, the creation of a chain of military hierarchy) would appear to fulfil such a function.[52]

Indeed, international bodies and scholars have interpreted the words "each Party" in Common Article 3 as referring to NSAGs, besides state armed forces, to confirm that such groups have certain international obligations once they become parties to a NIAC.[53] Correspondingly, the 2020 ICRC Commentary holds that "it is today accepted that common Article 3 is binding on non-State armed groups, both as treaty and customary law", and expressly relies on the wording of the provision to support this assertion.[54] Further support is found in the *Tablada* case, in which the Inter-American Commission on Human Rights indicated: "Common Article 3's mandatory provisions expressly bind and apply equally to both parties to internal conflicts, i.e., government and dissident forces".[55] Similarly, the Appeals Chamber of the Sierra Leone Special Court stated in 2004:

> it is well-settled that all parties to an armed conflict, whether states or non-state actors, are bound by international humanitarian law, even though only states may become parties to international treaties. Customary international law represents the common standard of behaviour within the international community, thus even armed groups hostile to a particular government have to abide by these laws.[56]

Furthermore, there are ample examples of UN bodies, including the UN Security Council, calling on NSAGs, as parties to a NIAC, to respect IHL or condemning NSAGs' violations of IHL norms, including Common Article 3.[57]

52 *Prosecutor v Boškoski and Tarčulovski* (n 51) paras 202–203; Schmalenbach (n 3) 499; Katharine Fortin, *The Accountability of Armed Groups under Human Rights Law* (Oxford University Press 2017) 125–134.

53 See regarding scholarly contributions, e.g. Erik Castrén, *Civil War* (Suomalainen Tiedeakatemia 1966) 87; Liesbeth Zegveld, *The Accountability of Armed Opposition Groups* (Cambridge University Press 2002) 9; Annyssa Bellal, 'International Law and Armed Non-State Actors in Afghanistan' (2011) 93 International Review of the Red Cross 47, 55; Clapham (n 37) 770; Sassòli (n 37) para 6.67.

54 ICRC (n 46) paras 539–540, 542. Similarly in Pictet's commentary of 1952, see Jean Pictet, *Geneva Convention I for the Amelioration of the Condition of the Wounded and Sick in Armed Forces in the Field: Commentary* (ICRC 1952) 51.

55 IACHR, 'Report No 55/97 Case No 11.137 Argentina' OEA/Ser/L/V/II.97 Doc 38 (30 October 1997) para 174. See also *Case Concerning the Military and Paramilitary Activities in and against Nicaragua (Nicaragua v United States of America)* ICJ (Merits Judgment) [1986] ICJ Rep 14 paras 218–219, in which the International Court of Justice confirmed that Common Art 3 is applicable to NSAGs.

56 *Prosecutor v Sam Hinga Norman* SCSL (Decision on Preliminary Motion Based on Lack of Jurisdiction (Child Recruitment)) SCSL-2004–14-AR72(E) (31 May 2004) para 22. The wording of the relevant paragraph clarifies that the Court uses the term 'non-state actor' to refer to NSAGs.

57 See, i.a., UNGA, Res 54/96B (21 December 1999) UN Doc A/RES/54/96A-D Preamble; UNGA, Res 62/6 (13 December 2007) UN Doc A/RES/62/6 para 22; UNSC,

Similarly, UN-mandated investigative bodies, such as commissions of inquiry, have investigated violations of Common Article 3 as well as Additional Protocol II and customary IHL carried out by NSAGs.[58] As considered by the UN Group of Eminent International and Regional Experts on Yemen:

> Non-State armed groups are bound by Common Article 3 of the Geneva Conventions and – provided that the necessary requirements as to level of organization and exercise of territorial control are reached – also by Additional Protocol II. The status of party to the conflict applies without distinction to States and non-State actors involved in the conflict, despite the fact that non-State armed groups are by nature not in a position to ratify IHL treaties.[59]

In contrast to Common Article 3, the treaty text of Additional Protocol II is less clear. According to Article 1(1), the Protocol applies to NIACs between government armed forces and "dissident armed forces or other organized armed groups". Yet, the drafting delegates deliberately formulated the other articles of the Protocol in a passive tense, without explicitly clarifying to whom they are addressed. Moreover, the deletion of the term 'parties to the conflict' as well as the provision on the equality of obligations in the draft text would appear to suggest that the Protocol is not binding on NSAGs as collective entities.[60] Nevertheless, the ICRC Commentary to Additional Protocol II clarifies that the deletion of the term only affects the drafting of the instrument, but does not change its structure from a legal point of view: "All the rules are based on the existence of *two or more parties* confronting each other. These rules grant the same rights and impose the same duties on both the established government and the *insurgent party*".[61] Furthermore, the organisational requirements in Article

Res 2098 (28 March 2013) UN Doc S/RES/2098 Preamble; UNGA, Res 70/234 (9 March 2016) UN Doc A/RES/70/234 Preamble; UNSC, Res 2340 (8 February 2017) UN Doc S/RES/2340 Preamble; UNSC, Res 2461 (27 March 2019) UN Doc S/RES/2461 para 16; UNSC, Res 2502 (19 December 2019) UN Doc S/RES/2502 para 12; UNGA, Res 74/169 (23 January 2020) UN Doc A/RES/74/169 para 13; UNSC, Res 2624 (28 February 2022) UN Doc S/RES/2624.

58 See, e.g., 'Report of the International Commission of Inquiry on Darfur' (25 January 2005) para 172, see also Section VI(6); UNSC, 'Final Report of the International Commission of Inquiry on the Central African Republic' (22 December 2014) UN Doc S/2014/928 paras 84–85, 110, 170.

59 UNHRC, 'Report of the Detailed Findings of the Group of Eminent International and Regional Experts on Yemen' (3 September 2019) UN Doc A/HRC/42/CRP.1 paras 45–47, 49.

60 Antonio Cassese, 'The Status of Rebels under the 1977 Geneva Protocol on Non-International Armed Conflicts' (1981) 30 International and Comparative Law Quarterly 416, 420–421; ICRC, *Commentary on the Additional Protocols of 8 June 1977 to the Geneva Conventions of 12 December 1949* (Martinus Nijhoff 1987) paras 4413–4415.

61 ICRC (n 60) para 4442 see also para 4444 [emphasis added].

1(1) Additional Protocol II indicate that an NSAG should be collective in nature for it to be considered a party to a NIAC within the scope of the Protocol (e.g. the requirement of responsible command).[62] The provision holds that satisfying these requirements should enable the group to implement the Protocol. This strongly suggests that to be capable of complying as a collectivity with the greater body of obligations imposed by Additional Protocol II, the group is required to have a higher degree of organisation than under Common Article 3.[63] This is further supported by the function of Protocol II. It only develops and supplements Common Article 3, which clearly binds NSAGs, "without modifying its existing conditions of application".[64] The discussion demonstrates that Additional Protocol II is directed at both states and NSAGs. This conclusion is supported by practice and legal scholarship.[65]

A final aspect that needs to be addressed is the following clause included in Common Article 3: "The application of the preceding provisions shall not affect the legal status of the Parties to the conflict."[66] The clause responds to the concern of states that the application of the Convention could interfere with a government's lawful suppression of armed activity. To this end, the clause affirms that its application to NSAGs does not confer any legitimacy or authority upon said groups. It clarifies its main objective as being of a purely humanitarian nature. The second motivation underpinning the clause is to exclude the recognition of belligerency, which would bring a greater body of international law into effect.[67] In other words, "it merely ensures respect for the essential rules of humanity which all nations consider as valid everywhere, in all circumstances".[68] Common Article 3 would most probably not have been

62 Rodenhäuser (n 36) 47–50.

63 Sivakumaran (n 46) 184–185.

64 Art 1(1) Additional Protocol II. Cassese (n 60) 424–425; Jean-Marie Henckaerts and Louise Doswald-Beck (eds), *Customary International Humanitarian Law*, vol I: Rules (Cambridge University Press 2005) 497; Murray (n 10) 109; Kjeldgaard-Pedersen (n 39) 52.

65 See some of the previously cited examples of practice as well as *Prosecutor v Akayesu* ICTR (Trial Judgment) ICTR-96-4-T (2 September 1998) para 611; UNCHR, 'Report of the United Nations High Commissioner for Human Rights on the Human Rights Situation in Colombia' (17 February 2004) UN Doc E/CN.4/2004/13 para 41; UNHRC, 'Report of the International Commission of Inquiry to Investigate All Alleged Violations of International Human Rights Law in the Libyan Arab Jamahiriya' (12 January 2012) UN Doc A/HRC/17/44 para 64; UNHRC, 'Report of the Special Rapporteur on Extrajudicial, Summary or Arbitrary Executions on Armed Non-State Actors: The Protection of the Right to Life' (5 June 2018) UN Doc A/HRC/38/44 para 25. See also Sivakumaran (n 46) 236; Konstantinos Mastorodimos, *Armed Non-State Actors in International Humanitarian and Human Rights Law: Foundation and Framework of Obligations, and Rules on Accountability* (Ashgate 2016) 99; Sassòli (n 37) para 6.67.

66 Common Art 3(4).

67 Murray (n 10) 36–37.

68 ICRC (n 46) paras 900–908.

adopted without this clause, which indicates its importance.[69] From a broader perspective, it is a reflection of the ambivalent standpoint of states, which, on the one hand, have the desire to ignore NSAGs as inherently controversial entities and, on the other, are confronted with the pragmatic need to legally regulate the behaviour of such groups.[70]

In a similar vein, Additional Protocol II has a purely humanitarian purpose. Although the Protocol does not include an analogous clause, the deletion of every mention of "parties to the conflict" was deemed sufficient.[71] Importantly, despite this disclaimer, scholars have clarified that it does not affect the conferral by Common Article 3 and Additional Protocol II of a certain measure of international legal personality on NSAGs to the extent that they become holders of certain obligations under these norms.[72] Instead, as previously noted, the clause was included to address the concerns of states, by excluding the possibility that the application of direct IHL obligations to NSAGs would grant legitimacy or the recognition of belligerency to such groups. The latter implies that NSAGs do not attain the status of full subject of international law.[73]

1.3.3 Theories on how international humanitarian law binds non-state armed groups

The previous section has established that it is generally accepted that IHL norms applicable to situations of NIAC bind NSAGs when they are party to such armed conflicts. Importantly, the preceding discussion suggests that NSAGs are bound by such norms as collective entities, distinct from their constituent members. The question whether IHL binds NSAGs directly or, alternatively, indirectly through their members can be considered further through an examination of various theories that have been presented to explain *how* IHL may bind NSAGs as non-signatories to IHL treaty law. Although these theories form the focus of continuing

69 Frédéric Siordet, 'Les Conventions de Genève et La Guerre Civile' (1950) 32 Revue Internationale de la Croix-Rouge et Bulletin International des Sociétés de la Croix-Rouge 104, 119. With regard to Common Art 3, see ICRC, *Commentary on the First Geneva Convention: Convention (I) for the Amelioration of the Condition of the Wounded and Sick in Armed Forces in the Field* (Cambridge University Press 2016) paras 862–863. See, for example, the statements made by the representatives of the United Kingdom and the United States in 'Final Record of the Diplomatic Conference of Geneva of 1949' (n 39) 10, 12. See with regard to Additional Protocol II the statement made by the representative of the Italian delegation in 'Official Records of the Diplomatic Conference on the Reaffirmation and Development of International Humanitarian Law Applicable in Armed Conflicts (Geneva 1974–1977)' (n 39) 129 para 30. See also the statement made by the representative of the Republic of Zaire ibid. 219 paras 124–127.

70 Bílková (n 22) 112.

71 ICRC (n 60) paras 4415, 4439–4440.

72 Lindsay Moir, *The Law of Internal Armed Conflict* (Cambridge University Press 2002) 65–66; Murray (n 10) 39–41; ICRC (n 46) para 902 n 853.

73 Murray (n 10) 35–38.

scholarly debate, the discourse has not involved questioning the validity of the obligations imposed on NSAGs.[74] The objective of the analysis is not to determine which theory might be the most satisfactory. Instead, the aim is to evaluate the different ways in which these theories have conceptualised NSAGs as duty bearers under IHL. This provides an advantageous approach to further elucidate the exact identity of the duty bearer. These predominant theories include: the customary law, territorial control, third-party consent, and legislative jurisdiction theories.[75]

The customary law theory holds that NSAGs are bound by IHL as a matter of customary international law. Significantly, the main approach taken to this theory asserts that NSAGs are bound as independent subjects of international law by customary IHL applicable to NIACs.[76] This results from the implicit conferral of international legal personality, necessary to have obligations under this body of law, to NSAGs by states.[77] At the same time, according to this theory, customary IHL provides the basis for the prosecution of individual members for international crimes.[78] As previously demonstrated, the Appeals Chamber of the Special Court for Sierra Leone relied on this theory by arguing that: "Customary international law represents the common standard of behaviour within the international community, thus even armed groups hostile to a particular government have to abide by these laws."[79] Similarly, the International Commission of Inquiry on Darfur turned to custom to explain the binding force of IHL *vis-à-vis* NSAGs as distinct legal entities:

> The SLM/A and JEM, like all insurgents that have reached a certain threshold of organization, stability and effective control of territory, possess international legal personality and are therefore bound by the relevant rules of customary international law on internal armed conflicts referred to above. The same is probably true also for the NMRD.[80]

74 Siordet (n 69) 105; ICRC (n 60) para 4444; Daragh Murray, 'How International Humanitarian Law Treaties Bind Non-State Armed Groups' (2014) 20 Journal of Conflict & Security Law 101, 101–102; Kjeldgaard-Pedersen (n 39) 52; Sassòli (n 37) para 6.68–6.70; ICRC (n 46) paras 541–542.

75 Note that not all scholars adopt the same categorisation or explain the theories in the same manner. Compare for instance Murray (n 74) 102; Fortin (n 52) 178. Another prominent theory that explains NSAGs being bound as a result of the domestic implementation of treaty law by states is not considered since it addresses the legal personality of NSAGs under domestic rather than international law. See further Cassese (n 60) 429; Fortin (n 52) 185–187.

76 Kleffner (n 37) 454–455; Murray (n 74) 105–109; Fortin (n 52) 204.

77 Sassòli (n 37) para 6.68.

78 *Tadić Jurisdiction Decision* (n 44) paras 128–136; Clapham (n 37) 779; Yoram Dinstein, *Non-International Armed Conflicts in International Law* (Cambridge University Press 2014) 72.

79 *Prosecutor v Sam Hinga Norman* (n 56) para 22.

80 'Report of the International Commission of Inquiry on Darfur' (n 58) para 172. The Commission included in its final report a list of the customary rules on NIAC applicable to the armed conflict in Darfur, see ibid. 166.

This entails that at least Common Article 3, given its customary nature, applies to NSAGs as groups. However, this does not explain the application of certain provisions of Additional Protocol II which have not attained this status.

According to the second theory, NSAGs are bound by IHL by virtue of exercising control over territory.[81] Kleffner argues that "[s]uch an approach shifts the focus away from the binding force of IHL on the individual to the collective entity of the organized armed group", while Zegveld adds that "[a]rmed opposition groups are then regarded as independent entities that exist side-by-side with the established authorities".[82] Although the theory conceptualises an NSAG as a distinct duty bearer, it fails to explain the binding force of Common Article 3, which does not require control over territory by an NSAG for its application.[83]

The third approach is the third-party consent theory advanced by Cassese. The theory draws from the customary rules on the binding nature of treaties on third parties as codified in the Vienna Convention on the Law of Treaties (VCLT).[84] In accordance with Articles 34–36 VCLT, the theory involves enquiring whether the contracting states had the intent to bind NSAGs as third parties as well as determining whether the concerned third party has accepted the obligations. As clarified by Cassese, the latter requires the consent of the insurgents expressed through, for example, a unilateral declaration addressed to the government. Although Cassese speaks in terms of 'rebels', such measures would imply that action is taken by the group rather than by individual members on their personal behalf.[85] Accordingly, the theory conceptualises NSAGs as subjects of IHL in their own right.[86]

The legislative jurisdiction theory holds that the individual members of an NSAG are bound as a result of the parent state's acceptance of IHL treaty law. This treaty law would become binding on all nationals within the jurisdiction of the given state due to its capacity to legislate for all its nationals.[87] This entails that IHL only imposes direct obligations on individuals. The question of NSAGs' subjectivity under international law is thus bypassed.[88] As such, contrary to the other theories discussed, the legislative jurisdiction theory does not recognise NSAGs as distinct duty bearers under IHL. Kleffner has referred to this approach as a "fundamental conceptual defect, inasmuch as it derives the binding force of IHL on organized armed groups as collective entities from the binding force on *individual members*".[89]

81 Fortin (n 52) 199.
82 Zegveld (n 53) 15; Kleffner (n 37) 452.
83 Kjeldgaard-Pedersen (n 39) 56.
84 Vienna Convention on the Law of Treaties (1969) 1155 UNTS 331.
85 Cassese (n 60) 423–429.
86 Confirmed by Murray (n 74) 112, 121.
87 Moir (n 72) 53–54.
88 Fortin (n 52) 185–186.
89 Kleffner (n 37) 449.

As Fortin points out, this would imply that NSAGs are not bound by the whole corpus of IHL norms applicable during NIACs. In accordance with the rationale of the legislative jurisdiction theory, the obligations of an NSAG under IHL would be identical to those of its individual members since the latter form the basis for the law's binding force on the group.[90] This opens a problematic gap, in that it is questionable whether all of the obligations included in Common Article 3 and Additional Protocol II are binding upon individuals.[91] This can be discerned from the language of the provisions in question and the lack of capacity on the part of an individual to carry out particular duties alone. For example, Article 5, concerning the restriction of a person's liberty, and Article 6, dealing with penal prosecutions and fair trial rights, of Additional Protocol II are clearly directed only to NSAGs as duty bearers since they require the group to take collective action to comply. The same holds for Common Article 3(1)(d), which concerns: "the passing of sentences and the carrying out of executions without previous judgment pronounced by a regularly constituted court, affording all the judicial guarantees which are recognized as indispensable by civilized peoples". An individual member clearly lacks the necessary capacity to perform such a task.[92] This is also reflected in the application requirements included in Article 1(1) Additional Protocol II: "*organized armed groups* which, under responsible command, exercise such control over a part of its territory *as to enable them* [...] *to implement this Protocol*" [emphasis added].

These examples indicate that the obligations of NSAGs and their members do not always correspond. They further suggest that, contrary to the legislative jurisdiction theory, NSAGs bear obligations under IHL independently from their members as individuals.[93] Zegveld makes a similar observation, contending that individuals and NSAGs should be distinguished as duty bearers. She argues that the obligations of individuals are limited to prohibitions to commit certain international crimes, while Common Article 3 and Additional Protocol II require a greater effort on the part of NSAGs than solely refraining from committing certain acts. Consequently, individuals alone cannot adhere to the obligations under IHL.[94]

The legislative jurisdiction theory also goes against the fundamental principle of equality of belligerents in IHL, which entails that "each party to the conflict" bears the same rights and obligations as a matter of law. As determined in the previous section, the law of NIAC understands such parties as being collective entities and not isolated individuals. Moreover, the very idea behind this

90 Fortin (n 52) 193–194.
91 Sassòli (n 37) para 6.73.
92 However, one could argue that individuals could in fact adhere to this provision by simply refraining from engaging in such activities. Kleffner (n 37) 451; Fortin (n 52) 194.
93 Fortin (n 52) 194–195.
94 Zegveld (n 53) 16.

principle would be largely set aside if NSAGs would be bound by a more limited set of obligations than state parties to armed conflicts.

Taking this all into account, the theory of legislative jurisdiction does not satisfactorily explain the binding force of the full body of IHL and is thus rejected. Nevertheless, some prominent commentators have adopted a broader understanding of the theory by including, aside from private individuals, any collectivity, such as NSAGs, present in the domestic jurisdiction of a given state.[95] If one follows this broader approach to the legislative jurisdiction theory, NSAGs would indeed be conceptualised as distinct collective duty bearers. Consequently, all four theories agree on these points.

In sum, the analysis of the various theories explaining how IHL treaty law binds NSAGs shows that all conceptualise NSAGs engaged in NIACs as distinct duty bearers. As such, the theories provide further support for the conclusion that NSAGs have direct primary obligations under IHL. They do not rely on their individual members to explain their subjectivity. Consequently, the international legal personality of NSAGs is separate from that of their members. This satisfies the precondition to consider the possible international responsibility of such groups as collective entities or, rather, as subjects of international law.

1.3.4 The scope of the international legal personality of non-state armed groups

Having concluded that NSAGs which are party to NIACs have a distinct international legal personality under IHL, the discussion now turns to an examination of the scope of this legal personality. An NSAG bears certain obligations under IHL once it becomes party to a NIAC. In other words, the fulfilment of the threshold test to determine the existence of a NIAC can be understood as the tipping point at which a group of individuals matures into an identifiable and distinct subject for the purposes of IHL.[96] It is at this point that an NSAG starts to hold certain primary obligations under, at least, Common Article 3. Hence, as is explained in Pictet's commentary on this provision, Common Article 3 applies to a non-signatory party to the Geneva Conventions "which was not yet in existence and which was not even required to represent a legal entity capable of undertaking international obligations".[97]

Once it is a party to a NIAC, an NSAG may be bound solely by the minimum obligations listed in Common Article 3 and customary IHL or it may also

95 E.g., Sandesh Sivakumaran, 'Binding Armed Opposition Groups' (2006) 55 International and Comparative Law Quarterly 369, 382; Clapham (n 37) 772, 778; Mastorodimos (n 65) 79; Murray (n 10) 106. See also the ICRC Commentary on Additional Protocol II and the 'extended legislative jurisdiction theory' introduced by Fortin: ICRC (n 60) para 4444; Fortin (n 52) 196–198.

96 Fortin (n 52) 369.

97 Pictet (n 54) 51.

be subject to the complementary and more detailed body of norms included in Additional Protocol II, when the Protocol's supplementary requirements for applicability are satisfied.[98] In light of this distinction, different NSAGs may be bound by a varying spectrum of international obligations, depending on context and circumstance. As held by Sassòli, the higher threshold of application under Protocol II introduces "a sliding scale of obligations".[99] Only NSAGs that have a greater degree of organisation, which involves the additional requirement of territorial control, are also duty holders under this Protocol. Sivakumaran argues that there is thus "a close nexus between the organization of the armed group and the content of the applicable law".[100] Following this line of reasoning, the nexus suggests that the degree of organisation of an NSAG is used as an indicator to determine the ability of the group to comply with the greater body of international obligations. This function is already reflected in the organisation test under Common Article 3. It emphasises factors relating to, i.a., the presence of a command structure and a disciplinary system to ascertain whether an NSAG has a minimum level of organisation capable of ensuring adherence to the provision by its members.[101] Organisational competence is not only assessed on the basis of, for example, an NSAG's code of conduct when it exists, but also considers the context in which the group operates.[102] These observations are expressed in the argumentation of the Trial Chamber in the *Boškoski* case:

> This difference in the required degree of organisation is logical in view of the more detailed rules of international humanitarian law that apply in Additional Protocol II conflicts [...] By contrast, Common Article 3 reflects basic humanitarian protections, and a party to an armed conflict only needs a minimal degree of organisation to ensure their application.[103]

Significantly, this reasoning is supported by Article 1(1) Additional Protocol II, which states that NSAGs should be under a responsible command and in control over a part of the territory "as to enable them [...] to implement this Protocol". The ICRC Commentary to this provision clarifies that the ability to implement the Protocol is fundamental in nature and justifies the other listed requirements. It recognises that although the threshold for application seems

98 See Art 1(1) Additional Protocol II.
99 Marco Sassòli, 'Introducing a Sliding-Scale of Obligations to Address Fundamental Inequality Between Armed Groups and States?' (2011) 93 International Review of the Red Cross 426, 430–431.
100 Sivakumaran (n 46) 185.
101 *Prosecutor v Boškoski and Tarčulovski* (n 51) paras 194–203; Fortin (n 52) 134. See also Section 1.3.2.
102 Sivakumaran (n 46) 171–172.
103 *Prosecutor v Boškoski and Tarčulovski* (n 51) para 197. See in relation to Common Art 3 also para 196: "[t]he leadership of the group must, as a minimum, have the ability to exercise some control over its members so that the basic obligations of Common Article 3 of the Geneva Conventions may be implemented."

fairly high, it has a "degree of realism".[104] In this regard, the Commentary asserts that in such circumstances it is reasonable to expect that the parties apply "the rules developed in the Protocol" given they have "the minimum infrastructure required therefor".[105] This confirms the conclusion that there exists a close nexus between the higher degree of organisational capacity required of an NSAG and the greater body of applicable law under Additional Protocol II.[106] As a result, the organisation requirements can be understood as having the function of ascertaining a group's ability to fulfil the international obligations imposed upon it. Moreover, this contributes to a more realistic international legal regulation of NIACs.[107]

All in all, the discussion indicates that within the same category of subject of international law – i.e. NSAGs involved in a NIAC – individual groups can differ amongst themselves in the extent of their international obligations. This variance depends on their organisational capacities.[108] This provides a legal response to the heterogeneous nature of NSAGs active in NIACs. These findings concretise some of the conclusions that were drawn from the International Court of Justice's Advisory Opinion in the *Reparation for Injuries* case in Section 1.2. Namely, legal subjects may vary in the extent of their obligations (even within the same category) and their international legal personality should not be determined in an abstract manner but depends partly on the capacity of the actor to bear certain obligations.

NSAGs enjoy limited international legal personality for the functions they assume as parties to a NIAC.[109] In keeping with the objectives of IHL, there is a functional need to ensure the protection of civilians and minimize suffering by holding NSAGs to certain minimum obligations.[110] Moreover, from an international legal perspective, NSAGs only exist as legal entities alongside a NIAC. Indeed, they derive their legal personality from their status as a party to such conflicts.[111] Accordingly, they are recognised in law as long as they meet the organisation requirement, while taking part in armed hostilities of certain

104 ICRC (n 60) para 4470.
105 Ibid.
106 Similarly Fortin (n 52) 134–136, 154–155.
107 Ibid. 137; Sassòli (n 37) para 10.232.
108 This understanding finds support in the conclusion of Fortin that: "international legal personality is a concept that exists along a spectrum", see Fortin (n 52) 152–153. See also Rodenhäuser (n 36) 12–13.
109 Veronika Bílková, 'Establishing Direct Responsibility of Armed Opposition Groups for Violations of International Humanitarian Law?' in Noemi Gal-Or, Cedric Ryngaert and Math Noortmann (eds), *Responsibilities of the Non-State Actor in Armed Conflict and the Market Place* (Brill Nijhof 2015) 265; UNHRC, 'Report of the Special Rapporteur on Extrajudicial, Summary or Arbitrary Executions on Armed Non-State Actors: The Protection of the Right to Life' (n 65) para 43.
110 Worster (n 10) 238.
111 Zegveld (n 53) 151–152; Ezequiel Heffes and Brian Frenkel, 'The International Responsibility of Non-State Armed Groups: In Search of the Applicable Rules' (2017) 8 Goettingen Journal of International Law 39, 45.

intensity.[112] NSAGs are "provisional subjects of international law", this status stands in contrast to states, which are relatively stable and permanent subjects, which continue, unlike NSAGs, to legally exist beyond the conclusion of a NIAC.[113]

1.4 International human rights law

1.4.1 The application of human rights law beyond the state

Since the beginning of the 1990s, the question as to whether NSAGs should bear additional obligations under IHRL during situations of NIAC has become increasingly prominent in both international practice and legal scholarship. The international human rights regime has evolved to a point where it is no longer deemed applicable only during peacetime, but also, alongside IHL, in situations of armed conflict.[114] Nevertheless, the application of IHRL to NSAGs is not without controversy. Traditionally, IHRL only imposes direct obligations on states, particularly to respect, protect and fulfil the human rights of the persons under their jurisdiction, while being predicated on the responsibility of states.[115] States are required to tackle any possible human rights concerns emanating from NSAGs within this framework, which supposedly renders the regime adequate.[116] The state-centric nature of the human rights regime can be traced back to its historical origins. It developed as a means of curbing an entity's abuse of power over individuals who had been subjected to its public authority.[117] Considering that states are the primary entities holding and exercising such public authority, human rights law is first and foremost concerned with states as duty bearers.[118] Accordingly,

112 Bílková (n 109) 282. Here a slight nuance can be made. Although a NIAC only exists once there is a sufficient level of organisation of the parties and of the violence, it is generally recognised that IHL can continue to apply even when these levels are no longer met. According to Sassòli, the general close of military operations can serve as a criterion to determine when a NIAC has ended. Sassòli (n 37) para 6.59.

113 'Fourth Report on State Responsibility, by Mr Roberto Ago, Special Rapporteur' Yearbook of the International Law Commission (1972) Vol II UN Doc A/CN.4/264 and Add.1 para 154.

114 *Advisory Opinion on the Legality of the Threat or Use of Nuclear Weapons* ICJ [1996] ICJ Rep 226 para 25; *Advisory Opinion on Legal Consequences of the Construction of a Wall in the Occupied Palestinian Territory* ICJ [2004] ICJ Rep 136 para 106; *Case Concerning Armed Activities on the Territory of the Congo (Congo v Uganda)* ICJ (Judgment) [2005] ICJ Rep 168 para 216.

115 Charles R Beitz, *The Idea of Human Rights* (Oxford University Press 2011) 13.

116 Clapham (n 15) 25.

117 Maya Hertig Randall, 'The History of International Human Rights Law' in Gloria Gaggioli and Robert Kolb (eds), *Research Handbook on Human Rights and Humanitarian Law* (Edward Elgar Publishing 2013) 7.

118 Nigel S Rodley, 'Can Armed Opposition Groups Violate Human Rights?' in Kathleen E Mahoney and Paul Mahoney (eds), *Human Rights in the Twenty-First Century: A Global Challenge* (Martinus Nijhoff Publishers 1993) 298–299.

IHRL has been designed to regulate the vertical relationship between governments and the persons under their jurisdiction.[119] This is also reflected in the international and regional human rights treaties, which have been concluded by and for states. In such a context, NSAGs have generally not been included as duty bearers.[120] Moreover, it has been argued that bestowing direct human rights obligations on NSAGs could afford them unwarranted legitimacy, which would undermine the authority of the state and potentially dilute the state's human rights responsibilities.[121] If this traditional conceptualisation is favoured, IHRL only imposes additional obligations on the state party to a NIAC, while an NSAG is only bound by IHL. Indeed, in concert with this traditionalist view, some scholars have questioned the added value of extending the application of IHRL from states to NSAGs engaged in NIACs. Their underlying argument is that Common Article 3 and Additional Protocol II already provide the most essential protections.[122]

However, in taking a contrary position, Fortin convincingly demonstrates the added value of applying IHRL to NSAGs, alongside IHL, in territories under the control of such groups. Recent social science research has shown that, during times of armed conflict, civilians' everyday lives are not solely characterised by a concern for physical security or survival. Their everyday lives may actually persist in the midst of conflict.[123] Consequently, individual rights that may not exhibit a particular nexus to situations of armed conflict retain significant importance (e.g. the freedom of movement, the right to work).[124] However, states are unlikely to have the capacity to guarantee the human rights of the civilian population in rebel-held areas. Their ability to effectively exercise due diligence obligations in such areas may also be significantly restricted.[125]

119 Manfred Nowak and Karolina Miriam Januszewski, 'Non-State Actors and Human Rights' in Math Noortmann, August Reinisch and Cedric Ryngaert (eds), *Non-State Actors in International Law* (Hart Publishing 2015) 116–117; Rodenhäuser (n 36) 121–123.

120 Art 2 ICCPR (1966) 999 UNTS 171 and Art 2 ICESCR (1966) 993 UNTS 3 speak, e.g., in terms of "each State Party to the present Covenant". See also HR Committee, 'General Comment No 31 (The Nature of the General Legal Obligation Imposed on States Parties to the Covenant)' (26 May 2004) UN Doc CCPR/C/21/Rev1/Add13 para 8; HR Committee, 'General Comment No 35 (Article 9: Liberty and Security of Person)' (16 December 2014) UN Doc CCPR/C/GC/35 para 7. For two notable exceptions, see Art 4 Optional Protocol to the Convention on the Rights of the Child on the involvement of children in armed conflict (2000) 2173 UNTS 222; Art 7(5) African Union Convention for the Protection and Assistance of Internally Displaced Persons in Africa (Kampala Convention) (2009).

121 Clapham (n 15) 25.

122 See Zegveld (n 53) 52; Jelena Pejic, 'Conflict Classification and the Law Applicable to Detention and the Use of Force' in Elizabeth Wilmshurst (ed), *International Law and the Classification of Conflicts* (Oxford University Press 2012) n 22.

123 Katharine Fortin, 'The Application of Human Rights Law to Everyday Civilian Life Under Rebel Control' (2016) 63 Netherlands International Law Review 161, 167–169.

124 Ibid. 169–170.

125 Cedric Ryngaert, 'Human Rights Obligations of Armed Groups' (2008) 41 Belgian Review of International Law 355, 368–369; Rodenhäuser (n 36) 143–144; UNHRC,

Hence, persons living under the control of an NSAG are *de facto* deprived of the protections afforded under IHRL, with no viable recourse to make any sort of meaningful claim in respect of these rights.[126] Although NSAGs are still bound by IHL, these obligations will only cover a number of core human rights in instances that have a certain nexus to the armed conflict.[127]

Applying IHRL to NSAGs which exercise control over territory, alongside states, may mitigate the protection and accountability gaps in the human rights system.[128] In addition, the underlying rationale of IHRL, that being the regulation of the vertical relationship between the governor and the governed, would be *de facto* satisfied.[129] In contrast to assumptions made within legal scholarship, NSAGs are in fact often engaged in governance activities and regularly exercise a considerable degree of control and organisation over the territory and persons they rule.[130] The ICRC estimates that, as of July 2022, at least 175 million people live in areas controlled by armed groups (including NSAGs), of which many engage in *de facto* governance and the provision of public services.[131] As such, IHRL has a potentially important role to play in this context.

1.4.2 Non-state armed groups as duty bearers

The analysis in Section 1.3 allowed extracting a picture of NSAGs as duty bearers, rendering a comparable review of the theories on how NSAGs are bound by IHRL unnecessary.[132] Under this approach, to be subjected to the obligations of IHRL, an NSAG would need to have a certain level of organisation that would allow identifying it as a collective legal entity and distinguishing it, as such, from its constituent members.[133] In addition, the organisational structure would need to provide the group with the reasonable capacity to

'Report of the Special Rapporteur on Extrajudicial, Summary or Arbitrary Executions on Armed Non-State Actors: The Protection of the Right to Life' (n 65) para 23.

126 For a concrete example, see UNCHR, 'Report of the Special Rapporteur on Extrajudicial, Summary or Arbitrary Executions: Mission to Sri Lanka' (27 March 2006) UN Doc E/CN.4/2006/53/Add.5 paras 34–35.

127 Yaël Ronen, 'Human Rights Obligations of Territorial Non-State Actors' (2013) 46 Cornell International Law Journal 21, 23; Fortin (n 123) 172–177.

128 Fortin (n 123) 179; UNHRC, 'Report of the Special Rapporteur on Extrajudicial, Summary or Arbitrary Executions on Armed Non-State Actors: The Protection of the Right to Life' (n 65) paras 8, 28, 51.

129 Rodley (n 118) 313; Zegveld (n 53) 148–149; Murray (n 74) 157–158, 274.

130 Fortin (n 123) 163. See, e.g., Jeremy M Weinstein, *Inside Rebellion: The Politics of Insurgent Violence* (Cambridge University Press 2009) 69–70, 180, 265, 268–269; 'Islamic State-Controlled Parts of Syria, Iraq Largely Out of Reach: Red Cross' *Reuters* (13 March 2015); Geneva Call, 'Administration of Justice by Armed Non-State Actors' (2018) 5.

131 Matthew Bamber-Zryd, 'ICRC Engagement with Armed Groups in 2022' (*ICRC Humanitarian Law & Policy Blog*, 12 January 2023).

132 See, for an overview of such theories, Fortin (n 52) 18–21.

133 *Advisory Opinion on Western Sahara* (n 2) para 148.

implement the applicable obligations.[134] If this were not the case, the purpose of imposing IHRL obligations on NSAGs would risk being lost from the very start and remaining a legal fiction.[135] However, this approach would not entail that an NSAG actually respects IHRL in practice or accepts its applicability.[136]

Under the IHL framework, it was previously demonstrated that an NSAG is required to have a certain degree of organisation to become a party to a NIAC. Moreover, the evaluation of the organisation requirement, pursuant to the factors identified in the case law of the ICTY, functions as a means of determining the organisational unity of an NSAG in terms of it being separate from its members. This is based on the understanding that one of the aims of the organisation requirement is to determine whether an NSAG has a sufficient level of organisation to be treated as a distinct legal entity, which can ensure compliance with the imposed obligations. This can be illustrated by way of the factors which signal the presence of a command structure. These include, amongst others, the establishment of a general staff or high command and the existence of internal regulations that create a chain of military hierarchy between the various levels of commanders.[137] In a similar fashion, these factors could also inform the appraisal that would have to be made regarding the distinct existence of an NSAG under an IHRL framework. This is justified on the basis that the same type of NSAG is being examined here in the IHRL context as that examined in the IHL context. This NSAG would acquire human rights obligations alongside its IHL obligations for the duration of the armed conflict.[138]

In Section 1.3.4, it was argued that there exists a nexus between the organisation requirements under IHL and the content of the obligations imposed on NSAGs. This reasonably ensures that such groups have the capacity to fulfil the obligations to which they are bound. Correspondingly, Additional Protocol II requires a higher degree of organisation on the part of an NSAG than Common Article 3 considering the greater body of applicable norms. Following this logic, the application of certain human rights obligations to NSAGs may require a higher degree or even a distinct form of organisation from such groups due to the nature and scope of IHRL norms as contrasted to those under the IHL framework. For instance, the fulfilment of the right to health requires the satisfaction of, at the very least, a minimum core of obligations, namely to ensure, amongst others, the rights to access to health facilities, goods and services; access to basic shelter, housing and sanitation; and, the provision of

134 This is in line with the argument that international legal personality should not be determined *in abstracto* (see Section 1.2). Murray (n 10) 75.

135 Antonio Cassese, *International Law* (2nd edn, Oxford University Press 2005) 12–13.

136 Kelsen (n 34) 414; Rodenhäuser (n 36) 147. Compare to *Prosecutor v Boškoski and Tarčulovski* (n 51) para 205.

137 *Prosecutor v Boškoski and Tarčulovski* (n 51) para 199. See Section 1.3.2.

138 Fortin (n 52) 158–159.

appropriate training for health personnel.[139] It comes as no surprise that such obligations require considerable financial resources and institutional capacity.[140] Hence, in order to determine whether an NSAG is capable of applying such human rights obligations, it may be necessary to identify and evaluate distinct organisational factors compared to those required under IHL. The latter are largely defined regarding an NSAG's level of organisation in military terms. This is of less relevance to IHRL, which basically regulates a governance relationship between a governing entity and a population within a particular territory. As such, an organisational factor that could be more relevant in the context of IHRL is the group's capacity to administer the territory under its control.[141]

1.4.3 A context-dependent approach to the application of human rights law

Although the debate continues among international law scholars, it is increasingly accepted in both international practice and legal literature that NSAGs may acquire human rights obligations in addition to those under IHL. UN organs and bodies, including the UN Security Council and the UN General Assembly, as well as the Human Rights Council's Special Procedures and commissions of inquiry have produced a considerable body of resolutions, decisions and reports which recognise the application of IHRL to NSAGs. Hence, this practice puts the traditional state-centric nature of this body of law into question.[142] This is particularly deemed to be the case when NSAGs exercise some degree of *de facto* control over a territory and population.[143]

139 Art 12 ICESCR; CESCR, 'General Comment No 14: The Right to the Highest Attainable Standard of Health (Art 12)' (11 August 2000) UN Doc E/C.12/2000/4 paras 43–44.

140 For an extensive discussion of the application of the right to health to NSAGs, see Murray (n 10) ch 8.

141 Gilles Giacca, *Economic, Social, and Cultural Rights in Armed Conflict* (Oxford University Press 2014) 270–271; Fortin (n 52) 159–160; UNHRC, 'Report of the Special Rapporteur on Extrajudicial, Summary or Arbitrary Executions on Armed Non-State Actors: The Protection of the Right to Life' (n 65) para 59.

142 According to a review of UN Security Council practice conducted by Constantinides, the Council did not address NSAGs in human rights terms up until 1995. By the end of the 1990s, this became a more systematic practice. Aristoteles Constantinides, 'Direct Human Rights Obligations and Accountability of Armed Opposition Groups: The Practice of the UN Security Council' (2010) 4 Human Rights & International Legal Discourse 89, 98–99. A more recent systematic study identified over 125 UN Security Council resolutions and approx. 65 UN General Assembly resolutions that pertain to what might be conceptualised as possible human rights obligations of certain NSAGs, see Jessica S Burniske, Naz K Modirzadeh and Dustin A Lewis, 'Armed Non-State Actors and International Human Rights Law: An Analysis of the Practice of the U.N. Security Council and U.N. General Assembly – Briefing Report with Annexes' (Harvard Law School Program on International Law and Armed Conflict 2017). See in relation to UN Human

For example, it was held in a 2008 report of the UN High Commissioner for Human Rights on the Occupied Palestinian Territories:

> [w]ith respect to Hamas, it is worth recalling that non-State actors that exercise government-like functions and control over a territory are obligated to respect human rights norms when their control affects the human rights of the individuals under their control.[144]

Similarly, the Commission of Inquiry on Libya considered: "it is increasingly accepted that where non-State groups exercise de facto control over territory, they must respect fundamental human rights of persons in that territory".[145] A further example can be found in General Recommendation No. 30 of 2013 on Women in Conflict Prevention, Conflict and Post-Conflict Situations, in which the Committee on the Elimination of Discrimination against Women recognised:

> although non-State actors cannot become parties to the Convention, the Committee notes that under certain circumstances, in particular where an armed group with an identifiable political structure exercises significant

Rights Council practice: Annyssa Bellal, 'Human Rights Obligations of Armed Non-State Actors: An Exploration of the Practice of the UN Human Rights Council' (Geneva Academy of International Humanitarian Law and Human Rights 2016).

143 Regarding scholarship, see Christian Tomuschat, 'The Applicability of Human Rights Law to Insurgent Movements' in Horst Fischer and others (eds), *Krisensicherung und Humanitärer Schutz – Crisis Management and Humanitarian Protection. Festschrift für Dieter Fleck* (Berliner Wissenschafts-Verlag 2004); Sivakumaran (n 46) 96; Jean-Marie Henckaerts and Cornelius Wiesener, 'Human Rights Obligations of Non-State Armed Groups: A Possible Contribution from Customary International Law?' in Robert Kolb and Gloria Gaggioli (eds), *Research Handbook on Human Rights and Humanitarian Law* (Edward Elgar Publishing 2013) 159, 161; Murray (n 10) 151; Fortin (n 52) 385.

144 UNHRC, 'Human Rights Situation in Palestine and Other Occupied Arab Territories' (6 June 2008) UN Doc A/HRC/8/17 para 9 see also para 6. This assertion is supported in footnote 12 by reference to a joint report on Lebanon and Israel by a group of four Special Rapporteurs, see UNHRC, 'Report of the Special Rapporteur on Extrajudicial, Summary or Arbitrary Executions; the Special Rapporteur on the Right of Everyone to the Enjoyment of the Highest Attainable Standard of Physical and Mental Health; the Representative of the Secretary-General on Human Rights of Internally Displaced Persons; and the Special Rapporteur on Adequate Housing as a Component of the Right to an Adequate Standard of Living: Mission to Lebanon and Israel' (2 October 2006) UN Doc A/HRC/2/7 para 19.

145 UNHRC, 'Report of the International Commission of Inquiry to Investigate All Alleged Violations of International Human Rights Law in the Libyan Arab Jamahiriya' (n 65) para 62. The Commission makes in this regard reference in footnote 51 to the following report: UNSG, 'Report of the Secretary-General's Panel of Experts on Accountability in Sri Lanka' (31 March 2011) para 188.

control over territory and population, non-State actors are obliged to respect international human rights.[146]

The UN Special Rapporteur on extrajudicial, summary or arbitrary executions concluded, in 2018, based on a review of UN practice, that "ANSAs [armed non-state actors] that have displaced the *de jure* government and established (exclusive) territorial control are responsible for the protection (and violations) of human rights in the areas under their control".[147] Moreover, there is also practice which suggests that NSAGs that lack control over territory must still respect certain human rights obligations, such as core human rights norms which are part of *jus cogens*.[148]

Within this framework, the discourse appears to be leaning towards a context-dependent approach to the application of IHRL to NSAGs. The approach takes account of the organisational capacity of an NSAG and the circumstances in which it operates. In particular, the extent to which the group exercises control over a territory and population is central to determining the breadth of obligations applicable in each context.[149] In practice, this results in the application of human rights obligations in a graduated manner. NSAGs that factually resemble states, for example by controlling and exercising quasi-governmental functions over a certain part of the territory, would bear IHRL obligations akin to states. Others, lacking a state-like structure but controlling territory, would be bound by a more limited scope of obligations.[150]

146 CEDAW, 'General Recommendation No 30 on Women in Conflict Prevention, Conflict and Post-Conflict Situations' (18 October 2013) UN Doc CEDAW/C/GC/30 para 16.

147 UNHRC, 'Report of the Special Rapporteur on Extrajudicial, Summary or Arbitrary Executions on Armed Non-State Actors: The Protection of the Right to Life' (n 65) para 19 see also paras 9–18, 20. See also UNHRC, 'Report of the Special Rapporteur on the Promotion of Truth, Justice, Reparation and Guarantees of Non-Recurrence: Role and Responsibilities of Non-State Actors in Transitional Justice Processes' (12 July 2022) UN Doc A/HRC/51/34 para 50.

148 UNHRC, 'Report of the Independent International Commission of Inquiry on the Syrian Arab Republic' (22 February 2012) UN Doc A/HRC/19/69 para 106; Tilman Rodenhäuser, 'Human Rights Obligations of Non-State Armed Groups in Other Situations of Violence: The Syria Example' (2012) 3 Journal of International Humanitarian Legal Studies 263; Giacca (n 141) 257–258.

149 Rodenhäuser evaluates e.g. an NSAG's infrastructure and degree of power exercised over persons under its control as well as the extent to which the *de jure* government continues to provide certain human rights functions in the controlled area. Rodenhäuser (n 36) 210–211.

150 See Giacca (n 141) 267–271; Annyssa Bellal, 'Establishing the Direct Responsibility of Non-State Armed Groups for Violations of International Norms: Issues of Attribution' in Noemi Gal-Or, Cedric Ryngaert and Math Noortmann (eds), *Responsibility of the Non-State Actor in Armed Conflict and the Market Place* (Brill Nijhof 2015) 308–309; UNHRC, 'Report of the Special Rapporteur on the Promotion and Protection of Human Rights and Fundamental Freedoms While Countering Terrorism, Ben Emmerson' (16 June 2015) UN Doc A/HRC/29/51 paras

This necessitates the making of case-by-case assessments of each situation at hand.[151] The aforementioned UN Special Rapporteur proposes such an approach when applying obligations concerning the right to life to NSAGs. It could entail that the negative obligation to not violate individuals' right to life applies to all NSAGs, while certain groups may be also under an obligation to, for instance, deliver some minimum policing functions or justice depending on the sophistication of their governance capacity.[152] As a result, this involves a differentiated rather than an all-or-nothing approach. The latter approach would have implied that only those groups that can ensure the full range of human rights obligations would be bound by them.[153] Significantly, the context-dependent approach responds to concerns raised by some commentators that NSAGs may not have the required capacity to be bound by IHRL.[154] Such concerns are formulated against the backdrop that NSAGs typically do not have the same level of resources and institutional capacity as states. The capabilities of NSAGs may also differ significantly across examples.[155] At one extreme, some groups have a centralised command structure, with a strict hierarchy and discipline, are well financed, and control large portions of the territory; while other groups are characterised by their minimum level of organisation, a lack of resources, and a decentralised organisational structure that brings together a series of autonomous sub-groups.[156] Correspondingly, the context-dependent approach ensures the effectiveness of the obligations to a greater degree or, put differently, it ensures that the legal framework remains realistic.[157]

30–31; Murray (n 10) 275–276; Andrew Clapham, 'Detention by Armed Groups under International Law' (2017) 91 International Law Studies US Naval War College 1, 27; Fortin (n 52) 162; Andrew Clapham, 'Human Rights Obligations for Non-State Actors: Where Are We Now?' in Fanny Lafontaine and Francois Larocque (eds), *Doing Peace the Rights Way: Essays in International Law and Relations in Honour of Louise Arbour* (Intersentia 2018) 1; Rodenhäuser (n 36) 147, 210–211; UNHRC, 'Report of the Special Rapporteur on Extrajudicial, Summary or Arbitrary Executions on Armed Non-State Actors: The Protection of the Right to Life' (n 65) para 8.

151 Rodenhäuser (n 36) 211.

152 UNHRC, 'Report of the Special Rapporteur on Extrajudicial, Summary or Arbitrary Executions on Armed Non-State Actors: The Protection of the Right to Life' (n 65) paras 67–78 see particularly paras 69, 74.

153 Fortin (n 52) 161–162; Murray (n 10) 172.

154 See Moir (n 72) 194; Sandesh Sivakumaran, 'Re-Envisaging the International Law of Internal Armed Conflict' (2011) 22 European Journal of International Law 219, 255–256.

155 Rodenhäuser (n 36) 148, 210.

156 ICRC, 'Strengthening International Humanitarian Law Protecting Persons Deprived of Their Liberty: Concluding Report' (2015) 33; ICRC, 'The Roots of Restraint in War' (2018) 38, 46.

157 Murray (n 10) 177–179; Fortin (n 52) 169.

As a lesser body of obligations would bind NSAGs with a lesser degree of organisational capacity, this approach overlaps with that taken under IHL.[158] In further similarity to the IHL approach, NSAGs may be bound by a different scope of obligations and the degree of organisation of a group is used as an indicator to reasonably ensure its capacity to implement the imposed obligations.[159] The approach enables stakeholders to deal with the challenges posed by the structural diversity present among NSAGs and in comparison to states. Lastly, it shows sensitivity towards ensuring that the applicable obligations are feasible in practice.

Some scholars have argued that NSAGs exercising territorial control may also hold human rights obligations in the absence of an armed conflict. They recognise that such groups can legally exist at all times.[160] However, there appears to be little international practice, at present, that supports such an argument in contrast to the application of IHRL to NSAGs which are engaged in NIACs.[161] Furthermore, it is questionable as to how the notion of '*armed* group' might apply in non-conflict situations, since the manner in which it has been conceptualised, in legal practice and scholarship, is premised on the involvement of the group in a NIAC.[162] It triggers the question 'what does it mean for an entity to be armed in such circumstances?' As confirmed by Sassòli, "the requirements of organization that an entity must fulfil to qualify as an armed group have thus far exclusively been discussed in relation to IHL of NIACs and they do not make sense absent an armed conflict".[163] Accordingly, the organisation requirement would have to be defined in a distinct manner and be disconnected from situations of armed conflict.[164] This would imply a different approach to that suggested in the previous section. It would further require an explanation as to how such non-conflict non-state entities still relate to NSAGs and, correspondingly, how they can be understood as belonging to the same category of legal subjects under international law.

158 Fortin (n 52) 162.

159 Murray (n 10) 275; Rodenhäuser (n 36) 211; UNHRC, 'Report of the Special Rapporteur on Extrajudicial, Summary or Arbitrary Executions on Armed Non-State Actors: The Protection of the Right to Life' (n 65) paras 50–51.

160 See Murray (n 10) ch 5; Rodenhäuser (n 36) 118, 181.

161 For a notable exception, see UNHRC, 'Report of the Independent International Commission of Inquiry on the Syrian Arab Republic' (n 148) para 106; UNHRC, 'Report of the Independent International Commission of Inquiry on the Syrian Arab Republic' (16 August 2012) UN Doc A/HRC/21/50 para 12.

162 See, e.g., Schmitt (n 51) 131–132.

163 Marco Sassòli, 'Two Fascinating Questions: Are All Subjects of a Legal Order Bound by the Same Customary Law and Can Armed Groups Exist in the Absence of Armed Conflict? Book Discussion' (*EJIL: Talk!*, 4 November 2016).

164 Tom Gal, 'The International Legal Status of Armed Groups: Can One Be Determined Outside the Scope of Armed Conflict? (Book Review Essay)' (2018) 51 Israel Law Review 321, 325, 329.

1.5 Conclusions

Several conclusions can be drawn from the analysis of the international legal personality of NSAGs that have subsequent relevance when examining the possible collective responsibility of such groups and their duty to repair within the international legal system. First, it has been established that an NSAG that is party to a NIAC constitutes a distinct subject of international law, with legal personality under IHL and potentially IHRL in certain circumstances. An NSAG begins its legal existence within the international legal system once the threshold requirements to determine the existence of a NIAC are fulfilled. It is at this point that the collectivity transcends the collection of individuals and attains a separate legal existence. The requirements under both bodies of law for an NSAG to have a certain degree of organisation allows treating that group as a legal entity distinct from its individual members, which can fulfil and ensure compliance with the applicable international obligations. The international legal personality of an NSAG thus satisfies the necessary precondition to subsequently consider the status of such groups in the law of international responsibility.

Second, it has been determined that NSAGs enjoy limited international legal personality. Contrary to states that continue to exist beyond the conclusion of a NIAC, an NSAG is a temporary subject of international law. This conclusion poses significant challenges when seeking to hold an NSAG legally responsible for breaches of its international obligations in the aftermath of an armed conflict. In such a context, the group would have ceased to exist from an international legal perspective. As illustrated by Clapham, "one can not really indict something that does not exist in law".[165] This challenge presents itself starkly with respect to the question of reparations, which is generally dealt with after a conflict has ended.[166] Consequently, this must be considered when developing a regime of international responsibility for NSAGs.[167]

Third, it has been argued that the international legal personality of NSAGs should not be determined in an abstract manner. Instead, the reasonable capacity of a group to fulfil the concerned international obligations is one of the elements that should be considered. The analysis of the IHL and IHRL frameworks has indicated that the degree of organisation of an NSAG is used as an indicator of such normative capacity. This results in an international legal framework which takes a differentiated approach to the regulation of NSAGs

165 Andrew Clapham, 'The Question of Jurisdiction Under International Criminal Law over Legal Persons: Lessons from the Rome Conference on an International Criminal Court' in Menno T Kamminge and Saman Zia-Zarifi (eds), *Liability of Multinational Corporations under International Law* (Kluwer 2000) 157; Frédéric Mégret, 'The Subjects of International Criminal Law' in Philip Kastner (ed), *International Criminal Law in Context* (Routledge 2017) 38.

166 Heffes and Frenkel (n 111) 71.

167 Íñigo Álvarez (n 1) 68.

which are party to armed conflicts. Hence, a varied range of international obligations may bind NSAGs which exhibit different levels of organisation and control over territory. Such an approach responds to two concerns: namely that NSAGs generally do not have the same capabilities as states and that they also differ amongst themselves. Fundamentally, this approach indicates that international law can accommodate such diversity and is, consequently, capable of surmounting these challenges. Ultimately, it ensures that the international obligations imposed on NSAGs are realistic and effective.

Similar challenges confront the discussion about a possible duty of NSAGs to repair under international law. Scholars have indicated that such groups, in contrast to states, may have neither the organisational capacity nor the resources to provide reparations.[168] In addition, the structural disparity among NSAGs could render the development of a uniform legal framework difficult.[169] A similar differentiated approach could underpin the development of a potential set of secondary rules of international law concerning reparation applicable to NSAGs. This could provide a viable solution to such concerns. Indeed, this analysis of the international legal personality of NSAGs has opened the door to considering such an approach and thus warrants further exploration. Nothing appears to prevent such considerations from equally applying to the question of international responsibility of NSAGs. These considerations will be further examined in Chapter 4.

Last, the discussion has shown that the position of NSAGs in international law is marked by a tension between the need to regulate the behaviour of these controversial actors and the desire of states to simply disregard them as not to confer any legitimacy or recognition upon them. Within this context, states have regularly labelled NSAGs as 'terrorists', which has been used by some to deny the application of IHL to counterterrorism operations and justify exceptional responses.[170] This attitude by states has the adverse effect of challenging the development of a regime of international responsibility of NSAGs and a role for such actors in reparations. This could be considered as an unwarranted step that would treat NSAGs more akin to states. Although the development of such a regime would expand NSAGs' legal personality, at least in terms of

168 See, e.g., Cecily Rose, 'An Emerging Norm: The Duty of States to Provide Reparations for Human Rights Violations by Non-State Actors' (2010) 33 Hastings International and Comparative Law Review 307, 309–310; Luke Moffett, 'Beyond Attribution: Responsibility of Armed Non-State Actors for Reparations in Northern Ireland, Colombia and Uganda' in Noemi Gal-Or, Cedric Ryngaert and Math Noortmann (eds), *Responsibilities of the Non-State Actor in Armed Conflict and the Market Place* (Brill Nijhof 2015) 325, 334.

169 Jann K Kleffner, 'The Collective Accountability of Organized Armed Groups for System Crimes' in Andre Nollkaemper and Harmen Gijsbrecht van der Wilt (eds), *System Criminality in International Law* (Cambridge University Press 2009) 258; Bellal (n 150) 306–307.

170 ICRC, 'International Humanitarian Law and the Challenges of Contemporary Armed Conflicts' (2019) 58–59.

additional obligations, it would not be concerned with extending any legitimacy or privilege towards such groups. The overarching objective is, instead, to take NSAGs serious as violators, by attaching legal consequences to their violations of the norms that the international legal system seeks to promote.[171] This should not be considered a controversial proposal, since it goes to the very essence of the notion of law itself and, correspondingly, any legal system.[172] In addition, from a justice and accountability perspective, it is an imperative in the context of the fight against impunity that responsible NSAGs remedy the harm they have caused during situations of armed conflict.[173] The international community has recognised impunity on various occasions as constituting a serious obstacle to ensuring accountability and consolidating the rule of law.[174] Excluding NSAGs, as international legal entities, from any responsibility would contradict the very objectives which states have collectively sought to promote and achieve. This is further true given the assumption that the law of international responsibility contributes, at least in theory, to rendering the legal system effective for the benefit of all subjects, including states towards which NSAGs also owe obligations.[175]

171 Kleffner (n 169) 269.
172 Pellet (n 1) 3–4.
173 Íñigo Álvarez (n 1) 59–61.
174 UNSC, 'The Rule of Law and Transitional Justice in Conflict and Post-Conflict Societies – Report of the Secretary-General' (23 August 2004) UN Doc S/2004/616 4; Kleffner (n 169) 259–260; UNSC, 'The Rule of Law and Transitional Justice in Conflict and Post-Conflict Societies – Report of the Secretary-General' (12 October 2011) UN Doc S/2011/634; Security Council Report, 'The Rule of Law: Retreat from Accountability' (2019) 28.
175 Kleffner (n 169) 258–259; Bílková (n 109) 277–278; Sten Verhoeven, 'International Responsibility of Armed Opposition Groups: Lessons from State Responsibility for Actions of Armed Opposition Groups' in Noemi Gal-Or, Cedric Ryngaert and Math Noortmann (eds), *Responsibilities of the Non-State Actor in Armed Conflict and the Market Place* (Brill Nijhof 2015) 303.

Chapter 2

Existing international law frameworks, approaches and building blocks for reparations by non-state armed groups

2.1 Introduction

The purpose of this chapter is to examine whether existing international law requires NSAGs to provide reparation where they violate their primary obligations during situations of NIAC. The duty to provide reparation constitutes one of the legal consequences of holding an entity legally responsible under international law. It follows, that the ensuing examination determines whether an NSAG can be held internationally responsible and whether this results in a duty of reparation. It builds on the findings of the previous chapter, which identified these groups as distinct subjects of international law with certain primary obligations under IHL and possibly IHRL. The confirmation of their independent legal existence was recognised as a necessary precondition for the following analysis of NSAGs' position within the law of international responsibility. As part of this examination, the chapter aims to identify, compare and evaluate international law approaches concerning how the duty of NSAGs to provide reparation has been conceptualised and put into practice when recognised. The analysis of these approaches provides some preliminary building blocks useful for the following chapters, which explore how the reparation duty of NSAGs could be operationalised in international law. Over the course of the present chapter, a study will be carried out of various primary and secondary sources of international law, particularly those concerning IHL, IHRL and ICL, as well as the various responses, applied under the auspices of international law, to violations committed by NSAGs during situations of armed conflict.

2.2 International responsibility of non-state armed groups and their duty to repair: a preliminary assessment

2.2.1 Reparation for wrongful acts as a fundamental principle of international law

The principle of reparation is generally understood as involving the obligation of a responsible person, or entity, to provide redress for the injury resulting

DOI: 10.4324/9781003401292-4

from an unlawful act. Besides constituting a fundamental legal principle in domestic legal systems, reparation has also gained a firm basis in international law. As early as 1927–1928, the Permanent Court of International Justice invoked the principle in the landmark *Factory at Chorzów* case, stating, "it is a principle of international law, and even a general conception of law, that any breach of an engagement involves an obligation to make reparation".[1] Therefore, reparation is the "indispensable complement" of the failure to comply with an international obligation, which needs not to be stated in the concerned legal instrument.[2] In this sense, reparation is the natural consequence of committing an internationally wrongful act, that gives rise to the responsibility of the wrongdoer under international law.[3] It showcases the intrinsic relation between responsibility and reparation.[4]

This classical framework underlies the approach of the International Law Commission (ILC) to reparation, as set out in Article 31 of the Articles on the Responsibly of States for Internationally Wrongful Acts (ARS). The duty of reparation is formulated as "the immediately corollary of a State's responsibility, i.e. as an obligation of the responsible State resulting from the breach".[5] Similarly, Judge Cançado Trindade has conceptualised this framework as follows, "breach and reparation go together, conforming an indissoluble whole: the latter is the indispensable consequence or complement of the former", "so

1 *Case concerning the Factory at Chorzów (Germany v Poland)* PCIJ (Merits) [1928] PCIJ Rep Series A No 17 29.

2 *Case Concerning the Factory at Chorzów (Germany v Poland)* PCIJ (Jurisdiction) [1927] PCIJ Rep Series A No 9 21; *Factory at Chorzów Case (Merits)* (n 1) 29. This general rule has been reaffirmed in the case law of the International Court of Justice, see *LaGrand (Germany v United States of America)* ICJ (Judgment) [2001] ICJ Rep 466 para 48; *Advisory Opinion on Legal Consequences of the Construction of a Wall in the Occupied Palestinian Territory* ICJ [2004] ICJ Rep 136 para 152; *Case Concerning Armed Activities on the Territory of the Congo (Democratic Republic of the Congo v Uganda)* ICJ (Judgment) [2005] ICJ Rep 168 para 259; *Armed Activities on the Territory of the Congo (Democratic Republic of the Congo v Uganda)* ICJ (Reparations Judgment) [2022] ICJ Rep 13 para 100. See also *Case of El Amparo v Venezuela* IACtHR (Judgment Reparations and Costs) Series C No 28 (14 September 1996) para 14; *Scordino v Italy (No 1)* ECtHR (Judgment) App No 36813/97 (29 March 2006) para 246; *Case of Dimitrovi v Bulgaria* ECtHR (Judgment) App No 12655/09 (21 October 2016) para 17; African Court on Human and Peoples' Rights, 'Comparative Study on the Law and Practice of Reparations for Human Rights Violations' (2019) 4.

3 Ian Brownlie, *Principles of Public International Law* (6th edn, Oxford University Press 2003) 420–421; Carla Ferstman, *International Organizations and the Fight for Accountability: The Remedies and Reparations Gap* (Oxford University Press 2017) 69–70.

4 Laura Íñigo Álvarez, *Towards a Regime of Responsibility of Armed Groups in International Law* (Intersentia 2020) 159. See also Chapter 4 Section 4.3.

5 ILC, Articles on the Responsibility of States for Internationally Wrongful Acts with Commentaries, Yearbook of the International Law Commission (2001) Vol II Part Two (ARS) Art 31, 91 para 4.

as to cease all the effects of this latter [the breach], and to secure respect for the legal order".[6] As a result, the duty of reparation is fundamental in nature as it is "an imperative of justice".[7] The UN Basic Principles and Guidelines echo the latter notion by stating that "reparation is intended to promote justice by redressing gross violations of international human rights law or serious violations of international humanitarian law", as also reflected more broadly in the area of transitional justice.[8] Similarly, the International Criminal Court held, in the *Lubanga* case, that one of the purposes of reparations, besides obliging those responsible to repair the harm caused, is that they enable the Court to ensure that wrongdoers account for their acts.[9]

The traditional doctrine of reparation in international law developed as an exclusive matter of inter-state responsibility. This is not surprising considering that states were historically considered as the primary and exclusive subjects of international law. Yet, the international legal system has gradually recognised certain non-state actors as bearing rights and obligations. This raises the question whether a broader interpretation of the principle invoked in the *Factory at Chorzów* case could extend its application to these new actors, resulting in a duty to repair as a direct and fundamental consequence of violating international law obligations.[10] Recent developments in international law, with respect to international organisations and individuals, demonstrate that the principle of reparation is no longer solely reserved to states as duty bearers.[11] The Articles on the Responsibility of International Organizations (ARIO) prescribe that an international organisation, which is responsible for an internationally wrongful act, has an obligation to make full reparation, while the International Criminal Court can order reparation

6 *Separate Opinion of Judge Cançado Trindade in the Case of Ahmadou Sadio Diallo (Republic of Guinea v Democratic Republic of the Congo)* ICJ [2012] ICJ Rep 324 para 40; *Separate Opinion of Judge Cançado Trindade in the Case of Certain Activities Carried Out by Nicaragua in the Border Area (Costa Rica v Nicaragua)* ICJ [2018] ICJ Rep 15 paras 11–12.

7 *Separate Opinion of Judge Cançado Trindade in the Case of Ahmadou Sadio Diallo* (n 6) paras 32–35, 40, 97.

8 UNGA, Basic Principles and Guidelines on the Right to a Remedy and Reparation for Victims of Gross Violations of International Human Rights Law and Serious Violations of International Humanitarian Law adopted by UNGA Res 60/147 on 16 December 2005 (21 March 2006) UN Doc A/RES/60/147 (UN Basic Principles and Guidelines) principle 15; UNGA, 'Promotion of Truth, Justice, Reparation and Guarantees of Non-Recurrence – Note by the Secretary-General' (14 October 2014) UN Doc A/69/518 paras 9–11.

9 *Prosecutor v Thomas Lubanga Dyilo* ICC (Amended Order for Reparations) ICC-01/04–01/06–3129-AnxA (3 March 2015) para 2.

10 Heidi Rombouts, Pietro Sardaro and Stef Vandeginste, 'The Right to Reparation for Victims of Gross and Systematic Violations of Human Rights' in Koen de Feyter and others (eds), *Out of the Ashes: Reparation for Victims of Gross and Systematic Human Rights Violations* (Intersentia 2005) 363.

11 Íñigo Álvarez (n 4) 161.

against a criminally convicted individual.[12] These developments might signal that a duty of reparation is emerging as an attribute of subjectivity, ensuing from the condition of being at least a bearer of duties in international law.[13]

Based on this discussion, it appears coherent to include NSAGs, as distinct subjects that hold certain primary obligations, in the domain of international responsibility. This follows from the traditional conceptualisation of reparation in international law, as the indispensable complement of failing to comply with an obligation.[14] Moreover, the aforementioned international legal developments demonstrate that the duty of reparation is no longer an exclusive matter of state responsibility; indeed, it can be extended to non-state actors. The need to include NSAGs in this recent development is reinforced by the understanding of reparation as an important justice and accountability measure for victims. Finally, the inclusion of NSAGs in reparations practice would also respond to the present realities of armed conflicts, which predominantly involve such groups as violent actors.

2.2.2 *International humanitarian law*

In Chapter 1, it was determined that an NSAG bears primary obligations under IHL as a distinct subject of international law. Consequently, it would appear logical, in light of the fundamental principle of international law invoked in the *Factory at Chorzów* case, that the group's responsibility and resulting duty of reparation would arise upon breaching an obligation of IHL. Several legal scholars have reached the same preliminary conclusion.[15] Nevertheless, current

12 Art 75 ICC Statute; Art 31 ILC, Articles on the Responsibility of International Organizations with Commentaries, Yearbook of the International Law Commission (2011) Vol II Part Two (ARIO).

13 *Separate Opinion of Judge Cançado Trindade in the Case of Ahmadou Sadio Diallo* (n 6) para 32.

14 Similarly, Marco Sassòli, 'Taking Armed Groups Seriously: Ways to Improve Their Compliance with International Humanitarian Law' (2010) 1 Journal of International Humanitarian Legal Studies 5, 46–47; Konstantinos Mastorodimos, *Armed Non-State Actors in International Humanitarian and Human Rights Law: Foundation and Framework of Obligations, and Rules on Accountability* (Ashgate 2016) 116–117; Paloma Blázquez Rodríguez, 'Does an Armed Group Have an Obligation to Provide Reparations to Its Victims? Construing an Obligation to Provide Reparations for Violations of International Humanitarian Law' in James Summers and Alex Gough (eds), *Non-State Actors and International Obligations* (Brill Nijhof 2018) 408–410; Íñigo Álvarez (n 4) 34.

15 Emanuela-Chiara Gillard, 'Reparation for Violations of International Humanitarian Law' (2003) 85 International Review of the Red Cross 529, 535; Zakaria Dabone, 'International Law: Armed Groups in a State-Centric System' (2011) 93 International Review of the Red Cross 395, 412; Ezequiel Heffes, 'The Responsibility of Armed Opposition Groups for Violations of International Humanitarian Law: Challenging the State-Centric System of International Law' (2013) 4 Journal of International Humanitarian Legal Studies 81, 84; Katharine Fortin, *The*

IHL lacks any secondary norm in treaty law providing for such international responsibility on the part of NSAGs. More broadly, international law does not provide for a legal framework or instrument which is similar to those developed in relation to the responsibility of states and international organisations. Additionally, there is no international forum through which victims can seek to establish the collective responsibility of NSAGs with the objective of claiming reparations. Evans concludes that "this illustrates a major lacuna in international humanitarian law", especially considering the contemporary dominance of NIACs involving NSAGs.[16]

This is affirmed in the 2020 ICRC Commentary to Common Article 3: "[i]nternational law is unclear as to the responsibility of a non-State armed group, as an entity in itself, for acts committed by members of the group".[17] However, the ICRC appears to leave some room regarding NSAGs that are also bound by Additional Protocol II. More specifically, the ICRC study on customary IHL of 2005 recognises that it could be argued that NSAGs incur responsibility for acts committed by persons forming part of such groups since these groups must respect IHL and operate under a "responsible command" (while explicitly referencing Article 1(1) Additional Protocol II).[18] Nevertheless, the same ICRC study indicates that the consequences of such responsibility are not clear.[19] It is particularly "unclear to what extent armed opposition groups are under an obligation to make full reparation".[20] The latter conclusion has been confirmed by more recent scholarly contributions on the topic.[21]

Accountability of Armed Groups under Human Rights Law (Oxford University Press 2017) 277.

16 Christine Evans, *The Right to Reparation in International Law for Victims of Armed Conflict* (Cambridge University Press 2012) 31.

17 ICRC, 'Commentary on the Third Geneva Convention: Convention (III) Relative to the Treatment of Prisoners of War' (2020) para 931.

18 However, note that these obligations also apply to NSAGs solely falling under Common Art 3, see Rule 139 Jean-Marie Henckaerts and Louise Doswald-Beck (eds), *Customary International Humanitarian Law*, vol I: Rules (Cambridge University Press 2005); ICRC (n 17) para 938.

19 Henckaerts and Doswald-Beck (n 18) 536.

20 Ibid. 550.

21 Jann K Kleffner, 'The Collective Accountability of Organized Armed Groups for System Crimes' in Andre Nollkaemper and Harmen Gijsbrecht van der Wilt (eds), *System Criminality in International Law* (Cambridge University Press 2009) 255; Sassòli (n 14) 47; ILA Committee on Non-State Actors, 'Washington Conference Non State Actors' (2014) 11; Luke Moffett, 'Beyond Attribution: Responsibility of Armed Non-State Actors for Reparations in Northern Ireland, Colombia and Uganda' in Noemi Gal-Or, Cedric Ryngaert and Math Noortmann (eds), *Responsibilities of the Non-State Actor in Armed Conflict and the Market Place* (Brill Nijhof 2015) 346; Blázquez Rodríguez (n 14); Luke Moffett, 'Violence and Repair: The Practice and Challenges of Non-State Armed Groups Engaging in Reparations' (2020) 102 International Review of the Red Cross 1057, 1062.

In this regard, the ICRC study refers to the ARS. The Commentary of the ILC to this authoritative instrument recalls that it is not concerned with the international responsibility of NSAGs but, at the same time, leaves this issue open: "[a] further possibility is that the insurrectional movement may itself be held responsible for its own conduct under international law, for example for a breach of international humanitarian law by its forces."[22] The ILC clarifies that the essential idea of such a movement is reflected in Article 1(1) Additional Protocol II:

> dissident armed forces or other organized armed groups which, under responsible command, exercise such control over a part of [the relevant State's] territory as to enable them to carry out sustained and concerted military operations and to implement this Protocol.[23]

Thus, the term 'insurrectional movement' certainly encompasses at least one type of NSAG examined in this study, namely those groups that are also bound by Additional Protocol II. However, since the ILC only refers to Additional Protocol II as a definitional "guide", NSAGs solely bound by Common Article 3 are not necessarily excluded.[24]

Going back to 1972, ILC Special Rapporteur Ago recognised an insurrectional movement as a "separate subject of international law [...] perfectly capable of committing internationally wrongful acts", which can involve that subject's responsibility.[25] However, from 1975 onwards, the ILC avoided addressing the international legal personality or status of such movements, "since that was a question outside the scope of the article" concerned.[26] Correspondingly, Article 14 paragraph 3 of an older draft of the ARS, which dealt with the "conduct of organs of an insurrectional movement", held that "paragraph 1 is without prejudice to the attribution of the conduct of the organ of the insurrectional movement to that movement in any case in which such attribution may be made under international law".[27] The Commentary to this draft article clarifies that the ILC did not intend to take a position on matters of

22 ILC Commentary to Art 10 ARS 52 para 16.

23 ILC Commentary to Art 10 ARS 51 para 9.

24 ILC Commentary to Art 10 ARS 51 para 9; Zakaria Daboné, *Le Droit International Public Relatif Aux Groupes Armés Non Étatiques* (Schulthess 2012) 172–174.

25 'Fourth Report on State Responsibility, by Mr Roberto Ago, Special Rapporteur' Yearbook of the International Law Commission (1972) Vol II UN Doc A/CN.4/264 and Add.1 129 para 153.

26 Compare Ago's draft Art 12(2) to the reworked Art 12ter, see Yearbook of the International Law Commission (1975) Vol I UN Doc A/CN.4/SER.A/1975 42 para 1 and 216 paras 41,43. Daboné (n 24) 172.

27 ILC, Draft Articles on State Responsibility with Commentaries provisionally adopted by the ILC on first reading at its forty-eight session (6 May-26 July 1996) Yearbook of the International Law Commission (1996) Vol II UN Doc A/CN.4/SER.A/1996/Add.1 (Part 2) (draft ARS of 1996).

attribution in relation to such movements, but rather sought to provide for the mere possibility in light of existing international practice (see Section 2.3.1 of this chapter for a discussion of this practice and its relation to the work of the ILC).[28]

In his first report of 1998, ILC Special Rapporteur Crawford held that the responsibility of insurrectional movements falls beyond the scope of the ARS considering their focus on state responsibility. He did, however, recognise that such responsibility for IHL breaches "can certainly be envisaged".[29] Eventually, the paragraph was deleted and deferred to the commentary, as demonstrated in the final version of the ARS of 2001 (see *supra*).[30] All things considered, the respective work of the ICRC and ILC do not firmly affirm nor reject the international responsibility of NSAGs, particularly those also bound by Additional Protocol II, for violations of IHL.[31]

In legal scholarship, it also remains a contentious matter whether the international responsibility of an NSAG arises when breaching a primary obligation of IHL. Some scholars contend that NSAGs' international responsibility in IHL has been recognised or even go as far as arguing that this assertion is no longer controversial.[32] For these scholars, the contemporary debate focuses not on whether NSAGs have international responsibility, but on issues of attribution, content and implementation.[33] Nevertheless, the majority of scholars have taken a more tentative position on the matter. They argue for the necessity of a

28 ILC Commentary to draft Art 14 ARS (1996) 99 para 31, Yearbook of the International Law Commission (1975) Vol II UN Doc A/CN.4/SER.A/1975/Add.1.

29 'First Report on State Responsibility, by Mr James Crawford, Special Rapporteur' (1998) UN Doc A/CN.4/490 and Add.1–7 53 para 272.

30 Yearbook of the International Law Commission (1998) Vol I UN Doc A/CN.4/SER.1/1998 290 para 86.

31 Eyassu Gayim, 'Reflections on the Draft Articles of the International Law Commission on State Responsibility: Articles 14; 15; & 19 in the Context of the Contemporary International Law of Self-Determination' (1985) 54 Nordic Journal of International Law 85, 102; Liesbeth Zegveld, 'Accountability of Non-State Actors in International Law', *Proceedings of the Bruges Colloquium: Relevance of International Humanitarian Law to Non-State Actors, Collegium Special Edition* (2003) 157.

32 For instance, in the *Nicaragua* case, the International Court of Justice implicitly recognised that the *Contras* might potentially be held responsible for their own violations of IHL. The Court took the view that "the *contras* remain responsible for their acts". *Case Concerning the Military and Paramilitary Activities in and against Nicaragua (Nicaragua v United States of America)* ICJ (Merits Judgment) [1986] ICJ Rep 14 para 116; Veronika Bílková, 'Armed Opposition Groups and Shared Responsibility' (2015) 62 Netherlands International Law Review 69, 77.

33 Liesbeth Zegveld, *The Accountability of Armed Opposition Groups* (Cambridge University Press 2002) 133–134; Sassòli (n 14) 47; Marco Sassòli, *International Humanitarian Law: Rules, Controversies, and Solutions to Problems Arising in Warfare* (Edward Elgar Publishing Limited 2019) paras 5.44, 10.255; Elizabeth Salmón and Juan-Pablo Pérez-León-Acevedo, 'Reparation for Victims of Serious Violations of International Humanitarian Law: New Developments' (2022) 104 International Review of the Red Cross 1315, 1325–1326.

new regime of responsibility for NSAGs and generally identify increased support for the idea that NSAGs have international responsibility. Yet, at the same time, these scholars acknowledge the difficulty of drawing any definite conclusions given the little practice that currently exists.[34]

Contrary to the responsibility gap *vis-à-vis* NSAGs in IHL, Article 91 of Additional Protocol I to the Geneva Conventions requires a responsible state party to an international armed conflict to make reparation: "[a] Party to the conflict which violates the provisions of the Conventions or of this Protocol shall, if the case demands, be liable to pay compensation."[35] Given its scope of application, it also applies to wars of national liberation. Moreover, state practice has established this rule as a norm of customary IHL, a norm which is also applicable to situations of NIAC. However, its application does not extend to NSAGs engaged in such conflicts, hence creating an inequality in the parties' secondary obligations.[36]

The ICRC Commentary to the provision reveals that the underlying justification for the rule was of a preventative nature, more specifically the need to provide an additional measure to avoid violations of the law.[37] It is clear that NSAGs were not as prominent on the international agenda as they are today. Nevertheless, at present, the same concerns relating to compliance can be raised just as easily with regard to NSAGs.[38] More generally, a strong argument can be made that legal consequences must follow from violations, in order to uphold the very norms which the international legal system aims to promote.[39]

34 Éric David, *Principes de Droit Des Conflits Armés* (3rd edn, Bruylant 2002) 643; Veronika Bílková, 'Establishing Direct Responsibility of Armed Opposition Groups for Violations of International Humanitarian Law?' in Noemi Gal-Or, Cedric Ryngaert and Math Noortmann (eds), *Responsibilities of the Non-State Actor in Armed Conflict and the Market Place* (Brill Nijhof 2015) 276–277, 284; Kirsten Schmalenbach, 'International Responsibility for Humanitarian Law Violations by Armed Groups' in Heike Krieger (ed), *Inducing Compliance with International Humanitarian Law: Lessons from the African Great Lakes Region* (Cambridge University Press 2015) 497; Sten Verhoeven, 'International Responsibility of Armed Opposition Groups: Lessons from State Responsibility for Actions of Armed Opposition Groups' in Noemi Gal-Or, Cedric Ryngaert and Math Noortmann (eds), *Responsibilities of the Non-State Actor in Armed Conflict and the Market Place* (Brill Nijhof 2015) 303; Íñigo Álvarez (n 4) 3, 181–182, 216–217.

35 The provision constitutes a literal reproduction of Art 3 of Convention (IV) respecting the Laws and Customs of War on Land and its annex: Regulations concerning the Laws and Customs of War on Land (1907). Protocol Additional to the Geneva Conventions of 12 August 1949, and relating to the Protection of Victims of International Armed Conflicts (Additional Protocol I) (1977) 1125 UNTS 3.

36 Rules 149 and 150 Henckaerts and Doswald-Beck (n 18); Ezequiel Heffes and Brian Frenkel, 'The International Responsibility of Non-State Armed Groups: In Search of the Applicable Rules' (2017) 8 Goettingen Journal of International Law 39, 42.

37 ICRC, *Commentary on the Additional Protocols of 8 June 1977 to the Geneva Conventions of 12 December 1949* (Martinus Nijhoff 1987) paras 3645–3646.

38 Daboné (n 24) 188–189.

39 Annyssa Bellal, 'Establishing the Direct Responsibility of Non-State Armed Groups for Violations of International Norms: Issues of Attribution' in Noemi Gal-Or,

From a strict legal perspective, international responsibility remains one of the most credible measures to render this legal system effective.[40]

2.2.3 International human rights law

The increasing doctrinal and practical acceptance that certain NSAGs hold human rights obligations during situations of armed conflict necessitates considering their international responsibility and particularly their duty of reparation under IHRL. Scholarly debate and practice continue to be very much focused on NSAGs' primary obligations under IHRL.[41] A recent and notable exception to this tendency is a 2018 report of the UN Special Rapporteur on extrajudicial, summary or arbitrary executions, which, among other observations, concludes that the binding of NSAGs to IHRL "provides for a legal foundation for access to remedies and reparation for victims of ANSAs [armed non-State actors] violations".[42] An important additional rationale for binding NSAGs to IHRL is that "the current legal framework to hold them accountable has unacceptably large deficits with regard to access to justice, remedies, and reparations".[43] This may provide a tentative sign that this issue may become the next frontier in human rights scholarship on NSAGs and may experience developments in practice. Nevertheless, the sophisticated human rights system of remedies, which is highly developed in comparison to IHL, remains state-centric in its nature. It exhibits neither immediate signs of extending its scope, nor signs of comprehensive development concerning the establishment of a tailored forum, which might deal exclusively with human rights claims filed against NSAGs.[44] Moreover, as long as there is no uniform consensus on the

Cedric Ryngaert and Math Noortmann (eds), *Responsibility of the Non-State Actor in Armed Conflict and the Market Place* (Brill Nijhof 2015) 304.

40 Alain Pellet, 'The Definition of Responsibility in International Law' in James Crawford, Alain Pellet and Simon Olleson (eds), *The Law of International Responsibility* (Oxford University Press 2010) 3; Sassòli (n 14) 43.

41 However, see Art 5(2) Res No 2/2010 Reparation for Victims of Armed Conflict (ILA Committee on Reparation for Victims of Armed Conflict 2010); ILA Committee on Reparation for Victims of Armed Conflict, 'The Hague Conference Reparation for Victims of Armed Conflict' (2010) 12; Mastorodimos (n 14) 198–199, 203 (he concludes that NSAGs' "accountability for human rights violations is in an embryonic stage").

42 UNHRC, 'Report of the Special Rapporteur on Extrajudicial, Summary or Arbitrary Executions on Armed Non-State Actors: The Protection of the Right to Life' (5 June 2018) UN Doc A/HRC/38/44 para 98.

43 Ibid. 21.

44 See, for relevant human rights provisions, i.a., Art 8 Universal Declaration of Human Rights (1948), adopted by UNGA Res 217 A (III) (1948); Arts 2(3)(a), 9(5), 14(6) ICCPR; Art 6 Convention on the Elimination of All Forms of Racial Discrimination (1966) 660 UNTS 195; Art 14 Convention against Torture (1984) 1465 UNTS 85; Art 39 Convention on the Rights of the Child (1989) 1577 UNTS 3. At the regional human rights level, see Arts 13, 33–34 European Convention on

primary obligations of NSAGs under IHRL, developments regarding their legal responsibility are unlikely to proceed, at least for the time being.[45]

2.2.4 International criminal law

Although international law lacks a regime of responsibility for NSAGs, the International Criminal Court has recently embarked on an innovative course. The International Criminal Court not only has a mandate to hold group members criminally responsible for their part in the commission of core international crimes, but can also oblige those responsible to repair the harm they have caused.[46] Indeed, one of the essential principles upon which the Court's system of reparation is based, is that an order for reparations must be directed against the convicted person.[47] Accordingly, "reparation orders are intrinsically linked to the *individual* whose criminal liability is established in a conviction and whose culpability for those criminal acts is determined in a sentence".[48] This clearly follows from the context in which such orders arise at the Court, which is a legal regime concerned with establishing *individual* criminal responsibility for the crimes included in the Rome Statute.[49] This makes it very clear that the Court does not have the jurisdiction to obligate the NSAG, to which the convicted person belonged and in whose service the crimes were committed, to contribute to providing reparations. However, Article 75(6), which provides for the convicted person's duty to repair in paragraph 2, holds that such reparation does not prejudice "the rights of victims under national or international law",

Human Rights (1950) ETS No. 005; Arts 25, 33(b), 63 American Convention on Human Rights (1969) OAS Treaty Series No 36 1144 UNTS 123; Art 28(h) Protocol on the Statute of the African Court of Justice and Human Rights (2008). See the following statement by the Inter-American Commission on Human Rights for an illustration of the state centricity of the human rights system: IACHR, 'Third Report on the Human Rights Situation in Colombia' OEA/SER.L/II.102 Doc 9 rev 1 (26 February 1999) ch IV para 5. However, see UNHRC (n 42) para 100(e) in which the UN Special Rapporteur on extrajudicial, summary or arbitrary executions recommends to states to explore the establishment of specialized human rights court(s) to prosecute NSAGs.

45 Íñigo Álvarez (n 4) 174.

46 Art 75(2) ICC Statute.

47 *Prosecutor v Thomas Lubanga Dyilo* ICC (Judgment on the Appeals against the "Decision establishing the Principles and Procedures to be applied to Reparations" of 7 August 2012) ICC-01/04–01/06–3129 (3 March 2015) paras 1, 32, 65–70, 87, 99; *Prosecutor v Germain Katanga* ICC (Order for Reparations pursuant to Article 75 of the Statute) ICC-01/04–01/07–3728 (24 March 2017) paras 30–31; *Prosecutor v Ahmad Al Faqi Al Mahdi* ICC (Reparations Order) ICC-01/12–01/15–236 (17 August 2017) paras 25–26, 38; *Prosecutor v Bosco Ntaganda* ICC (Reparations Order) ICC-01/04–02/06 (8 March 2021) paras 96–97.

48 *Prosecutor v Thomas Lubanga Dyilo* (n 47) para 65.

49 Ibid.

therefore leaving open the possibility for the development of victims' rights beyond this individual responsibility framework.

In all reparations orders issued thus far by the International Criminal Court, the convicted persons have been declared indigent.[50] This raises a legitimate question as to whether it might be beneficial to provide for a legal basis that would enable the Court, in cooperation with the relevant state parties, to pursue the illegal assets and property of the NSAG and its other members, where possible.[51] The Rome Statute does not give the Court the power to formally request the cooperation of NSAGs, nor does it require them, as a matter of law, to comply with any requests regarding reparations. Nonetheless, McCarthy argues that this might prove significant when the Court makes a reparations order to victims residing in territories controlled by such groups. It may, for instance, be necessary for the NSAG to grant safe access to communities to facilitate the provision of redress.[52] Blázquez Rodríguez adds a practical consideration to the discussion by pointing out that convicted persons may easily move their assets, while the group itself may be able to assist the Court if they know about the location of such assets.[53]

Despite the apparent appeal of such proposals, they can be challenged on at least two grounds. State parties may be unlikely to grant such power to the Court, given that it might imply some form of recognition of the NSAG itself and the power it wields. Moreover, it might be considered doubtful that an NSAG would be willing to cooperate without some kind of incentive, especially considering the fact that a criminal conviction of one of its members, possibly a leader or high-level commander, would lie at the basis of proceedings.[54] Beyond these challenges, it is questionable how any request could be enforced where domestic authorities have not been able to restrain the power of an NSAG which holds *de facto* territorial control. Depending on the circumstances of a given case, it might be more effective to request the convicted person to call upon the group to cooperate as a positive contribution to his or her duty to repair. In the *Lubanga* case, the Legal Representatives of Victims V01 observed that the convicted person continues to wield significant political influence in the Ituri province of the Democratic Republic of the Congo. This, it was argued,

50 *Prosecutor v Thomas Lubanga Dyilo* ICC (Decision Establishing the Principles and Procedures to Be Applied to Reparations) ICC-01/04–01/06–2904 (7 August 2012) paras 269, 277; *Prosecutor v Germain Katanga* (n 47) para 327; *Prosecutor v Ahmad Al Faqi Al Mahdi* (n 47) para 113; *Prosecutor v Bosco Ntaganda* ICC (Addendum to the Reparations Order of 8 March 2021, ICC-01/04–02/06–2659) ICC-01/04–02/06 (14 July 2023) para 21; Verhoeven (n 34) 285–286; Íñigo Álvarez (n 4) 177–178.

51 Salmón and Pérez-León-Acevedo (n 33) 1339.

52 Connor McCarthy, *Reparations and Victim Support in the International Criminal Court* (Cambridge University Press 2012) 317, 322–323.

53 Blázquez Rodríguez (n 14) 426–427.

54 Geneva Academy of International Humanitarian Law and Human Rights, 'Rules of Engagement: Protecting Civilians through Dialogue with Armed Non-State Actors' (2011) 22–24.

could impact the implementation of the reparations process by the Trust Fund, and could influence how the participating victims are perceived by their immediate communities, sometimes even by their own families. In a letter from their counsel to the Defence, the victims asked whether Lubanga, as a positive action in favour of the victims, would call on the members of the *Forces Patriotiques pour la Libération du Congo* (FPLC), which he headed, and on the population of Ituri to: cooperate with officials of the Trust Fund responsible for implementing the reparations plan; and, refrain from any negativity towards victim-beneficiaries. Yet, it appears that Lubanga, who had failed up to then to admit responsibility for the crimes for which he was convicted, gave no response to this proposal.[55]

2.2.5 Contemporary responses to violations committed by non-state armed groups

International law responds in several ways to violations of primary obligations committed by NSAGs during armed conflict, despite the lack of a treaty or other instrument setting out the secondary rules for their possible international responsibility. There are a number of actors and mechanisms that have progressively engaged in monitoring, reporting and even sanctioning such groups. This section identifies the significance and limitations of these efforts from the perspective of international responsibility.

UN bodies, including the Security Council and the General Assembly, have regularly called in their resolutions on NSAGs to respect and comply with their primary obligations under international law. Moreover, these bodies have condemned NSAGs' violations and have called upon such groups to put an end to their commission.[56] This has been done by calling upon all parties and/or by referring to the respective groups by name.[57] Other bodies within the UN human rights machinery have also not shied away from drawing attention to violations committed by NSAGs. A call was made as early as 1990, during a session of the Commission on Human Rights, to pay increased attention to violations committed by NSAGs, on the basis that such violations could have a negative impact on the enjoyment of human rights. This discourse led to an

55 *Prosecutor v Thomas Lubanga Dyilo* ICC (Public Redacted Version of Filing regarding Symbolic Collective Reparations Projects with Confidential Annex: Draft Request for Proposals) ICC-01/04–01/06–3223-Conf (19 September 2016) 23–25.

56 See, e.g., UNSC, Res 1574 (19 November 2004) UN Doc S/RES/1574 Preamble; UNSC, Res 2277 (30 March 2016) UN Doc S/RES/2277 para 16.

57 For further examples see the following database, which contains excerpts of UN Security Council and General Assembly practice concerning NSAGs (covering 1995 to 2017): Jessica S Burniske, Naz K Modirzadeh and Dustin A Lewis, 'Armed Non-State Actors and International Human Rights Law: An Analysis of the Practice of the U.N. Security Council and U.N. General Assembly – Briefing Report with Annexes' (Harvard Law School Program on International Law and Armed Conflict 2017) 33–77.

eventual decision that existing mechanisms should pay particular attention to the atrocities committed by these groups.[58] This example illustrates that the accountability of NSAGs was already on the UN agenda more than 30 years ago, even in the face of the traditional state-centricity of the human rights system. Over the years, the Human Rights Council and human rights experts, appointed under its system of Special Procedures, have identified and condemned violations of both IHL and IHRL perpetrated by NSAGs.[59] Similarly, the Inter-American Commission on Human Rights has proven to be a prominent monitor of NSAGs' compliance with IHL and IHRL.[60]

The UN Security Council, inter-governmental organisations, such as the European Union, and individual states have imposed sanctions, such as assets freezes and travel bans, on NSAGs and their members. This has been done in an effort to reduce the danger to peace and security that such groups may pose.[61] For instance, a Sanctions Committee established by the Security Council can impose sanctions on entities, such as NSAGs, that are "involved in planning, directing, or committing acts that violate international human rights law or international humanitarian law".[62] While these measures intend first and foremost to preserve international peace and security and provide for a measure of accountability, they are not designed to deal with issues of international responsibility of NSAGs.[63]

58 David Matas, 'Armed Opposition Groups' (1997) 24 Manitoba Law Journal 621, 621–622.

59 For instance, UNHRC, Res 28/20 (8 April 2015) UN Doc A/HRC/RES/28/20 para 6; UNHRC, Res 31/27 (20 April 2016) UN Doc A/HRC/RES/31/27 para 11; UNGA, 'Interim Report on the Situation of Human Rights in the Sudan Prepared by the Special Rapporteur of the Commission on Human Rights' (16 October 1995) UN Doc A/50/569 paras 72–74; UNHRC, 'Report of the Special Rapporteur on Extrajudicial, Summary or Arbitrary Executions' (15 May 2012) UN Doc A/HRC/20/22/Add.2 paras 40–44; UNHRC (n 42) 5–6.

60 See, e.g., IACHR, 'Country Report Colombia: Truth, Justice and Reparation' OEA/Ser.L/V/II. Doc 49/13 (31 December 2013) para 56. Zegveld (n 33) 158–162; Sassòli (n 14) 39–40.

61 See, for instance, with regard to the Democratic Republic of the Congo UNSC, Res 2293 (23 June 2016) UN Doc S/RES/2293; UNSC, Res 2424 (29 June 2018) UN Doc S/RES/2424; UNSC, Res 2478 (26 June 2019) UN Doc S/RES/2478. See also Jeremy M Weinstein, *Inside Rebellion: The Politics of Insurgent Violence* (Cambridge University Press 2009) 346–347; Nigel D White, 'Autonomous and Collective Sanctions in the International Legal Order' (2018) 27 The Italian Yearbook of International Law Online 1, 22.

62 UNSC, Res 2134 (28 January 2014) UN Doc S/RES/2134 para 37(b); Tilman Rodenhäuser, *Organizing Rebellion: Non-State Armed Groups under International Humanitarian Law, Human Rights Law, and International Criminal Law* (Oxford University Press 2018) 156–157.

63 Kleffner (n 21) 252–255; Agata Kleczkowska, 'Filling the Gap: The New Regime of Responsibility for Armed Non-State Actors' (2018) 25 Australian International Law Journal 137, 159; Íñigo Álvarez (n 4) 52.

In 2005, the UN Security Council established a Monitoring and Reporting Mechanism (MRM) to foster accountability in the area of children's rights in armed conflict and the compliance of parties to armed conflicts with international child protection standards and norms.[64] The Special Representative of the Secretary-General on Children and Armed Conflict serves as the UN focal point for the Security Council agenda and the implementation of the MRM.[65] The MRM systematically monitors, documents and reports on six grave violations against children, including the killing and maiming of children and the recruitment or use of children as soldiers, whether committed by state or non-state parties to a conflict.[66] NSAGs that engage in such violations can be listed in the annexes of the UN Secretary-General's annual report on children and armed conflict, which may lead to sanctions being imposed against the group by the Security Council. This is complemented by the possibility for NSAGs to commit themselves to action plans, concerned with the halting of violations.[67] All in all, the MRM plays an important role in this area of international law by contributing to accountability, compliance and the prevention of future violations through naming and shaming, dialogue and sanctions.[68] Yet, the purpose of the mechanism is not to provide a legal tool through which the international responsibility of NSAGs could be assessed. Instead, it constitutes a policy instrument.[69]

Finally, mechanisms dealing with truth seeking have frequently addressed violations of IHL and IHRL committed by NSAGs. This is the case for truth-seeking efforts established by the UN in the forms of commissions of inquiry, fact-finding missions or other investigative bodies. Íñigo Álvarez completed a comprehensive analysis of the practice of these mechanisms, which focused on the collective responsibility of NSAGs. She concluded that most of the mechanisms' reports do indeed map NSAGs' violations of primary IHL and IHRL obligations.[70] However, she further concluded that almost all these

64 UNICEF, 'Guidelines: Monitoring and Reporting Mechanism on Grave Violations against Children in Situations of Armed Conflict' (2014) 7.

65 Ibid. 10.

66 UNSC, Res 1612 (26 July 2005) UN Doc S/RES/1612.

67 Cedric Ryngaert and Anneleen Van de Meulebroucke, 'Enhancing and Enforcing Compliance with International Humanitarian Law by Non-State Armed Groups: An Inquiry into Some Mechanisms' (2011) 16 Journal of Conflict & Security Law 443, 458–460; Andrew Clapham, 'Focusing on Armed Non-State Actors' in Andrew Clapham and Paola Gaeta (eds), *The Oxford Handbook of International Law in Armed Conflict* (Oxford University Press 2014) 800–802.

68 UNICEF (n 64) 20.

69 Íñigo Álvarez (n 4) 51.

70 See, e.g., UNHRC, 'Report of the International Commission of Inquiry to Investigate All Alleged Violations of International Human Rights Law in the Libyan Arab Jamahiriya' (1 June 2011) UN Doc A/HRC/17/44 paras 261–263; UNSC, 'Final Report of the International Commission of Inquiry on the Central African Republic' (22 December 2014) UN Doc S/2014/928 Annex B; UNHRC, 'Report of the Independent International Fact-Finding Mission on Myanmar' (12 September 2018)

reports subsequently refer to the individual criminal responsibility of group members as the exclusive accountability mechanism through which NSAGs can be dealt with.[71] In contrast, violations committed by states and their agents were considered from the perspectives of both state and individual criminal responsibility.[72] Nevertheless, Bellal argues that such mechanisms may be "useful tools for establishing *as a preliminary step* the responsibility of non-state armed groups during a particular conflict".[73]

Another prominent truth-seeking mechanism is the truth commission. Truth commissions have been identified as mechanisms which, due to their general focus on patterns of past abuses, allow for an understanding of the collective role of NSAGs in armed conflict.[74] Such commissions have similarly reported on international law violations committed by NSAGs, while some have even recognised the direct responsibility of such groups as collective entities.[75]

UN Doc A/HRC/39/64 paras 54, 66; UNHRC, 'Report of the Independent International Commission of Inquiry on the Syrian Arab Republic' (2 July 2020) UN Doc A/HRC/44/61; UNHRC, 'Report of the International Commission of Human Rights Experts on Ethiopia' (5 October 2022) UN Doc A/HRC/51/46.

71 Notable exceptions to this dominant approach recognising the direct international responsibility of NSAGs include: 'Report of the International Commission of Inquiry on Darfur' (25 January 2005) para 175; UNSG, 'Report of the Secretary-General's Panel of Experts on Accountability in Sri Lanka' (31 March 2011) para 191; UNHRC, 'Report of the Detailed Findings of the Group of Eminent International and Regional Experts on Yemen' (3 September 2019) UN Doc A/HRC/42/CRP.1 para 867; UNHRC, 'Detailed Findings on Attacks and Restrictions on and Harassment of Civil Society Actors, by All Duty Bearers – Independent International Commission of Inquiry on the Occupied Palestinian Territory, Including East Jerusalem, and Israel' (2 June 2023) UN Doc A/HRC/53/CRP.1 para 12.

72 Íñigo Álvarez (n 4) 40–45. Similarly, Zegveld concluded earlier in 2002 that "while international bodies have given due consideration to accountability of individual leaders of armed opposition groups, they have so far largely ignored the accountability of the groups in favour of the accountability of individual members" Zegveld (n 33) 223.

73 Annyssa Bellal, 'Non-State Armed Groups in Transitional Justice Processes: Adapting to New Realities of Conflict' in Roger Duthie and Paul Seils (eds), *Justice Mosaics: How Context Shapes Transitional Justice in Fractured Societies* (ICTJ 2017) 238.

74 Olivia Herman, 'Holding Armed Groups to Account Under International Human Rights Law: An Analysis of the Under-Explored Practice of Truth Commissions' (2019) 13 Human Rights & International Legal Discourse 48, 68; UNHRC, 'Report of the Special Rapporteur on the Promotion of Truth, Justice, Reparation and Guarantees of Non-Recurrence: Role and Responsibilities of Non-State Actors in Transitional Justice Processes' (12 July 2022) UN Doc A/HRC/51/34 paras 60–61.

75 See Sierra Leone Truth and Reconciliation Commission, 'Witness to Truth' (2004) Vol 1 ch 5 para 66; Sierra Leone Truth and Reconciliation Commission, 'Witness to Truth' (2004) Vol 2 ch 2 pp 38, 44, 48–49; Truth and Reconciliation Commission of Liberia, 'Consolidated Final Report' (2009) Vol II 336; Truth Commission of Colombia, 'Informe Final: Hasta La Guerra Tiene Límites' (2022) 39–40. For further discussion of the practice of truth commissions concerning IHL and IHRL violations by NSAGs, see Herman (n 74); Íñigo Álvarez (n 4) 46–49.

Notably, the Commission on the Truth for El Salvador held that the "FMLN must provide [moral and material] compensation where it is found to have been responsible".[76] This approach converges with the traditional understanding of responsibility in international law.

The overall significance of these efforts lies in a recognition of the need to address, at the international level, the collective and detrimental role that NSAGs play in situations of armed conflict. All such efforts contribute to the current accountability framework concerning NSAGs, by monitoring and scrutinizing their behaviour against international law and by potentially imposing some sort of sanction.[77] While a majority of the mechanisms emphasise violations of primary obligations by NSAGs, some go further by invoking the international responsibility of the group on this basis. However, the mechanisms that have taken the latter step have not been explicit about the underlying legal framework, or the set of rules and principles used to assess the question of the international responsibility of NSAGs.[78] As Kleffner rightly argues, this is wholly unsatisfactory within an international order which is supposedly governed by the rule of law, which requires certain, predictable and stable rules, legal certainty and transparency, among other requirements.[79] Moreover, the various mechanisms have not provided an avenue for victims to claim reparations from responsible groups.[80] Nonetheless, a more focused examination of this accountability practice, conducted through the prism of a specific aspect of international responsibility, may still prove beneficial. Bellal, for instance, explored how some of the mechanisms have linked internationally wrongful acts to NSAGs in the context of their monitoring activities, with the purpose of identifying possible attribution rules.[81] A similar analysis will be carried out in Sections 2.3.4 and 2.3.5, but through the lens of the duty to provide reparation.

2.2.6 *A responsibility gap in current international law regulating armed conflict*

The prior examination demonstrated that, although NSAGs bear certain primary obligations, current international law does not include a secondary norm, nor a uniform set of rules and principles, which govern the possible legal responsibility of NSAGs where they violate these obligations.[82] The present situation is not remedied in a satisfactory manner by the existing regimes of

76 Commission on the Truth for El Salvador, 'From Madness to Hope: The 12-Year War in El Salvador' (1993) UN Doc S/25500 148, 185. See further Section 2.3.5.
77 See the Introduction to this book, Section I.2.2, for a definition of the concept of accountability versus responsibility.
78 Similarly, Kleffner (n 21) 257; Íñigo Álvarez (n 4) 57.
79 Kleffner (n 21) 259–260; Íñigo Álvarez (n 4) 58–59.
80 Kleczkowska (n 63) 150–151.
81 See Bellal (n 39).
82 Kleczkowska (n 63) 138.

state responsibility and individual criminal responsibility, which only partially cover violations committed by NSAGs. This conclusion is based on several limitations of both regimes that will be briefly outlined here (see Chapter 3 for an extensively discussion). As a general rule, a state is not responsible for the wrongful acts committed by an NSAG operating independently in its territory. An exception is when an NSAG succeeds in establishing a new government or state. However, this does not address the responsibility of unsuccessful groups. A state may also incur responsibility for failing to exercise due diligence concerning the wrongful act, but this originates in the state's own conduct, and it is practically unlikely that it will be triggered in times of armed conflict. Furthermore, an NSAG can in a way be held indirectly responsible for its violations through the criminal responsibility of individual members. However, this only concerns violations that amount to crimes under international law, whereas others are not covered.[83]

Consequently, a responsibility gap is left in current international law regulating situations of armed conflict.[84] In accordance with the foregoing conclusions, Bílkova finds that such a gap manifests itself at both the theoretical level, by way of the existing asymmetry between the primary and secondary rules applicable to NSAGs, and in practice, because of the *de facto* impunity for certain violations of international law.[85] In order to overcome this gap, several scholars have called for the introduction of the international responsibility of NSAGs, including a proposed duty to provide reparation.[86] The analysis carried out here has not revealed an apparent legal reason or justification for neglecting the international responsibility of NSAGs. Some scholars have reinforced this call by relying on additional justifications, such as the need for an international legal order governed by the rule of law.[87] This study emphasises the importance of such developments for the advancement of victims' efforts to obtain reparations, within the broader context of the fight against impunity. The lack of a legal responsibility framework and of an avenue for victims of armed conflict to rely upon, become an even more pressing issue when taking into account that NSAGs have become some of the leading protagonists in present-day conflicts.[88]

83 Similarly, Zegveld (n 33) 223–224; Bílková (n 34) 275; Schmalenbach (n 34) 495–496; Verhoeven (n 34) 285–286, 303; Íñigo Álvarez (n 4) 54, 56, 70.

84 Similarly, Zegveld speaks of an "accountability gap" in Zegveld (n 33). Íñigo Álvarez describes the "responsibility gap" in the following terms: "The existing consensus on the IHL primary rules applicable to armed groups contrasts with the lack of agreement that exists in relation to the application of secondary rules." Íñigo Álvarez (n 4) 54.

85 Bílková (n 34) 275.

86 Zegveld (n 33) 220; Bílková (n 34) 275; Moffett, 'Beyond Attribution: Responsibility of Armed Non-State Actors for Reparations in Northern Ireland, Colombia and Uganda' (n 21); Schmalenbach (n 34) 496; Verhoeven (n 34) 303; Blázquez Rodríguez (n 14).

87 Kleffner (n 21) 259–260; Íñigo Álvarez (n 4) 58–63.

88 See also Section 2.2.1.

Indeed, within the framework of this responsibility gap, it is particularly unclear whether an NSAG is subject to a duty to make reparation. However, one could argue that reparation is the natural consequence of an internationally wrongful act. As discussed in Section 2.2.1, reparation for wrongful conduct constitutes a fundamental principle of international law. Nonetheless, an argument for extending this principle to NSAGs requires further support in state practice or at least an authoritative court or tribunal decision.[89] This will be further considered over the course of the analysis in the subsequent part of this chapter. Moreover, the analysis requires the additional examination of a diverse set of legal sources and materials concerning NSAGs and reparations. Hence, these preliminary findings concerning the possible duty of NSAGs to provide reparation are further explored over the following section.

2.3 Recognition that non-state armed groups should provide reparation

Having preliminarily concluded that the existence of the duty of NSAGs to provide reparation remains unclear in current international law, this section will delve deeper into the question. To this end, an examination of tentative evidence in international practice, soft law instruments and other legal materials recognising a role for NSAGs in providing reparation is conducted. The aim of this mapping exercise is twofold. The first objective is to determine whether a duty to repair is recognised for NSAGs based on international law. This involves looking for indications as to whether developments in state practice might contribute to the formation of a customary international norm. Although the 2005 ICRC study on customary IHL found that the duty of NSAGs to provide reparation remained unclear, both previously underexplored and subsequent practice need to be considered.[90] However, this examination does not claim to be exhaustive and, therefore, the conclusions are necessarily preliminary. The same disclaimer holds for the second objective of this section, which concerns itself with identifying, comparing and evaluating approaches as to how the role of NSAGs in reparations and, in particular, NSAGs' possible duty of reparation have been conceptualised and put into practice in these instances. The general conclusions resulting from these research objectives are brought together in Section 2.4.

89 Similarly, Schmalenbach (n 34) 502; Mastorodimos (n 14) 117.

90 The ICRC found some limited instances of state and other practice to the effect that NSAGs are required to provide reparation for the damage resulting from violations of IHL. Reference is made to the Comprehensive Agreement on Respect for Human Rights and International Humanitarian Law in the Philippines (see further Section 2.3.2.3), a public apology made by a provisional arm of the National Liberation Army (ELN) in Colombia in 2001 and three examples of UN practice (see further Section 2.3.4). Henckaerts and Doswald-Beck (n 18) 549–550.

2.3.1 Historical precedent in the laws of insurgency and belligerency

Having been largely replaced by the compulsory rules of modern IHL, the laws of belligerency and insurgency are generally considered as being out-dated. Nevertheless, an analysis of these old laws can still contribute to a better understanding of the status of NSAGs within the domain of international responsibility. Indeed, state practice and scholarship both indicate that these legal frameworks did not preclude states from claiming reparations directly from NSAGs in situations of belligerency and insurgency. As a result, they provide something of a historical precedent. An analysis of these frameworks, which remain underexplored from the current perspective, will reveal the circumstances in which these claims were presented. The conclusions drawn will offer perspective with respect to NSAGs' responsibility under contemporary international law. Before commencing this examination however, it is necessary to outline the general legal frameworks of insurgency and belligerency.

2.3.1.1 The general legal frameworks of insurgency and belligerency

During the nineteenth and a large part of the twentieth centuries, there was a general reluctance on the part of states to regulate situations of internal strife by means of international law. States feared that this would enhance the legal status of the NSAG involved, as warfare was considered to be an exclusive privilege of states. Moreover, these situations of violence were deemed to belong to the domestic affairs of states, which preferred to treat such groups as being merely criminal in nature. In this sense, it was both their non-state character and their defiant stance towards the state which played a particular role in the development of international law in relation to such actors.[91] Because of these factors, such situations were regulated in a somewhat *ad hoc* manner, with states retaining the upper hand.[92] Situations of internal violence could fall into three categories, which were largely based on the intensity of the violence: rebellion, insurgency and belligerency. Rebellion involved violence of a short duration and low level of intensity, that could easily be suppressed by the parent state. It was deemed as belonging to the state's domestic affairs and therefore subjected to domestic regulation.[93] In contrast, states had to recognise a rebel group as an insurgency or belligerency for it to attain a limited international legal personality.

To be recognised as an insurgency, the violence had to have escalated to such an extent that the government was no longer able to adequately suppress it. Third states could be forced to recognise the factual situation in order to protect their own national interests, whilst entering into regular, but provisional,

91 Daboné (n 15) 397.

92 Sandesh Sivakumaran, *The Law of Non-International Armed Conflict* (Oxford University Press 2012) 9.

93 Ibid.

relations with the insurgents regarding shipping and trading matters, among other issues. There was no clear set of criteria that allowed for an objective determination of a situation as an insurgency. On the contrary, the recognising state had a great discretion in this regard. Following from this recognition, NSAGs were considered as bearing certain international rights and obligations of an *ad hoc* nature. Instead of being predetermined, they depended on the terms of the recognition.[94] The act of recognition would not confer any formal status on either party to the conflict.[95]

Those groups that fulfilled certain objective criteria and that were recognised as belligerents acquired certain international rights and obligations, which were normally applicable to states involved in international armed conflicts.[96] Belligerent fighters would, for example, acquire prisoner of war status and immunity for lawful acts of war. Moreover, they could also stop and search vessels and institute blockades.[97] An act of recognition could be granted by the parent state and third states at their discretion. However, it was unlikely for a government to take the step of recognition until it was clear that the rebellion could not be put down quickly or effectively. Recognition granted by third states would trigger the application of the law of neutrality. Consequently, belligerent ships were, e.g., admitted entering the ports of the recognising states.[98] Such an act of recognition came down to recognising a factual situation, i.e. the existence of war, and, in principle, did not constitute a recognition of the insurgent party as the legitimate government of the state.[99] The American Civil War (1861–1865) was the last conflict in which insurgents were recognised as belligerents.[100]

2.3.1.2 Reparations by non-state armed groups in situations of belligerency and insurgency

THE LAW OF BELLIGERENCY

One of the objective criteria that justified the recognition of belligerency consisted of the NSAG's *de facto* control over a substantial part of the national territory, where it exercised government-like functions. An understanding of the

94 Ibid. 10.
95 Lindsay Moir, *The Law of Internal Armed Conflict* (Cambridge University Press 2002) 4–5.
96 Sivakumaran (n 92) 11–14; Daragh Murray, *Human Rights Obligations of Non-State Armed Groups* (Hart Publishing 2016) 55.
97 Sivakumaran (n 92) 16; Konstantinos Mastorodimos, 'Belligerency Recognition: Past, Present and Future' (2014) 29 Connecticut Journal of International Law 301, 307–308.
98 Yair M Lootsteen, 'The Concept of Belligerency in International Law' (2000) 166 Military Law Review 109, 110.
99 Moir (n 95) 5–10.
100 Lootsteen (n 98) 110.

latter part of this requirement is made more concrete by reference to a statement made by President Grant of the United States of America (US), in 1875, in relation to the insurrection in Cuba:

> I fail to find in the insurrection the existence of such a substantial political organization, real, palpable, and manifest to the world, having the forms and capable of the ordinary functions of government toward its own people and to other states, with courts for the administration of justice, with local habitation, possessing such organization of force, such material, such occupation of territory, as to take the contest out of the category of a more rebellious insurrection or occasional skirmishes and place it on the terrible footing of war, to which a recognition of belligerency would aim to elevate it.[101]

This passage reveals the high standard of government-like functions that had to be reached by the group. As a result of a recognition of belligerency, the parent state was released from all responsibility towards third states in relation to acts occurring in territory under the control of the belligerents.[102] Instead, the rules of international responsibility, including the duty to make reparation, would become applicable to the belligerent NSAG.[103] Therefore, the group would become responsible for its own wrongful actions, and responsible to third states for the damages perpetrated against that state's assets and nationals in the areas under belligerent control. In the words of Hall, this followed from "the inability of the state to perform its international obligations in such parts of its dominions as are not under its actual control".[104] This view is confirmed by Whiteman, who explained that

> the incapacity of government to protect aliens against injurious acts committed by the insurrectionists will in practically all cases be so clear that no rational ground can exist for exacting an obligation to prevent injuries or losses or to make compensation for such as have been sustained.[105]

101 Seventh Annual Message to Congress reprinted in George Grafton Wilson, 'Insurgency and International Maritime Law' (1907) 1 The American Journal of International Law 46, 48; John Y Simon (ed), *The Papers of Ulysses S. Grant: 1875* (Southern Illinois University Press 2003) 393–394.

102 John Bassett Moore, *A Digest of International Law*, vol I (US Government Printing Office 1906) 185; Hersch Lauterpacht, *Recognition in International Law* (Cambridge University Press 1947) 247–250.

103 Moore (n 102) 208–209; Hans Kelsen, *Principles of International Law* (Rinehart & Company 1952) 292; Jochen Frowein, *Das de Facto-Regime Im Völkerrecht* (Carl Heymanns Verlag KG 1968) 74 (for a concrete example of a claim for pecuniary compensation see footnote 23); Roscoe Oglesby, *Internal War and the Search for Normative Order* (Martinus Nijhoff 1971) 73, 76–77; 'Fourth Report on State Responsibility, by Mr Roberto Ago, Special Rapporteur' (n 25) 139; Mastorodimos (n 97) 308.

104 William Edward Hall, *International Law* (Clarendon Press 1880) 26.

105 Marjorie M Whiteman, *Digest of International Law* (US Government Printing Office 1963) 648.

This reveals that the justification for such international responsibility followed from an NSAG's territorial control in default of a parent state, which had been rendered incapable of exerting its power. This reflected, therefore, a shifting of responsibility from the state to the NSAG.[106] This forced third states to address the NSAG directly for any claims relating to the protection of their assets and nationals present in the area under exclusive control of the group. As pointed out by Fortin, this shift of responsibility was often advantageous for both third states and the parent state, since it allowed for an aligning of the new situation on the ground with the legal framework. Third states had a better chance of receiving reparation for damages by being allowed to engage directly on responsibility matters with the entity holding control on the ground, whereas the parent state was released from responsibility with respect to the areas of territory outside of its control.[107] The ILC Special Rapporteur on state responsibility, Roberto Ago, has drawn further attention to the vital role of the belligerent group's legal personality while citing the work of the Institute of International Law: "if the 'insurrectional government' had been recognised as a 'belligerent power', and therefore as a separate subject of international law, it was to that government that injured States should address their claims for reparation of injuries sustained".[108] This suggests that NSAGs which were recognised as belligerents could be held responsible for breaches of their obligations as a result of their independent legal personality under international law.[109]

THE LAW OF INSURGENCY

There are several examples of state practice involving situations of insurgency which also tend to support an obligation for NSAGs to make reparation. In these cases, the responsible NSAGs held exclusive territorial control. On 9 April 1914, members of the crew of the US vessel *Dolphine* anchored at Tampico in Mexico. They were arrested by a squad of armed men belonging to the forces of General Huerta, who had temporarily seized control of most of the country during the last half of February, March and April 1913, before his power rapidly diminished between January and July 1914.[110] On 11 April, the US admiral requested various forms of reparations, including formal disavowal and

106 See in this regard also Frowein (n 103) 84.

107 Fortin (n 15) 278–279.

108 'Fourth Report on State Responsibility, by Mr Roberto Ago, Special Rapporteur' (n 25) 140 para 183 (footnote 402), 142 para 188. See also Institute of International Law, 'Annuaire de l'Institut de Droit International' (1900) Vol 18 243–244 (art 2 paras 2–3); Institute of International Law, 'Règlement Sur La Responsabilité Des Etats à Raison Des Dommages Soufferts Par Des Étrangers En Cas D'émeute, D'insurrection Ou de Guerre Civile' (1900).

109 Oglesby (n 103) 78; Fortin (n 15) 282.

110 *George W Hopkins (USA) v United Mexican States* General Claims Commission between the United States and Mexico (1926) IV RIAA 42 42, 46.

apologies, punishment of the officer in command of the squad and a salute to the American flag, hence treating them akin to a state. The Department of State supported this request. It is significant that the US drew attention to the illegality of the arrest under international law, clearly viewing international law as a basis for the reparations claim. While General Huerta expressed regret and undertook to investigate the responsibility of the officer, consent to the latter part of the demand was declined. This ultimately led to the occupation of Veracruz by US forces on 21 April.[111]

Similar examples can be found in the Spanish Civil War, which was never recognised as a belligerency, mainly due to political reasons, despite the fact that the Franco rebels held at least two-thirds of continental Spain and practically all of her overseas territories.[112] Several states – including the US, Norway,[113] Britain, France[114] and Portugal – directly called upon the Franco rebels, instead of the Spanish government as parent state, for reparations claims relating to damages caused to foreign property and nationals located in the territory under their exclusive control. Similarly, as in the case of belligerency, third states were confronted with the need to protect their interests within the territory over which the incumbent government had lost control. This forced them to initiate dialogue and legal relations with the insurgents.[115] Significantly, this involved correspondence regarding the insurgents' responsibilities to repair the damages caused.[116]

The injured British government categorically requested, on three occasions, reparations from the Nationalist government of Franco, located at Burgos or

111 The case is described in Green Haywood Hackworth, *Digest of International Law*, vol 2 (US Government Printing Office 1941) 420–421; Frowein (n 103) 75, 81; 'Fourth Report on State Responsibility, by Mr Roberto Ago, Special Rapporteur' (n 25) 139.

112 UK HC Deb 8 November 1937 vol 328 col 1385; Fortin (n 15) 104.

113 The Norwegian government claimed monetary compensation from the Nationalist authorities for the damages sustained due to an attack on its cargo ship *Gulnes*, on 7 December 1936, near Seville. See Charles Rousseau, 'La Non-Intervention En Espagne' (1938) 19 Revue de Droit International et de Législation Comparée 473, 508.

114 According to Rousseau, the relations of the French government and the Franco authorities were manifested within the domain of "international responsibility", when the former addressed a claim for reparations to the Nationalist authorities referred to as "the responsible authority" for the summary execution of one of its nationals. Their refusal was met by a measure of retaliation. See Charles Rousseau, 'La Non-Intervention En Espagne' (1938) 19 Revue de Droit International et de Législation Comparée 217, 273–274 [own translation]; Jean Siotis, 'Le Droit de La Guerre et Les Conflits Armés d'un Caractère Non-International' (Université de Genève 1958) 164.

115 Records of a debate held in the United Kingdom House of Commons confirm this observation: UK HC Deb 8 November 1937 vol 328 cols 1385–1387. Similar challenges confronted the US and other states. See Norman J Padelford, *International Law and Diplomacy in the Spanish Civil Strife* (The Macmillan Company 1939) 169, 171; Lauterpacht (n 102) 53.

116 Fortin (n 15) 105.

Salamanca. These examples have been described by Ago as "by far the most important cases". They were issued in response to: the loss of the destroyer *Hunter*, blown up on 13 May 1937 by a mine laid by the Nationalists, four miles off Almeria (in this case monetary compensation was requested); the destruction of the steamer *Aleyra/L'Alcira*, sunk 20 miles off Barcelona on 4 February 1938 by seaplanes from the Nationalist base in Majorca; and, the attack on the British merchant vessel *Stanwell* by a Nationalist aircraft.[117] A further request for reparations was made for the bombing of the British steamer *Jean Weems*. In response, the Nationalist authorities were prepared "to express their official regret and to give an assurance that orders will be given to their forces to take all possible precautions against further incidents of this nature", while furthermore agreeing that "so far as liability and payment of compensation are concerned, to submit the case, if necessary, to arbitration and to abide by the result".[118] Although it is not clear from the records whether the British government considered international law as the basis of these claims, the Nationalist's obligation to repair, which it accepted on several occasions, could be understood as one of the *ad hoc* international obligations that arose between the third state and the insurgents.[119] This supports the argument that it considered the Franco insurgents responsible as a matter of law regardless of the lack of any specific agreement to that end.[120]

The US, in its turn, addressed a note to the insurgent administration of Franco, which provided for a *caveat*, which could be relied upon at a later date, in terms of eliciting protection of their property and compensation for any delinquencies in that respect.[121] According to Rousseau, "the most typical case of international responsibility" concerns a case between the Portuguese government and the Nationalist authorities, relating to a violation of Portuguese territory by "numerous groups of armed Spaniards" in August 1936.[122] While initially presenting its claim for moral and material reparations to the

117 UK HC Deb 7 February 1938 vol 331 col 648; UK HC Deb 28 February 1938 vol 332 col 729; UK HC Deb 30 March 1938 vol 333 col 1973; Rousseau (n 114) 277–278; Rousseau (n 113) 508–509; 'Fourth Report on State Responsibility, by Mr Roberto Ago, Special Rapporteur' (n 25) 139.

118 UK HC Deb 8 November 1937 vol 328 col 1381; Rousseau (n 113) 509–510.

119 Lauterpacht (n 102) 53–54.

120 Fortin (n 15) 106.

121 See Padelford (n 115) 170; Green Haywood Hackworth, *Digest of International Law*, vol 3 (US Government Printing Office 1942) 655. Indeed, on at least three occasions, protests were lodged for damaged property against the Franco insurgents, who expressed regret and provided guarantees of non-repetition and restitution (in the case of the tanker *Nantucket Chief*, the insurgents released the vessel and the members of the crew upon informal representations made by the US government). See Padelford (n 115) 172–173; Green Haywood Hackworth, *Digest of International Law*, vol 1 (US Government Printing Office 1940) 362–363; Green Haywood Hackworth, *Digest of International Law*, vol 7 (US Government Printing Office 1943) 172–173.

122 The case is described in Rousseau (n 114) 278 [own translation].

incumbent government, the latter held that the insurgents were responsible "in accordance with international conventions".[123] This indicates that the Spanish government itself considered the Franco insurgents as internationally responsible. Following this response, the Portuguese government presented a note in which it reproduced the claims originally presented to the Spanish government and observed that, in fact, the insurgents exercised sovereignty over the Spanish territories along the common borders with Portugal. The Nationalist authorities accepted the claim because the Spanish government had lost its power to protect its borders and the properties and lives of foreign nationals. As a result, it was responding as "the representative exercising national sovereignty over its entire territory".[124]

CONCLUSIONS CONCERNING THE RESPONSIBILITY OF NON-STATE ARMED GROUPS IN CURRENT INTERNATIONAL LAW

These examples of state practice demonstrate that the insurgents were deemed to have gained sufficient international legal personality to be held responsible for wrongful acts, even in situations falling short of the recognition of belligerency. Such practice was a result of the effective control the relevant NSAGs were deemed to have held over territory and the state's lack of capacity to exert its influence in these areas.[125] Significantly, these considerations have also been identified as constituting the justification for shifting the regime of international responsibility, originally applicable to the parent state, to NSAGs recognised as belligerents. This shows an interesting overlap between the insurgency and belligerency frameworks, which is of importance to the question of responsibility. More specifically, the practice suggests that the capacity of an NSAG to be held responsible for reparation does not follow from a recognition of belligerency, but rather from its exclusive control over territory. Although such an obligation is generally associated with the law of belligerency, in which it was natural for the belligerent party to have effective territorial control, these aspects of past state practice appear to indicate that the duty to repair could also exist outside of this framework.[126] The practice suggests that where a third state wished to pursue a claim for redress, it made both legal and practical sense to call directly on the responsible NSAG. The NSAG was deemed to have gained sufficient international legal personality to answer the claim, while it made little sense to pursue the incumbent government for matters outside of its control.[127] Concerns over recognition, or conferral of unwarranted legitimacy,

123 Ibid. 279 [own translation].
124 Ibid. 278–280 [own translation]; Fortin (n 15) 106.
125 Lauterpacht (n 102) 278; Rousseau (n 114) 280; Fortin (n 15) 107, 112–113.
126 Similar conclusions have been presented by Frowein (n 103) 84; Fortin (n 15) 116, 156; Patrick Dumberry, *Rebellions and Civil Wars: State Responsibility for the Conduct of Insurgents* (Cambridge University Press 2021) 200–204.
127 Frowein (n 103) 79; Fortin (n 15) 112–113, 278–279.

did not prevent states from making claims, even where armed hostilities were ongoing.

As discussed in Section 2.2.2 of this chapter, the ILC Commentary to Article 14(3) of the draft version of the ARS, which was provisionally adopted in 1996,[128] leaves the international responsibility of insurrectional movements as something of an open question, whilst simultaneously providing some support for the conclusions made in the preceding analysis. The Commentary draws attention to the difference between the injurious conduct of an insurrectional movement that assumes power over a portion of the state's territory and cases of riots or demonstrations by a rebellious mob. It makes this distinction based on the fact that in the former situation "there is a possibility of holding the movement itself responsible for the wrongful acts of its organs".[129] When such a movement takes shape, "there is in existence [...] an organization which has its own machinery and whose organs may act on behalf of the insurrectional movement".[130] The Commentary explains that:

> as soon as they begin their *separate existence on the international scene*, such movements may be capable within certain limits of committing internationally wrongful acts of their own. [...] It will rarely be possible to accuse a State of failing its own obligations of vigilance and protection in relation to the conduct of organs of an insurrectional movement because, most of the time, the actions in question are entirely beyond its control. *Even more rarely will such accusation be levelled against the State in cases where, after the insurrectional movement has succeeded in entrenching its authority over a sufficient portion of the State's territory, third States come to hold the movement itself responsible for internationally wrongful acts of its own organs.*[131]

Thus, the Commentary makes clear that once an NSAG has legal personality under international law, it may be held responsible for violations of its international obligations. In such circumstances, claims would generally be addressed directly to the movement and not to the parent state that has lost control.[132] This Commentary is based on several examples of state practice, including those previously discussed from the American Civil War, Mexico and the Spanish Civil War. In light of this practice, the ILC wanted to provide, in draft

128 Art 14 of draft ARS of 1996 deals with the 'conduct of organs of an insurrectional movement'. Paragraph 3 holds that "[s]imilarly, paragraph 1 is without prejudice to the attribution of the conduct of the organ of the insurrectional movement to that movement in any case in which such attribution may be made under international law."

129 ILC Commentary to draft Art 14 ARS (1996) (n 28) 98 para 28.

130 Ibid. 91 para 3.

131 Ibid. 92 para 4 [emphasis added].

132 Fortin (n 15) 277–278.

Article 14(3), for the possibility that wrongful conduct could be legally attributed to an insurrectional movement. However, it did not take a specific stance on its modalities.[133] It must again be noted, that paragraph 3 was eventually deferred to the ILC Commentary to the ARS of 2001.[134]

Turning to current international law, the examination of the law of belligerency and insurgency has revealed that there is historical precedent which suggests that, where an NSAG has exclusive control over part of a state's territory, it might be held internationally responsible for its wrongs. The analysis has also clarified that it made, and therefore arguably makes, both legal and practical sense to directly address an NSAG, wherever it has international legal personality and where its wrongful conduct has been perpetrated beyond the control of the parent state. These observations appear to be especially relevant in respect of NSAGs that are currently bound by Additional Protocol II, according to which an NSAG must exercise territorial control. However, the analysis has not uncovered similar evidence with respect to groups that do not exercise territorial control. Hence, it remains unclear whether such groups could hold international responsibility.[135]

The work of the ILC, discussed *supra*, allows us to connect these conclusions regarding the law of belligerency and insurgency in a more direct and at least preliminary manner to NSAGs' responsibility under contemporary IHL. First, the ILC considered the possibility of holding insurrectional movements internationally responsible. This was contemplated in light of some of the previously cited state practice concerning belligerency and insurgency. Second, the ILC used the term 'insurrectional movement' in its work. As explained in Section 2.2.2 of this chapter, the ILC has clarified that the essential idea of such movements is reflected in Article 1(1) Additional Protocol II. More specifically, "the threshold for the application of the laws of armed conflict contained in [...] Protocol II [...] may be taken as a guide".[136] It was concluded, on this basis, that the term insurrectional movement certainly encompasses NSAGs bound by Additional Protocol II, in addition to Common Article 3. Taken together, the ILC's work suggests that it considered past belligerency and insurgency practice as being generally relevant when considering the responsibility of NSAGs. More specifically, it reinforces the significance of this historical precedent, in terms of considering the possible responsibility of at least those NSAGs which both exercise exclusive territorial control and satisfy the higher threshold requirements of Additional Protocol II.

The discussion has further shown that the international responsibility of such NSAGs has generally been conceptualised as akin to that of states.[137] Important

133 *Yearbook of the International Law Commission* (1975) Vol II UN Doc A/CN.4/SER.A/1975/Add.1 (n 28) 98–99 paras 28, 31.

134 See ILC Commentary to Art 10 ARS 52 para 16.

135 Verhoeven (n 34) 297; Fortin (n 15) 282.

136 ILC Commentary to Art 10 ARS 51 para 9.

137 Íñigo Álvarez concluded on the basis of an examination of the notion of international responsibility and its evolution over time that "[i]n principle, other entities

for the present discussion, such responsibility is understood as giving rise to a duty to make reparation for wrongful acts. The aforementioned state practice indicates that claims for several forms of reparations, normally requested from states, have been made against such groups, namely: restitution, compensation, satisfaction and guarantees of non-repetition. This suggests that they can be relevant for NSAGs in international law. Lastly, these instances show that NSAGs may be willing to address reparations claims and capable of satisfying them.[138]

2.3.2 Contemporary evidence in domestic jurisdictions and state practice[139]

Other than the Justice and Peace Law process in Colombia (discussed in Section 2.3.2.2 and Chapter 5), this study has identified no examples of international or domestic bodies having held NSAGs judicially responsible to make reparation for their violations of international law.[140] Nevertheless, there are a number of notable instances in which aggrieved parties have attempted to establish, through the national judicial system of the US, the civil responsibility of NSAGs based on international law. These attempts notwithstanding, the discussion does identify a case in Northern Ireland, in which the collective civil responsibility of an NSAG was successfully established, but based on domestic law. Additionally, a number of agreements concluded between states and NSAGs have recognised a role for these groups in the provision of reparations. All in all, the examination reveals some limited instances of state practice that recognise a duty of NSAGs to provide reparation for violations of international law.

2.3.2.1 United States of America

Several attempts have been made within the US domestic legal system to bring civil claims directly against NSAGs based on violations of international law. In the *Linder v Portocarrero* case, the plaintiffs sought damages against four individual defendants and three *Contra* organisations for violations of, i.a., Common Article 3 of the First Geneva Convention, the Second Geneva Convention and the Protocols thereto, customary international law, and other treaties in connection with the death of Mr. Linder in the midst of the Nicaraguan civil war.[141] The Court dismissed the tort claim based on a violation of

[than states] that exercise powers over territory or control over people could follow a similar understanding of international responsibility." Íñigo Álvarez (n 4) 70.

138 Fortin (n 15) 279.

139 A distinction is made between evidence in domestic jurisdictions and state practice in order to include domestic efforts to obligate responsible NSAGs to make reparation on the basis of national law, on the one hand, and the practice of states founded on international law, on the other.

140 Similarly, Kleczkowska (n 63) 138.

141 *Linder v Portocarrero* US District Court for SD Florida 747 F.Supp. 1452 (17 September 1990) paras 1453–1454.

customary international law against torture by arguing that torture by a non-state actor is not a violation of international law.[142] The Court also considered the claim resulting from a violation of Common Article 3[143] as non-justifiable, due to the political question doctrine. On the basis of the latter finding, the Court held, in accordance with case law of the US Supreme Court, that domestic tort actions are not appropriate remedies for injuries that occur outside the US during conflicts with belligerents.[144] While the case was not successful, it is significant that the Court did not expressly reject the possibility of holding an NSAG responsible for international law violations.

Further attempts have been made to bring claims against NSAGs under two domestic acts: the Alien Tort Claims Act (ATCA, also known as the Alien Tort Statute or ATS) and the Torture Victims Protection Act (TVPA).[145] They provide US courts with jurisdiction over civil claims brought by non-US nationals for torts committed in violation of international law. Numerous cases linked to armed conflict have been initiated under both acts.[146]

In the *Klinghoffer v S.N.C. Achille Lauro* case, which dealt with the liability of the Palestinian Liberation Organization (PLO), the Second Circuit Court of Appeals held that while "unrecognized regimes" are generally precluded from initiating proceedings in US courts without consent of the executive branch, there were no restrictions on such an entity being sued.[147] The case indicates that there was no principled objection against bringing a civil claim against at least such non-state actor. In a more recent case of 2011, the US Appeals Court for the District of Columbia Circuit had to determine whether the ATCA provided jurisdiction over civil actions for torture committed by a non-state actor such as the PLO.[148] The Court held:

> We do not purport to decide that the ATS can create no actions against private actors. *Sosa* makes clear that the analysis of whether 'international

142 Ibid. paras 1460–1462.

143 The Court did not consider the Additional Protocols to the 1949 Geneva Conventions, as the US was not a signatory party.

144 *Linder v Portocarrero* (n 141) paras 1463–1464; *Linder v Portocarrero* US Court of Appeals for 11th Cir 963 F.2d 332 (17 June 1992) para 337.

145 The landmark *Karadzic* case allowed, for the first time, ATCA claims to be presented against non-state actors: "We do not agree that the law of nations, as understood in the modern era, confines its reach to state action. Instead, we hold that certain forms of conduct violate the law of nations whether undertaken by those acting under the auspices of a state or only as private individuals." *Kadic v Karadzic* US Court of Appeals for 2d Cir 70 F.3d 232 (13 October 1995).

146 Judiciary Act, ch 20, § 9, 1 Stat 73, 76–77 (codified as amended at 28 U.S.C. § 1350 (2006)) 1789 (US); Gillard (n 15) 547–548.

147 *Klinghoffer v SNC Achille Lauro* US Court of Appeals for 2d Cir 937 F.2d 44 (21 June 1991) para 48; Elihu Lauterpacht and Christopher Greenwood (eds), *International Law Reports*, vol 96 (Cambridge University Press 1994) 70.

148 *Ali Mahmud Ali Shafi et al v Palestinian Authority and Palestinian Liberation Organization* US Court of Appeals for DC Cir No 10–7024 (14 June 2011) 5–6.

> law extends the scope of liability ... to the perpetrator being sued, if the defendant is a private actor' pertains to the 'given norm' being analysed.[149]

It was concluded that at present there was insufficient consensus that torture by private actors violates international law.[150] Nevertheless, the case suggests that a US court could potentially consider the civil responsibility of such an actor when dealing with an actionable violation of a clearly binding norm of international law.

In the case *Doe v Islamic Salvation Front*, civil action was initiated against the Islamic Salvation Front (FIS) and a member of the organisation. The US District Court for the District of Columbia found that the crimes allegedly committed by the defendant FIS were in violation of Common Article 3 of the Geneva Conventions, which fulfilled the condition to establish jurisdiction under the ATCA.[151] In *Islamic Salvation Front II* it was observed in a footnote that the "FIS has never been served and indeed may not exist. It was banned by the Algerian government in February 1992".[152] The judicial proceedings primarily dealt with the allegations against the individual defendant and the motions he brought forward. Curiously, it appears that this was not deemed as an obstacle for the continuation of the action against FIS. The case was ultimately dismissed for reasons unrelated to the question whether organisations, such as the FIS, could be sued under the Act. Accordingly, the case provides further support for the assertion that there is no principle barring NSAGs from being held responsible for reparation in such civil proceedings. Nevertheless, it also reveals some of the challenges that such litigation might involve: starting with the intricacies of serving an illegal group and extending to the enforcement of any potential judgment on reparations.[153]

Moving to the TVPA, the US Supreme Court held in *Mohamad v Palestinian Authority and Palestinian Liberation Organization* of 2012 that the Statute only imposes liability on natural persons and not the organisations they serve.[154] Hence, the decision excludes the potential liability of organisations, such as NSAGs, for torture or extrajudicial killing. In an *amici curiae* brief relating to this case and the linked *Kiobel* case, the Center for Justice and Accountability argued against this limitation while drawing attention to the collective nature of such system crimes, and the resulting necessity of addressing organisational

149 Ibid. 13. See *Sosa v Alvarez-Machain* US Supreme Court 542 US 692 (29 June 2004).

150 *Ali Mahmud Ali Shafi et al v Palestinian Authority and Palestinian Liberation Organization* (n 148) 14–16. Reference is made in this regard to *Sosa v Alvarez-Machain* (n 149) n 20.

151 *Doe v Islamic Salvation Front* US District Court for DC 993 F Supp 3 (3 February 1998) para 8.

152 *Doe v Islamic Salvation Front* US District Court for DC 257 F Supp 2d 115 (31 March 2003) n 3.

153 Kleffner (n 21) 256–257.

154 *Mohamad v Palestinian Authority* US Supreme Court 132 SCt 1702 (18 April 2012).

liability and providing effective remedies to that end.[155] This further concretises the important role which the collective responsibility of NSAGs may perform in the context of providing effective redress to victims.

2.3.2.2 Northern Ireland and Colombia

While none of the civil suits in the US were successful, the High Court of Justice of Northern Ireland held that the Real Irish Republican Army (Real IRA) was responsible for a bombing carried out in 1998.[156] Although the case was decided on the basis of domestic law, it still recognises that an NSAG could be subjected to a court claim for reparations and could ultimately be held collectively responsible to that end. The case and its significance are further discussed in Section 4.5.2.2 of Chapter 4.

In Colombia, the Constitutional Court brought forward the notion of "solidarity civil responsibility" of NSAGs. This responsibility results from criminal conduct carried out within the confines of those groups that are subjected to a special criminal procedure regulated by the Justice and Peace Law of 2005.[157] Although criminal responsibility remains individual, civil responsibility flows from the criminal conduct so that compensation can be sought not only from the criminally convicted member, but also – in subsidy and by way of the principle of solidarity – from the NSAG to which the perpetrator belonged. The civil responsibility of the NSAG arises from serious crimes which have been committed during and on the occasion of the convicted individual's membership in the relevant group. Significantly, these are recognised as involving conduct which amounts to serious violations of IHL and IHRL.[158] Thus, it constitutes a notable instance of state practice, which recognises that NSAGs can be held to a duty to provide compensation for violations of international law. This type of responsibility concerning NSAGs is legally operationalised by holding the constituent members of the group jointly and severally liable to compensate the damages caused. It provides for an interesting approach to dealing with the

155 Center for Justice and Accountability, 'Brief of Amici Curiae Dr Juan Romagoza Arce, Cecilia Santos Moran, and Ken Wiwa in Support of Petitioners, Submission in Kiobel v Royal Dutch Petroleum Co and Mohamad v Palestinian Authority Nos 10–1491 & 11–88' (2011) 2–3.

156 *Mark Christopher Breslin and Others v Seamus McKenna and Others* High Court of Justice in Northern Ireland [2009] NIQB 50.

157 Law No 975 of 2005 (Justice and Peace Law) (Colombia); *Judgment C-370/06* Constitutional Court of Colombia (18 May 2006) [own translation].

158 As an example, *Case against Fredy Rendón Herrera* Superior Tribunal of Bogotá (Colombia) Justice and Peace Chamber (16 December 2011) 412–413. Moreover, as noted by Moffett, "[t]he Colombian situation represents the ability of armed groups to be held responsible for reparations on the basis of violating human rights law, not only by individuals, but by the organisation as a whole." Moffett, 'Beyond Attribution: Responsibility of Armed Non-State Actors for Reparations in Northern Ireland, Colombia and Uganda' (n 21) 343.

responsibility of NSAGs within the surprising setting of a criminal justice procedure. This case is more extensively discussed in Chapter 5.

2.3.2.3 Agreements concluded between states and non-state armed groups

This section examines several peace and other types of agreements concluded between states and NSAGs in the context of an armed conflict, particularly in Burundi, the Central African Republic, Colombia, Guatemala, Nepal, the Philippines, Sierra Leone, Somalia, South Sudan, Sudan and Uganda. All deal in some manner with the question of reparation. The purpose of the examination is to determine how they dealt with this question in relation to violations committed by the respective NSAGs and, particularly, whether the practice evidences any recognition of a duty of NSAGs to repair under international law. Over the course of the analysis, four general approaches have been identified.

In the first approach, agreements place the obligation to provide reparation exclusively on the state. This was the case in, for instance, the Comprehensive Agreement on Human Rights in Guatemala (1994) and the Lomé Peace Agreement in Sierra Leone (1999).[159]

In the second approach, parties recognise the importance of providing reparations, but do so without explicitly designating the NSAG as a collective duty holder.[160] Although the 2007 Agreement on Accountability and Reconciliation between the Government of Uganda and the Lord's Resistance Army (LRA) has been cited by several authors as recognising a duty for NSGAs to make reparation for IHL violations, a strict reading of the agreement warrants more nuance.[161] While the parties agreed that it is essential to address the suffering of the victims, no explicit obligation was placed on the LRA as such. Rather, the terminology used in the agreement suggests that group members were to provide reparations: "[a]lternative penalties and sanctions shall, as relevant [...] require perpetrators to make reparations to victims";

159 Comprehensive Agreement on Human Rights (Guatemala) (29 March 1994) VIII; Peace Agreement Between the Government of Sierra Leone and the Revolutionary United Front of Sierra Leone (Lomé Peace Agreement) (7 July 1999) XXIX; Agreement between the Government of the Republic of South Sudan (GRSS) and the South Sudan Democratic Movement/Army (SSDM/A) (27 February 2012) para 7(b).

160 See Darfur Peace Agreement (5 May 2006) paras 194, 199–200 (para 205[g] does state that the Compensation Commission will take into account the "capacity of the perpetrator or perpetrators to pay monetary compensation", but this appears to involve individuals rather than NSAGs).

161 E.g. Moffett, 'Beyond Attribution: Responsibility of Armed Non-State Actors for Reparations in Northern Ireland, Colombia and Uganda' (n 21) 343–344; Schmalenbach (n 34) 502; Francesca Capone, 'From the Justice and Peace Law to the Revised Peace Agreement between the Colombian Government and the FARC: Will Victims' Rights Be Satisfied at Last?' (2017) 77 Heidelberg Journal of International Law 125, 159.

and, "[r]eparations, which may be ordered to be paid to a victim as part of penalties and sanctions in accountability proceedings".[162] Article 9.2 of the Agreement arguably left room to further negotiate the collective role of the LRA in the reparations process: "[t]he Parties agree that collective as well as individual reparations should be made to victims through mechanisms to be adopted by the Parties upon further consultation." However, the annexure to the Agreement, which set out the proposed implementation framework, did not provide further clarification to that end.[163] Moreover, the LRA's post-conflict role in terms of reparations also remains unclear, as the group had no political ambitions and would have ceased to exist had the agreement come to fruition.[164] Ultimately, the peace process collapsed due to the LRA's failure to sign the final agreement.

The third approach recognises that NSAGs should contribute to providing reparations, at times expressly as a consequence of international law violations. Significantly, the following agreements, which are illustrative of this approach, cover the five main forms of reparations included within the UN Basic Principles and Guidelines.[165] Additionally, they suggest that at least some NSAGs may exhibit a willingness to provide such measures, and that states may accept their role in a reparations process. A first illustration is the Somali Agreement on Implementing the Cease-fire and on Modalities of Disarmament (1993), which provides for a measure of restitution: "[a]ll sides agree in principle that properties unlawfully taken during the fighting shall be returned to the lawful owners."[166] Another example is the Comprehensive Agreement concluded between the government of the Philippines and the National Democratic Front of the Philippines (1998), which is grounded in IHRL and IHL. It provides that, "[t]he Parties [...] shall take concrete steps to stop and prevent the violations of human rights, ensure that those found guilty of such violations are punished, and provide for the indemnification, rehabilitation and restitution of the victims."[167] In 2001, a peace agreement with another NSAG, the Moro Islamic Liberation Front (MILF), was signed in which the parties agreed to "safely return evacuees to their place of origin; provide all the necessary financial/

162 Agreement on Accountability and Reconciliation between the Government of Uganda and the Lord's Resistance Army (29 June 2007) Arts 6.4, 8.1, 9.1–9.3.

163 Annexure to the Agreement on Accountability and Reconciliation between the Government of Uganda and the Lord's Resistance Army (19 February 2008) clauses 1, 16–18.

164 Barney Afako, 'Between Revulsion and Realism: Policies and Dilemmas in Responding to the LRA' (IFIT 2020) 35.

165 UN Basic Principles and Guidelines principles 18–23.

166 Somali Agreement on Implementing the Cease-fire and on Modalities of Disarmament (15 January 1993) III.

167 Comprehensive Agreement on Respect for Human Rights and International Humanitarian Law between the Government of the Republic of the Philippines and the National Democratic Front of the Philippines (16 March 1998) Preamble paras 1 and 6, Part II Art 5, Part III Arts 2(3) and 10.

material and technical assistance to start a new life, as well as allow them to be awarded reparations for their properties lost or destroyed by reason of the conflict", while the MILF also committed to "determine, lead and manage rehabilitation and development projects in conflict affected areas".[168] A further example is the Arusha Peace and Reconciliation Agreement for Burundi (2000), in which the parties undertook to implement the following principles and measures relating to reparations for genocide, war crimes and crimes against humanity: the "[e]rection of a national monument in memory of all victims"; the "[i]nstitution of a national day of remembrance for victims" for such crimes; and, the "taking of measures that would facilitate the identification of mass graves and ensure a dignified burial for the victims".[169] More recently, the 2013 Agreement between the government of Sudan and the Justice and Equality Movement-Sudan holds that "[t]he parties shall expeditiously take measures to commence the payment of compensation to returning IDPs [internationally displaced people], refugees as well as all other victims of the conflict".[170] In a 2019 peace agreement, the government of the Central African Republic and several armed groups agreed "to take appropriate measures, including the establishment of a trust fund, to guarantee the rehabilitation and reparation due to victims".[171] Last, the Final Peace Agreement between the Colombian government and the FARC-EP (2016) recognises the group's duty to contribute to material and symbolic reparations for the damages resulting from violations of international law.[172] While concrete steps have been taken to implement this last agreement, further research is needed to establish the extent to which this is true of the other agreements discussed in this section. Evidence of their implementation would bolster their legal significance and shed light on the NSAGs' capacity to implement these measures.

The last approach includes agreements which embrace certain measures that could theoretically fall within the definition of some of the reparations forms, but are not characterised as such. Therefore, it is to be assumed that the measures were not designed to be reparative in nature. Nevertheless, such agreements do indicate that it is possible to agree upon such actions with an NSAG and that such groups can have a potential role in their implementation.[173]

168 Agreement on Peace between the Government of the Republic of the Philippines and the Moro Islamic Liberation Front (22 June 2001) Section B paras 2–3.

169 Arusha Peace and Reconciliation Agreement for Burundi (28 August 2000) Arts 4 (2), 6(7)-(8).

170 Agreement between the Government of Sudan and the Justice and Equality Movement-Sudan on the Basis of the Doha Document for Peace in Darfur (6 April 2013) Art 17 para 43. See also Sudan Peace Agreement (Juba Agreement) (2020) 33 para 6 and 34 para 12.1.

171 Political Agreement for Peace and Reconciliation in the Central African Republic (Khartoum Accord) (February 2019) Art 12, see also Art 5(i).

172 The reparations process involving the FARC-EP is extensively examined in Chapter 6.

173 For instance, the Government of Nepal and the Communist Party of Nepal (Maoist) agreed "to set up a High-level Truth and Reconciliation Commission

In sum, the discussion has revealed some limited instances of state practice that recognises a duty for NSAGs to provide reparation for harm resulting from their violations of international law committed during armed conflict.[174] Other practice, at least, recognises a role for NSAGs in a reparations process, but without a clear basis in international law. Still, this practice is of importance for the further development of this area of international law.[175] In this regard, Schmalenbach argues that "the existing agreements on reparations cannot be treated as irrelevant; they contribute to the emerging foundations of international obligation of armed groups to make reparation in cases of humanitarian law violations".[176] Similarly, Francioni and Ronzitti conclude that "the practice concerning the obligation incumbent upon armed opposition groups to grant reparation is at an emerging stage".[177]

2.3.3 UN Basic Principles and Guidelines

Some of the previously discussed instances of state practice provide recognition of a duty of NSAGs to make reparation under international law. Further support is found in the 2005 UN Basic Principles and Guidelines, also dubbed as "an international bill of rights of victims".[178] Principle 15 of this international soft law instrument deals with reparation for gross violations of IHRL and serious violations of IHL. This principle recognises, besides the obligation of states to provide reparation, that:

through mutual agreement in order to investigate truth about people seriously violating human rights and involved in crimes against humanity"; to pledge to abandon all types of war, attacks and violence; to allow "the people displaced due to the armed conflict to return back voluntarily to their respective ancestral or former residence"; and to "reconstruct the infrastructure destroyed as a result of the conflict". Comprehensive Peace Agreement between the Government of Nepal and the Communist Party of Nepal (Maoist) (21 November 2006) paras 5.2.5, 5.2.6, 5.2.8.

174 While the legal status of such agreements remains unclear, they can be treated as instances of state practice relevant for the process of customary international law formation. ILA Committee on Non-State Actors (n 21) 7–8; Daniëlla Dam-de Jong, 'Building a Sustainable Peace: How Peace Processes Shape and Are Shaped by the International Legal Framework for the Governance of Natural Resources' (2019) 29 Review of European, Comparative & International Environmental Law 21, 30.

175 According to Dam-de Jong, "the interaction between peace agreements and international law goes two ways. First, international law provides a normative and interpretative framework for the design and implementation of the arrangements set out in peace agreements. Second, peace agreements can also shape and further develop international law, most notably by providing novel interpretations to existing norms and principles in international law". Dam-de Jong (n 174) 23–24.

176 Schmalenbach (n 34) 502.

177 Francesco Francioni and Natalino Ronzitti, *War by Contract: Human Rights, Humanitarian Law, and Private Contractors* (Oxford University Press 2011) 260.

178 M Cherif Bassiouni, 'International Recognition of Victims' Rights' (2006) 6 Human Rights Law Review 203, 203.

> In cases where *a person, a legal person, or other entity* is found liable for reparation to a victim, such a party *should* provide reparation to the victim or compensate the State if the State has already provided reparation to the victim [emphasis added].

The principle thus acknowledges that in addition to states, non-state entities may also be required to make reparation for gross or serious violations of IHRL and IHL. Importantly, this arguably includes NSAGs.[179] However, this preliminary interpretation is subject to debate in legal scholarship. Moffett argues that the UN Basic Principles clearly outline that NSAGs have an obligation to provide reparation to victims.[180] Yet, Dudai and Rose question this, by noting that the instrument does not explicitly address NSAGs' duty to repair and, more generally, appears to have left this controversial matter open. Instead of operating to clarify the notion of responsibility for reparation, the Basic Principles and Guidelines are primarily centred on the rights of victims.[181]

To provide clarity on the issue, an analysis of the drafting process and of the commentaries provided by the former Special Rapporteurs, van Boven and Bassiouni, is needed. While reflecting on the drafting process, van Boven identified the question of non-state actors as one "of the main issues that came up in the process of discussion and negotiation":[182]

> While the Principles and Guidelines are drawn up on the basis of State responsibility, the issue of responsibility of non-State actors was also raised

179 Andrew Clapham, *Human Rights Obligations of Non-State Actors* (Oxford University Press 2006) 73.

180 Moffett, 'Beyond Attribution: Responsibility of Armed Non-State Actors for Reparations in Northern Ireland, Colombia and Uganda' (n 21) 331.

181 Cecily Rose, 'An Emerging Norm: The Duty of States to Provide Reparations for Human Rights Violations by Non-State Actors' (2010) 33 Hastings International and Comparative Law Review 307, 320–321; Ron Dudai, 'Closing the Gap: Symbolic Reparations and Armed Groups' (2011) 93 International Review of the Red Cross 783, 789–790.

182 In his 1999 report, Bassiouni identified the following as one of the main issues to be resolved: "who is responsible for providing any of these modalities of redress: the violator in his/her personal capacity, the State, non-State actors, or legal entities under private law?". UNCHR, 'Report of the Independent Expert on the Right to Restitution, Compensation and Rehabilitation for Victims of Grave Violations of Human Rights and Fundamental Freedoms, Mr M Bassiouni, Submitted Pursuant to Commission on Human Rights Resolution 1998/43' (8 February 1999) UN Doc E/CN.4/1999/65 para 77; UNCHR, 'The Right to a Remedy and Reparation for Victims of Violations of International Human Rights and Humanitarian Law – Note by the High Commissioner for Human Rights' (27 December 2002) UN Doc E/CN.4/2003/63 para 48; Theo van Boven, 'Victims' Rights to a Remedy and Reparation: The New United Nations Principles and Guidelines' in Alan Stephens, Mariana Goetz and Carla Ferstman (eds), *Reparations for Victims of Genocide, War Crimes and Crimes Against Humanity: Systems in Place and Systems in the Making* (Martinus Nijhoff Publishers 2009) 27.

> in the discussions and negotiations, notably insofar as *movements or groups exercise effective control over a certain territory and people in that territory*, but also with regard to business enterprises exercising economic power. It was *generally felt that non-State actors are to be held responsible for their policies and practices*, allowing victims to seek redress and reparation on the basis of *legal liability* and human solidarity, and not on the basis of State responsibility.
>
> The Principles and Guidelines provide for equal and effective access to justice, "*irrespective of who may ultimately be the bearer of responsibility for the violation*" (principle 3 (c)). In this connection reference is also made to the following provision: "In cases where a person, a legal person, or other entity is found liable for reparation to a victim, such party should provide reparation to the victim or compensate the State if the State has already provided reparation to the victim" (principle 15, last sentence). It is a *victim-oriented perspective* that was kept in mind in extending, albeit in a *modest and cautious way*, the scope of the Principles and Guidelines to include the *responsibility and liability of non-State actors*.[183]

These insights into the drafting of the instrument show general support for the obligation of NSAGs with effective control over territory and people to provide reparation on the basis of their responsibility. However, the drafters adopted a 'modest and cautious' approach and refrained from making any conclusive decisions, while maintaining a victim-centred perspective. Although the preparatory work confirms that a particular focus was placed on the significant levels of victimisation caused by NSAGs with effective control, this was not incorporated into the final text.[184] This was likely because the instrument

183 Theo van Boven, 'The United Nations Basic Principles and Guidelines on the Right to a Remedy and Reparation for Victims of Gross Violations of International Human Rights Law and Serious Violations of International Humanitarian Law' 1, 3 [emphasis added].

184 UNCHR, 'Study Concerning the Right to Restitution, Compensation and Rehabilitation for Victims of Gross Violations of Human Rights and Fundamental Freedoms, Final Report Submitted by Mr Theo van Boven, Special Rapporteur' (2 July 1993) UN Doc E/CN.4/Sub.2/1993/8 56 (see footnote to proposed principle 2: "[w]here these principles refer to States, they also apply, as appropriate to other entities exercising effective power"); UNCHR, 'Report of the Independent Expert on the Right to Restitution, Compensation and Rehabilitation for Victims of Grave Violations of Human Rights and Fundamental Freedoms, Mr M Bassiouni, Submitted Pursuant to Commission on Human Rights Resolution 1998/43' (n 182) para 20 (this language is absent in the 1996 version); UNCHR, 'The Right to a Remedy and Reparation for Victims of Violations of International Human Rights and Humanitarian Law – Note by the High Commissioner for Human Rights' (n 182) para 106 (representative of Argentina clarified that it understood 'non-State entities' as including those recognised in Common Art 3 and Additional Protocol II); UNCHR, 'The Right to a Remedy and Reparation for Victims of Violations of International Human Rights and Humanitarian Law – Note by the High

wanted to prioritize victims, regardless of who was responsible for the harm (state or non-state actors).[185]

As the Basic Principles contend not to introduce new international legal obligations, but rather to consolidate existing ones, the text has been drafted to reflect this reality. It uses the term 'shall' where a binding norm is in effect and 'should' where a norm is not strictly binding.[186] Accordingly, the formulation of principle 15, which uses the term 'should', indicates an "emerging concept of the responsibility" of NSAGs in international law.[187] The principle recognises that an NSAG *could* be obliged to provide reparation under international law, particularly for serious violations of IHL; however, the application of the principle in IHRL was faced with greater resistance. This is reflected in a conclusion of the Chairperson-Rapporteur, which was itself based on discussions recorded during a consultative meeting between representatives of a large number of Member States, non-governmental organisations and international agencies:

> With regard to [former] principle 17, while recognizing that non-State actors, such as armed groups, may indeed commit violations, more clarity in the text was seen as necessary with regard to the responsibility of non-State actors [...] in order to correctly reflect differences between human rights law and IHL in their application to non-State actors.[188]

Commissioner for Human Rights' (10 November 2003) UN Doc E/CN.4/2004/57 27–28 and Appendix 1 Preamble para 12 of 2003 version.

185 UNCHR, 'The Right to a Remedy and Reparation for Victims of Violations of International Human Rights and Humanitarian Law – Note by the High Commissioner for Human Rights' (n 182) 63 Annex I para 114; Marten Zwanenburg, 'The Van Boven/Bassiouni Principles: An Appraisal' (2006) 24 Netherlands Quarterly of Human Rights 641, 646, 650. See also UN Basic Principles and Guidelines principle 3(c).

186 Preamble of the UN Basic Principles and Guidelines para 7; UNCHR, 'The Right to a Remedy and Reparation for Victims of Violations of International Human Rights and Humanitarian Law – Note by the High Commissioner for Human Rights' (n 184) paras 10–11.

187 The Chairperson-Rapporteur noted that: "The Principles and Guidelines have been built on international law and practice as they have evolved in the course of the development of the Principles; thus, the emerging concept of the responsibility of non-State actors is reflected in the Principles and Guidelines." Ibid. 13.

188 Former principle 17 stated, "[i]n cases where the violation is not attributable to the State, the party responsible for the violation should provide reparation to the victim". A further insightful conclusion is the following: "As the concept of the accountability of non-State actors is evolving, care should be taken in the wording [...] While everyone recognized non-State accountability under IHL and international criminal law, some delegations held that only States (and their agents) can violate human rights law as such." UNCHR, 'The Right to Restitution, Compensation and Rehabilitation for Victims of Gross Violations of Human Rights and Fundamental Freedoms – Final Report of the Special Rapporteur' (18 January 2000) UN Doc E/CN.4/2000/62 Annex para 17; UNCHR, 'The Right to a Remedy and

The Basic Principles and Guidelines take a judicial approach to reparations. This is indicated in principle 15, which suggests that a formal legal judgment is a necessary prerequisite to reparation ("a person, legal person, or other entity is found liable for reparation to a victim").[189] Although this consequently provides a stringent threshold for reparations, van Boven admits that, in reality, non-judicial schemes and programmes also contribute to reparative justice alongside judicial reparations.[190] In addition, the primary focus of the Basic Principles and Guidelines appears to be the domestic rather than the international level.

As a result of its victim-centred perspective, the concepts of social and human solidarity play a particular role in the Basic Principles and Guidelines.[191] Principle 16 appears to be an expression of that.[192] It provides for a subsidiary responsibility for the state to establish national reparations programmes and other assistance to victims when "the parties liable for the harm suffered are *unable or unwilling to meet their obligations*".[193] This suggests that, although NSAGs would bear a primary duty to repair, reparations should not be solely dependent on such entities. Instead, states play a crucial role in guaranteeing effective redress.

Notably, the UN General Assembly, which enjoys virtually universal participation, adopted the Basic Principles and Guidelines in 2005 without a vote.[194] The ILC has emphasised the weight of such resolutions in identifying rules of customary international law, stating that they "offer important evidence of the collective opinion of its Members".[195] At the same time, a resolution adopted by the General Assembly cannot independently create a norm of custom.[196] It

Reparation for Victims of Violations of International Human Rights and Humanitarian Law – Note by the High Commissioner for Human Rights' (n 182) paras 18, 48. See also ibid. 12, 14, 17, 19 and Annex I paras 15, 18, 29, 33, however, see para 38 (response van Boven); UNCHR, 'The Right to a Remedy and Reparation for Victims of Violations of International Human Rights and Humanitarian Law – Note by the High Commissioner for Human Rights' (n 184) para 15; Bassiouni (n 178) 252–255.

189 See also UN Basic Principles and Guidelines principle 17.

190 Bassiouni (n 178) 266 n 317; van Boven (n 182) 37.

191 Preamble of the UN Basic Principles and Guidelines para 11; UNCHR, 'The Right to a Remedy and Reparation for Victims of Violations of International Human Rights and Humanitarian Law – Note by the High Commissioner for Human Rights' (n 184) 26, 28.

192 Zwanenburg (n 185) 648.

193 [emphasis added]; Moffett, 'Beyond Attribution: Responsibility of Armed Non-State Actors for Reparations in Northern Ireland, Colombia and Uganda' (n 21) 331.

194 UNGA, Res 60/147 adopted on 16 December 2005 (21 March 2006) UN Doc A/RES/60/147.

195 ILC, Draft Conclusions on Identification of Customary International Law with Commentaries (2018) UN Doc A/73/10 Commentary to Draft Conclusion 12 para 2.

196 Ibid. 12(1) para 4.

can, however, play an important role in the development of customary international law, where it provides inspiration and impetus for the growth of a general practice accepted as law (accompanied by *opinio juris*) conforming to its terms.[197] It is true that this instrument has become a key point of reference for states and other actors to interpret and apply the concept of reparation in international law.[198] Yet, the previous discussion in Section 2.3.2 did not identify any instance of state practice expressly relying on this basis to recognise a duty for NSAGs to provide reparation.[199] Even if this was implied, only little practice has been identified. This certainly does not satisfy the high threshold for the identification of customary international law.[200] Thus, although the instrument tentatively recognises an emerging concept of responsibility of NSAGs involving a duty to make reparation for at least IHL violations, it cannot be concluded that this soft norm has turned hard.[201] However, given the Basic Principles and Guidelines' authoritative character, it also cannot be excluded that this might occur in the future.

2.3.4 UN practice

This section examines whether there are instances of UN practice which recognise a duty of NSAGs to make reparation under international law. The general practice of UN bodies and Special Rapporteurs is considered, while a more systematic study is conducted of the reports of 30 UN-established commissions of inquiry, fact-finding missions or other investigative mechanisms dealing with conflicts in the Central African Republic, Colombia, Côte d'Ivoire, Democratic Republic of the Congo, Ethiopia, Iraq, Libya, Mali, Myanmar, Nepal, Nigeria, Palestine/Israel, South Sudan, Sri Lanka, Sudan, Syria and Yemen. This selection focuses on mechanisms established to investigate violations of international law that are committed in situations that have been classified as NIAC.[202] These mechanisms are of particular interest because they

197 Ibid. 12(2) para 7.

198 See, for example, Clara Sandoval, 'The Legal Standing and Significance of the Basic Principles and Guidelines on the Right to a Remedy and Reparation' (2018) 78 Heidelberg Journal of International Law 565, 567; Íñigo Álvarez (n 4) 166–167.

199 Following Sandoval, "any discussion whether the Basic Principles reflect current international law should not take place in general terms. Various principles are included in the document [...] which would need to be studied, one by one, to arrive at a conclusion about their legal status" Sandoval (n 198) 566.

200 The identified practice is, for instance, clearly not general, meaning that it must be sufficiently widespread and representative, as well as consistent. ILC Draft Conclusions on Customary International Law (n 195) Draft Conclusion 8(1).

201 Christine Chinkin, 'The Challenge of Soft Law: Development and Change in International Law' (1989) 38 International and Comparative Law Quarterly 850, 857.

202 The selection was made based on the UN Research Guide on International Commissions of Inquiry, Fact-Finding Missions and Other Investigations and the UN Human Rights Council's online database, both available at <www.ohchr.org/en/hr-bodies/hrc/co-is>. The mechanisms' selection and the examination of their practice cover the period up until the end of August 2023.

have investigated violations committed by NSAGs and often deal with the question of accountability.[203] This is notable considering the lack of a dedicated forum to deal with the violations and potential responsibility of NSAGs.

In 2003, the UN Security Council, rather exceptionally, recognised the need for "developing further measures to promote the responsibility of armed groups".[204] However, it does not appear as if the Council has subsequently gone as far as imposing an obligation of reparation on NSAGs which stands on equal footing with that held by states.[205] Other UN bodies have at times addressed the reparative obligations of NSAGs. In relation to the situation in Afghanistan, both the UN Commission on Human Rights and, subsequently, the UN General Assembly urged "all the Afghan parties" to provide "sufficient and effective remedies for the victims of grave violations and abuses of human rights and of accepted humanitarian rules".[206] A similar call was made in a 2019 report of the UN Assistance Mission in Afghanistan (UNAMA) and the UN Office of the High Commissioner for Human Rights (UNOHCHR).[207] Likewise, the UNOHCHR recently called upon all parties to the Libyan conflict, "including those with de facto control of territory", to provide reparations.[208] The UN Secretary-General has made similar statements to the Security Council, in several reports on the protection of civilians in armed conflict, most notably:

203 See Section 2.2.5; UNOHCHR, 'Commissions of Inquiry and Fact-Finding Missions on International Human Rights and Humanitarian Law: Guidance and Practice' (2015) 12.

204 Ten-Point Platform on the Protection of Civilians in Armed Conflict (15 December 2003) UN Doc S/PRST/2003/27; UNSC, 'Report of the Secretary-General to the Security Council on the Protection of Civilians in Armed Conflict' (28 May 2004) UN Doc S/2004/431 para 16.

205 See Section 2.2.5; Gérard Cahin, 'The Responsibility of Other Entities: Armed Bands and Criminal Groups' in James Crawford, Alain Pellet and Simon Olleson (eds), *The Law of International Responsibility* (Oxford University Press 2010) 340. A review of the records of the open debate on transitional justice, held by the UN Security Council in February 2020, did not identify attention by the Member States to a possible duty to repair of NSAGs as part of such processes. However, see UNSC, Res 1071 (30 August 1996) UN Doc S/RES/1071 ("calls upon the leaders of the factions to ensure the immediate return of looted property"); Henckaerts and Doswald-Beck (n 18) 550.

206 UNCHR, Res 1998/70 (21 April 1998) UN Doc E/CN.4/RES/1998/70 70; UNGA, Res 53/165 (25 February 1999) UN Doc A/RES/53/165; Henckaerts and Doswald-Beck (n 18) 550.

207 UNAMA and UNOHCHR, 'Afghanistan Protection of Civilians in Armed Conflict' (2019) 73. "It is essential that the parties to the conflict [...] repair the harm they have caused."

208 UNHRC, 'Report of the UN High Commissioner for Human Rights on the Situation of Human Rights in Libya' (4 February 2019) UN Doc A/HRC/40/46 13–14; UNHRC, 'Report of the UN High Commissioner for Human Rights on the Situation of Human Rights in Libya' (23 January 2020) UN Doc A/HRC/43/75 15.

> Significant developments in advancing individual criminal responsibility should not distract us from another critical dimension of accountability: the responsibility of parties to conflict to comply with international humanitarian law and human rights law, and the duty to make reparations for violations thereof.[209]

Some independent human rights experts, mandated by the Special Procedures of the UN Human Rights Council, have shown an increased recognition that NSAGs should provide reparations. The UN Special Rapporteur on the promotion of truth, justice, reparation and guarantees of non-recurrence held, in a 2019 report, that "[i]n many contexts, State and non-State actors, including armed groups, are responsible for the atrocities and should contribute to reparations".[210] The assertion is based on scholarship and the 2016 peace agreement concluded between the Colombian government and the FARC-EP as an example of state practice. The Rapporteur's subsequent report on public apologies does not limit itself to states, but elaborately discusses apologies issued by NSAGs.[211] His 2022 report specifically focused on the role and responsibilities of NSAGs in transitional justice processes, including reparations. The Rapporteur recognised the primary duty of responsible NSAGs to contribute to material, symbolic and post-conflict or post-authoritarian reparations, with a subsidiary responsibility for the state if the group lacks capacity.[212] The Special Rapporteur on extrajudicial, summary or arbitrary executions also addressed, in a 2018 report, the duty of NSAGs to provide reparation, specifically in relation to violations of the right to life. The Rapporteur stated that "[w]hen they [NSAGs] are the perpetrators of right to life violations, ANSAs [armed non-State actors] should provide reparations [...]

209 UNGA and UNSC, 'The Causes of Conflict and the Promotion of Durable Peace and Sustainable Development in Africa – Report of the Secretary-General' (13 April 1998) UN Doc A/52/871-S/1998/318 para 50; UNSC, 'Report of the Secretary-General to the Security Council on the Protection of Civilians in Armed Conflict' (30 March 2001) UN Doc S/2001/331 11, 17; UNSC, 'Report of the Secretary-General on the Protection of Civilians in Armed Conflict' (29 May 2009) UN Doc S/2009/277 paras 61, 68; UNSC, 'Report of the Secretary-General on the Protection of Civilians in Armed Conflict' (11 November 2010) UN Doc S/2010/579 paras 82, 93; UNSC, 'Report of the Secretary-General on the Protection of Civilians in Armed Conflict' (7 May 2019) UN Doc S/2019/373 paras 61–62; UNSC, 'Report of the Secretary-General on the Protection of Civilians in Armed Conflict' (10 May 2022) UN Doc S/2022/381 para 87(c); Henckaerts and Doswald-Beck (n 18) 550.

210 UNHRC, 'Report of the Special Rapporteur on the Promotion of Truth, Justice, Reparation and Guarantees of Non-Recurrence' (11 July 2019) UN Doc A/HRC/42/45 para 95. See also UNHRC, 'Report of the Special Rapporteur on the Promotion of Truth, Justice, Reparation and Guarantees of Non-Recurrence' (21 August 2017) UN Doc A/HRC/36/50 8–10.

211 UNGA, 'Report of the Special Rapporteur on the Promotion of Truth, Justice, Reparation and Guarantees of Non-Recurrence' (12 July 2019) UN Doc A/74/147.

212 UNHRC (n 74) paras 78, 82, 87.

ANSAs should also provide public apologies, and contribute to national memorials and commemoration ceremonies."[213] It is further recognised that NSAGs could contribute to disclosing the truth about what happened and to publicly acknowledging the harm inflicted on victims within the framework of truth commissions.[214] Aside from symbolic reparations, the Special Rapporteur proposed, in relation to compensation, "the possibility to tie forfeiture of ANSAs assets to peace-process, and/or truth and reconciliation. Otherwise, there would need to be a means of seizing, for example, ANSAs-held bank accounts".[215] All in all, the Special Rapporteur ties NSAGs' duty to repair to their responsibility for violations of the right to life, which can involve obligations to provide compensation and symbolic reparations.[216] A final interesting aspect of the report is the suggestion that transitional justice mechanisms, such as truth commissions, may constitute an important opportunity for new developments relating to the collective responsibility of NSAGs and their duty to repair.[217]

Finally, the examination of the various UN investigative mechanisms identified four inquiries – Darfur, Syria, Libya and Yemen[218] – that recognise a duty of NSAGs to provide reparation as a consequence of, at least, IHL violations.[219] The three latter inquiries also expressly deemed IHRL to be applicable where an NSAG exercises *de facto* control over territory, hence providing for an additional legal basis to consider the duty of reparation.[220] Although not expressed in such strong terms, the International Commission of Inquiry on Darfur also appears to have recognised an obligation of NSAGs to provide compensation for serious violations of IHRL (see *infra*). It is notable that these

213 UNHRC (n 42) para 94.
214 Ibid.
215 Ibid. 91.
216 Íñigo Álvarez (n 4) 172–173.
217 UNHRC (n 42) paras 89–90.
218 Although the investigative mechanism dealing with the conflict in Sri Lanka did not explicitly recognise a duty to repair for the Liberation Tigers of Tamil Eelam (LTTE), which was militarily defeated, it did propose that "funds acquired by the LTTE [...] should be secured for the purpose of making reparations". UNSG (n 71) paras 419, 442.
219 For the application of IHL to these cases, see 'Report of the International Commission of Inquiry on Darfur' (n 71) paras 75, 157–158, 172; UNHRC, 'Report of the International Commission of Inquiry to Investigate All Alleged Violations of International Human Rights Law in the Libyan Arab Jamahiriya' (12 January 2012) UN Doc A/HRC/17/44 para 64; UNHRC, 'Report of the Independent International Commission of Inquiry on the Syrian Arab Republic' (2 February 2017) UN Doc A/HRC/34/64 Annex I para 7; UNHRC, 'Report of the Detailed Findings of the Group of Eminent International and Regional Experts on Yemen' (n 71) paras 46–47.
220 UNHRC, 'Report of the International Commission of Inquiry to Investigate All Alleged Violations of International Human Rights Law in the Libyan Arab Jamahiriya' (n 219) para 62; UNHRC, 'Report of the Independent International Commission of Inquiry on the Syrian Arab Republic' (n 219) para 5; UNHRC, 'Report of the Detailed Findings of the Group of Eminent International and Regional Experts on Yemen' (n 71) paras 82–83.

mechanisms conceptualise the duty of such groups as akin to that of states under international law, while, in some cases, NSAGs and states were treated alike. Moreover, the mechanisms on Darfur and Yemen drew attention to the state-like nature of the groups when considering their duty of reparation.[221]

The report of the International Commission of Inquiry on Darfur held:

> *Serious violations of human rights law and humanitarian law* may amount to international crimes [and …] may entail individual criminal liability […] These violations may also involve the *international responsibility* of the State or of the *international non-state entity* to which those authors belonged as officials (or for which they act as de facto organs), with the consequences that the State or the non-state-entity may have to pay *compensation* to the victims of those violations.[222]

The Commission further clarified that it recognises such international responsibility for both the state and "the state-like entity" on whose behalf the perpetrator was acting.[223] The approach suggests a certain complementarity between collective responsibility resulting in a duty of compensation and individual criminal responsibility. The Commission proposed to fund the compensation measures for victims of rebels (whether or not the perpetrators were identified and punished) through a trust fund to be established on the basis of international voluntary contributions.[224] The UN Security Council ultimately referred the situation in Darfur to the International Criminal Court, but did not take up the recommendation on reparations.[225] A further instance can be found in the work of the International Commission of Inquiry on Libya, which made the same recommendation to both the state and the National Transitional Council: to grant adequate reparations for IHL and IHRL violations and to take all appropriate measures

221 A notable exception to this conclusion is the report of the Goldstone Commission, which did not include a recommendation for Hamas to provide reparations, even though it held overall control of the territory and population in Gaza. This would have made it particularly fitting for such a recommendation. However, the Commission did argue that the Gaza authorities are obligated under international law to control the activities of NSAGs operating on the territory under their control. If they fail to take the necessary measures to prevent the groups from endangering the civilian population by conducting hostilities in a manner incompatible with IHL, they would bear responsibility for the damage done to the civilians living in Gaza. UNHRC, 'Report of the United Nations Fact-Finding Mission on the Gaza Conflict' (25 September 2009) UN Doc A/HRC/12/48 paras 280, 304–305, 498, 1953–1954; Dudai (n 181) 791.

222 'Report of the International Commission of Inquiry on Darfur' (n 71) para 175 [emphasis added].

223 Ibid. 593; Christian Tomuschat, 'Darfur–Compensation for the Victims' (2005) 3 Journal of International Criminal Justice 579, 588.

224 'Report of the International Commission of Inquiry on Darfur' (n 71) paras 600, 603.

225 UNSC, Res 1593 (31 March 2005) UN Doc S/RES/1593.

to prevent the recurrence of such violations.[226] Hence, the Commission treated the NSAG and the state in a similar manner. The Independent International Commission of Inquiry on the Syrian Arab Republic recommended, in a 2013 report, that the relevant NSAGs should provide "effective redress for victims based on international standards", apparently for IHRL and IHL violations.[227] Yet, this is not a consistent element in the Commission's reports. Lastly, the 2019 report of the Group of Eminent International and Regional Experts on Yemen noted that, although logic suggests that NSAGs bear responsibility for IHL violations, it is less clear what the implications of such responsibility entail.[228] The Group of Experts argued, that "there is increasing recognition that non-State entities must also provide reparations. This is particularly pertinent when these entities are considered to be de facto authorities".[229] Accordingly, they have reviewed reparation practices of the *de facto* authorities.[230] Interestingly, the recommendation of the Group of Experts to the "de facto authorities, including affiliated armed actors as relevant" went beyond the call to provide reparations, by including recommendations to adopt a comprehensive policy and package of measures regarding the fulfilment of the right to reparation of victims of serious IHRL and IHL violations and abuses; to ensure compensation is provided for wrongful civilian deaths, injuries and harm; and, to ensure systems are in place for civilians to request such compensation. The exact same recommendation was formulated towards the government of Yemen, hence treating both alike.[231]

To conclude, the preceding examination has revealed several instances of UN practice which recognise a duty of NSAGs to make reparation, resulting from

226 UNHRC, 'Report of the International Commission of Inquiry to Investigate All Alleged Violations of International Human Rights Law in the Libyan Arab Jamahiriya' (n 219) paras 258(e), 259(c).

227 UNHRC, 'Report of the Independent International Commission of Inquiry on the Syrian Arab Republic' (5 February 2013) UN Doc A/HRC/22/59 25 para 177(d). See also the Commission's policy paper: 'Civilians Under Attack in Syria: Towards Preventing Further Civilian Harm' (28 June 2022) 10.

228 UNHRC, 'Report of the Detailed Findings of the Group of Eminent International and Regional Experts on Yemen' (n 71) para 859(c). The report finds the attribution of responsibility to non-state entities particularly reasonable when such entities are equipped with organs that have the capacity to act on their behalf, similar to a state's structure. Ibid. 867.

229 Ibid. para 868. However, little substantiation for this claim is given.

230 See, e.g., (29 September 2020) UN Doc A/HRC/45/CRP.7 para 408.

231 UNHRC, 'Report of the Detailed Findings of the Group of Eminent International and Regional Experts on Yemen' (n 71) 224–225. Similar recommendations were made in subsequent reports of 2020 and 2021. See also the communication addressed to the *de facto* authorities by the Working Group on Enforced or Involuntary Disappearances, Working Group on Arbitrary Detention, Special Rapporteur on the promotion and protection of the right to freedom of opinion and expression, and Special Rapporteur on torture and other cruel, inhuman or degrading treatment or punishment AL OTH 55/2019 (3 December 2019) 2, 7.

violations of IHL and IHRL. Notably, this responsibility is consistently conceptualised as being akin to states' duty to repair under international law. While some instances of practice generally speak of redress, others refer to specific forms of reparations, including compensation, satisfaction and guarantees of non-repetition. This provides a certain recognition of their adequacy when dealing with NSAGs. Additionally, some practice deems the recovery of assets from NSAGs as being relevant for reparation purposes. The examination has identified several more recent examples, which could indicate that the role of NSAGs in reparations is gaining some momentum at the UN level. This is particularly true for UN mandate holders and investigative mechanisms. Although their reports do not constitute a traditional source of international law, they could still be considered as "subsidiary means for the determination of rules of law" akin to "judicial decisions" or "the teachings of the most highly qualified publicists of the various nations".[232] The reports attain further authority when produced by reputable impartial experts and endorsed by the UN. Moreover, given the diplomatic context in which these experts present their work, such reports inform discussions on the international level and have the potential of influencing states' views and practice.[233]

2.3.5 The practice of truth commissions

The following section analyses the final reports of eight truth commissions, which concluded their work with a publicly available report seeking to uncover the truth about the NIACs that took place in Colombia, El Salvador, Guatemala, Liberia, Peru, Sierra Leone, Solomon Islands and Timor-Leste, respectively. As noted in Section 2.2.5, truth commissions have scrutinised the conduct of NSAGs from an international legal perspective. The objective here is to determine how these commissions dealt with the question of reparations for victims of NSAGs, and, particularly, whether their practice involved recognition of a duty of NSAGs to provide reparation under international law. Similar to the UN reports discussed in the previous section, the legal significance of this practice can be equated to subsidiary sources of international law that may become more authoritative when endorsed by the concerned state or an international organisation such as the UN.

Most of the truth commissions recommended that the state should bear the primary responsibility for providing reparation to victims of both the states' and NSAGs' violations by way of administrative reparations programmes.[234]

232 Art 38(1)(d) ICJ Statute (1945) XV UNCIO 355.
233 Rodenhäuser (n 62) 150–152; Íñigo Álvarez (n 4) 102–105, 171.
234 Guatemalan Commission for Historical Clarification, 'Memory of Silence: Conclusions and Recommendations' (1999) 49–50; Truth and Reconciliation Commission (Peru), 'Programa Integral de Reparaciones' 142–143 <www.cverdad.org.pe/ifinal/pdf/TOMO%20IX/2.2.%20PIR.pdf>; Sierra Leone Truth and Reconciliation Commission, 'Witness to Truth' (n 75) Vol 2 ch 1 p 20, ch 4 p 231–232; Commission for Reception, Truth, and Reconciliation Timor-Leste, 'Chega! (Executive Summary)' (2005) 200–202;

Some commissions still recognised that NSAGs could make *contributions* to reparations through the delivery of satisfaction measures and asset recovery. The Guatemalan Commission for Historical Clarification recommended symbolic measures, including a public apology and recognition of responsibility (both by way of the ex-command), and the defunct group's involvement in the search for the disappeared.[235] In contrast, the Sierra Leone Truth and Reconciliation Commission recommended the tracing of the NSAG's assets to be recouped and placed in a fund for war victims, and apologies by all conflict actors.[236] Although this practice indicates that an NSAG may play an appropriate contributory role in such reparations measures, and even in a post-conflict setting through its former members, it would not appear that these commissions grounded their recommendations on any internationally binding duty of reparation *vis-à-vis* the NSAGs.

Differently, the Commission on the Truth for El Salvador truly recognised a reparation duty for NSAGs. The Commission recommended that the relevant NSAG should provide moral and material compensation "where it is found to have been responsible" and also stressed the need for the group to provide guarantees of non-repetition in order to prevent similar violations in the future.[237] Notably, these recommendations were not only submitted to the state, but also to the former leadership of the NSAG.[238] This further suggests that there is a role for former members of NSAGs in post-conflict reparations.[239] Besides IHL, the Commission considered the NSAG to be bound by IHRL, particularly when the group had assumed "government powers in territories under their control [... which] would make them responsible for breaches of those obligations".[240] It is noteworthy that the Commission generally qualified the unlawful conduct as either a violation of IHL or of both IHL and IHRL, which could indicate a certain hesitance to address the responsibility of the group on the mere basis of IHRL.[241]

The Colombian Truth Commission was tasked with clarifying the extra-judicial collective responsibilities of the FARC-EP and other entities involved in the conflict for IHRL and IHL violations.[242] Within this context, the Commission promoted processes concerning the acknowledgment of responsibility in which the FARC-EP assumed collective responsibility as a contribution to

Truth and Reconciliation Commission of Liberia (n 75) 378; Solomon Islands Truth and Reconciliation Commission, 'Final Report: Confronting the Truth for a Better Solomon Islands' (2012) Vol III 752, 754–755; Rose (n 181) 328–332.

235 Guatemalan Commission for Historical Clarification (n 234) 49, 52.

236 Sierra Leone Truth and Reconciliation Commission, 'Witness to Truth' (n 75) Vol 2 ch 3 pp 183 and 199 para 518.

237 Commission on the Truth for El Salvador (n 76) 175, 185.

238 Ibid. 188.

239 See further Chapter 4 Section 4.5.2 on reparations in post-conflict settings.

240 Commission on the Truth for El Salvador (n 76) 20.

241 Herman (n 74) 63.

242 Truth Commission of Colombia (n 75) 30, 39–40.

reparation.[243] In 2021, for instance, the defunct FARC-EP, by way of its former commander-in-chief, recognised the group's responsibility as principal perpetrator of kidnappings.[244] As such, this practice accepts the collective role of NSAGs in symbolic reparations for internationally wrongful acts, possibly delivered by former members in a post-conflict context. The transitional justice system, of which the Truth Commission is part, recognises that the FARC-EP is obliged to contribute to other forms of reparations as well, as further discussed in Chapter 6.

2.3.6 International expert documents

In the following section, several international expert documents are examined. All address a possible duty of NSAGs to provide reparation under international law. As discussed in Section 2.2.2, the authoritative ILC Commentary to the ARS leaves the international responsibility of NSAGs open.[245] Although no express mention is made of NSAGs' duty to repair, recognising an implied duty of this nature would be the logical consequence of following the ARS approach to responsibility. Moreover, Special Rapporteur Ago expressly dealt with such a duty when discussing the challenges that could arise when claiming reparations from NSAGs.[246] This discussion incorporated analysis of several reparations claims that had been presented to such groups.[247]

Another instrument which dealt with the issue is the Chicago Principles on Post-Conflict Justice (2007), which was the result of an extensive process involving scholars, jurists, journalists and others. It presents basic guidelines for designing and implementing policies to address past atrocities.[248] Principle 3.3 holds that "[w]here non-state actors are responsible for violations, they should provide reparations to victims. Where these actors are unable or unwilling to meet their obligations, states should assume this responsibility". Similar to the UN Basic Principles and Guidelines, the instrument provides for a clear primary obligation for non-state actors, potentially NSAGs, and a subsidiary role for states. Yet, use of the term 'should' indicates "a suggested action based on

243 Acuerdo Final para la Terminación del Conflicto y la Construcción de una Paz Estable y Duradera (Government of Colombia – FARC-EP) (24 November 2016) 134, 136.

244 Truth Commission of Colombia (n 75) 261.

245 ILC Commentary to Art 10 ARS 52 para 16.

246 Namely, NSAGs' temporary legal existence; changing extent, size and control over territory; possible lack of property as a means to offer compensation; and, states' fear of conferring implied recognition.

247 'Fourth Report on State Responsibility, by Mr Roberto Ago, Special Rapporteur' (n 25) paras 154, 180–181. See Section 2.3.1.2 for a discussion of these reparations claims.

248 The Chicago Principles on Post-Conflict Justice (International Human Rights Law Institute 2007) v.

international norms", rather than an obligation which is established in international law.[249]

In the same year, the civil society-led Nairobi Declaration on Women's and Girl's Right to a Remedy and Reparation was adopted by women's rights advocates, activists and survivors of sexual violence in situations of conflict. In contrast to the Chicago Principles, the Declaration places the primary responsibility to provide redress with the state, while, at the same time, stating that reparations programmes must address the responsibility of all actors, including NSAGs, based on the "fundamental nature of the struggle against impunity".[250] Hence, the responsibility of NSAGs is not disregarded.

The International Law Association (ILA) Declaration of International Law Principles on Reparation for Victims of Armed Conflict (2010) also recognises NSAGs as a 'responsible party', which should make reparation for violations of international law applicable in armed conflict. The commentary recognises "the possibility that non-State actors are already liable to pay reparation for violations of the law of armed conflict",[251] while also strongly encouraging "the further development of a regime of responsibility for such actors" as mandated by the rule of law.[252] Another ILA Committee on Non-State Actors was more cautious in a 2014 report. While it considered reparations as a desirable consequence of NSAGs' responsibility, it questioned whether a reparation regime for NSAGs should mirror the existing regimes for states and international organisations. Reparations in the form of compensation, and to that effect an international indemnity fund composed of blocked assets, was at least contemplated. Nevertheless, it was concluded that, from an empirical point of view, the direct responsibility of NSAGs appears to be, at the very best, "a doctrine *in statu nascendi*".[253] The seminal 2005 ICRC study on customary IHL made a similar conclusion, on the basis of an analysis of law and practice up to 2005, that the existence of an obligation for NSAGs to make full reparation, as a result of their international responsibility, is unclear.[254] Although more recent instances of practice have been identified in this chapter, it remains sparse and fragmented.

249 Ibid. 3.

250 Nairobi Declaration on Women's and Girl's Right to a Remedy and Reparation (2007) paras 5–6.

251 The term 'non-state actor' appears to include NSAGs. The commentary notes that some developments indicate that NSAGs may have a secondary obligation to make reparation, referring to the report of the International Commission of Inquiry on Darfur, principle 15 of the UN Basic Principles and Guidelines, and examples of US case law.

252 Declaration of International Law Principles for Victims of Armed Conflict (ILA Committee on Reparation for Victims of Armed Conflict 2010) Arts 5(2) and 6; ILA Committee on Reparation for Victims of Armed Conflict (n 41) 11–13.

253 ILA Committee on Non-State Actors (n 21) 10–11.

254 Henckaerts and Doswald-Beck (n 18) 549–550. See also Section 2.2.2.

More recently, the practice-informed Belfast Guidelines on Reparations in Post-Conflict Societies (2022) share good practice on NSAGs' engagement in reparations. In legal terms, the Guidelines recognise that reparation is a legal obligation of responsible actors including NSAGs. The Guidelines hold that the latter should *contribute* to reparations at the end of hostilities and reimburse the state, *as far as possible*, for the cost of reparations. Thus, the Guidelines acknowledge possible capacity concerns on the part of NSAGs and that the state may step in to ensure victims' redress. Similar to state responsibility, the Guidelines suggest that reparations can involve compensation, satisfaction, restitution, guarantees of non-recurrence, and asset recovery. NSAGs should also contribute to domestic reparations programmes.[255]

In sum, some notable expert documents, which are understood as "subsidiary means for the determination of rules of law", suggest or at least leave open the possibility that NSAGs should provide reparation to victims when they are found responsible for violations of international law.[256] However, these instruments generally recognise that such an obligation is not firmly established in current international law. For their part, the Belfast Guidelines take a progressive position on the responsibility of NSAGs in reparations processes. Although most appear to follow the classical framework of state responsibility when considering NSAGs, the ILA Committee on Non-State Actors differs by suggesting that this conception of responsibility should be tweaked to fit NSAGs' distinct nature. Moreover, the discussion raises the question as to whether the state should bear a primary or subsidiary responsibility. This discourse is being reinforced by an increasing number of legal scholars who argue that NSAGs should be under a duty to provide reparation, and generally use the international responsibility of states as an initial blueprint to frame NSAGs' responsibility.[257] This issue is further supported or at least addressed within the work of prominent non-governmental organisations working in the fields of human rights, IHL and transitional justice.[258]

255 Belfast Guidelines on Reparations in Post-Conflict Societies (Queen's University Belfast 2022) 8, 12–14.

256 Art 38(1)(d) ICJ Statute.

257 Kleffner (n 21); Dudai (n 181) 785; Bílková (n 34) 280–281; Moffett, 'Beyond Attribution: Responsibility of Armed Non-State Actors for Reparations in Northern Ireland, Colombia and Uganda' (n 21); Verhoeven (n 34) 286; Blázquez Rodríguez (n 14); Iñigo Álvarez (n 4) ch V.

258 Human Rights Watch, 'Turning a Blind Eye: Impunity for Laws-of-War Violations During the Gaza War' (2010) 47; Geneva Call, 'Deed of Commitment for the Prohibition of Sexual Violence in Situations of Armed Conflict and towards the Elimination of Gender Discrimination'; ICTJ, 'More Than Words: Apologies as a Form of Reparation' (2015) 16–17; Amnesty International, 'Released and Exiled: Torture, Unfair Trials and Forcible Exile of Yemenis under Houthi Rule' (2021) 33; Mwatana for Human Rights and Lowenstein International Human Rights Clinic Yale Law School, 'Returned to Zero: The Case for Reparations to Civilians in Yemen' (2022) 131–143.

2.4 Conclusions

This chapter has dealt with the question whether an NSAG is under a duty to provide reparation when violating its primary obligations under international law. To that end, a considerable body of legal sources and international practice was examined. This has led to the conclusion that the international responsibility of NSAGs continues to be a topic of unsettled debate and, within this context, the existence of NSAGs' duty to provide reparation remains unclear. No firmly established secondary norm imposing such a duty was found in either international treaty or customary law. Moreover, no explicit support was found for extending the fundamental principle of reparation for wrongful acts to NSAGs under international law. However, as further discussed in Chapter 6, the government of Colombia relied on this international legal principle for the FARC-EP's responsibility concerning reparations. At present, a duty of reparation for NSAGs finds its most authoritative recognition in the UN Basic Principles and Guidelines. As an international soft law instrument, it tentatively recognises an emerging concept of international responsibility for NSAGs, resulting in a duty to make reparation for at least IHL violations.

Some notable instances of affirmative state and other international practice have been identified. Although such practice remains sparse, it does help set the initial groundwork for NSAGs' duty to provide reparation under international law. Some of the most prominent instances of state practice can be found in Colombia, which will be elaborated upon in Part 3 of this book. In addition, historical precedent for holding NSAGs to a duty of reparation was identified in some older instances of state practice, particularly where such groups exercised effective control over territory. Finally, there is a prominent and increasing trend among international experts and legal scholars to emphasise the need to develop a reparation duty for NSAGs in international law, as they seek to counter the responsibility gap in contemporary conflicts.

Taking these findings together, it is concluded that the duty of NSAGs to provide reparation is primarily a question of *lex ferenda*. The adjective 'primarily' is chosen quite deliberately, because, at the same time, the matter finds itself at an incipient stage in current international law. This acknowledges that there exists at least some legal precedent and recognition that NSAGs should provide reparation when violating their primary obligations in situations of armed conflict. Together, they provide the initial foundations of a duty of NSAGs to provide reparation under international law. This conclusion recognises that international law presently lacks an established secondary norm on the matter and that further clarification is needed.

In a subsequent step, the examination sought to determine how a possible duty to repair of NSAGs has been conceptualised and put into practice in those instances in which such a duty was recognised, particularly based on international law. The different existing approaches to operationalising an NSAG's duty to repair can be brought together into five broad findings. The purpose is not to argue that they are emerging or established customary rules. Instead, the findings constitute initial building blocks that are considered useful for exploring, in Part 2 of this book, how a duty of NSAGs to provide reparation could be operationalised in international law from a *de lege ferenda* perspective. Even so, their preliminary nature must be recognised, especially given that the study of practice and legal materials carried out in this chapter does not claim to be exhaustive. Within this context, some of the materials analysed, such as documents of UN-established investigative mechanisms and truth commissions, have been identified as being akin to subsidiary sources of international law. They are considered as valuable tools of interpretation concerning the international responsibility of NSAGs, especially in light of their potential authoritative character; the lack of a dedicated forum dealing with NSAGs' responsibility within the current international legal system; and, the limited guidance offered by the traditional sources of international law, including the existence of limited state practice on the issue.[259]

The first finding is that NSAGs' apparent duty to repair has been generally conceptualised as being akin to that of states, as traditionally developed in international law. The duty has commonly found its legal basis in internationally wrongful acts, involving violations of primary IHL and possibly IHRL obligations. Moreover, the five main forms of reparation listed in the UN Basic Principles and Guidelines have come forward over the course of the examination. This indicates that all should be considered when exploring a possible duty of NSAGs to repair. The discussion thus suggests that the law of state responsibility and, particularly, the rules concerning reparation can function as possible baselines in such an exploration. At the same time, international experts have cautioned against a simple copy-and-paste exercise.

Second, a possible duty of reparation for NSAGs that hold effective control over territory and for those that are state-like has been emphasised.[260] This finding may hint to the existence of greater support for the possible role of such groups in reparations. It is apparent in older instances of state practice concerning the laws of insurgency and belligerency. Aspects of this practice have indicated that it makes practical and legal sense to call upon a group for reparations considering its territorial control, the state's incapacity and the group's own legal subjectivity. The element of territorial control has continued to appear in, for instance, the work of the ILC and the drafting process concerning the UN Basic Principles and Guidelines. Other relevant examples can be found in UN practice where commissions of inquiry have alluded to state-like groups in this context. Legal scholars such as Heffes and Frenkel have also suggested that "highly organized armed groups exercising long-term control over a territory and having developed State-like institutions would be bound by rules on international responsibility".[261] Similarly, Dabone found that

259 Similarly, Bellal (n 39) 310; Íñigo Álvarez (n 4) 103–108.
260 This element also appears in the case of Colombia (see Part 3 of this book).
261 Heffes and Frenkel (n 36) 70.

reparations from an NSAG are more credible when "it has existed over an extended period, it has effective and prolonged control over a part of a state's territory, and it has an almost quasi-state dimension".[262]

Third, the potentials of national and international, as well as judicial and extra-judicial, efforts to hold NSAGs to a duty of reparation have been identified.[263] Thus, all are considered pertinent when examining questions concerning forum. Additionally, the examination of state practice in Sections 2.3.1.2 and 2.3.2.3 suggests that some groups may be willing and capable to commit to reparations for their wrongs.

The fourth finding is that NSAGs have been called upon to provide reparations both during and after NIACs. Concerns over granting unwarranted legitimacy during an ongoing conflict seem not to have stopped states, or other actors, from calling upon NSAGs to provide reparations. It appears sensible to argue that such groups incur international responsibility for their own wrongful acts as long as they legally exist, i.e. for the duration of the conflict.[264] However, the question of a group's international responsibility appears to remain pertinent in the aftermath of an armed conflict, when the NSAG has legally ceased to exist. The practice of some truth commissions suggests that former members, such as commanders, could still fulfil a role in such contexts.

Finally, the discussion has raised some questions concerning the relationship of the possible international responsibility of an NSAG and that of other subjects of international law. Instruments, such as the UN Basic Principles and Guidelines and the Chicago Principles on Post-Conflict Justice, suggest that the state should bear a subsidiary responsibility when an NSAG is unable or unwilling to meet its duty of reparation. Differently, several truth commissions, among other instances, have placed the primary responsibility with the state, and some seem to have additionally proposed a contributing role for NSAGs. Regardless of these differences, all these approaches appear to implicitly acknowledge that reparations cannot be solely dependent on NSAGs. The International Commission of Inquiry on Darfur has further suggested a certain complementarity between the responsibility of NSAGs, involving a duty of compensation, and the criminal responsibility of individual members.

262 Daboné (n 15) 412.

263 Compare, e.g., domestic efforts in civil and criminal courts; a possible role for NSAGs in truth commissions as proposed by the UN Special Rapporteur on extra-judicial, summary or arbitrary executions; and, the provision of reparations through a fund as recommended by the International Commission of Inquiry on Darfur and the Sierra Leone Truth and Reconciliation Commission.

264 Fortin (n 15) 277.

Part 2

Establishing a duty for non-state armed groups to provide reparation

Chapter 3

Character of an international responsibility regime for non-state armed groups

3.1 Introduction

Part 1 of this book came to the conclusion that the international responsibility of NSAGs remains controversial. Within this context, the existence under international law of an NSAG's duty to provide reparation largely constitutes a question of *lex ferenda*. To bring the discussion forward, the aim of this chapter is to investigate what the character of a future international responsibility regime for NSAGs should be. This examination will be framed by the existing international legal regimes of state responsibility and individual criminal responsibility. An assessment will be made whether NSAGs' responsibility could be construed as analogous to, or integrated with, these existing regimes of either state or individual criminal responsibility, or whether a new, separate type of responsibility is required.[1] As a preliminary step, it is necessary to determine to what extent these regimes already address the international responsibility of NSAGs and, if they do, which implications manifest as a result. The analysis in the present chapter will determine the methodological approach adopted in Chapter 4. This subsequent chapter will delve into the operationalisation of the content of a potential responsibility regime concerning NSAGs, with a specific focus on their duty to make reparation within the framework of international law.

More specifically, these two main regimes of international responsibility – the law of state responsibility and individual criminal responsibility – are analysed to determine their limitations and potential with respect to the possible responsibility of NSAGs under international law.[2] An evaluation will be made

1 Veronika Bílková, 'Establishing Direct Responsibility of Armed Opposition Groups for Violations of International Humanitarian Law?' in Noemi Gal-Or, Cedric Ryngaert and Math Noortmann (eds), *Responsibilities of the Non-State Actor in Armed Conflict and the Market Place* (Brill Nijhof 2015) 278–279.

2 The ILC, Articles on the Responsibility of International Organizations with Commentaries, Yearbook of the International Law Commission (2011) Vol II Part Two (ARIO), which find their basis in the work of the ILC on state responsibility, are based on limited practice, in contrast to the regimes of state responsibility and individual criminal responsibility that are well established in international law. As a result, it has been characterised as mostly an exercise of progressive development

DOI: 10.4324/9781003401292-6

of the extent to which both legal regimes in their current form allow the direct responsibility of NSAGs to be addressed under international law. The limitations of this exercise will be identified and their implications for framing a specific regime of responsibility for NSAGs will be considered. On the other hand, the potential of both regimes for conceptualising such international responsibility will be examined. The perspective of the analysis is different depending on the regime being considered. Regarding the classical law of state responsibility, a preliminary analysis is carried out of the extent to which its existing reparation rules and principles could constitute a starting point for devising the content of NSAGs' possible responsibility. In contrast, the analysis of criminal responsibility will consider to what extent the responsibility of NSAGs could be integrated into international criminal law by introducing the collective criminal responsibility of such groups. Following recent developments in this body of law, this new form of criminal responsibility could provide a basis to address the civil consequences of NSAGs' criminal conduct. In terms of the structure of the chapter, the regime of state responsibility will be analysed first, followed by the regime of individual criminal responsibility. Based on the outcomes of the overall analysis, a proposal for how NSAGs' international responsibility might be characterised will be presented.

3.2 The law of state responsibility

3.2.1 Non-state armed groups in the ILC Articles on the Responsibility of States for Internationally Wrongful Acts

As the name suggests, the ILC ARS only deal with the responsibility of states and not with that of non-state entities.[3] According to a general principle of the law of state responsibility, states are not responsible for the harmful acts of NSAGs engaged in a struggle against them, both during the fighting and after the group has been defeated.[4] Although a state may incur responsibility when

rather than codification of recognised principles. The ARIO do not hold the same authority as the ARS, but rather depend upon the "reception by those to whom they are addressed" (ILC Commentary to the ARIO 46–47 para 5). Considerations arising from the ARIO are included in this chapter when relevant for the discussion, whilst a closer examination is carried out in Chapter 4.

3 ILC, Articles on the Responsibility of States for Internationally Wrongful Acts with Commentaries, Yearbook of the International Law Commission (2001) Vol II Part Two (ARS) 32 para 4(d).

4 *Sambiaggio* Italian-Venezuelan Claims Commission (1903) X RIAA 499 513; *GL Solis (USA) v United Mexican States* United States-Mexican Claims Commission (1928) IV RIAA 358 361; ILC Commentary to Art 10 ARS 50 paras 2–3. For a further discussion of affirmative practice, see 'Fourth Report on State Responsibility, by Mr Roberto Ago, Special Rapporteur' Yearbook of the International Law Commission (1972) Vol II UN Doc A/CN.4/264 and Add.1 132–141; Gérard Cahin, 'Attribution of Conduct to the State: Insurrectional Movements' in James

failing to prevent or punish injurious conduct carried out by an NSAG, it does not bring about the state's obligation to take responsibility for the actual conduct itself. Instead, the state's responsibility results from its lack of due diligence, i.e. for its own failure to act.[5] Even so, since the principle of due diligence is predominantly an obligation of means, state responsibility is rarely incurred in situations of armed conflict where NSAGs act completely beyond the state's control.[6] Differently, the state can be held directly responsible for the conduct of entities when it may be attributed to the state at the international level, which involves the conduct of the state's organs or of others who have acted under the direction, instigation or control of those organs.[7]

The ARS recognise that there are several exceptions to this general principle of the law of state responsibility, particularly when there is a sufficiently strong link between an armed group and the state.[8] One such exception is Article 10 ARS, which is particularly pertinent to the present discussion. It provides a rule of attribution that encompasses the conduct of an NSAG operating independently from the state, which forms the focus of this study. The conduct of such an NSAG is attributed to the state when that NSAG is successful in establishing a new government or state. In this sense, there is certain continuity between the

Crawford, Alain Pellet and Simon Olleson (eds), *The Law of International Responsibility* (Oxford University Press 2010) 252–253; Patrick Dumberry, *Rebellions and Civil Wars: State Responsibility for the Conduct of Insurgents* (Cambridge University Press 2021) rules no 3 and 9.

5 See Art 1 European Convention on Human Rights; Art 1(1) American Convention on Human Rights; Art 1 African Charter on Human and Peoples' Rights (1981) OAU Doc CAB/LEG/67/3 rev 5, 21 ILM 58; HR Committee, 'General Comment No 31 (The Nature of the General Legal Obligation Imposed on States Parties to the Covenant)' (26 May 2004) UN Doc CCPR/C/21/Rev1/Add13 para 8; *Case of Velásquez Rodríguez v Honduras* IACtHR (Judgment Merits) Series C No 4 (29 July 1988) para 172. See Art 1 common to the Geneva Conventions in relation to the duty 'to ensure respect' in times of armed conflict, which involves a state's due diligence obligation to prevent and repress violations committed by NSAGs operating on its territory: ICRC, *Commentary on the First Geneva Convention: Convention (I) for the Amelioration of the Condition of the Wounded and Sick in Armed Forces in the Field* (Cambridge University Press 2016) Commentary to Common Art 1.

6 'Fourth Report on State Responsibility, by Mr Roberto Ago, Special Rapporteur' (n 4) 130 para 154; Bílková (n 1) 271; Kirsten Schmalenbach, 'International Responsibility for Humanitarian Law Violations by Armed Groups' in Heike Krieger (ed), *Inducing Compliance with International Humanitarian Law: Lessons from the African Great Lakes Region* (Cambridge University Press 2015) 496.

7 ILC Commentary to the ARS 38–39 paras 1–3. See in relation to the conduct of state organs Art 4 ARS and particularly the ILC Commentary to Art 4 ARS 40 para 2. See also Jean-Marie Henckaerts and Louise Doswald-Beck (eds), *Customary International Humanitarian Law*, vol I: Rules (Cambridge University Press 2005) Rule 149 on the responsibility of a state for IHL violations attributable to it.

8 See Arts 5, 8–11 ARS; Cedric Ryngaert, 'State Responsibility and Non-State Actors' in Math Noortmann, August Reinisch and Cedric Ryngaert (eds), *Non-State Actors in International Law* (Hart Publishing 2015).

group and the responsible state entity. For these reasons, Article 10 ARS will be examined more closely below. On the other hand, Article 9 ARS is of limited relevance to the present analysis, as it relates to the performance of certain essential public functions by NSAGs, such as taxation or the exercise of policing and judiciary functions, and not the full range of possible harmful acts. Moreover, it would result in the attribution of responsibility to the adversarial state and not to the NSAG itself.[9]

3.2.1.1 State responsibility in the case of government or state formation

Article 10 ARS reads as follows:

> 1 The conduct of an insurrectional movement which becomes the new Government of a State shall be considered an act of that State under international law.
> 2 The conduct of a movement, insurrectional or other, which succeeds in establishing a new State in part of the territory of a pre-existing State or in a territory under its administration shall be considered an act of the new State under international law. [...]

The general rule that the conduct of an NSAG is not attributable to a state is premised on the assumption that the structures and organisation of the group remain independent of those of the state. Differently, if an NSAG is successful in achieving its aims and either installs itself as the new government or forms a new state, the new regime or state will incur responsibility for the violations committed by the group in question. As a result, the two scenarios included in Article 10 ARS constitute exceptions to this general rule.[10]

The justification for this attribution lies in the organisational continuity of the movement and the new government or state.[11] When a new government is established, the state itself would not cease to exist as a subject of international law despite internal structural changes. Hence, it constitutes the only entity to which responsibility can be attributed. As a result, the acts committed during the struggle for power by the NSAG, as well as the group's acts in its capacity as newly established government, will be attributed to the state in question.[12]

9 See further Katharine Fortin, 'The Relevance of Article 9 of the Articles on State Responsibility for the Internationally Wrongful Acts of Armed Groups' in James Summers and Alex Gough (eds), *Non-State Actors and International Obligations* (Brill 2018).
10 ILC Commentary to Art 10 ARS 50 para 4; ICRC, 'Commentary on the Third Geneva Convention: Convention (III) Relative to the Treatment of Prisoners of War' (2020) paras 929–930.
11 ILC Commentary to Art 10 ARS 50–51 paras 4–6; Patrick Dumberry, 'New State Responsibility for Internationally Wrongful Acts by an Insurrectional Movement' (2006) 17 The European Journal of International Law 605, 611–612.
12 ILC Commentary to Art 10 ARS 50 para 5.

Regarding situations where a new state is created, the former ILC Special Rapporteur Ago explains that "an existing subject of international law would merely change category: from a mere embryo State it would become a State proper, without any interruption in its international personality resulting from the change".[13] He further clarifies that "it would not be a question of attributing to a subject of international law the conduct of organs of another subject, but merely of continuing to attribute to the same subject – which would have reached the final stage of its progressive evolution the act of its own organs".[14] Hence, it would only be a normal application of the general rule providing for the attribution of the conduct of its organs to a subject of international law.[15]

Article 10(1) ARS applies to 'insurrectional movements'. Although the ARS do not provide a comprehensive definition of the types of groups encompassed by this term, the ILC Commentary suggests that the threshold for the application of Additional Protocol II to the Geneva Conventions may be taken as a guide. Thus, this would include organised NSAGs that, under responsible command, exercise territorial control so as to enable them to carry out sustained and concerted military operations and to implement said Protocol.[16] As the threshold only serves as guidance, this arguably does not apply in every situation.[17] What is of primary importance instead is that the NSAG, aiming to become the new government, is successful by way of an armed struggle. As a result, the conduct of NSAGs that only trigger the application of Common Article 3 may still be subject to the attribution of responsibility pursuant to Article 10 ARS.[18] Nonetheless, in practice, it is doubtful that NSAGs falling below the threshold of Additional Protocol II will be successful. Paragraph 2 of Article 10 ARS broadens the scope to include "insurrectional or other"

13 'Fourth Report on State Responsibility, by Mr Roberto Ago, Special Rapporteur' (n 4) 131–132.
14 Ibid. 131.
15 Ibid. 132 para 159.
16 Art 1 Additional Protocol II; ILC Commentary to Art 10 ARS 51 para 9.
17 See also 'Fourth Report on State Responsibility, by Mr Roberto Ago, Special Rapporteur' (n 4) 145 para 198.
18 Marco Sassòli, 'State Responsibility for Violations of International Humanitarian Law' (2002) 84 International Review of the Red Cross 401, 410; Liesbeth Zegveld, *The Accountability of Armed Opposition Groups* (Cambridge University Press 2002) 157; James Crawford and Simon Olleson, 'The Character and Forms of International Responsibility' in Malcolm Evans (ed), *International Law* (4th edn, Oxford University Press 2014) 463; Sten Verhoeven, 'International Responsibility of Armed Opposition Groups: Lessons from State Responsibility for Actions of Armed Opposition Groups' in Noemi Gal-Or, Cedric Ryngaert and Math Noortmann (eds), *Responsibilities of the Non-State Actor in Armed Conflict and the Market Place* (Brill Nijhof 2015) 288–289, 294; ICRC (n 10) paras 929–930. However, see Ezequiel Heffes, 'The Responsibility of Armed Opposition Groups for Violations of International Humanitarian Law: Challenging the State-Centric System of International Law' (2013) 4 Journal of International Humanitarian Legal Studies 81, 95.

movements, which reflects the existence of a greater variety of movements, whose actions may result in the formation of a new state, such as national liberation movements.[19]

Although Article 10 ARS takes account of NSAGs, it only reduces the existing responsibility gap *vis-à-vis* such groups in international law to a limited extent. This is due to several reasons. Taken together, they provide for a first justification to explore the possibility of establishing a new regime of responsibility for NSAGs in international law.[20]

First, the provision does not apply when a government of national reconciliation is formed following an agreement between the existing authorities and the leadership of an NSAG.[21] The responsibility of the group dissolves and is reduced to the individual member level. The underlying rationale is that questions of responsibility may challenge the conclusion of a negotiated agreement and may thus endanger the achievement of peace through negotiations.[22] This exception would serve as an enticement for NSAGs to partake in a negotiated power-sharing solution, rather than seeking to take control of the state by force.[23] This exception is problematic from an accountability perspective as it provides a clear incentive to leave responsibility concerns unaddressed.[24] In addition, it is not substantiated by any practice. Instead, it relies on a policy-based justification which contends that the rule in Article 10 should "not be pressed too far", as a state should not be made responsible for the conduct of an NSAG "merely because, in the interests of an overall peace agreement, elements of the opposition are drawn into a reconstructed Government".[25] In cases

19 ILC Commentary to Art 10 ARS 51 para 10; Dumberry (n 11) 618–619.

20 Gérard Cahin, 'The Responsibility of Other Entities: Armed Bands and Criminal Groups' in James Crawford, Alain Pellet and Simon Olleson (eds), *The Law of International Responsibility* (Oxford University Press 2010) 337–338; Bílková (n 1) 275; Schmalenbach (n 6) 295–296.

21 ILC Commentary to Art 10 ARS 51 para 7.

22 However, Ago envisaged that the rule of attribution would also apply "in the case of an agreement between the legitimate government and the insurrectional government under which members of the insurrection are called upon to participate in the government of the State" further nothing that there is "nothing surprising in the attribution to the State of the acts not only of members of its preceding organization but also of members of the organization that grew during the insurrection and is subsequently united with the preceding organization", but he signals that this has occurred very rarely. 'Fourth Report on State Responsibility, by Mr Roberto Ago, Special Rapporteur' (n 4) 146 para 199, 149 para 209.

23 Jean d'Aspremont, 'Rebellion and State Responsibility: Wrongdoing by Democratically Elected Insurgents' (2009) 58 International and Comparative Law Quarterly 427, 436.

24 See, for further critical reflection on the ILC's line of reasoning, ibid. 436–437; Verhoeven (n 18) 291–292.

25 ILC Commentary to Art 10 ARS 51 para 7; Tatyana Eatwell, 'State Responsibility, "Successful" Insurrectional Movements and Governments of National Reconciliation' in James Summers and Alex Gough (eds), *Non-State Actors and International Obligations* (Brill Nijhof 2018).

of national reconciliation governments, a valid argument can be made that at least the successor entity of an NSAG in the form of a political party could be held responsible for past wrongful behaviour when there is sufficient organisational continuity between the NSAG and the new party. It is questionable as to why responsibility should simply disappear when a former NSAG has obtained a seat at the table.[26] A political party could at least inherit the legal consequences of the wrongful conduct of its predecessor, when its existence is the direct result of a collective transformation process by which the NSAG abandoned its weapons to continue its political engagement within the legal and democratic arena.[27] Such an approach would address the responsibility gap by preventing responsibility from being evaded and safeguarding victims' redress. Otherwise, the successor entity could at best agree to assume the consequences of responsibility within, e.g., the peace agreement that provided for the group's political transformation. However, this approach can be challenged on at least two fronts. First, such a political party is not a subject of international but rather national law. This complicates the argument from an international legal perspective. Second, there is little state practice to substantiate the argument.[28]

The second issue regarding Article 10 ARS is that although the two positive attribution rules contained within it were applied in several arbitral decisions of the first half of the 20th century, state practice since that time appears to be scarce.[29] Consequently, the relevance of their application to present-day conflicts can be questioned.[30] Third, Article 10 ARS contains rules of attribution of conduct and not of responsibility. As a result, the question of NSAGs' direct

26 Konstantinos Mastorodimos, *Armed Non-State Actors in International Humanitarian and Human Rights Law: Foundation and Framework of Obligations, and Rules on Accountability* (Ashgate 2016) 134, 136; Eatwell (n 25) 396–397.

27 Veronique Dudouet, Katrin Planta and Hans J Giessmann, 'The Political Transformation of Armed and Banned Groups' (Berghof Foundation and UNDP 2016) 7.

28 See the following example of state practice: Linas-Marcoussis Agreement (23 January 2003) 3) a-, c-, d- and Annex 'Programme of the Government of National Reconciliation' VI- 2), 4).

29 See *Bolívar Railway Company* Mixed Claims Commission Great Britain-Venezuela (1903) IX RIAA 445 453; *Puerto Cabello and Valencia Railway Company* Mixed Claims Commission Great Britain-Venezuela (1903) IX RIAA 510 513; *Dix Case* Mixed Claims Commission United States-Venezuela (1903) IX RIAA 119 120; *French Company of Venezuelan Railroads* Mixed Claims Commission United States-Venezuela (1905) X RIAA 285 354; *Georges Pinson (France) v United Mexican States* Mixed Claims Commission France-Mexico (1928) V RIAA 327 353. See also ILC Commentary to Art 10 ARS 51–52 paras 12–14 and for more recent examples of practice UNHRC, 'Situation of Human Rights in the Central African Republic – Report of the United Nations High Commissioner for Human Rights' (12 September 2013) UN Doc A/HRC/24/59 para 25; Dumberry (n 4) 88–92.

30 Zegveld (n 18) 156; d'Aspremont (n 23) 431–432; Verhoeven (n 18) 287–288; Ezequiel Heffes and Brian Frenkel, 'The International Responsibility of Non-State Armed Groups: In Search of the Applicable Rules' (2017) 8 Goettingen Journal of International Law 39, 59.

responsibility is sidestepped.[31] As discussed in Chapter 2, the ILC Commentary to Article 10 ARS mentions the further possibility that NSAGs may themselves be held responsible for their own conduct under international law. However, one is quickly reminded that the responsibility of NSAGs falls outside the scope of the ARS, which are only concerned with the responsibility of states.[32] Fourth, this type of state responsibility cannot be called upon when a NIAC is ongoing. Consequently, its practical relevance is reduced.[33] Finally, the rule is limited to successful groups. However, NSAGs may not succeed in their aims, yet may remain active for a considerable period. Alternatively, they may simply pursue different goals than those foreseen in Article 10 ARS, such as gaining increased autonomy or greater social equality.[34]

3.2.2 *Taking the law of state responsibility as a baseline*

The ARS display certain limitations in mitigating the existing responsibility gap concerning NSAGs in international law. Nevertheless, the analysis conducted in Chapter 2 has found that it is still relevant to examine to what extent it can function as a baseline for the development of a new regime of responsibility for NSAGs.[35] The law of state responsibility is the regime of responsibility that is currently developed to the fullest extent. This is not surprising considering the historical primacy of the state as primary subject in the international legal system. As a result, state responsibility can be considered as "the paradigm form of responsibility on the international plane".[36] Accordingly, scholars have used this framework as a starting point when elaborating a future responsibility regime for NSAGs through analogical legal reasoning.[37] Importantly, such a perspective could facilitate a more consistent approach to the system of responsibility in international law.[38] This method of legal reasoning can be beneficial in bridging legal gaps, but it should not be interpreted as a mere

31 d'Aspremont (n 23) 431.
32 ILC Commentary to Art 10 ARS 52 para 16.
33 Annyssa Bellal, 'International Law and Armed Non-State Actors in Afghanistan' (2011) 93 International Review of the Red Cross 47, 70–71.
34 Francis Kofi Abiew and Noemi Gal-Or, 'International Responsibility of the AOG in International Law: Is There a Case for an African Approach?' in Noemi Gal-Or, Cedric Ryngaert and Math Noortman (eds), *Responsibilities of the Non-State Actor in Armed Conflict and the Market Place* (Brill Nijhof 2015) 352–353.
35 See Chapter 2 Section 2.4.
36 Crawford and Olleson (n 18) 443–444.
37 For example Verhoeven (n 18); Heffes and Frenkel (n 30) 60–65; Laura Íñigo Álvarez, *Towards a Regime of Responsibility of Armed Groups in International Law* (Intersentia 2020) 81–91.
38 Alain Pellet, 'International Organizations Are Definitely Not States. Cursory Remarks on the ILC Articles on the Responsibility of International Organizations' in Maurizio Ragazzi (ed), *Responsibility of International Organizations* (Martinus Nijhoff Publishers 2013) 53; Íñigo Álvarez (n 37) 91.

replication of existing legal rules and principles. Rather, the use of analogies entails a comparison of pertinent similarities and differences.[39]

NSAGs and states have similar characteristics. They are both collective legal entities and sufficiently organised to participate as distinct entities in organised armed violence whose intensity reaches the threshold of a NIAC. Additionally, some NSAGs can control territory, and may perform governmental tasks that are similar to the roles of states. For instance, the Sri Lanka's Liberation Tigers of Tamil Eelam (LTTE) controlled large parts of the territory from the 1990s until May 2009. The group operated as a *de facto* state in the territory it controlled, where it established its own police, court system, immigration department and social services, among other functions. It developed a sophisticated military, with ground, air and naval capabilities.[40] A further similarity between states and NSAGs lies in the legal regulation of both entities under the primary rules of international law. More specifically, the same international obligations bind NSAGs and states under at least IHL and possibly IHRL.[41]

However, Kleffner correctly notes that any transposition of the rules governing the responsibility of states to NSAGs must be approached with caution. In contrast to states, NSAGs have neither a right to exist nor presumptive legitimacy in international law.[42] A possible result may be that the underlying rationales for their international responsibility may not only involve rules on, e.g., attribution and reparation, but also on the effective dismantlement of the responsible group.[43] Furthermore, some groups have characteristics similar to states and may therefore be subject to similar rules that bind states. Others, however, operate through loose organisational structures, without control of territory and with limited or non-existent resources. The IHL framework already responds to this structural disparity among NSAGs by imposing a greater range of primary obligations on groups that exceed the minimum requirements of organisation under Common Article 3 and particularly exercise control over territory.[44] Similarly, the disparity

39 Ahlborn clarifies that the "use of analogical reasoning generally involves the application of a legal rule that covers a specific case to a different case that has similar characteristics but is unregulated by law". Christiane Ahlborn, 'The Use of Analogies in Drafting the Articles on the Responsibility of International Organizations An Appraisal of the 'Copy-Paste Approach" (2012) 9 International Organizations Law Review 53, 55–57; Íñigo Álvarez (n 37) 81–83.

40 UNSG, 'Report of the Secretary-General's Panel of Experts on Accountability in Sri Lanka' (31 March 2011) para 33; ICRC, 'The Roots of Restraint in War' (2018) 38. For another example of similar NSAGs operating in the Central African Republic, see MINUSCA, 'Report on the Situation of Human Rights in the Central African Republic' (2015) para 14.

41 See Chapter 1. Íñigo Álvarez (n 37) 84–85.

42 Ibid. 86.

43 Jann K Kleffner, 'The Collective Accountability of Organized Armed Groups for System Crimes' in Andre Nollkaemper and Harmen Gijsbrecht van der Wilt (eds), *System Criminality in International Law* (Cambridge University Press 2009) 260–261.

44 See Chapter 1 Section 1.3.4.

that exists between NSAGs and states, and among NSAGs, must be factored into the secondary rules governing a potential system of international responsibility of NSAGs.[45] In terms of reparation specifically, this issue is challenging because of the varying capacity of NSAGs to provide reparations. As will be discussed further in Chapter 4, an NSAG's capacity to provide reparations may differ significantly to other groups, as well as in comparison to states. This is especially true given that the capacity to deliver reparations correlates with an NSAG's level of organisation and its availability of resources. Accordingly, there is a need to accommodate these differences in organisational capacity to ensure the effectiveness of a future regime of international responsibility. Ultimately, it is necessary to devise abstract rules that can be applied generally, and which can at the same time provide enough flexibility to regulate the entire spectrum of NSAGs.[46]

It follows from this discussion that the implementation of analogical reasoning needs to consider these similarities and respond to the listed particularities of NSAGs. It will be necessary to bear in mind that "the subjects of law [...] are not necessarily identical in their nature or in the extent of their rights",[47] and accordingly develop *sui generis* rules.[48] Following this understanding, it's quite possible that the international responsibility of distinct subjects may be governed by different rules. Still, this methodology allows balancing a more unified approach to responsibility in international law while simultaneously considering the distinct characteristics of NSAGs. The ILC took a similar approach when elaborating the responsibility of international organisations based on the ARS, as the general model of international responsibility. Rather than assuming that the same principles outlined in the ARS applied to such organisations, each principle was examined in light of the responsibility of international organisations. This required to take a number of considerations into account: the differences of such organisations in comparison to states; the significant diversity amongst them in terms of, e.g., powers, functions, size of membership, structure and the primary rules to which they are bound; and, differences in relevant practice.[49]

In Chapter 4, the principles of reparation in the law of state responsibility will be taken as a baseline for elaborating the duty of NSAGs to provide

45 Kleffner (n 43) 261; Marco Sassòli, 'Taking Armed Groups Seriously: Ways to Improve Their Compliance with International Humanitarian Law' (2010) 1 Journal of International Humanitarian Legal Studies 5, 47; Íñigo Álvarez (n 37) 67, 85–86, 90–91.

46 Kleffner (n 43) 258, 261.

47 *Advisory Opinion on Reparation for Injuries Suffered in the Service of the United Nations* ICJ [1949] ICJ Rep 174 178. Similarly, the ARIO are in many respects akin to the ARS, while seeking to give appropriate weight to the specific and different character of international organisations in comparison to states. ILC Commentary to the ARIO 46–47.

48 Bílková (n 1) 279, 284; Íñigo Álvarez (n 37) 108.

49 ILC Commentary to the ARIO 46 paras 3–7; Ahlborn (n 39); Pellet (n 38); Íñigo Álvarez (n 37) 81.

reparation from a *de lege ferenda* perspective. Still, other approaches to reparations by other subjects, particularly international organisations and individuals, will provide additional information for analysis. Together, a broad reference framework, which is grounded in international law, is established to guide the examination.

3.3 Individual criminal responsibility

The focus of this section turns to the regime of individual criminal responsibility. In the first instance, the analysis will evaluate whether and, if so, to what extent this regime includes considerations for the responsibility of NSAGs as such for international crimes, the limitations which attach to the approach followed and the implications thereof. Based on this evaluation, two paths will be proposed as ways forward and will be explored. The first is the introduction of collective criminal responsibility of NSAGs (Section 3.3.2). The second is the suggestion of a potential new regime of international responsibility for NSAGs which is not criminal in character (Section 3.4).

3.3.1 The criminal responsibility of group members and its limitations

It is no longer controversial that individual members of NSAGs can be held criminally responsible for their participation in certain international crimes, such as war crimes, crimes against humanity and genocide. This might involve, for instance, leaders or commanders of an NSAG who are held responsible for the acts committed by their subordinates, or ordinary members who are responsible in respect of their direct participation in such crimes. This is only a recent development in international law. Its origins date to the 1990s, with the establishment of the ICTY in 1993 and the International Criminal Tribunal for Rwanda (ICTR) in 1994. These developments were followed by the entering into force of the Rome Statute of the International Criminal Court in 2002 and the work of the Special Court for Sierra Leone, amongst others.[50]

Although criminal responsibility under international law does not extend to the NSAG as such, the legal framework and definitions governing these international crimes recognise that such groups can constitute the context or the

50 See, i.a., *Prosecutor v Tadić* ICTY (Decision on the Defence Motion for Interlocutory Appeal on Jurisdiction) IT-94-1-AR72 (2 October 1995) para 134; *Prosecutor v Sesay, Kallon and Gbao* SCSL (Appeals Judgment) SCSL-04-15-A (26 October 2009); *Prosecutor v Thomas Lubanga Dyilo* ICC (Trial Judgment) ICC-01/04-01/06-2842 (14 March 2012); *Prosecutor v Jean-Pierre Bemba Gombo* ICC (Trial Judgment) ICC-01/05-01/08 (21 March 2016) (overturned on appeal); UNSC, 'Report of the Secretary-General Pursuant to Paragraph 5 of Security Council Resolution 955' (13 February 1995) UN Doc S/1995/134 para 12; William A Schabas, 'Punishment of Non-State Actors in Non-International Armed Conflict' (2002) 26 Fordham International Law Journal 907, 922; ICRC (n 10) paras 909–919.

system in which the criminal acts are carried out. The category of war crimes illustrates this observation. War crimes comprise of serious violations of IHL perpetrated during situations of armed conflict, which involve armed hostilities between parties of a collective nature with a sufficient degree of organisation. Correspondingly, war crimes have been perpetrated with the involvement of NSAGs, which bear obligations under IHL. Put differently, certain violations of IHL, perpetrated by NSAGs, can entail the individual criminal responsibility of their members.[51] An analogous example can be found within the category of crimes against humanity, which are perpetrated as part of "a widespread or systematic attack directed against any civilian population [...] pursuant to or in furtherance of a State or organizational policy to commit such attack".[52] Recent practice has confirmed that such organisational policy may also involve that of an NSAG.[53]

It can be said that the international community has concentrated its efforts on criminalising the acts of individuals during times of NIAC, while largely ignoring the responsibility of the group as the broader collectivity in which the individual authors of these crimes are embedded. The latter notion is reflected in the concept of 'system criminality', which was put forward by Röling when discussing aspects of criminal responsibility for violations of the laws of war. It involves two key aspects.

The first aspect is the organisational or collective context in which the crimes are committed. Röling speaks of governments as 'systems' that order, encourage, tolerate or even permit the commission of crimes. The crime is caused by the structure of the system, rather than personal inclinations. In this sense, the commissions of such crimes "serves the system, and is caused by the system", as opposed to incidental criminality that involves crimes committed by the individual for personal reasons.[54] Nollkaemper builds on Röling's work by extending the

51 Art 8(1) ICC Statute provides that the Court has jurisdiction over such crimes, particularly "when committed as part of a plan or policy or as part of a large-scale commission of such crimes". Yet, it also provides for the possibility that a single act performed by an individual could constitute a war crime. ICC, Elements of Crimes, ICC-PIDS-LT-03–002/11 (2011) 13–42; Kleffner (n 43) 247–248; ICRC (n 10) paras 920–927.

52 Art 7(1) and (2)(a) ICC Statute.

53 *Prosecutor v Sesay, Kallon and Gbao* SCSL (Trial Judgment) SCSL-04–15-T (2 March 2009) (upheld on appeal); *Prosecutor v Germain Katanga* ICC (Trial Judgment) ICC-01/04–01/07 (7 March 2014); *Prosecutor v Jean-Pierre Bemba Gombo* (n 50). For a discussion Tilman Rodenhäuser, 'Beyond State Crimes: Non-State Entities and Crimes against Humanity' (2014) 27 Leiden Journal of International Law 913. See also Neha Jain, *Perpetrators and Accessories in International Criminal Law: Individual Modes of Responsibility for Collective Crimes* (Hart Publishing 2014) 2–3; Frédéric Mégret, 'The Subjects of International Criminal Law' in Philip Kastner (ed), *International Criminal Law in Context* (Routledge 2017); Anna Marie Brennan, 'Prospects for Prosecuting Non-State Armed Groups under International Criminal Law: Perspectives from Complexity Theory' in Jamie Murray, Thomas Webb and Steven Wheatley (eds), *Complexity Theory and Law: Mapping an Emergent Jurisprudence* (Routledge 2019) 137–138.

54 Bert VA Röling, 'The Significance of the Laws of War' in Antonio Cassese (ed), *Current Problems of International Law: Essays on U.N. Law and on the Law of*

notion of system involved in international crimes to non-state actors. Accordingly, system criminality is defined as "a situation where collective entities order or encourage international crimes to be committed, or permit or tolerate the committing of international crimes".[55] This conceptualisation is closely related to Kelman's idea of 'crimes of obedience' as "crimes that take place, not in opposition to the authorities, but under explicit instructions from the authorities to engage in these acts, or in an environment in which such acts are implicitly sponsored, expected, or at least tolerated by the authorities" or, as defined by Kelman and Hamilton, as "an act performed in response to orders from authority that is considered illegal or immoral by the larger community".[56] Kleffner further explores this notion of system criminality, specifically in respect of NSAGs. He convincingly argues that such groups can be understood as systems, which follows primarily from the organisation requirement that determines whether a group is to be considered a party to a NIAC under IHL. For this requirement to be satisfied, it is necessary that the group is at least to some degree structurally organised, which becomes even more apparent in respect of armed conflicts which fall under Additional Protocol II. Indeed, as was established in Chapter 1, the organisational requirement serves as a key tool to determine when a loose collection of individuals matures into a distinct, collective entity. From a socio-psychological perspective, military organisations involved in warfare are generally characterised by their group spirit, loyalties, morals, values and expectations, which replace individual drives. NSAGs may also succeed in creating a climate in which crimes are considered as being in conformity with and justified by the group's values and norms.[57]

The second aspect relating to system criminality is the collective nature of the crimes themselves. As was already demonstrated *supra*, international crimes committed in a context of armed conflict are often not only committed by one person, but rather by a group of individuals gathered *in casu* within the confines of an NSAG, which expresses a form of collective criminality.[58] While the

Armed Conflict (Giuffrè 1975) 138; Mark A Drumbl, 'Collective Violence and Individual Punishment: Criminality of Mass Atrocity' (2005) 99 Northwestern University Law Review 539, 571.

55 André Nollkaemper, 'Introduction' in André Nollkaemper and Harmen Van der Wilt (eds), *System Criminality in International Law* (Cambridge University Press 2009) 16.

56 Herbert C Kelman, 'The Policy Context of International Crimes' in André Nollkaemper and Harmen Van der Wilt (eds), *System Criminality in International Law* (Cambridge University Press 2009) 27; Elies Van Sliedregt, *Individual Criminal Responsibility in International Law* (Oxford University Press 2012) 20–21.

57 Laurel E Fletcher and Harvey M Weinstein, 'Violence and Social Repair: Rethinking the Contribution of Justice to Reconciliation' (2002) 24 Human Rights Quarterly 573, 606–611; Kleffner (n 43) 242–247.

58 *Prosecutor v Tadić* ICTY (Appeals Judgment) IT-94–1-A (15 July 1999) para 191; George P Fletcher, 'The Storrs Lectures: Liberals and Romantics at War: The Problem of Collective Guilt' (2002) 111 Yale Law Journal 1499, 1514; Drumbl (n 54) 567–568; Antonio Cassese, 'The Proper Limits of Individual Responsibility under

traditional modes of liability, such as direct commission, instigation and aiding and abetting, are not always able to grasp this kind of criminality, joint criminal enterprise, common purpose liability and command responsibility can be of more use.[59] These modes of liability allow for the holding of one person responsible for the acts committed by others. The latter mode can, for instance, provide a basis to hold a military commander responsible when failing to take measures to prevent or punish the commission of war crimes by a subordinate.[60] Nevertheless, these modes of liability do not focus on holding a group as such responsible. Any criminal conviction will still find its fundamental basis in the principle of individual fault and not in that of the collectivity of which the convicted person was a part.[61] As clarified by the Special Court for Sierra Leone: "[t]he trial, officially titled the *Prosecutor v. Sesay, Kallon and Gbao*, has been commonly referred to as the RUF trial due to the fact that the three Accused persons were members of the Revolutionary United Front ("RUF"), The Trial Chamber [...] observed that this trial is not a trial of the RUF organisation itself, but rather a trial against three individuals".[62] This shows that although international crimes are characterised by their collective nature, international justice focuses on the role of the involved individuals.[63]

Holding individual members of NSAGs criminally responsible for the commission of international crimes undeniably forms a fundamental part of

the Doctrine of Joint Criminal Enterprise' (2007) 5 Journal of International Criminal Justice 109, 110.

59 Van Sliedregt (n 56) 21–22.

60 Joint criminal enterprise provides the possibility of holding all participants in a common plan criminally responsible for agreed upon crimes and also for those which were a "natural and foreseeable consequence" of the execution of the plan. On the other hand, common purpose liability, applied by the International Criminal Court, involves holding an individual criminally responsible for contributing to crimes committed by a group acting with a common purpose. Art 25(3)(d) ICC Statute; *Prosecutor v Kvočka et al* ICTY (Appeals Judgment) IT-98–30/1-A (28 February 2005) para 83; Shane Darcy, *Collective Responsibility and Accountability under International Law* (Brill 2007) 197–198.

61 Even so, these modes of liability have caused much discussion amongst international criminal law scholars and practitioners. Darcy contends, for instance, that aspects of joint criminal enterprise and superior responsibility fall short of basic principles of criminal law, including the *mens rea* requirement and causation. Convictions on the basis of these modes of liability may not adequately reflect the personal wrongdoing of the accused. Shane Darcy, 'Imputed Criminal Liability and the Goals of International Justice' (2007) 20 Leiden Journal of International Law 377, 403. See also James G Stewart, 'The End of "Modes of Liability" for International Crimes' (2012) 25 Leiden Journal of International Law 165, 171–185; Marjolein Cupido, 'Group Acting with a Common Purpose' in Jérôme de Hemptinne, Robert Roth and Elies van Sliedregt (eds), *Modes of Liability in International Criminal Law* (Cambridge University Press 2019).

62 *Prosecutor v Sesay, Kallon and Gbao* (n 53) para 4.

63 Íñigo Álvarez (n 37) 37–39.

affording justice and is a significant step in the fight against impunity. Along with upholding the key objectives of criminal justice, it may play an important role in providing a measure of retribution and deterrence, as well as facilitating the prevention of future crime.[64] However, criminal trials also have their limits, especially to the extent that they only account for an individual's culpability, whereas the (collective) responsibility of the system as a whole is left aside. As a result, a fragmented picture of collective violence is given, in which an NSAG is deconstructed to a limited number of its individual members.[65] In addition, individual criminal responsibility only considers the most serious violations of IHL and IHRL, whereas a range of other harmful abuses in which NSAGs engage are left unaddressed. At best, but also unsatisfactorily, this provides for a broad measure of so-called 'indirect responsibility' of individual members for violations perpetrated by NSAGs, when their behaviour overlaps.[66] A fundamental limitation from the perspective of this study is the limited reach of the principle of individual criminal responsibility in respect of reparations.[67] As a result, redress cannot be offered for the full spectrum of violations perpetrated and resulting harms that have taken place at the hands of NSAGs in situations of NIAC.[68]

The current limits of international criminal justice result in at least two possible suggestions to move forward. First, international criminal law should be extended to NSAGs as legal entities and a form of collective criminal responsibility should be established as a consequence (see the following section). Alternatively, the regime of individual criminal responsibility should be complemented with a new type of responsibility relevant to NSAGs, which should be non-criminal in character (see Section 3.4).[69]

64 Florian Jessberger and Julia Geneuss (eds), *Why Punish Perpetrators of Mass Atrocities?: Purposes of Punishment in International Criminal Law* (Cambridge University Press 2020).
65 Zegveld (n 18) 223–224.
66 Bílková (n 1) 272.
67 Art 75(2) ICC Statute.
68 Katharine Fortin, 'Armed Groups and Procedural Accountability: A Roadmap for Further Thought', *Yearbook of International Humanitarian Law*, vol 19 (TMC Asser Press 2016) 159.
69 The latter was also recognised by the UN Secretary-General in his 2009 report on the protection of civilians in armed conflict to the UN Security Council: "Significant developments in advancing individual criminal responsibility should not distract us from another critical dimension of accountability: the responsibility of parties to conflict to comply with international humanitarian law and human rights law, and the duty to make reparations for violations thereof." UNSC, 'Report of the Secretary-General on the Protection of Civilians in Armed Conflict' (29 May 2009) UN Doc S/2009/277 para 68.

3.3.2 The collective criminal responsibility of non-state armed groups

3.3.2.1 An appraisal

There are several reasons that justify exploring the possibility of holding NSAGs criminally responsible under international law. It would involve stretching the fundamental principle of individual criminal responsibility to encompass the responsibility of such groups as distinct legal entities. Following from the previous discussion, the notion of collective responsibility would assist in addressing the wrongs of the larger system, or organisation, in which the behaviour of individual authors and participants of international crimes is embedded.[70] It would provide a more comprehensive picture of the reality of international crimes, which, in contrast to common crimes, generally involve collective instead of individual action.[71] As a result, a greater measure of justice could be afforded by ensuring that the larger system or organisation that played a decisive role in the perpetration of international crimes is not let off the hook. Indeed, in contrast, it would become possible to directly target the perpetrating NSAG through prosecution.[72] This would contribute to some of the principal aims of international justice: "to put an end to impunity for the perpetrators" of international crimes as "to contribute to the prevention of such crimes".[73] Accordingly, the impunity gap could be mitigated, while at the same time furthering the deterrent and preventive functions of criminal law.[74] In sum, at least from a purely legal perspective, such an approach could render the international legal system more effective.

Such a proposal is not necessarily inconceivable in international law, especially when one considers the conclusions of Chapter 1 which clarified that NSAGs are legal subjects in their own right with a limited legal personality under at least IHL.[75] Crucially, for present purposes, confirmation of collective criminal responsibility could provide a basis to claim reparations from the convicted group. Such an approach would be in line with the recent course set by the International Criminal Court, where a duty to provide reparation attaches to a finding of international criminal responsibility.

Despite these valid arguments, the criminal prosecution of a collective entity sits uneasy with one of criminal law's national and international fundamental principles: *nulla poena sine culpa*. The concept of criminal responsibility is premised on this principle of individual fault or culpability, which holds that

70 Nollkaemper (n 55) 1.
71 Darcy (n 60) 197.
72 Brennan (n 53) 129–130, 137–138; Ilya Nuzov, 'Post-Conflict Justice: Extending International Criminal Responsibility to Non-State Entities' in Ezequiel Heffes, Marcos D Kotlik and Manuel J Ventura (eds), *International Humanitarian Law and Non-State Actors* (TMC Asser Press 2020).
73 Preamble of the ICC Statute.
74 Brennan (n 53) 130.
75 Ibid. 142.

"nobody may be held criminally responsible for acts or transactions in which he had not personally engaged or in some other way participated".[76] It draws from long-standing Western legal traditions, which consider the individual to be an autonomous agent with an individual will to act, rather than a passive actor whose responsibility flows from a relation to others.[77] The emergence of individual criminal responsibility as a general principle of law, both domestically and internationally, formed a break from its collective past.[78] In modern criminal law, the notion of collective guilt, which served to hold an entire group responsible for acts performed by a member in their individual capacity, is no longer acceptable. It is considered as being unfair and morally detrimental.[79] Instead, a concept of individual justice has replaced such form of collective responsibility. One factor behind this development, was the prevention of never-ending revenge taking and retaliatory measures against a group.[80] In this sense, this shift provided a means to break with "the collective cycle of guilt" that group or collective responsibility might perpetuate.[81]

The introduction of the principle of individual criminal responsibility in the international legal system can be traced to the criminal justice initiatives established in the aftermath of World War II. As famously declared in the judgment

76 *Tadić Appeals Judgment* (n 58) para 186; ICRC, *Commentary on the Additional Protocols of 8 June 1977 to the Geneva Conventions of 12 December 1949* (Martinus Nijhoff 1987) para 4603.

77 Mark Osiel, *Making Sense of Mass Atrocity* (Cambridge University Press 2009) 187; Kirsten Campbell, 'Victims and Perpetrators of International Crimes: The Problem of the "Legal Person"' (2011) 2 Journal of International Humanitarian Legal Studies 325, 331–332; Elies Van Sliedregt, 'The Curious Case of International Criminal Liability' (2012) 10 Journal of International Criminal Justice 1171, 1172–1173.

78 M Cherif Bassiouni, *Introduction to International Criminal Law* (2nd edn, Martinus Nijhoff Publishers 2014) 66.

79 See also ILC Special Rapporteur Crawford's review of Art 19 draft ARS on state crimes (eventually deleted), noting that punishing a criminal state could indirectly amount to punishing the population that is often victimised by state crimes in the first place. 'First Report on State Responsibility, by Mr James Crawford, Special Rapporteur' (1998) UN Doc A/CN.4/490 and Add.1–7 22 para 87; James Crawford and Jeremy Watkins, 'International Responsibility' in John Tasioulas and Samantha Besson (eds), *The Philosophy of International Law* (Oxford University Press 2010) 290.

80 Albert Levy, 'Criminal Responsibility of Individuals and International Law' (1945) 12 The University of Chicago Law Review 313, 313–314; Francesco Parisi and Giuseppe Dari-Mattiacci, 'The Rise and Fall of Communal Liability in Ancient Law' (2004) 24 International Review of Law and Economics 489, 490–491; Antonio Cassese, *International Criminal Law* (2nd edn, Oxford University Press 2008) 33–34; M Cherif Bassiouni, 'Perspectives on International Criminal Justice' (2010) 50 Virginia Journal of International Law 269, 277.

81 Mark R Reiff, 'Terrorism, Retribution, and Collective Responsibility' (2008) 34 Social Theory and Practice 209, 234–239; Shachar Eldar, 'Exploring International Criminal Law's Reluctance to Resort to Modalities of Group Responsibility' (2013) 11 Journal of International Criminal Justice 331, 337.

of the Nuremberg International Military Tribunal (IMT): "Crimes against international law are committed by men, not by abstract entities, and only by punishing individuals who commit such crimes can the provisions of international law be enforced."[82] These origins on the international level were grounded in the need to break with the immunity of state officials, who before this time were able to shelter themselves behind the collective notion of state responsibility, which could not be brought back to its agents.[83] Contrary to state responsibility, criminal law concerns itself with the punishment of an individual's conduct. Namely, by violating the law, this individual has committed a crime.[84] Subsequent international justice instruments and initiatives have reiterated the fundamental principle of individual criminal responsibility, which can be considered as being firmly embedded at the core of modern international criminal law.[85]

3.3.2.2 An evaluation of the law and practice of international criminal courts and tribunals

Despite the dominant focus on individual responsibility and fault, the collective nature of international crimes has left its mark on international criminal law. This body of law not only criminalises direct perpetration, but also provides for concepts such as command responsibility, joint criminal enterprise and common purpose liability.[86] While this does not go as far as providing for the possibility of holding a group or organisation criminally responsible, there is some limited past practice that did not shy away from dealing with this question and devising responses to address it. This practice is retraced and analysed, over the following sections, through the lens of the collective criminal responsibility of NSAGs.

82 'Trial of the Major War Criminals before the International Military Tribunal' (Nuremberg 1947) Vol I 223; Art 6 Charter of the Nuremberg IMT in Agreement for the Prosecution and Punishment of the Major War Criminals of the European Axis (1945) 82 UNTS 279 (Nuremberg IMT Charter).

83 'Trial of the Major War Criminals before the International Military Tribunal' (n 82) 223–224; Van Sliedregt (n 56) 18–19.

84 Hans Kelsen, 'Collective and Individual Responsibility in International Law with Particular Regard to the Punishment of War Criminals' (1943) 31 California Law Review 530, 532–534.

85 UNGA, Affirmation of the Principles of International Law Recognized by the Charter of the Nuremberg Tribunal (11 December 1946) UN Doc A/RES/95; Art IV Convention on the Prevention and Punishment of the Crime of Genocide (1948) 78 UNTS 277; Arts 7(1), 23(1) ICTY Statute, adopted by UNSC Res 827 (1993); Arts 6 (1), 22(1) ICTR Statute, adopted by UNSC Res 955 (1994); Art 25 ICC Statute; Art 6(1) SCSL Statute (2002) 2178 UNTS 138; ILC, Draft Code of Crimes against the Peace and Security of Mankind, Yearbook of the International Law Commission (1996) Vol II Part Two.

86 Van Sliedregt (n 56) 19–20.

NUREMBERG INTERNATIONAL MILITARY TRIBUNAL

The notion of collective criminal responsibility is marked by its controversial history in international criminal law. Although the Nuremberg IMT propagated the principle of individual responsibility, it was also faced with the challenge of dealing with mass crimes, which resulted from a highly advanced form of system criminality. The Tribunal devised a controversial theory of collective or group criminality, which involved the notion of criminal organisations.[87] This allowed the IMT to declare certain Nazi organisations or groups, such as the Gestapo, the SS and the Nazi party, as criminal in nature.[88] For a criminal organisation of this nature to exist, it must have been "a group bound together and organized by a common purpose" which was "formed or used in connection with the commission of crimes" under consideration.[89] Interestingly, one of the objectives of criminalising these organisations was to control their assets, partly with the purpose of directing them to the provision of reparations.[90] This offered a subsequent basis for national courts to prosecute members of these organisations, as they had been declared as criminal by the Tribunal.[91] Membership was considered as proof of participation in an organisation's crimes. More specifically, individual criminal responsibility was determined on the basis of one's membership within the criminal organisation, provided it was voluntary and the person had knowledge of its criminal purpose or was personally implicated.[92] The rationale behind this model of criminal organisations was that the prosecutorial and judicial workload would be significantly reduced and, at the same time, the evasion of justice could be avoided.[93]

The relevance of the IMT's criminal organisations model for the present discussion is limited for at least three reasons. First, it was devised to apply to state-linked organisations and does not provide any indication that it might be extended to non-state actors, such as NSAGs. When one considers the highly

87 The judges recognised its controversial nature, see 'Trial of the Major War Criminals before the International Military Tribunal' (n 82) 256. See also Hans Kelsen, 'Will the Judgment in the Nuremberg Trial Constitute a Precedent in International Law?' (1947) 1 The International Law Quarterly 153, 165–167; UN War Crimes Commission, *History of the United Nations War Crimes Commission and the Development of the Laws of War* (His Majesty's Stationery Office 1948) 289; Van Sliedregt (n 56) 36.

88 Art 9 Nuremberg IMT Charter.

89 'Trial of the Major War Criminals before the International Military Tribunal' (n 82) 256.

90 Zegveld (n 18) 55.

91 Arts 10–11 Nuremberg IMT Charter; Art II(1)(d), (2)(e) Control Council Law No 10 Punishment of Persons Guilty of War Crimes, Crimes against Peace and against Humanity (20 December 1945) Official Gazette of the Control Council For Germany No 3 Berlin (1946).

92 'Trial of the Major War Criminals before the International Military Tribunal' (n 82) 256.

93 Darcy (n 60) ch V.

sophisticated and bureaucratic nature of the Nazi regime, it becomes a very open question as to how easily an NSAG characterised by a loose organisational structure, a fluctuating pool of members, and/or a general lack of information about its workings might relate to the Nuremberg concept of criminal organisation.[94] Second, it brings forward a precedent for collective criminal responsibility in international criminal law to the extent that a person could be subjected to a criminal sanction because of the behaviour of other members of the same criminally declared organisation. Yet, the judgment on the criminality of the Nazi organisations was merely declaratory in nature and did not provide the IMT with the power to hold the organisations themselves criminally responsible and to punish them accordingly.[95] Instead, it was a means of holding the individual members responsible.[96] The focus of the present enquiry is different, as it seeks to explore whether NSAGs can be held criminally responsible in their own right.[97] Third, and as will be discussed further below, the concept of criminal organisations was short lived. It did not experience a revival after the post-World War II trials. In this sense, the notion that the Nuremberg model might provide any significance for the present discussion in terms of precedent is seriously tempered.

INTERNATIONAL CRIMINAL TRIBUNALS FOR THE FORMER YUGOSLAVIA AND RWANDA

During the drafting process of the Statute of the ICTY, a committee of French jurists proposed the inclusion of a notion of criminal organisations that was similar to that included in the Nuremberg Charter.[98] However, the controversial proposal did not attract the necessary support and was eventually set aside. Concerns were raised that findings of guilt by association would be fundamentally unjust and unfair, and that the limits of relying on membership alone to prove individual guilt were problematic.[99] The UN Secretary-General also questioned the concept in his report on the establishment of the ICTY. He queried "whether a juridical person, such as an association or organization, may be considered criminal as such and thus its members, for that reason alone, be made subject to the jurisdiction of the International Tribunal".[100] It was concluded that such a concept should not be retained on the basis that

94 Nina Jørgensen, 'Criminality of Organizations Under International Law' in André Nollkaemper and Harmen Van der Wilt (eds), *System Criminality in International Law* (Cambridge University Press 2009) 220.
95 Ibid. 204.
96 Cassese (n 80) 34–35.
97 Zegveld (n 18) 55–56, 58.
98 Nina Jørgensen, 'A Reappraisal of the Abandoned Nuremberg Concept of Criminal Organisations in the Context of Justice in Rwanda' (2001) 12 Criminal Law Forum 371, 375.
99 Darcy (n 60) 282–283.
100 UNSC, 'Report of the Secretary-General Pursuant to Paragraph 2 of Security Council Resolution 808 (1993)' (3 May 1993) UN Doc S/25704 para 51.

international crimes are carried out by natural persons, who should be subjected to international criminal jurisdiction irrespective of their membership within a particular group.[101] Despite the harmful activities of armed militias and groups in Rwanda, the model of criminal organisations was not reconsidered within the context of the establishment of the ICTR.[102]

INTERNATIONAL CRIMINAL COURT

It is notable that Draft Article 23 of the Statute of the International Criminal Court, discussed at the Rome Conference in 1998, included the possibility of prosecuting not only natural persons but also legal persons, excluding states.[103] This despite Draft Article 23 being a provision on 'individual criminal responsibility'. Under such a provision, the Court would have had jurisdiction "when the crimes committed were committed on behalf of such legal persons or by their agencies or representatives".[104] In accordance with Draft Article 76(vi), appropriate forms of reparations could have been imposed against convicted legal persons as a possible penalty, besides fines, dissolution and forfeiture of proceeds, property and assets obtained by criminal conduct, among other penalties. In the draft, it was suggested that this concept be further examined in the context of reparations to victims, which is in line with the general rejection of punitive damages in international law.[105] The draft Statute went in fact further than the Nuremberg IMT, as it provided a means to prosecute and punish legal persons as such. The footnote to Draft Article 23 clarifies that there was

101 Ibid. 51, 53. Further rejection of the concept of collective criminal responsibility can be found in the first annual report of the ICTY submitted by its President Cassese, see UNGA and UNSC, 'Report of the International Tribunal for the Prosecution of Persons Responsible for Serious Violations of International Humanitarian Law Committed in the Territory of the Former Yugoslavia since 1991' (29 August 1994) UN Doc A/49/342-S/1994/1007 para 16.

102 Jørgensen (n 98) 375.

103 For an in-depth discussion Andrew Clapham, 'The Question of Jurisdiction Under International Criminal Law over Legal Persons: Lessons from the Rome Conference on an International Criminal Court' in Menno T Kamminge and Saman Zia-Zarifi (eds), *Liability of Multinational Corporations under International Law* (Kluwer 2000).

104 'Report of the Preparatory Committee on the Establishment of an International Criminal Court' in UN Diplomatic Conference of Plenipotentiaries on the Establishment of an International Criminal Court (Rome 15 June-17 July 1998) UN Doc A/CONF.183/13 (Vol III) 30–31.

105 Ibid. 63; Observations of the Trust Fund for Victims on the Appeals against Trial Chamber I 's "Decision Establishing the Principles and Procedures to be Applied to Reparations" ICC-01/04–01/06 (8 April 2013) para 106; ILC Commentary to the ARS 99 n 516; Nina Jørgensen, 'A Reappraisal of Punitive Damages in International Law' (1998) 68 The British Yearbook of International Law 247; Rolf Einar Fife, 'Penalties' in Roy S Lee (ed), *The International Criminal Court: The Making of the Rome Statute: Issues, Negotiations, Results* (Kluwer Law International 1999) 335.

"a deep divergence of views as to the advisability of including criminal responsibility of legal persons in the Statute".[106] Although some delegations strongly favoured the inclusion, and even argued for the addition of organisations lacking legal status (presumably criminal and terrorist organisations when following the account of Clapham), it appears that many strongly opposed the proposal. It was feared that the provision could be used against those struggling for self-determination, amongst others.[107] Some delegations proposed, as a middle ground, to only provide for the "civil or administrative responsibility/liability of legal persons", which was, however, not thoroughly discussed.[108]

At the Rome Conference, a French proposal, based on Draft Article 23, revived the discussion on the concept of criminal organisations, but this time without the controversial crime of membership. It was proposed that when "a crime was committed by a natural person on behalf or with the assent of a *group or organization of every kind*, the Court may declare that this group or organization is a *criminal organization*" and "[a]ppropriate forms of reparation" could be imposed as a penalty.[109] The proposal was deemed attractive from the perspective of obtaining reparations for victims.[110] Nevertheless, concerns were raised over the definition of 'criminal organisation' or 'legal person', the exclusive focus of the Statute on individual criminal responsibility, and the absence of the concept in some domestic legal systems of State Parties, among other issues.[111]

The concepts of legal person and, later, criminal organisation were not clearly defined. On the one hand, the concept of legal person could have potentially included NSAGs, given their limited international legal personality under IHL. On the other hand, as was mentioned *supra*, an argument was made to extend the concept of legal persons to include organisations lacking legal status. NSAGs are commonly illegal under domestic law. Consequently, NSAGs can at the same time be qualified as organisations with no legal status at the domestic level.[112] A similar argument can be made regarding international law when following the perspective of those who do not recognise NSAGs as

106 'Report of the Preparatory Committee on the Establishment of an International Criminal Court' (n 104) 31 n 71.
107 Clapham (n 103) 157.
108 'Report of the Preparatory Committee on the Establishment of an International Criminal Court' (n 104) 31 n 71.
109 'Proposal Submitted by France: Article 23 Individual Criminal Responsibility Legal Persons' (16 June 1998) UN Doc A/CONF.183/C.1/L.3 [emphasis added].
110 Clapham (n 103) 147; Darcy (n 60) 283–284; Kai Ambos, 'Article 25 - Individual Criminal Responsibility' in Otto Triffterer and Kai Ambos (eds), *The Rome Statute of the International Criminal Court: A Commentary* (3rd edn, Hart 2016) 986.
111 'Summary Records of the Meetings of the Committee of the Whole' in UN Diplomatic Conference of Plenipotentiaries on the Establishment of an International Criminal Court (Rome 15 June-17 July 1998) UN Doc A/CONF.183/13 (Vol II) 133–136.
112 Zegveld (n 18) 56–57.

international legal persons, or subjects, despite their limited legal personality.[113] This could indicate that Draft Article 23 may initially have covered NSAGs. However, there are no further indications to that end. This differs from the criminal responsibility of corporations, which was even considered as a separate item during the discussions.[114] Furthermore, the final French proposal substituted the concept of 'legal person' in the draft Statute with 'juridical person', partly because the term 'legal' suggested a degree of inappropriate legitimacy.[115] The term juridical person was understood as being "a corporation whose concrete, real or dominant objective is seeking private profit or benefit".[116] This clearly excluded considerations for NSAGs. Eventually, any references to 'legal person', 'criminal organisation' or 'juridical person' were left out of final Article 25 of the Rome Statute, which only provides for the individual criminal responsibility of natural persons.[117]

CONCLUDING OBSERVATIONS

From the above discussion, it can be clearly seen that developments in modern international criminal law and practice provide little support for the creation of a notion of collective criminal responsibility for NSAGs. Nevertheless, there have been some occasions, at both the domestic and international levels, when courts, tribunals and non-judicial mechanisms have implicitly relied on the notion that NSAGs can commit international crimes. While this involved indirect considerations about their responsibility under international criminal norms, it did not result in establishing their criminal responsibility as such. For instance, the International Commission of Inquiry on Darfur seems to suggest that serious violations of IHRL and IHL amounting to international crimes may involve the international responsibility of NSAGs.[118] Another example can be found in the case law of the Special Court of Sierra Leone. When exploring the

113 Brennan (n 53) 142–144.

114 See, for instance, 'Summary of the Proceedings of the Preparatory Committee during the Period 25 March-12 April 1996' (7 May 1996) UN Doc A/AC.249/1 26. The term 'legal persons' also appears in Art 46C of the Protocol on Amendments to the Protocol on the Statute of the African Court of Justice and Human Rights (2014), which provides the Court with the jurisdiction to determine the criminal liability of corporations with no reference to other entities such as NSAGs.

115 Clapham (n 103) 152.

116 'Working Paper on Article 23, Paragraphs 5 and 6' (3 July 1998) UN Doc A/CONF.183/C.1/WGGP/L.5/Rev.2 para 5(d). Note that, at the outset, the various proposals concerning the prosecution of non-natural persons did not only have corporate entities in mind, but also political parties and even racist groups. Andrew Clapham, 'Extending International Criminal Law Beyond the Individual to Corporations and Armed Opposition Groups' (2008) 6 Journal of International Criminal Justice 899, 919.

117 Clapham (n 103) 156–157. However, see Art 25(3)(d) ICC Statute.

118 'Report of the International Commission of Inquiry on Darfur' (25 January 2005) para 175.

contextual elements of crimes against humanity, the Trial Chamber identified the RUF on several occasions as the author of attacks carried out against the civilian population.[119] Likewise, in the *Limaj* case, the Trial Chamber of the ICTY considered "the allegation of an attack against a civilian population perpetrated by a non-state actor [i.e. the Kosovo Liberation Army or KLA] with extremely limited resources, personnel and organisation".[120] Similarly, a federal class-action civil lawsuit, brought on behalf of affected Colombian families under the US Alien Tort Statute, was initiated against the corporation Chiquita for complicity in international crimes allegedly committed together with a Colombian paramilitary group. The case depended on proving that the protection money offered by Chiquita facilitated the commission of these crimes by the group, instead of certain named individuals.[121] In other words, the complainants needed to rely on the notion that an armed group can commit violations of international criminal law as a group.[122]

3.4 A proposal for a new *sui generis* regime of international responsibility for non-state armed groups

The failure of the law of state responsibility to mitigate the existing responsibility gap, which concerns violations committed by NSAGs in international law, provides a first justification to explore the possibility of establishing a new regime of international responsibility for NSAGs. This conclusion is reinforced by the findings of the analysis regarding the regime of individual criminal responsibility. The collective criminal responsibility of NSAGs could have provided a means to hold such groups responsible for their role in international crimes and a potential legal basis to claim reparations. However, the analysis in this chapter has revealed a clear rejection of this possibility. As shown, the extension of international criminal law to NSAGs is, first, fraught with a variety of legal concerns over fairness, justice and conformity with the foundational principles of criminal law and, second, characterised by a lack of practice which would corroborate such an assertion. Instead of trying to find solace in the area of international criminal law, there is more merit in complementing existing initiatives, which concern the criminal responsibility of individual group members, with a new regime of international responsibility of NSAGs, which is

119 *Prosecutor v Sesay, Kallon and Gbao* (n 53) paras 944–945, 947, 953, 955–956.

120 *Prosecutor v Fatmir Limaj Haradin Bala Isak Musliu* ICTY (Trial Judgment) IT-03–66-T (30 November 2005) para 191. For further implicit practice relating to NSAGs and crimes against humanity, see Katharine Fortin, *The Accountability of Armed Groups under Human Rights Law* (Oxford University Press 2017) 300–303.

121 *John Doe et al v Chiquita Brands International* US District Court for DNJ (2007).

122 For a discussion of further relevant examples under the US Alien Tort Statute, see Andrew Clapham, 'Focusing on Armed Non-State Actors' in Andrew Clapham and Paola Gaeta (eds), *The Oxford Handbook of International Law in Armed Conflict* (Oxford University Press 2014) 807–808.

comparable to state responsibility.[123] Such a constellation would correspond to the observation that the remedies which attach to the responsibility of collective entities and individuals are generally different, with the former leading to reparations and the latter to punishment.[124] This conclusion finds further support in the analysis of international practice and legal materials carried out in Chapter 2 and within scholarly opinion, which tend towards a responsibility regime similar to that of states as opposed to the criminalisation of an NSAG's wrongful conduct.[125] As established in Section 3.2.2, the elaboration of the content of a future responsibility regime, particularly the duty to repair, can commence from an analogical analysis of the reparation rules and principles as expressed in the law of state responsibility. Such an exercise can be further informed by the approaches to reparation applied within the responsibility regimes dealing with international organisations and individuals. On the contrary, if the examination had resulted in an affirmation of the establishment of collective criminal responsibility *vis-à-vis* NSAGs, it would have required, first of all, an analysis of the reparation standards developed in the field of international criminal law relevant to NSAGs.

The responsibility of NSAGs could be conceptualised as being civil in character due to its reparatory function and by analogy with national legal systems, which generally distinguish civil from criminal responsibility. Here, however, it is preferred to characterise it as a *sui generis* responsibility. This is based on two main considerations. First, the legal consequences of this form of responsibility could go beyond an obligation to make reparation. As an example, it could also entail the dismantlement of the responsible NSAG, thereby incorporating a measure of coercion or punishment, which results from the distinct nature of NSAGs. Second, state responsibility forms a unified system in international law. It neither distinguishes between degrees of liability according to the source of the obligations breached (e.g. crime, tort or contract), nor embodies the national law classifications of civil or criminal. This explains the

123 Zegveld (n 18) 58; André Nollkaemper and Harmen Van der Wilt, 'Conclusions and Outlook' in André Nollkaemper and Harmen Van der Wilt (eds), *System Criminality in International Law* (Cambridge University Press 2009) 345; Mark A Drumbl, 'Accountability for System Criminality' (2010) 8 Santa Clara Journal of International Law 373, 377; Luke Moffett, 'Beyond Attribution: Responsibility of Armed Non-State Actors for Reparations in Northern Ireland, Colombia and Uganda' in Noemi Gal-Or, Cedric Ryngaert and Math Noortmann (eds), *Responsibilities of the Non-State Actor in Armed Conflict and the Market Place* (Brill Nijhof 2015) 330; Daragh Murray, *Human Rights Obligations of Non-State Armed Groups* (Hart Publishing 2016) 67–69; Fortin (n 120) 286–307.

124 Andre Nollkaemper, 'Concurrence between Individual Responsibility and State Responsibility in International Law' (2003) 52 International and Comparative Law Quarterly 615, 636.

125 See Kleffner (n 43) 269; Bílková (n 1) 279; Moffett (n 123) 332; Íñigo Álvarez (n 37) 73–74.

characterisation of state responsibility as being "neither civil nor criminal".[126] For this reason, the notion of international responsibility cannot be simply assimilated to notions of domestic law.[127] In addition, the *sui generis* character of NSAGs' international responsibility is further reflected in the need to accommodate the particularities of these groups within the legal rules and principles that purport to govern such responsibility.

When devising the *sui generis* notion of collective responsibility for NSAGs, the question of perpetuating a form of collective guilt among the members of the group becomes less of a concern. Contrary to criminal justice, the obligation to repair which attaches to NSAGs' responsibility is not traced back to individual members' contributions to a given crime in terms of personal fault, culpability or blameworthiness. Instead, it finds its basis in the agency of the collectivity or, in other words, in the breaches of the obligations by the collective or group actor. Although members may bear divergent degrees of personal guilt, this approach provides for a measure in which group members collectively share in the remedying of harmful consequences of an internationally wrongful act perpetrated by the group they are or were a part of. They may also play a collective role in preventing similar harms from occurring. The distribution of costs of compensation and reconstitution of the victims is not to be equated with the distribution of guilt, and thus says nothing about a person's individual responsibility.[128] Besides their bases, the aims and nature of retributive and reparative forms of justice differ. When it comes to reparative forms of justice, instead of focusing on the punishment and condemnation of blameworthy wrongdoers, the focus lies on remedying the harm that persons or communities have experienced as a broader process of healing. This further underscores the distinct role of various forms of responsibility and their complementary nature. From a moral perspective, it also appears fair and right that reparative obligations are jointly incurred when the harms are caused in a group context, regardless of the extent of one's involvement.[129]

This does not nullify the possibility that a certain complementarity could exist between the criminal responsibility of an individual member and the possible international responsibility of the NSAG they belong to. Both forms of responsibility could complement one another, as those bearing personal

126 Ian Brownlie, *Principles of Public International Law* (6th edn, Oxford University Press 2003) 421; Alain Pellet, 'The Definition of Responsibility in International Law' in James Crawford, Alain Pellet and Simon Olleson (eds), *The Law of International Responsibility* (Oxford University Press 2010) 12–15.

127 ILC Commentary to Art 1 ARS 33 paras 3, 5; Crawford and Olleson (n 18) 449–452.

128 Nollkaemper (n 55) 10–11; Michael Walzer, *Just and Unjust Wars: A Moral Argument with Historical Illustrations* (5th edn, Basic Books 2015).

129 Thomas Franck, 'Individual Criminal Liability and Collective Civil Responsibility: Do They Reinforce or Contradict One Another?' (2007) 6 Washington University Global Studies Law Review 567; Erin I Kelly, 'Reparative Justice' in Tracy Isaacs and Richard Vernon (eds), *Accountability for Collective Wrongdoing* (Cambridge University Press 2011).

culpability cannot hide behind the collectivity, while the group or system also needs to answer for its role.[130] This approach responds to two concerns. First, "if all are accountable, no one is accountable" or, as formulated by Lauterpacht, "unless responsibility is imputed and attached to persons of flesh and blood, it rests with no one".[131] Second, it satisfies the call to directly address the system, i.e. an NSAG, engaged in violations of international law. This idea of turning to complementarity in the context of dealing with collective entities is not new to international law. Article 58 ARS holds that the "articles are without prejudice to any question of the individual responsibility under international law of any person acting on behalf of a State". The ILC Commentary further clarifies that when "crimes against international law are committed by State officials, it will often be the case that the State itself is responsible for the acts in question or for failure to prevent or punish them".[132] Similarly, Article 25(4) of the Rome Statute of the International Criminal Court provides that "[n]o provision in this Statute relating to individual criminal responsibility shall affect the responsibility of States under international law." The most discussed practical manifestation of such complementarity can be found in the *Bosnian Genocide* case. In the case, the International Court of Justice was requested to decide on the international responsibility of Serbia for alleged violations of the Convention on the Prevention and Punishment of the Crime of Genocide. The Court concluded that the acts of the individuals, who committed the crime of genocide at Srebrenica, could not be attributed to Serbia.[133] However, it did hold that Serbia "failed to comply both with its obligation to prevent and its obligation to punish genocide", consequently engaging its state responsibility.[134] In response to Serbia's argument that the nature of the Convention excludes state responsibility from its scope, the Court observed that "duality of responsibility continues to be a constant feature of international law", reflected in both the Rome Statute of the International Criminal Court and the ARS.[135]

130 Nollkaemper and Van der Wilt (n 123) 345–347.

131 Hersch Lauterpacht, *International Law: Being The Collected Papers of Hersch Lauterpacht*, vol 2 The Law of Peace, Part 1 International Law in General (Elihu Lauterpacht ed, Cambridge University Press 1975) 520; Christopher Kutz, *Complicity: Ethics and Law for a Collective Age* (Cambridge University Press 2000) 113; Nollkaemper (n 55) 8.

132 ILC Commentary to Art 58 ARS 142 para 3. This is similarly stated with regard to international organisations, see ILC Commentary to Art 3 ARIO 53 para 6 and Art 66 ARIO.

133 *Application of the Convention on the Prevention and Punishment of the Crime of Genocide (Bosnia and Herzegovina v Serbia and Montenegro)* ICJ (Judgment) [2007] ICJ Rep 43 202–219, 237.

134 Ibid. 226–229.

135 Ibid. 115–117. Similarly, the ICTY held that "[u]nder current international humanitarian law, in addition to individual criminal liability, State responsibility may ensue as a result of State officials engaging in torture or failing to prevent torture or to punish torturers." *Prosecutor v Furundžija* ICTY (Trial Judgment) IT-95–17/1-T (10 December 1998) para 142.

Such an understanding indicates that complementarity between these two forms of responsibility serves different purposes. Individual criminal responsibility aims to combat impunity and punish the perpetrator, while state responsibility seeks to restore the international order to its *status quo* and repair the damage caused.[136] The argument that a similar logic can be applied to NSAGs and their individual members finds express support in the work of the International Commission of Inquiry on Darfur and the Panel of Experts on Accountability in Sri Lanka, as well as in legal scholarship.[137]

3.5 Conclusions

The aim of this chapter has been to determine what the character of a future regime of international responsibility for NSAGs should be. To this end, the limitations and potential of the existing regimes of state responsibility and individual criminal responsibility have been evaluated. Considering the limitations of these responsibility regimes, it has been concluded that the responsibility of NSAGs warrants a new and separate regime in international law. It has been proposed based on this discussion to conceptualise the international responsibility of NSAGs as being both analogous to that of states and *sui generis* in character. The latter observation refers to the new regime's characterisation as being neither civil nor criminal and to the need to accommodate the particularities of NSAGs when conceptualising such international responsibility. Accordingly, it has been determined that the elaboration of this regime of responsibility can make use of analogical legal reasoning that takes the existing rules and principles of the law of state responsibility as a starting point, while being additionally informed by the legal rules governing the responsibility of international organisations and individuals. The exercise of elucidating a possible duty of NSAGs to repair, as one of the legal consequences of international responsibility, will be conducted in the following chapter. The objective is to devise abstract rules that can be applied generally, while at the same time providing the necessary flexibility to accommodate the particularities of NSAGs. Finally, it has been argued that a certain complementarity could exist between the possible international responsibility of an NSAG and the individual criminal responsibility of its members. It is conceivable, by way of analogy with state responsibility, that these forms of responsibility could complement each other in dealing with harmful acts by way of the distinct actors they focus on, the violations they address and the distinct purposes they serve.

136 Íñigo Álvarez (n 37) 63–64.

137 'Report of the International Commission of Inquiry on Darfur' (n 118) para 175; UNSG (n 40) para 191; Fortin (n 120) 378–379; Íñigo Álvarez (n 37) 65.

Chapter 4

Operationalising a duty for non-state armed groups to provide reparation

4.1 Introduction

This chapter examines how a possible duty of NSAGs to provide reparation for internationally wrongful acts could be operationalised as part of a future law of international responsibility. Given that such a duty of reparation remains unsettled in international law, the examination has been carried out with a view to *lex ferenda*. It involves exploring how such a duty could be conceptualised and put into practice. The chapter starts with addressing the feasibility of holding NSAGs to a duty of reparation, while shedding light on some of the concerns that may arise with such an endeavour. This discussion forms the cornerstone of the further analysis in this chapter. The chapter then proceeds by evaluating the possible application of certain reparation standards to NSAGs under international law. Building on the conclusions of Chapter 3, the legal principles and rules on reparation in the law of state responsibility are used to draw parallels to possible standards for NSAGs. The analysis is additionally informed by the existing approaches to reparation *vis-à-vis* international organisations and individuals in international law, the corresponding scholarly debates and the practice of NSAGs. The question when an NSAG could be called upon to provide reparations is also addressed. All in all, the chapter presents a multifaceted proposal for operationalising a duty of NSAGs to provide reparation under international law.

4.2 Feasibility of obtaining reparations from non-state armed groups

NSAGs must have a minimum level of organisation to function as parties in a NIAC. The organisational structure of some groups may be more sophisticated than others and even display state-like characteristics. Nevertheless, compared to states, NSAGs usually lack the equivalent institutional capacity and resources needed to provide effective reparations to victims in situations of armed conflict.[1]

1 Sten Verhoeven, 'International Responsibility of Armed Opposition Groups: Lessons from State Responsibility for Actions of Armed Opposition Groups' in Noemi Gal-Or, Cedric Ryngaert and Math Noortmann (eds), *Responsibilities of the Non-State Actor*

DOI: 10.4324/9781003401292-7

Such contexts are characterised by mass victimisation involving a complex set of harms and needs. This reality can easily exceed the practical capabilities of the responsible NSAG. The group may lack the resources or other organisational features to provide or even contribute to repairing the harms caused, may only be able to provide certain forms of reparations, or may simply cease to exist making redress infeasible. Consequently, victims may have few prospects of obtaining reparations for any harm suffered.[2] This has also been recognised by the International Center for Transitional Justice, which, on the one hand, recommended that the rebel groups active in Darfur should acknowledge responsibility for the violations committed by their forces and ensure that these violations cease and, on the other, held that "it is usually not feasible to hold armed groups, whether pro or anti-government, directly accountable for reparations".[3] This differs from states which through their institutions, infrastructure and resources will be typically better equipped to implement reparations programmes.[4] These capacity concerns are common in discussions regarding the role of NSAGs in reparations processes. Similar ones have also been raised vis-á-vis other non-state actors, such as individuals and international organisations.[5] Similarly, the capabilities of states concerning reparations have been taken as a benchmark.[6]

The capacity of NSAGs to provide certain measures of redress, or to collectively engage in a reparations mechanism, may also vary greatly from one group to another. NSAGs may "range from hierarchically complex, well-financed

in Armed Conflict and the Market Place (Brill Nijhof 2015) 299; Daragh Murray, *Human Rights Obligations of Non-State Armed Groups* (Hart Publishing 2016) 172.

2 Cecily Rose, 'An Emerging Norm: The Duty of States to Provide Reparations for Human Rights Violations by Non-State Actors' (2010) 33 Hastings International and Comparative Law Review 307, 309–310; Ron Dudai, 'Closing the Gap: Symbolic Reparations and Armed Groups' (2011) 93 International Review of the Red Cross 783, 785–786; Luke Moffett, 'Beyond Attribution: Responsibility of Armed Non-State Actors for Reparations in Northern Ireland, Colombia and Uganda' in Noemi Gal-Or, Cedric Ryngaert and Math Noortmann (eds), *Responsibilities of the Non-State Actor in Armed Conflict and the Market Place* (Brill Nijhof 2015) 334.

3 ICTJ, 'Providing Meaningful Reparations to Victims' (2009) 2.

4 Moffett (n 2) 325.

5 Natalia Szablewska, 'Non-State Actors and Human Rights in Non-International Armed Conflicts' (2007) 32 African Yearbook of International Law 345, 356.

6 In relation to individuals, see Octavio Amezcua-Noriega, 'Reparation Principles under International Law and Their Possible Application by the International Criminal Court: Some Reflections' (2011) Reparations Unit, Transitional Justice Network, Briefing Paper No 1, 8; Christine Evans, *The Right to Reparation in International Law for Victims of Armed Conflict* (Cambridge University Press 2012) 4; Moffett (n 2) 329–330. Concerning international organisations, see Art 40 ILC, Articles on the Responsibility of International Organizations with Commentaries, Yearbook of the International Law Commission (2011) Vol II Part Two (ARIO); Alain Pellet, 'International Organizations Are Definitely Not States. Cursory Remarks on the ILC Articles on the Responsibility of International Organizations' in Maurizio Ragazzi (ed), *Responsibility of International Organizations* (Martinus Nijhoff Publishers 2013) 49–53.

armed groups that exercise control over large swathes of territory at one extreme, to minimally organized, poor, and mobile groups at the other".[7] Thus, NSAGs' remedial capabilities necessarily vary with the organisational and resource level of a specific group. These capabilities may also fluctuate over the course of an armed conflict as an NSAG may, for example, have a more rudimentary organisation at the beginning of an armed conflict and become more sophisticated in later years, or vice versa.[8] Still, an NSAG must maintain a minimum organised structure to be considered a party to the conflict and, hence, be recognised as a subject of international law.[9] Additionally, the organisational structure of an NSAG may mutate, fragment, merge into another group, or even dissolve.[10] The unstable and temporary nature of NSAGs can make it difficult to pursue reparations claims against the very group that is responsible.[11] Hence, the overall capacity of an NSAG to fulfil a duty to provide reparation may vary significantly compared to other groups, may change over time and may even become impractical. Besides questions of organisational and resource capacity, NSAGs may also simply lack the will to provide reparations. This could result in, for example, hiding or laundering their assets, misusing public apologies as a technique of denial of responsibility, or even in a complete lack of engagement.[12]

Although reparations from NSAGs may not be feasible in all cases, Dudai argues that it is wrong to assume that they will simply never be feasible.[13] He demonstrates, based on an analysis of reparation processes involving the African National Congress (ANC) in South Africa and the Irish Republican Army (IRA) in Northern Ireland, that "at least in some cases, and in relation to at least some forms of reparations, it would indeed be feasible to discuss the question of reparations from armed groups".[14] Moffett comes to a similar

7 ICRC, 'Strengthening International Humanitarian Law Protecting Persons Deprived of Their Liberty: Concluding Report' (2015) 33.

8 Verhoeven (n 1) 299; ICRC, 'The Roots of Restraint in War' (2018) 24.

9 See Chapter 1. Laura Íñigo Álvarez, *Towards a Regime of Responsibility of Armed Groups in International Law* (Intersentia 2020) 87–88.

10 ILA Committee on Non-State Actors, 'Washington Conference Non State Actors' (2014) 10; Moffett (n 2) 334.

11 Jann K Kleffner, 'The Collective Accountability of Organized Armed Groups for System Crimes' in Andre Nollkaemper and Harmen Gijsbrecht van der Wilt (eds), *System Criminality in International Law* (Cambridge University Press 2009) 265; Zakaria Daboné, *Le Droit International Public Relatif Aux Groupes Armés Non Étatiques* (Schulthess 2012) 192–193.

12 Dudai (n 2) 785; Moffett (n 2) 334; UNGA, 'Report of the Special Rapporteur on the Promotion of Truth, Justice, Reparation and Guarantees of Non-Recurrence' (12 July 2019) UN Doc A/74/147 para 23.

13 See also Paloma Blázquez Rodríguez, 'Does an Armed Group Have an Obligation to Provide Reparations to Its Victims? Construing an Obligation to Provide Reparations for Violations of International Humanitarian Law' in James Summers and Alex Gough (eds), *Non-State Actors and International Obligations* (Brill Nijhof 2018) 415.

14 Dudai (n 2) 786.

conclusion on the basis of his study of the state practice of holding NSAGs responsible for reparation in Northern Ireland, Colombia and Uganda. He concludes that while there may be difficulties in ensuring that NSAGs can fulfil their obligation, it is apparent from these cases that they can still play a significant role in ensuring effective remedies for victims.[15]

All in all, the discussion indicates that there is a need to develop an international legal framework that accommodates the varying degrees of organisational capacity amongst NSAGs, and their differences in comparison to states. To this end, possible secondary rules and principles concerning reparation should be designed in such a way as to ensure that they could be applied to all types of NSAGs and in all situations. Thus, as concluded in Chapter 3, the challenge is to arrive at abstract rules that allow for this required flexibility while ensuring the concrete application of the obligations imposed and excluding the creation of legal fictions.[16] Put differently, it should render the international legal framework realistic, while avoiding a schism between the normative framework itself and the facts on the ground.[17] Additionally, victims may have difficulty in seeking redress from NSAGs not only because of their limited or non-existent capacity. They may also experience a lack of willingness on the part of NSAGs. To address the potential lack of capacity or willingness, it is essential that the proposed legal framework includes a mechanism that guarantees, to the greatest extent possible, satisfactory redress for the victims.

4.3 Cascading regime of responsibility for reparation

The concept of reparation is characterised by the intrinsic relation between responsibility for internationally wrongful acts and the duty of the responsible actor to provide reparation.[18] This finds its expression in a fundamental principle of both domestic and international law that holds that those responsible for causing injury should repair it. This legal principle is found in myriad sources of international law, including in the case law of the Permanent Court of International Justice which conceptualises reparation as the indispensable complement of a failure to comply with an international obligation by affirming that "any breach of an engagement involves an obligation to make

15 Moffett (n 2) 345.

16 Compare to the similar approach taken in the ARIO in response to the diversity of international organisations, see ILC Commentary to Art 2 ARIO 51 para 15. Antonio Cassese, *International Law* (2nd edn, Oxford University Press 2005) 12–13; Salvatore Zappalà, 'Can Legality Trump Effectiveness in Today's International Law?' in Antonio Cassese (ed), *Realizing Utopia: The Future of International Law* (Oxford University Press 2012) 106; Taki Hiroshi, 'Effectiveness' in Rüdiger Wolfrum (ed), *The Max Planck Encyclopedia of Public International Law* (Oxford University Press 2013) para 1.

17 Íñigo Álvarez (n 9) 67; Katharine Fortin, *The Accountability of Armed Groups under Human Rights Law* (Oxford University Press 2017) 242.

18 Moffett (n 2) 324; Blázquez Rodríguez (n 13) 416–417; Íñigo Álvarez (n 9) 159.

reparation".[19] Correspondingly, the obligation of reparation is conceptualised in the law of state responsibility as "the immediate corollary" of international responsibility or, put differently, as the obligation of the responsible state resulting from the breach.[20] The ARIO equally adopt this approach to reparation.[21] The reparations orders of the International Criminal Court demonstrate the same intrinsic relationship, as they are "intrinsically linked to the *individual* whose criminal liability is established in a conviction".[22] Accordingly, one of the main purposes of reparation is to "oblige those responsible for serious crimes to repair the harm they caused to the victims".[23] More broadly, this is said to ensure that offenders account for their acts.[24] This conception of the duty to repair, resulting from breaches of international law, has profound historical roots, such as in the natural law principle of *neminem laedere* (to injure no one) and the ancient principles of corrective justice.[25]

The logical consequence of this intrinsic relationship between responsibility and the duty of reparation is then that the violator of an international norm – the responsible actor – is the first to bear the duty to provide reparation. Accordingly, an NSAG should incur the primary duty to repair the harm resulting from its own wrongful conduct, which is clearly in line with established principles in international law. Furthermore, ensuring there is a close and visible link between reparations and responsibility can appropriately redirect blame towards those responsible and relieve the guilt that survivors often feel.[26] Consequently, it can play an important role in a person's healing process. From the perspective of the responsible actor, the act of providing reparations can

19 *Case concerning the Factory at Chorzów (Germany v Poland)* PCIJ (Merits) [1928] PCIJ Rep Series A No 17 29. See also Chapter 2 Section 2.2.1.

20 ILC, Articles on the Responsibility of States for Internationally Wrongful Acts with Commentaries, Yearbook of the International Law Commission (2001) Vol II Part Two (ARS) Art 31, 91 para 4.

21 Art 31 ARIO.

22 *Prosecutor v Thomas Lubanga Dyilo* ICC (Judgment on the Appeals against the "Decision establishing the Principles and Procedures to be applied to Reparations" of 7 August 2012) ICC-01/04–01/06–3129 (3 March 2015) para 65.

23 Ibid. para 58.

24 Ibid.

25 *Separate Opinion of Judge Cançado Trindade in the Case of Certain Activities Carried Out by Nicaragua in the Border Area (Costa Rica v Nicaragua)* ICJ [2018] ICJ Rep 15 paras 9–11; David Daiches Raphael, *Concepts of Justice* (Oxford University Press 2001) 49–50; M Cherif Bassiouni, 'International Recognition of Victims' Rights' (2006) 6 Human Rights Law Review 203, 207 (n 13 for historical references); Luke Moffett, 'Transitional Justice and Reparations: Remedying the Past?' in Cheryl Lawther, Luke Moffett and Dov Jacobs (eds), *Research Handbook on Transitional Justice* (Edward Elgar Publishing 2017) 378.

26 Heidi Rombouts, Pietro Sardaro and Stef Vandeginste, 'The Right to Reparation for Victims of Gross and Systematic Violations of Human Rights' in Koen de Feyter and others (eds), *Out of the Ashes: Reparation for Victims of Gross and Systematic Human Rights Violations* (Intersentia 2005) 487.

help symbolise the perpetrator's commitment to apologise, make amends and take responsibility.[27]

However, as discussed in Section 4.2, an NSAG may lack the organisational capacity or resources to make reparations as a collectivity, may only be able to contribute to some reparations forms in whole or in part, or may cease to exist. Moreover, other NSAGs may simply be unwilling to provide any reparations to those who suffered harm. Consequently, any future responsibility regime for NSAGs should not make the provision of reparations only dependent upon these actors or, in other words, upon their practical capabilities or arbitrary willingness.[28] This was also evident from some of the legal materials examined in Chapter 2. Such challenges should rather inform the design of this responsibility regime, with a view to ensuring that effective reparations are offered to all victims, regardless of the identity of the perpetrator.[29]

The legal frameworks governing reparation by other non-state actors reflect similar considerations. For example, the ARIO contain an obligation for members of a responsible organisation to enable the organisation to fulfil its obligation to provide reparation.[30] Similarly, the International Criminal Court may order that the award of reparations be made through the Trust Fund for Victims when the convicted person's resources are insufficient.[31] To this end, the Trust Fund can, amongst others, raise funds and gather voluntary contributions.[32] The fact that all members of NSAGs convicted by the International Criminal Court thus far have been declared indigent in the corresponding reparations orders proves the Fund's vital importance for victims' redress.[33]

27 Brandon Hamber, 'Narrowing The Micro and Macro: A Psychological Perspective on Reparations in Societies in Transition' in Pablo de Greiff (ed), *The Handbook of Reparations* (Oxford University Press 2006) 566–567.

28 Íñigo Álvarez (n 9) 204.

29 UNGA, Basic Principles and Guidelines on the Right to a Remedy and Reparation for Victims of Gross Violations of International Human Rights Law and Serious Violations of International Humanitarian Law adopted by UNGA Res 60/147 on 16 December 2005 (21 March 2006) UN Doc A/RES/60/147 (UN Basic Principles and Guidelines) principles 3(c)-(d), 8 and 11(b).

30 Art 40(2) ARIO.

31 The possibility of holding the state responsible for reparation when a convicted individual is indigent did not make it into the final version of the ICC Statute. See Luke Moffett, 'Reparations for Victims at the International Criminal Court: A New Way Forward?' (2017) 21 The International Journal of Human Rights 1204, 1205.

32 Arts 75(2), 79 ICC Statute; Rules of Procedure and Evidence, Official Records of the Assembly of States Parties to the Rome Statute of the International Criminal Court, First Session, New York, ICC-ASP/1/3/ and Corr.1, part II.A (2002) Rule 98.

33 *Prosecutor v Thomas Lubanga Dyilo* ICC (Decision Establishing the Principles and Procedures to Be Applied to Reparations) ICC-01/04–01/06–2904 (7 August 2012) para 269, 277; *Prosecutor v Germain Katanga* ICC (Order for Reparations pursuant to Article 75 of the Statute) ICC-01/04–01/07–3728 (24 March 2017) para 327; *Prosecutor v Ahmad Al Faqi Al Mahdi* ICC (Reparations Order) ICC-01/12–01/15–236 (17 August 2017) para 113; *Prosecutor v Bosco Ntaganda* ICC (Addendum to the Reparations Order of 8 March 2021, ICC-01/04–02/06–2659) ICC-01/04–02/06 (14

This practically demonstrates that reparations cannot depend only on individual perpetrators.[34]

Consistent with the rationale behind these approaches, the UN Basic Principles and Guidelines require states to step in when the provision of reparations may be compromised by a lack of capacity or willingness of an NSAG. Principle 15 holds that "where a person, a legal person or other entity is found liable for reparation to a victim, such a party should provide reparation to the victim or compensate the State if the State has already provided reparation to the victim". Principle 16 adds that "States should endeavour to establish national programmes for reparation and other assistance to victims in the event that the parties liable for the harm suffered are unable or unwilling to meet their obligations." This recognises that an NSAG has a duty to provide reparation, whilst the state holds a subsidiary role when the group is unable or unwilling to meet its obligation. It ultimately ensures that victims have access to a remedy either way.[35] A similar approach has been included in other legal materials, such as the Declaration of Basic Principles of Justice for Victims of Crime and Abuse of Power, the Chicago Principles and the Belfast Guidelines on Reparations.[36] Furthermore, this approach is not voided by examples of international practice and enjoys support in legal scholarship.[37]

Following this approach, a subsidiary responsibility could fall on the territorial state to provide reparations for the wrongful acts of an NSAG that is unable or unwilling to take up responsibility for remedying the harm caused.[38] The state could implement this responsibility by, for example, creating a special

July 2023) para 21; Miriam Cohen, *Realizing Reparative Justice for International Crimes: From Theory to Practice* (Cambridge University Press 2020) 138–139, 141, 146–147.

34 African Court on Human and Peoples' Rights, 'Comparative Study on the Law and Practice of Reparations for Human Rights Violations' (2019) 13.

35 Moffett (n 2) 331.

36 UNGA, Declaration of Basic Principles of Justice for Victims of Crime and Abuse of Power adopted by UNGA Res 40/43 of 29 November 1985 (29 November 1985) UN Doc A/RES/40/34 para 12; Chicago Principles on Post-Conflict Justice (International Human Rights Law Institute 2007) principle 3.3; Belfast Guidelines on Reparations in Post-Conflict Societies (Queen's University Belfast 2022) 8, 12–14.

37 'Report of the International Commission of Inquiry on Darfur' (25 January 2005) paras 590–592; Moffett (n 2) 335; Francesca Capone, *Reparations for Child Victims of Armed Conflict* (Intersentia 2017) 102–103; Blázquez Rodríguez (n 13) 428; Joint Statement by Independent United Nations Human Rights Experts* on Human Rights Responsibilities of Armed Non-State Actors (25 February 2021); Reparations, Responsibility & Victimhood in Transitional Societies, 'Engaging Non-State Armed Groups on Reparations' (Queen's University Belfast 2022) 51; Luke Moffett, *Reparations and War: Finding Balance in Repairing the Past* (Oxford University Press 2023) 199, 223.

38 The term 'territorial state' is used to refer to the state on whose territory the NIAC takes place. As a NIAC can take place among NSAGs themselves, the territorial state is not necessarily the adversarial party in all NIACs.

trust fund or an administrative programme for reparations, or introducing a dedicated line in the yearly national budget.[39] This recognises that, within most conflict and post-conflict situations, reparations necessitate a comprehensive approach to address the full range of victims' needs, which responsible NSAGs alone are unlikely to meet. Current practice and legal scholarship are unclear on whether a state has a legal obligation to substitute an NSAG in providing redress for harm caused by the group's wrongdoings.[40] The responsibility arising from a state's failure to prevent or respond to acts by NSAGs does not provide a satisfactory basis, as it arises from the state's own wrongful conduct. Under human rights law, however, scholars have identified a more promising obligation for states to ensure the right to an effective remedy of all victims through reparations, particularly when a non-state perpetrator is indigent or unidentifiable.[41] The character of a state's subsidiary responsibility will eventually determine whether a state can be legally compelled, where it lacks political will, to step in. Regardless of its legal or at least moral nature, states have in some cases taken on, exclusively or along with the concerned NSAG, the provision of reparations to all victims of an armed conflict.[42]

Besides the territorial state, the international community could provide additional assistance in particularly weak states with limited resources, for instance through an international trust fund for victims of NSAGs' violations established under the auspices of the UN or another international process.[43] Processes involving third actors must ensure that reparations are accompanied by an acknowledgment of victimhood to ensure the measures' reparative nature

39 UN Basic Principles and Guidelines principle 16; UNOHCHR, 'Rule-of-Law Tools for Post-Conflict States: Reparation Programmes' (2008) 32; UNSG, 'Report of the Secretary-General's Panel of Experts on Accountability in Sri Lanka' (31 March 2011) 119, 122; Blázquez Rodríguez (n 13) 424–425.

40 Bassiouni (n 25) 223; Annyssa Bellal, 'Non-State Armed Groups in Transitional Justice Processes: Adapting to New Realities of Conflict' in Roger Duthie and Paul Seils (eds), *Justice Mosaics: How Context Shapes Transitional Justice in Fractured Societies* (ICTJ 2017) 243.

41 Rose (n 2) 316–317, 325–327; Luke Moffett, 'Violence and Repair: The Practice and Challenges of Non-State Armed Groups Engaging in Reparations' (2020) 102 International Review of the Red Cross 1057, 1062; Clara Sandoval, 'International Human Rights Adjudication, Subsidiarity, and Reparation for Victims of Armed Conflict' in Cristián Correa, Shuichi Furuya and Clara Sandoval (eds), *Reparation for Victims of Armed Conflict* (Cambridge University Press 2020) 180; Belfast Guidelines on Reparations in Post-Conflict Societies (n 36) 12.

42 See Comprehensive Agreement on Human Rights (Guatemala) (29 March 1994) VIII; Peace Agreement between the Government of Sierra Leone and the Revolutionary United Front of Sierra Leone (Lomé Peace Agreement) (7 July 1999) XXIX; Mark Freeman and Iván Orozco, *Negotiating Transitional Justice: Firsthand Lessons from Colombia and Beyond* (Cambridge University Press 2020) 153–154.

43 Similarly UNHRC, 'Report of the Special Rapporteur on Extrajudicial, Summary or Arbitrary Executions on Armed Non-State Actors: The Protection of the Right to Life' (5 June 2018) UN Doc A/HRC/38/44 paras 92, 100(a).

and distinguish them from humanitarian assistance, development or other initiatives.[44]

The different roles of these actors in repairing the harm caused by an NSAG culminate in a *cascading regime of responsibility for reparation*. Under this cascading regime, the responsible NSAG holds the principal duty to provide reparation, possibly complemented by the individual responsibility of group members;[45] the territorial state incurs a subsidiary responsibility to the extent that the NSAG is unable or unwilling to provide reparations; and, the international community takes a potential additional role. In practice, the state's subsidiary responsibility may be implemented as a complement to the partially exercised responsibility of the NSAG when, for example, the group does not have the capacity to fully meet victims' reparations needs (see further Section 4.4.1). This proposed scheme clarifies the potential relationships between the direct responsibility of an NSAG and the responsibility of other actors. A cascading regime not only ensures that an NSAG does not evade its obligations towards victims, but also seeks to better guarantee effective redress for victims.

4.4 Conceptualising a duty of non-state armed groups to provide reparation

4.4.1 Actor-specific approach

The duty to provide reparation is framed by the nature of the violation and the resulting harm that determine which forms of reparations are necessary in a particular case.[46] The type of entity responsible for the violation is not considered in this framing exercise.[47] Nevertheless, the ARS introduce elements of equity and reasonableness to allow for some flexibility in how full reparation should be accomplished. As will be discussed further in Section 4.4.2, restitution, for instance, should not result in a burden on the wrongdoer which is out of all proportion to the benefit obtained by the injured party.[48] As Ferstman correctly notes, this does not extend to limiting the amount or quality of redress that is required when the wrongdoer simply finds it challenging to comply.[49]

44 Rombouts, Sardaro and Vandeginste (n 26) 466.

45 See Chapter 3 Section 3.4.

46 *Case Concerning Avena and Other Mexican Nationals (Mexico v United States of America)* ICJ (Judgment) [2004] ICJ Rep 12 para 119; UNGA, 'Promotion of Truth, Justice, Reparation and Guarantees of Non-Recurrence – Note by the Secretary-General' (14 October 2014) UN Doc A/69/518 para 31; African Court on Human and Peoples' Rights (n 34) 2.

47 Carla Ferstman, *International Organizations and the Fight for Accountability: The Remedies and Reparations Gap* (Oxford University Press 2017) 68, 84. See, e.g., *Prosecutor v Bosco Ntaganda* ICC (Reparations Order) ICC-01/04–02/06 (8 March 2021) paras 97–98, 223; *Prosecutor v Bosco Ntaganda* (n 33) para 21.

48 ILC Commentary to Art 34 ARS 96 para 5.

49 Ferstman (n 47) 90.

However, it is proposed that the concrete application of a duty of reparation to a responsible NSAG could still consider that group's organisational capacity to provide the required forms of reparations. Despite diverging from the law of state responsibility, the proposal finds support in the current legal regulation of the conduct of NSAGs party to armed conflicts under the primary rules of international law. The examination in Chapter 1 regarding the primary obligations of NSAGs identified several elements that could equally inform the conceptualisation of NSAGs' international responsibility. Instead of determining the scope and/or content of the primary IHL and IHRL obligations of an NSAG in an abstract manner, these obligations are based on an evaluation of an NSAG's level of organisation to ensure the group's normative capacity. For example, a greater body of obligations likely binds an NSAG which exercises quasi-governmental authority in a certain part of the territory, compared to an NSAG with a minimum level of organisation sufficient for the sole application of Common Article 3 and potentially some core human rights norms. Consequently, this indicates that a different range of primary obligations may bind NSAGs, even though they belong to the same category of subjects of international law. At a fundamental level, international law exhibits a clear sensitivity to ensuring that a group can reasonably meet the obligations imposed.

A similar approach could be adopted for obligations of NSAGs under the secondary rules of international law. Particularly, *an actor-specific approach* could be taken to the application of the duty of a particular NSAG to provide reparation. This proposed approach involves a case-by-case evaluation of the responsible NSAG's level of organisation and resources, as indicators of the group's organisational capacity to meet the imposed obligations.[50] This evaluation aims to determine the concrete scope of the NSAG's duty of reparation.

Such an evaluation would consider two interrelated aspects, both of which concern the scope of the NSAG's duty to repair. The first aspect relates to the range of reparations forms which have been requested from the responsible NSAG to achieve *restitutio in integrum*. Following the proposed approach, an evaluation would help determine which of the requested forms of reparations could actually be provided by the NSAG. For example, an NSAG with a minimal organisational structure and few resources has been requested to provide satisfaction and monetary compensation. However, an evaluation made pursuant to the actor-specific approach reveals that the group lacks the capacity to provide for both. The NSAG could therefore be required to deliver the measures of satisfaction, such as a public apology, in the first place, as they require a lesser capacity that is within its capabilities. However, this approach depends on the state stepping in to ensure full reparation, as discussed below.

The second aspect focuses on the conduct necessary to deliver a specific form of redress or full reparation as such. In this regard, a particular NSAG may be required to contribute to, or at the very least facilitate, the provision of

50 Similarly Moffett (n 37) 199, 223.

reparations by states or other actors when it is unable to fully deliver the required redress. A similar argument is made by Mégret regarding the provision of symbolic reparations and guarantees of non-repetition by individuals. Although certain types of symbolic reparations may surpass the capacity of individual wrongdoers, he argues that individuals can still help deliver such reparations. Individuals may, for example, share information that is valuable in the search for the whereabouts of the disappeared, while being unable to conduct such a search entirely on their own. The same holds for guarantees of non-repetition. While no individual could be made wholly responsible for non-repetition, an individual could still contribute to maximising the chances of non-repetition (e.g. a convicted head of state that still retains significant influence with a part of the population).[51] This reasoning is also of relevance for NSAGs. For example, an NSAG may be unable to offer rehabilitation services to victims living under their control, but could still facilitate the provision of these services by, for example, allowing service providers access to these areas.[52] Similarly, a group could disclose information on certain violations or incidents, which could be an instrumental contribution to a truth-seeking process and the provision of satisfaction to victims. Overall, the proposed approach ensures that the diverse capabilities of NSAGs are considered, and translates into a differentiated and case-sensitive application of the duty to repair to these actors.

A crucial prerequisite for the viability of this proposed actor-specific approach is the application of the subsidiary responsibility of the territorial state. This would ensure that the state contributes to the extent that the responsible NSAG lacks capacity to provide the required redress (see Section 4.3 on this cascading regime). Hence, the fundamental principle of full reparation would be maintained through a division of responsibility between the NSAG and the state. The usefulness of the actor-specific approach combined with the subsidiary role for the state has been endorsed by the UN Special Rapporteur on the promotion of truth, justice, reparation and guarantees of non-recurrence.[53] The justification for this approach arises from the need to establish a realistic normative framework that reasonably ensures that reparation obligations of NSAGs can be effectively fulfilled in practice. Much like the primary rules of international law, this differentiated approach allows for a matching of

51 Frédéric Mégret, 'The International Criminal Court Statute and the Failure to Mention Symbolic Reparation' (2009) 16 International Review of Victimology 127, 137–138.

52 Similarly Jann K Kleffner and Liesbeth Zegveld, 'Establishing an Individual Complaints Procedure for Violations of International Humanitarian Law', *Yearbook of International Humanitarian Law*, vol 3 (2000) 400.

53 UNHRC, 'Report of the Special Rapporteur on the Promotion of Truth, Justice, Reparation and Guarantees of Non-Recurrence: Role and Responsibilities of Non-State Actors in Transitional Justice Processes' (12 July 2022) UN Doc A/HRC/51/34 paras 82, 87, 110.

the international legal framework with the realities on the ground by taking account of a particular NSAG's organisational capacity. In doing so, the concerns about the varying capabilities that may exist between, on the one hand, NSAGs themselves and, on the other, NSAGs and states are addressed.

As the organisational capacity of an NSAG would determine the extent to which it is concretely bound to make reparation, there is a need to consider what indicia might be employed to evaluate that capacity. According to Dudai, organisational features such as internal cohesion, discipline and strong leadership can be vital factors for the feasibility of engaging NSAGs in measures of truth-recovery and symbolic reparations.[54] Kleffner and Zegveld have argued for credible rather than illusory reparative measures from NSAGs, which, regarding monetary compensation, could entail taking account of the group's economic position.[55] Moffett draws, on his turn, distinctions between the capacities of centralised and community-based organisations to provide specific forms of reparations.[56] In addition, the indicative factors identified by the ICTY to evaluate the organisation requirement in IHL may also be useful. The group of factors which point to an NSAG's ability to speak with one voice could indicate that the NSAG is able to authoritatively deliver public apologies or acknowledge responsibility on behalf of the group.[57] Factors signalling the presence of a command structure could function as indicators of an NSAG's ability to implement guarantees of non-repetition among its members through the issuance and dissemination of internal regulations.[58]

All in all, the proposed actor-specific approach facilitates the development of a legal framework which can govern a possible duty of NSAGs to repair. The framework consists of abstract rules and principles that in their application to a responsible group allow for certain flexibility, which assists in accommodating the specificities of the case at hand. As a result, the entire range of reparations forms, that may be situationally required to deliver full reparation, can be applied to wrongful conduct committed by all types of NSAGs. Still, some forms of reparations, such as a public apology or the return of property, may require less organisational capacity than other forms, such as rehabilitation or compensation. Although most NSAGs are likely able to provide these former types of redress, the discussion indicates that minimally organised groups may still be able to contribute to, or at least facilitate, the delivery of these latter measures.

The proposed approach can be applied to all types of NSAGs, ranging from NSAGs which have a minimum level of organisation to highly organised groups which exercise control over a territory through state-like institutions. As a

54 Dudai (n 2) 797–798.
55 Kleffner and Zegveld (n 52) 399.
56 Moffett (n 41) 1070.
57 *Prosecutor v Boškoski and Tarčulovski* ICTY (Trial Judgment) IT-04–82-T (10 July 2008) para 203.
58 Ibid. para 199.

result, a broader approach is taken which deviates from the tendency in international law to emphasise the responsibility of NSAGs with territorial control or state-like characteristics.[59] This position is supported by several arguments. In the words of the Permanent Court of International Justice, "[i]t is a principle of international law that the breach of an engagement involves an obligation to make reparation in an adequate form. Reparation is therefore the indispensable complement of a failure to apply a convention".[60] From such a strict legal perspective, it appears illogical that NSAGs lacking territorial control would be exempt from a duty to make reparation when violating their primary obligations under Common Article 3, contrary to other groups that are also bound by Additional Protocol II. Capacity concerns could be raised in respect of groups with very minimal levels of organisation. Yet, the proposed approach responds directly to these concerns, for example, by only obliging an NSAG to contribute to a specific selection or portion of the requested forms of reparation, while the subsidiary responsibility of the state is triggered. Furthermore, this broad approach prevents the potential opening of a responsibility gap when an NSAG no longer holds territorial control. As was discussed in Section 4.2, an NSAG's level of organisation can fluctuate considerably throughout an armed conflict. Such a situation would otherwise provoke the question: 'can such a group still be held to its duty to make reparation or does it no longer fall within the law of international responsibility?' Finally, it is morally unfair to create unequal legal treatment concerning reparation between the victims of different types of NSAGs. The actor-specific approach has the potential to avoid this situation.

4.4.2 Principle of full reparation

As formulated by the International Court of Justice, "it is well established in general international law that a State which bears responsibility for an internationally wrongful act is under an obligation to make full reparation for the injury caused by that act".[61] This principle of full reparation or *restitutio in integrum* demands that "reparations must, as far as possible, wipe out all consequences of the illegal act and reestablish the situation which would, in all probability have existed if that act had not been committed".[62] The principle can be found in Articles 31 and 34 of the ARS and ARIO respectively, as well as

59 See Chapter 2 Section 2.4.

60 *Case Concerning the Factory at Chorzów (Germany v Poland)* PCIJ (Jurisdiction) [1927] PCIJ Rep Series A No 9 21. See also Chapter 2 Section 2.2.1.

61 *Case Concerning Armed Activities on the Territory of the Congo (Congo v Uganda)* ICJ (Judgment) [2005] ICJ Rep 168 para 259.

62 *Factory at Chorzów Case (Merits)* (n 19) 47; *Case of Velásquez Rodríguez v Honduras* IACtHR (Judgment Merits) Series C No 4 (29 July 1988) para 166; *Papamichalopoulos v Greece (Article 50)* ECtHR (Judgment) Series A No 330-B (31 October 1995) para 36; *Scordino v Italy (No 1)* ECtHR (Judgment) App No 36813/97 (29 March 2006) paras 246–247.

in principle 18 of the UN Basic Principles and Guidelines. Following this standard, the obligation to make full reparation is presented in the law of responsibility as one of the main legal consequences arising from the commission of an internationally wrongful act.[63] However, the principle has been interpreted in different ways. The ARS place the emphasis on restitution and compensation, whereas certain human rights instruments and bodies have taken a broader approach to achieving full reparation.[64]

As Section 4.2 reveals, the application of this core principle to NSAGs may face significant challenges. These arise from differences in capacity between NSAGs and states. An NSAG may lack the necessary capacity to implement the full range of reparations measures required to restore the *status quo ante*. At the same time, similar concerns have been voiced in relation to states. Roht-Arriaza notes that there is "a basic paradox at the heart of reparations", given that the objective of full reparation is impossible to reach in practice: what could replace the loss of a loved one, or a whole family; a generation of friends; the destruction of one's home, culture and community?[65] Accordingly, there is a general recognition among scholars that this standard is difficult to satisfy, even for states, especially where cases concern serious or massive violations.[66] That being said, states will usually be better equipped to provide for reparations in comparison to NSAGs. They have, for instance, the power to raise taxes, the ability to reserve a line in the national budget for reparations and, often, the institutional capacity to set up sophisticated reparations programmes.[67]

Despite the associated practical difficulties, a lack of capacity does not provide a sufficient justification to exempt a responsible NSAG from the well-established principle of full reparation.[68] Allowing for such an exemption would result in a lower standard for NSAGs and unequal treatment between the victims of these groups and the victims of states. Instead, full reparation should remain the rule. The actor-specific approach, detailed in the previous section, would provide a tool to respond where an NSAG does not hold the

63 ILC Commentary to Art 31 ARS 91 paras 1–3.

64 Arts 34–37 ARS; UN Basic Principles and Guidelines principles 18–23; *Factory at Chorzów Case (Merits)* (n 19) 47; Jo Pasqualacci, *The Practice and Procedure of the Inter-American Court of Human Rights* (Cambridge University Press 2013) 188–250; Veronika Fikfak, 'Changing State Behaviour: Damages before the European Court of Human Rights' (2018) 29 European Journal of International Law 1091, 1099–1100.

65 Naomi Roht-Arriaza, 'Reparations Decisions and Dilemmas' (2004) 27 Hastings International and Comparative Law Review 157, 158.

66 Jemima García-Godos, 'Victim Reparations in the Peruvian Truth Commission and the Challenge of Historical Interpretation' (2008) 2 International Journal of Transitional Justice 63, 66; Evans (n 6) 29; Dinah Shelton, *Remedies in International Human Rights Law* (3rd edn, Oxford University Press 2015) 34.

67 Similarly, Pellet (n 6) 49–50.

68 Similarly regarding international organisations, ILC Commentary to Art 31 ARIO 77 paras 3–4.

capacity to provide the required forms of reparations, or where it can only contribute to a certain extent. Moreover, in such cases, the cascading regime of responsibility for reparation would ensure that the territorial state would complement the efforts of the NSAG, insofar it lacks capacity, in a subsidiary manner. This would ultimately secure full reparation to a greater extent than would otherwise be possible.[69] Nevertheless, certain forms of reparations, such as public apologies, cannot be substituted by the state. The role of the NSAG would thus be indispensable in attaining full reparation.[70]

The ILC Commentary to Article 34 ARS notes that concerns have been raised that the principle of full reparation may lead to disproportionate requirements for responsible states. In the ARS, the principle of proportionality is addressed within each form of redress: restitution is excluded when it involves a burden out of all proportion to the benefit gained by the injured party, while satisfaction must "not be out of proportion to the injury".[71] An analogous application to NSAGs would prevent the duty of full reparation from becoming a disproportionate burden, which might discourage groups from engaging in reparations processes.[72] Disproportionality could potentially also result in punitive damages, which are not recognised in international law.

The principle included in Article 32 ARS provides that a liable state may not invoke the provisions of internal law as a justification for its failure to provide full reparation. This rule could apply analogously to NSAGs. In such a context, internal law could be understood as codes of conduct or similar instruments, which groups may adopt to regulate members' internal behaviour and their relations outside of the group by imposing certain rules and responsibilities.[73]

4.4.3 Forms of reparations

Full reparation may include five principal forms: restitution, compensation, rehabilitation, satisfaction and guarantees of non-repetition.[74] Starting from their conceptualisation in international law, the analogous application of these reparations forms to NSAGs is examined. This attends to one of the findings of Chapter 2, which suggests that all forms should be considered when examining NSAGs' duty of reparation. Moreover, it provides the opportunity to make the proposed actor-specific approach more concrete and inform the operationalisation of NSAGs' duty of reparation by considering related practice. The examples expressed below should be read in conjunction with the practice covering

69 See Section 4.3.
70 Íñigo Álvarez (n 9) 197.
71 ILC Commentary to Art 34 ARS 96 para 5. See also UN Basic Principles and Guidelines principle 15.
72 Moffett (n 2) 335.
73 Similarly, Art 32 ARIO. Olivier Bangerter, 'A Collection of Codes of Conduct Issued by Armed Groups' (2011) 93 International Review of the Red Cross 483, 484.
74 UN Basic Principles and Guidelines principles 18–23.

the full range of reparations forms discussed in Chapter 2. In addition to these traditional forms, adjusted or new reparations forms tailored to the specific capabilities of an NSAG could also be considered, as further discussed in Chapter 6.

4.4.3.1 Restitution

The obligation to make restitution can be transposed to NSAGs without too many difficulties. In its simplest form, restitution can involve the release of persons wrongly detained or the return of property wrongly seized during times of NIAC.[75] As an example, a 2014 UN Human Rights Council resolution called on Syrian NSAGs to immediately and unconditionally release human rights defenders and all civilians they had detained.[76] There are cases of NSAGs agreeing to or engaging in restitution. All sides to the Somali Agreement on Implementing the Cease-fire and on Modalities of Disarmament agreed to return properties unlawfully taken during the hostilities.[77] The National Liberation Army (ELN) and the FARC-EP set up a joint reparations commission in Arauca, Colombia, which received victims' complaints and ordered restitution. Displaced persons were awarded a parcel of land and productive projects were financed, while farmers who lost their homes received financial support for the construction of new houses.[78]

4.4.3.2 Compensation

NSAGs can contribute with their resources, such as financial and material assets, to the reparation of harms suffered by victims through monetary payments. The International Commission of Inquiry on Darfur emphasised the duty of NSAGs to pay compensation, while some NSAGs such as the RUF in Sierra Leone have included compensatory measures within their codes of conduct.[79] The Syrian Democratic Forces reportedly provided compensation for the damage caused and the items stolen by its members during an attack against a Syrian hospital in 2021.[80] Monetary compensation is not without significant challenges in the context of armed conflict. NSAGs may have hid or laundered their assets, victimisation may be so immense that compensation can "actually

75 Art 35 ARS, see also ILC Commentary to Art 35 ARS 96–97 paras 1, 5; UN Basic Principles and Guidelines principle 19; Art 35 ARIO; Íñigo Álvarez (n 9) 201.
76 UNHRC, Res 27/16 (3 October 2014) UN Doc A/HRC/RES/27/16 paras 12, 15.
77 Somali Agreement on Implementing the Cease-fire and on Modalities of Disarmament (15 January 1993) III.
78 '¿Juntos Pero No Revueltos?' *El Espectador* (1 September 2013).
79 'Report of the International Commission of Inquiry on Darfur' (n 37) para 175; Bangerter (n 73) 489, 497.
80 UNHRC, 'Report of the Independent International Commission of Inquiry on the Syrian Arab Republic' (13 August 2021) UN Doc A/HRC/48/70 para 104.

bankrupt the [...] armed opposition group", or NSAGs may simply lack resources.[81] Nevertheless, limited resources can still be used to contribute, even symbolically, to compensation or the financing of other reparations measures through, for instance, a fund and/or an administrative reparations programme, which could also benefit from other financial contributors, such as the state or the international community. Within this context, the UN Secretary-General and the Sierra Leone Truth and Reconciliation Commission, respectively, have made recommendations to make NSAGs financially liable to their victims by seizing their assets for reparation purposes.[82] For instance, Colombia's Reparations Fund is made up of, i.a., the proceeds of fines imposed on NSAGs in judicial and administrative proceedings and voluntary contributions made by governments, international organisations and other entities.[83] Asset recovery for compensation purposes could also be linked to demobilisation and disarmament, or peace or justice processes, as is for instance the case in Colombia (see Part 3 of this book).[84]

4.4.3.3 Rehabilitation

Rehabilitation has been recognised as being crucial to ensuring that victims can successfully reintegrate into society, including through medical and psychological care, as well as legal, social and educational services.[85] It immediately becomes clear from the nature of these services, that an NSAG should have a significant level of institutional capacity somewhat comparable to that of states.[86] Despite this reality, NSAGs can still play a role in the provision, or at least the facilitation, of rehabilitation.[87] As explained by Dudai, whilst analysing actions taken by the IRA in Northern Ireland, some rehabilitative measures are not just aimed at the health of the victim, but also at their "civic status": for example, by restoring the good name of victims through public declarations of their innocence.[88] While seemingly inapplicable to NSAGs, the IRA engaged in

81 Kleffner and Zegveld (n 52) 399; Rose (n 2) 309–310.

82 UNGA and UNSC, 'The Causes of Conflict and the Promotion of Durable Peace and Sustainable Development in Africa, Report of the Secretary-General' (13 April 1998) UN Doc A/52/871-S/1998/318 para 50; Sierra Leone Truth and Reconciliation Commission, 'Witness to Truth' (2004) Vol 2 ch 3 p 183; UNGA (n 46) para 57(b).

83 Art 177 Law No 1448 of 2011 (Victims' Law) (Colombia).

84 UNHRC (n 43) para 91.

85 UN Basic Principles and Guidelines principle 21; Marco Sassòli, *International Humanitarian Law: Rules, Controversies, and Solutions to Problems Arising in Warfare* (Edward Elgar Publishing Limited 2019) para 5.70; UNHRC, 'Report of the Special Rapporteur on the Promotion of Truth, Justice, Reparation and Guarantees of Non-Recurrence' (11 July 2019) UN Doc A/HRC/42/45 paras 98, 103.

86 Anne-Marie La Rosa, 'Sanctions as a Means of Obtaining Greater Respect for Humanitarian Law: A Review of Their Effectiveness' (2008) 90 International Review of the Red Cross 221, 236.

87 Íñigo Álvarez (n 9) 201.

88 UNOHCHR (n 39) 25.

such a process regarding individuals who were killed by the group after being wrongfully accused of being informants. The relatives and friends of those killed sought such declarations, which involved the restoration of the good name and dignity of their loved ones, directly from the NSAG and not from the state. Dudai reported that the declarations had positive results *vis-à-vis* their rehabilitation.[89] In other instances, a responsible NSAG could at the least allow for rehabilitative measures by giving access to relevant aid organisations that provide such services.[90] For instance, NSAGs that are signatories to the Geneva Call's Deed of Commitment on sexual violence and gender discrimination, pledge to "encourage and facilitate", among other concerns:

- access to services, including medical, psychological, social and legal services, in cooperation with humanitarian and development organisations where appropriate;
- rehabilitation programmes and actions that facilitate social reintegration of victims.[91]

4.4.3.4 Satisfaction

Holding NSAGs responsible for satisfaction measures is not uncontested. Some scholars argue that this form of redress is a prerogative of states. Tomuschat, for example, argues that apologies presented by non-state actors are "no more than a gesture of courtesy and do not have the same weight as official apologies offered by a State".[92] Contrary to this view, a more sensible approach would be to give victims a central role in determining whether such reparations are actually wanted from an NSAG in a given case. Kleffner, in his turn, questions to what extent Article 37(3) ARS can be applied to NSAGs. The article provides that satisfaction "may not take a form humiliating to the responsible State" and, therefore, would imply that the law regulating NSAGs' responsibility should, by analogy, protect the dignity of such groups. Instead, he suggests that punitive damages could be imposed on NSAGs.[93] Although it is true that NSAGs' distinct nature in international law may affect the extent to which the content of state responsibility can be transposed, reparations should remain a victim- rather than a perpetrator-oriented effort. Following present tendencies in international law, reparations should be conceptualised as a compensatory

89 Dudai (n 2) 801–804.
90 Kleffner and Zegveld (n 52) 400.
91 Geneva Call, 'Deed of Commitment for the Prohibition of Sexual Violence in Situations of Armed Conflict and towards the Elimination of Gender Discrimination' para 4.
92 Christian Tomuschat, 'The Responsibility of Other Entities: Private Individuals' in James Crawford, Alain Pellet and Simon Olleson (eds), *The Law of International Responsibility* (Oxford University Press 2010) 320.
93 Kleffner (n 11) 264–265.

rather than punitive tool, all the while taking the principle of proportionality into account. Punitive practices may also disincentive NSAGs from engaging in reparations processes.[94]

The potential of NSAGs to provide measures of satisfaction and their reparative impact on victims should not be dismissed, as recognised by an increasing number of scholars and practitioners. NSAGs' acknowledgement of responsibility and apologies can, for instance, contribute to vindicating the experiences of victims and preventing the recurrence of harmful actions by conveying moral messages about their wrongfulness.[95] Their contributions to the search, localisation and recovery of the disappeared or the clarification of facts can be crucial, especially when they are the only entity holding the necessary information.[96] Moreover, as complex organisations, NSAGs are tied together through, i.a., bonds of loyalty and shared history, common values and objectives. When paired with a sufficiently strong organisational structure, this may provide the opportunity to maximise such relations by mobilising members to collectively crowd source information.[97] The IRA in Northern Ireland and the ANC in South Africa have, for instance, engaged in truth-recovery processes and other symbolic measures respectively, while other groups have contributed to the work of truth commissions or, alternatively, such commissions have recommended symbolic reparations from NSAGs in their final reports.[98] NSAGs, such as the FARC-EP as part of Colombia's transitional justice process and the Syrian Democratic Forces, have made statements of regret and apology for unlawful conduct and the resulting harm.[99] In Section 4.5.2.3 and in Part 3 of this book, public apologies by NSAGs are further explored, including practice from Colombia.

94 Moffett (n 41) 1082–1083.

95 Reparations, Responsibility & Victimhood in Transitional Societies (n 37) 36.

96 Lars Waldorf, 'Ex-Combatants and Truth Commissions' in Ana Cutter Patel, Pablo de Greiff and Lars Waldorf (eds), *Disarming the Past: Transitional Justice and Ex-combatants* (Social Science Research Council 2009) 120–121; Blázquez Rodríguez (n 13) 419–420.

97 Isabella Bueno, 'Mass Victimization and Restorative Justice in Colombia: Pathways towards Peace and Reconciliation?' (KU Leuven 2013) 352; Luke Moffett and others, 'Alternative Sanctions Before The Special Jurisdiction For Peace: Reflections on International Law and Transitional Justice' (Queen's University Belfast 2019) paras 130, 132; Stephen Oola and Luke Moffett, '"Cul Pi Bal" Reparations for the Northern Ugandan Conflict' (Queen's University Belfast 2020) 52.

98 Sierra Leone Truth and Reconciliation Commission (n 82) ch 3 p 199 para 518; Dudai (n 2); Lauren Dempster, 'The Republican Movement, "Disappearing" and Framing the Past in Northern Ireland' (2016) 10 International Journal of Transitional Justice 250, 255–257; UNHRC (n 43) para 94; Moffett and others (n 97) paras 127–128.

99 Ezequiel Heffes, 'Responsible Rebels: Exploring Correlations Between Compliance and Reparations in Non-International Armed Conflicts' (2022) 14 Journal of Human Rights Practice 415, 425–426.

4.4.3.5 Guarantees of non-repetition

NSAGs can play a potential role in contributing to guarantees of non-repetition. By analogy with some of the measures included in the UN Basic Principles and Guidelines, NSAGs could pass or modify their internal laws, such as codes of conduct, and provide training to their members to prevent the recurrence of wrongful conduct.[100] The UN Security Council, for example, has called on parties to armed conflict to make and implement commitments to combat sexual violence, which could include, i.a., the issuance of clear orders through chains of command that prohibit sexual violence and the prohibition of such violence in codes of conduct, military field manuals or the equivalent.[101] The NSAG *Alliance du Peuple pour un Congo Libre et Souverain*, from the Democratic Republic of Congo, modified their internal regulations to implement humanitarian norms, following engagement with Geneva Call.[102] Moreover, NSAGs can collectively commit to their disarmament, demobilisation and political transformation, and can give public assurances to never again engage in violence.[103] These are important aspects of the 2016 peace agreement with the FARC-EP and the related transitional justice system in Colombia, examined in Chapter 6. Another example is the Commission on the Truth for El Salvador which recommended the dismantlement of illegal armed groups as a preventative measure.[104] In Northern Ireland, former fighters have participated in community-based restorative justice schemes and educational programmes to deliver on non-recurrence of violence.[105]

4.5 Reparations by non-state armed groups during and after armed conflict

Reparations are not legally restricted in time to an ongoing armed conflict or to its aftermath. Generally, however, they have been claimed and granted after an

100 UN Basic Principles and Guidelines principle 23(e)(f)(h); Liesbeth Zegveld, *The Accountability of Armed Opposition Groups* (Cambridge University Press 2002) 222; Ezequiel Heffes and Brian Frenkel, 'The International Responsibility of Non-State Armed Groups: In Search of the Applicable Rules' (2017) 8 Goettingen Journal of International Law 39, 69; Íñigo Álvarez (n 9) 190–191.

101 UNSC, Res 1960 (16 December 2010) UN Doc S/RES/1960 para 5. See also, e.g., UNSC, Res 2121 (10 October 2013) UN Doc S/RES/2121 para 15.

102 Heffes (n 99) 426.

103 UNCHR, 'Report of the Independent Expert to Update the Set of Principles to Combat Impunity, Diane Orentlicher' (8 February 2005) UN Doc E/CN.4/2005/102/Add.1 principle 37; Moffett (n 2) 335; UNHRC, 'Report of the Special Rapporteur on the Promotion of Truth, Justice, Reparations and Guarantees of Non-Recurrence' (7 September 2015) UN Doc A/HRC/30/42 para 23; Bellal (n 40) 247.

104 Commission on the Truth for El Salvador, 'From Madness to Hope: The 12-Year War in El Salvador' (1993) UN Doc S/25500 179–180.

105 UNHRC (n 53) paras 94–95.

armed conflict has ended.[106] In Chapter 2, it was concluded that NSAGs have been called upon to provide reparations both during and after NIACs, indicating that the international responsibility of such actors is relevant in both situations.[107] It seems sensible to argue that an NSAG holds a duty of reparation for its own wrongful conduct at least for the duration of the conflict: when it still legally exists. In times of conflict, NSAGs may have different motivations to engage in reparations, which may be a way for these actors to, for example, maintain their relations with the civilian population on whose support they depend, seek legitimacy, improve moral and discipline within the group, or improve compliance with international law.[108] However, injured states may be reluctant to call on the responsible NSAG due to its temporary nature or the state's fear that this may imply some form of recognition.[109] Post-conflict reparations by NSAGs face a distinct legal challenge. As concluded in Chapter 1, NSAGs are temporary subjects of international law. Therefore, it is necessary to develop a regime of international responsibility that provides answers to whether and how NSAGs could still be called upon in a post-conflict setting.[110] Ultimately, a central question arises: 'how can an NSAG carry out a duty to repair when it no longer exists from an international legal perspective?' Put differently, 'upon whom can the victims call?'

4.5.1 Engagement on reparations during and at the end of an armed conflict

This section considers the engagement with NSAGs on the question of reparations during and at the end of an armed conflict. In this study, the concept of 'engagement' is used in two ways: on the one hand, it generally refers to the participation or involvement of NSAGs in the provision of redress (engagement *in*; see, e.g., Section 4.4.3) and, on the other hand, it concerns engagement *with* NSAGs *on* the issue of reparations. The following discussion deals with the latter notion.

In legal scholarship and practice concerning NSAGs, the concept of engagement generally features in discussions which are concerned with enhancing compliance by such groups with existing primary obligations of IHL through a

106 Jemima García-Godos and Knut Andreas O Lid, 'Transitional Justice and Victims' Rights before the End of a Conflict: The Unusual Case of Colombia' (2010) 42 Journal of Latin American Studies 487, 487–488; Konstantinos Mastorodimos, *Armed Non-State Actors in International Humanitarian and Human Rights Law: Foundation and Framework of Obligations, and Rules on Accountability* (Ashgate 2016) 133.

107 Íñigo Álvarez (n 9) 193.

108 Heffes (n 99) 428; Moffett (n 37) 201–202, 207.

109 Patrick Dumberry, *Rebellions and Civil Wars: State Responsibility for the Conduct of Insurgents* (Cambridge University Press 2021) 147, 205–206.

110 Kleffner (n 11) 265.

meaningful exchange on IHL matters.[111] Here, the notion is extended to the sphere of secondary norms. The objective is to conceptualise how a similar notion of engagement with NSAGs could be framed regarding reparations, and which potential opportunities and challenges could arise. The discussion can draw partly from insights offered by the aforementioned body of existing literature on engagement in IHL.

Based on the conceptualisation of 'engagement' offered by Bellal, engagement with an NSAG on reparations would entail that a meaningful contact is established with the group so as to exchange on the question of redress in an effort to promote its delivery.[112] Similar to efforts seeking to improve respect for primary norms, such engagement could take place through voluntary or non-coercive mechanisms, such as the use of dialogue or negotiation, which could even employ certain incentives to promote engagement.[113] In applying the words of Dudai and McEvoy, this would entail a consideration that, at least in some contexts, "armed groups can be part of the solution and not just the problem".[114] Such engagement could take place on the basis of at least two distinct purposes. First of all, from a *de lege ferenda* perspective, it could seek to make an NSAG comply voluntarily with its hard law duty to provide reparation. Depending on the context, this could potentially result in more effective compliance than if it were enforced. Second, it could take place regardless of any question of legal responsibility. Instead, it would start from the assumption that NSAGs themselves can play an important role in reparations, which can be stimulated through engagement. Monitoring and/or reporting systems could accompany voluntary commitments to reparations undertaken by NSAGs.[115]

111 See, e.g., Cedric Ryngaert and Anneleen Van de Meulebroucke, 'Enhancing and Enforcing Compliance with International Humanitarian Law by Non-State Armed Groups: An Inquiry into Some Mechanisms' (2011) 16 Journal of Conflict & Security Law 443; Annyssa Bellal, 'Welcome on Board: Improving Respect for International Humanitarian Law Through the Engagement of Armed Non-State Actors', *Yearbook of International Humanitarian Law*, vol 19 (TMC Asser Press 2016); Ezequiel Heffes, Marcos D Kotlik and Manuel J Ventura (eds), *International Humanitarian Law and Non-State Actors* (TMC Asser Press 2020) Part IV.

112 Bellal (n 111) 38.

113 Compare with engagement efforts to enhance NSAGs' compliance with international primary norms through, i.a., awareness raising, dissemination, persuasion, technical support or capacity building, negotiation, dialogue and advocacy as well as the role of incentives. See UNGA and UNSC, 'Report of the Secretary-General on Children and Armed Conflict' (15 May 2014) UN Doc A/68/878-S/2014/339 para 15; Bellal (n 111) 47–51; UNGA, 'One Humanity: Shared Responsibility, Report of the Secretary-General for the World Humanitarian Summit' (2 February 2016) UN Doc A/70/709 para 51.

114 Ron Dudai and Kieran McEvoy, 'Thinking Critically about Armed Groups and Human Rights Praxis' (2012) 4 Journal of Human Rights Practice 1, 17, 19.

115 Íñigo Álvarez (n 9) 194.

The first form of engagement could potentially take place between an NSAG and a state as part of a peace, demobilisation or political transformation process. It could result in reaffirming an NSAG's duty to repair in a special agreement or even in the inclusion of specific obligations in a mutual accord.[116] Instead of confining such groups to the roles of 'passive recipients of sanctions' or 'security threats to be managed', their potential as positive actors in the reparations process could be recognised.[117] It could promote a sense of active responsibility on the part of NSAGs to make amends, which would require them to comprehend the consequences of their actions and to form the willingness to repair.[118] Experts tend to agree that NSAGs should be allowed to take ownership by actively participating in initiatives for dealing with the past or, more broadly, in peace-making efforts, which are "more likely to be sustained if it is owned and driven by all relevant conflicting actors and their constituencies".[119] This involves understanding justice and security as being complementary and not mutually exclusive.[120]

The second form of engagement is more likely to take place with actors beyond the territorial state. During situations of armed conflict, actors such as international organisations or non-governmental organisations could focus their efforts on urging NSAGs to internalise rules on reparations in their internal codes of conduct or other relevant regulations, as a useful framework for engagement.[121] This could result in the setting of a useful internal benchmark for responsibility, on which, for instance, civilian communities could rely in their interactions with such groups. Research suggests that such an internalisation process creates a sense of

116 See Chapter 2 for concrete examples of such practice. Common Art 3(3) of the 1949 Geneva Conventions. Compare to Ryngaert and Van de Meulebroucke (n 111) 453–455.

117 Dudai and McEvoy (n 114) 16–17.

118 John Braithwaite, *Restorative Justice and Responsive Regulation* (Oxford University Press 2002) 129; Jennifer Larson Sawin and Howard Zehr, 'The Ideas of Engagement and Empowerment' in Gerry Johnstone and Daniel W Van Ness (eds), *Handbook of Restorative Justice* (Willan Publishing 2007) 45, 50.

119 Kieran McEvoy and Peter Shirlow, 'Re-Imagining DDR: Ex-Combatants, Leadership and Moral Agency in Conflict Transformation' (2009) 13 Theoretical Criminology 31; Véronique Dudouet and Hans J Giessmann, 'From Combatants to Peacebuilders: A Case for Inclusive, Participatory and Holistic Security Transitions' (Berghof Foundation 2012) 12, 34; Bellal (n 40) 236, 247; Moffett and others (n 97) para 123; Kieran McEvoy, Cheryl Lawther and Luke Moffett, 'Changing the Script: Non-State Armed Groups, Restorative Justice and Reparations' (2022) 14 Journal of Human Rights Practice 454.

120 Dudouet and Giessmann (n 119) 32.

121 Caroline Holmqvist, 'Engaging Armed Non-State Actors in Post-Conflict Settings' in Alan Bryden and Heiner Hänggi (eds), *Security Governance in Post-Conflict Peacebuilding* (DCAF 2005) 51–53; UNHRC (n 53) para 78. For example, civil society actors have called on the Ansar Allah (Houthi) armed group in Yemen to provide redress in accordance with international standards: Mwatana for Human Rights and Lowenstein International Human Rights Clinic Yale Law School, 'Returned to Zero: The Case for Reparations to Civilians in Yemen' (2022) 24–25.

ownership and commitment to ensure respect for the law, which, being normally imposed upon NSAGs, traditionally leaves their views and consent aside.[122] It could stimulate comprehension of the concept of reparation and how it could be appropriately granted, in line with international norms and standards, through, for instance, the NSAG's own administration of justice or mechanisms.[123] This can be illustrated more concretely through the work of Geneva Call, which, as a humanitarian organisation, recognises NSAGs as key actors in solving problems relating to the implementation of IHL in armed conflict. The organisation engages with NSAGs through an innovative tool, its so-called Deed of Commitment, which allows groups to formally commit to respecting and being held accountable to certain humanitarian norms.[124] Some of the agreed measures can be understood as reparations by NSAGs in times of armed conflict. As an example of guarantees of non-repetition, the Restoration Council of Shan State, from Myanmar, signed the Deed for the Protection of Children in 2019 and committed to implement an age verification mechanism to avoid the recruitment of children.[125] In the Deed of Commitment for the Prohibition of Sexual Violence in Situations of Armed Conflict and towards the Elimination of Gender Discrimination signatory NSAGs expressly commit themselves to encourage and facilitate the provision of reparations to victims.[126]

Another possibility is that measures akin to reparations under international law already form part of NSAGs' policies or practices. Under the FARC-EP's administration of justice, victims were, for instance, entitled to receive compensation for the harm done to them, including moral damages. This often included a community fine, which would be used to cover expenses benefitting the community as a whole (e.g. for the building of a school or repairing of a road).[127]

122 Marco Sassòli, 'Taking Armed Groups Seriously: Ways to Improve Their Compliance with International Humanitarian Law' (2010) 1 Journal of International Humanitarian Legal Studies 5, 29–30; Olivier Bangerter, 'Comment – Persuading Armed Groups to Better Respect International Humanitarian Law' in Heike Krieger (ed), *Inducing Compliance with International Humanitarian Law: Lessons from the African Great Lakes Region* (Cambridge University Press 2015) 113; Anne Quintin and Marie-Louise Tougas, 'Generating Respect for the Law by Non-State Armed Groups: The ICRC's Role and Activities' in Ezequiel Heffes, Marcos D Kotlik and Manuel J Ventura (eds), *International Humanitarian Law and Non-State Actors* (TMC Asser Press 2020) 359–360.

123 Geneva Academy of International Humanitarian Law and Human Rights, 'Rules of Engagement: Protecting Civilians through Dialogue with Armed Non-State Actors' (2011) 35.

124 See Ezequiel Heffes, 'Non-State Actors Engaging Non-State Actors: The Experience of Geneva Call in NIACs' in Ezequiel Heffes, Marcos D Kotlik and Manuel J Ventura (eds), *International Humanitarian Law and Non-State Actors* (TMC Asser Press 2020).

125 For more examples, Heffes (n 99) 427.

126 Geneva Call (n 91) para 4.

127 René Provost, 'FARC Justice: Rebel Rule of Law' (2018) 8 UC Irvine Law Review 227, 251.

Other examples can be found in the codes of conduct of other NSAGs. For instance, the New People's Army (NPA), from the Philippines, includes in their 'Basic Rules' as one of the 'Eight Points of Attention': "compensate all damages", while, in Sierra Leone, the RUF's 'Eight Codes of Conduct' provides that fighters should vis-á-vis civilians "pay for everything that you demand or damage".[128] In such cases, engagement could ensure that such measures are implemented in compliance with international legal standards.

In respect of both forms of engagement, legal-political challenges emanating from counter-terrorism legislation and the general concern of states about conferring legitimacy on NSAGs could stand in the way of any meaningful engagement.[129] To counter such obstacles, one must be clear about the legal and moral frameworks in which engagement takes place. These could emphasise the role of responsible NSAGs as duty bearers or the objective of providing redress and relief to victims.[130] Furthermore, in light of the sheer diversity of NSAGs involved in NIACs, research and practice on engagement suggests that a context-specific approach, which takes into account the particularities of the relevant NSAG, is essential.[131] Consequently, it requires obtaining a deep understanding of the specific conflict dynamics and a group's features in terms of their grievances, organisational structure, ideology, objectives, values and overall capacity regarding reparations, among other considerations.[132] This provides for a broader framework than just the law under which NSAGs can be engaged.[133] It can, for instance, shed light on which incentives can foster willingness.[134] This may be influenced by considerations regarding NSAGs' self-image; their moral, political and/or religious convictions; or their desire to strengthen their community ties, among other possibilities.[135] NSAGs are not neutral actors. Instead, they may seek to attain their own set of goals through their participation in processes of dealing with the past. In Colombia, for instance, the FARC-EP and the ELN began a joint initiative to provide reparations in

128 Bangerter (n 73) 489–490, 497; Geneva Call, 'Their Words: Directory of Armed Non-State Actor Humanitarian Commitments' <http://theirwords.org/>.

129 Bellal (n 40) 235; Sassòli (n 85) para 10.258; Quintin and Tougas (n 122) 380–382.

130 Ioana Cismas, *Religious Actors and International Law* (Oxford University Press 2014) 75; Compare, Aoife McCullough, 'The Legitimacy of States and Armed Non-State Actors: Topic Guide' (GSDRC University of Birmingham 2015) 23.

131 Michelle Mack, 'Increasing Respect for International Humanitarian Law in Non-International Armed Conflicts' (ICRC 2008) 11.

132 Holmqvist (n 121) 55–56; Heffes (n 124) 429–430, 434–436; Moffett (n 37) 204.

133 ICRC (n 8) 9, 65.

134 UNGA and UNSC (n 113) para 15.

135 Olivier Bangerter, 'Reasons Why Armed Groups Choose to Respect International Humanitarian Law or Not' (2011) 93 International Review of the Red Cross 353, 354, 358–383; Geneva Academy of International Humanitarian Law and Human Rights (n 123) 22–23.

their own territories as a way to increase community support.[136] Finally, the diverse nature of NSAGs may provide for its own set of challenges. Politically motivated NSAGs, whose struggle is based on grievances, may be hesitant to engage on reparations, as this could be seen as betraying or undermining their efforts or cause.[137] On the other end of the spectrum, there are groups, such as the Islamic State or Boko Haram, whose ideology implies a rejection of basic human rights. Although an inclusive approach should be favoured, NSAGs may simply reject any form of engagement.[138] Where an NSAG would be legally responsible, reparations claims could, in principle, still be enforced through a court of law or an administrative mechanism, where available, or, alternatively, their responsibility could ultimately trigger the states' subsidiary responsibility in accordance with the responsibility scheme proposed in Section 4.3.

4.5.2 Post-conflict reparations

The questions that must be addressed in a post-conflict setting are *whether* and *how* a responsible NSAG could fulfil its duty to provide reparation in this context when it legally ceases to exist. As discussed in Chapter 3, international law indirectly regulates the responsibility of NSAGs, in cases of government or state formation, following the end of a conflict. Beyond such instances, the challenging questions posed above remain unanswered. This study argues that it should still be possible to invoke the international responsibility of an NSAG even when it no longer exists as a legal entity. The focus of the discussion should thus be on how the resulting duty to repair could still be implemented. Importantly, the argument implies that victims could still call on the subsidiary responsibility of the territorial state, as a last resort, to obtain reparations when there is no possibility of claiming it from the responsible, now extinct, NSAG.

Several approaches will be explored, which illustrate different ways of operationalising an NSAG's duty to repair in a post-conflict setting when that group has, e.g., been defeated or dismantled. Yet, these approaches may also be relevant in ongoing conflicts where fragmentation or splintering has occurred

136 Ita Connolly and Colm Campbell, 'The Sharp End: Armed Opposition Movement, Transitional Truth Processes and the Rechtsstaat' (2012) 6 International Journal of Transitional Justice 11; International Crisis Group, 'Left in the Cold? The ELN and Colombia's Peace Talks' (2013) 9; Stuart Casey-Maslen (ed), *The War Report: Armed Conflict in 2013* (Oxford University Press 2014) 576; Dempster (n 98); '¿Juntos Pero No Revueltos?' (n 78).

137 Martien Schotsmans, 'Victims' Expectations, Needs and Perspectives after Gross and Systematic Human Rights Violations' in Koen de Feyter and others (eds), *Out of the Ashes: Reparation for Victims of Gross and Systematic Human Rights Violations* (Intersentia 2005) 122; Dudouet and Giessmann (n 119) 30, 31; Cheryl Lawther, 'The Truth about Loyalty: Emotions, Ex-Combatants and Transitioning from the Past' (2017) 11 International Journal of Transitional Justice 484.

138 Sassòli (n 85) para 10.257.

within a group, potentially leaving the initial collectivity, which holds responsibility for a violation, no longer intact.[139] These approaches draw largely from domestic and international practice, preliminary proposals made in legal scholarship and insights obtained from social science literature. They are further complemented by research carried out on Colombia. The approaches include: 1) asset tracing and recovery for reparations purposes; 2) a representation order in civil proceedings; and, 3) reparations provided by actors with representative authority. The first two approaches are particularly relevant when seeking to claim reparations from a defunct NSAG through legal processes. The third approach goes beyond the boundaries of the law and takes account of certain socio-political realities, which are pertinent for the issue of post-conflict reparations. These approaches should be understood as illustrations of how NSAGs' post-conflict duties to repair could potentially be operationalised. Other approaches may exist or could be developed. The overall significance in emphasising their potential uses lies in the acknowledgment that the engagement of NSAGs in post-conflict reparations should not be simply discarded. These approaches are not presented as reflecting emerging norms of custom, nor examples of best practice.

4.5.2.1 Asset tracing and recovery for reparations purposes

The first approach seeks to tackle the assets which defunct NSAGs have acquired over the course of armed hostilities. These assets could be used to provide restitution and compensation or finance other forms of reparation, such as rehabilitation programmes, the building of memorials, and the rebuilding of damaged or destroyed infrastructure in affected communities. Although the NSAG would have legally ceased to exist, such assets could still be recovered from former members, such as commanders and leaders, and third parties who were enriched by the activities of the group.[140] For example, although the LTTE was defeated, the Panel of Experts on Accountability in Sri Lanka still suggested that the "funds acquired by the LTTE from the diaspora and elsewhere, and which still exist, should be secured for the purpose of making reparations".[141] This could also contribute to guaranteeing non-repetition, by advancing the dismantlement of still existing economic power bases. Recovering assets from former members or third parties is a logical approach, given the fact that, even during a NIAC, it is unlikely that an NSAG would have

139 Kenny Paul, 'Structural Integrity and Cohesion in Insurgent Organizations: Evidence from Protracted Conflicts in Ireland and Burma' (2010) 12 International Studies Review 533, 535; Kathleen Gallagher Cunningham, 'Understanding Fragmentation in Conflict and Its Impact on Prospects for Peace' (Centre for Humanitarian Dialogue 2016) 4.

140 Daboné (n 11) 197; Belfast Guidelines on Reparations in Post-Conflict Societies (n 36) 14.

141 UNSG (n 39) paras 419, 442.

maintained assets in its own name due to its illegal nature in domestic law.[142] As a result of the link between any enrichment and the unlawful activity of the NSAG in question, recovered resources could be used to repair the victims of the group. A reparations fund could conceivably manage and distribute the assets for reparations purposes. For instance, the Sierra Leone Truth and Reconciliation Commission recommended tracing and recovering the material and financial assets of Charles Taylor, the National Patriotic Front of Liberia (NPFL) and the RUF, with the objective that it should become part of the War Reparations Fund and be used for financing the reparations programme recommended by the Commission. The Commission also recognised the role of internal and external actors who profited from the conflict. Their recovered assets should also be placed in this Fund.[143]

4.5.2.2 Representation order in civil proceedings

The second approach draws from the *Omagh bombing* case brought before the High Court of Justice of Northern Ireland. In this case, the Court rendered a judgement in the civil litigation initiated by several victims of a bombing carried out in the town of Omagh. The 1998 bombing was perpetrated by the Real IRA and killed 29 people, injuring over 220 others.[144] The case is of particular interest to the present discussion because the victims initiated civil proceedings, not only against a number of named individuals, but also directly against the Real IRA as an organisation. It was alleged that the defendants were responsible in various ways for the planning, production, planting and detonation of the bomb.[145] In other words, the victims sought to establish the civil responsibility of the Real IRA for the organisation's part in the bombing. During the proceedings, the Court was confronted with the lack of legal personality, albeit under domestic law, of the Real IRA. It is thus of interest to examine how the Court addressed this obstacle, and how it was eventually able to maintain the claim in spite of this legal challenge. The main objective of the analysis is to identify insights which are relevant for the international legal debate.

142 Andrew Clapham, 'Extending International Criminal Law Beyond the Individual to Corporations and Armed Opposition Groups' (2008) 6 Journal of International Criminal Justice 899, 920; Agata Kleczkowska, 'Filling the Gap: The New Regime of Responsibility for Armed Non-State Actors' (2018) 25 Australian International Law Journal 137, 158.

143 Sierra Leone Truth and Reconciliation Commission (n 82) ch 3 p 183 and ch 4 para 227(d).

144 The Real IRA emerged as a separate entity from the provisional IRA when a fracture occurred in 1997. *Mark Christopher Breslin and Others v Seamus McKenna and Others* High Court of Justice in Northern Ireland [2009] NIQB 50 para 80; Stanford University, 'Mapping Militant Organizations: Real Irish Republican Army (Last Modified August 2019)' <https://cisac.fsi.stanford.edu/mappingmilitants/content/mmp-real-irish-republican-army>.

145 *Mark Christopher Breslin and Others v Seamus McKenna and Others* (n 144) para 2.

The Court was "satisfied to a very high degree that the Real IRA were responsible for the Omagh bomb in that the directing minds of that organisation were committed to the carrying out of the terrorist campaign in every respect and were part of a concerted enterprise to that end".[146] Nevertheless, it was questioned whether, as a matter of law, it would be possible to maintain an action against the group. In legal terms, it is "an unincorporated association", which cannot be rendered a defendant to an action in its own right.[147] Such an association involves a simple legal structure comprising a group of people who have joined together in a common purpose. It lacks separate legal personality under the law of Northern Ireland.

The Court determined that Order 15 Rule 12 of the Rules of the Supreme Court in relation to representative proceedings could be applied. It provides that "where numerous persons have the same interest in any proceedings the proceedings may be begun and continued against any one or more of them as representing all or as representing all except one or more of them".[148] A judgment rendered under this rule would be binding on all represented persons, but enforcement against any person not a party to the proceedings would require the leave of the court. In a case where such leave is granted, the person may still dispute his or her liability.[149] Concretely, it provided a mechanism to maintain the action by empowering the court to make a representative order against one or more named members, as representatives of all those who were part of the unincorporated association (*in casu* the Real IRA), provided the persons represented had a common interest in defending the claim.[150]

However, the Court declined to make a representation order against any individual to represent all members of the Real IRA. It was argued that those who joined the organisation after the bombing would have a different defence or interest than those who had been members at the time of the attack.[151] Although the Court could not identify all of the members that participated in the attack, it could conclude, on the basis of the evidence tendered in the proceedings, that those who were members of the Army Council of the Real IRA at the time of the bombing bore responsibility for directing the attack.[152] On this basis, a representation order in respect of the fourth defendant (Liam Campbell, who was a senior Real IRA leader and a member of this Council at the time of the attack) was made, and Campbell was deemed to represent the other members of the Army Council.[153] He

146 Ibid. para 82.
147 Ibid. para 83.
148 Ibid. para 86; *Mark Christopher Breslin and Others v John Michael McKevitt and Others* Court of Appeal in Northern Ireland [2011] NICA 33 para 73.
149 Order 15 Rule 12 Rules of the Supreme Court (Northern Ireland) 1980.
150 *Mark Christopher Breslin and Others v Seamus McKenna and Others* (n 144) paras 83–84.
151 Ibid. paras 84–86.
152 The Army Council was the governing or decision-making body of the Real IRA.
153 *Mark Christopher Breslin and Others v Seamus McKenna and Others* (n 144) paras 267, 270; *Mark Christopher Breslin and Others v John Michael McKevitt and Others* (n 148) paras 72–73.

was held civilly responsible for their collective interests, aside from the other defendants who were held personally responsible.

As noted by Moffett, the judgment reflects that the bombing was the result of a concerted effort by the Real IRA. It did so by not only holding individuals who carried out the bombing responsible, but also those who commanded the organisation.[154] Although legal action could not be taken directly against the group at first, due to its lack of legal personality under domestic law, the rule of representative proceedings nevertheless allowed the victims to set forward their claim seeking compensation from the Real IRA, and allowed them to seek a determination which held the group civilly responsible by way of its leadership.[155] The case shows that establishing the civil responsibility of the group was of importance to the victims.

The *Omagh bombing* case provides for an interesting example of how a forum could potentially deal with the duty to repair of an NSAG that no longer has international legal personality. The case suggests that civil litigation could still be initiated against such a group by way of representative proceedings against one or more named members as representatives of some members (e.g. of a directive or military organ that participated in the unlawful act) or even all members of the NSAG when there is a common defence or interest. It should be noted that the Real IRA was still recognised by the Court as an unincorporated association. Although it did not hold separate legal personality, the group still existed in a factual sense. A similar situation could present itself when, e.g., an NSAG was neither entirely defeated, nor did it take full power in the aftermath of a NIAC. Instead, it continues to exist factually, as a non-state actor, while its military structures have become dormant.[156]

Nonetheless, application of the approach may prove difficult in practice. This is reflected in the reasoning of the Court of Appeal in the *Omagh bombing* case when it eventually rejected the representation order.[157] This included the consideration that the Real IRA was "a fluctuating body of persons involved in a criminal conspiracy with individual members being parties to distinct separate criminal enterprises, albeit carried out under the umbrella of the RIRA [Real IRA]".[158] Similar reasoning could easily apply to other NSAGs. There also may be evidentiary difficulties associated with the representation order approach. Although membership may provide some evidence that a member of an NSAG was a party to an unlawful act, it is questionable whether it sufficiently proves his or her personal liability, which would still need to be established. As a

154 Moffett (n 2) 338–340.

155 *Mark Christopher Breslin and Others v Seamus McKenna and Others* (n 144) para 270; Blázquez Rodríguez (n 13) 423; 'Omagh Bomb Families Win Multi-Million Pound Legal Case' *Belfast Telegraph* (8 June 2009).

156 See, e.g., Dudai (n 2) 808.

157 *Mark Christopher Breslin and Others v John Michael McKevitt and Others* (n 148) paras 72–75.

158 Ibid. para 74(a).

result, the common interest requirement, which underlies a representation order, may not be satisfied.[159] Nevertheless, the burden of proof remains less severe than in a criminal case, which requires proof beyond reasonable doubt. Given that no criminal charge is at issue, it is not for the court to determine whether a criminal offence has been committed. Instead, its role is to establish whether the defendant was responsible for causing harm and, if so, to determine whether damages are to be paid for that harm.[160]

4.5.2.3 Actors with representative authority

UNDERSTANDING NON-STATE ARMED GROUPS AS RESPONSIBLE ACTORS IN POST-CONFLICT SETTINGS

Although an NSAG legally ceases to exist with the end of a NIAC, research has shown that this does not necessarily entail that the defunct group no longer has any political, social or even moral authority and influence on segments of society. This follows from the observation that NSAGs do not come out of the blue but are rather embedded in pre-existing social structures and ties with communities.[161] It follows from this that, in some form or other, NSAGs may actually retain, in certain circumstances, an influential role in post-conflict settings, and may sometimes even have the potential of contributing to victims' redress.[162]

This is concretely demonstrated in Dudai's discussion of the IRA in Northern Ireland, which, following the 1998 Belfast Agreement, provided some measures of truth-recovery and symbolic reparation on behalf of the organisation. Dudai argues that the IRA case shows that, although the group ceased its military operations, it did not disappear. The group rather retained political and social authority in the communities that supported it, and its actions and statements still had the potential to affect people's lives. The IRA was neither totally eliminated, nor did it capture full power in the country. It rather remained an influential non-state actor.[163]

159 For the Court's reasoning in respect of the individual members of the Army Council of the Real IRA, see ibid. para 74(b), (d).

160 *Mark Christopher Breslin and Others v Seamus McKenna and Others* (n 144) para 6.

161 Teresa Koloma Beck, 'Staging Society: Sources of Loyalty in the Angolan UNITA' (2009) 30 Contemporary Security Policy 343; Dudai (n 2) 808; Lawther (n 137); David Brenner, 'Authority in Rebel Groups: Identity, Recognition and the Struggle over Legitimacy' (2017) 23 Contemporary Politics 408, 411; Philip A Martin, Giulia Piccolino and Jeremy S Speight, 'Ex-Rebel Authority after Civil War: Theory and Evidence from Côte d'Ivoire' (2021) 53 Journal of Comparative Politics 209.

162 Dudai (n 2) 807–808.

163 Since the declaration of a first ceasefire by the IRA in 1994, its command structures remained largely intact during the negotiations leading to the 1998 peace accord and the subsequent peacebuilding process. Even their political opponents accepted implicitly that maintaining a leadership structure was required to oversee the transition and demobilisation of the group, which ultimately helped to support the peace process. Dudouet and Giessmann (n 119) 16.

Importantly, this meant that victims seeking reparations could still call upon the IRA, as it remained an identifiable actor.[164]

Another example is the Colombian *Colectivo Nacional de Desmovilizados AUC*, which is a national collective of demobilised members of the AUC. Despite having gone through a demobilisation process more than a decade ago, demobilised members and commanders have convened within this organisation during their national conferences. The *Colectivo Nacional* issued, for instance, a communication in March 2019 in which it expressed its commitment to contribute to the work of the Truth Commission which was established as part of the peace process with the FARC-EP. Former high-level commanders of the AUC were among those who signed the communication.[165] The example suggests that the social bonds forged during a NIAC do not necessarily disappear in its aftermath. Ex-fighters may continue to organise themselves. Moreover, the former leadership can potentially remain an influential post-conflict factor, taking part in a transitional justice process, while retaining a degree of social and political authority. A further illustrative example can be found in the way the defunct FARC-EP has been carrying out its obligations to repair by way of a successor political entity in the wake of the 2016 peace agreement (see Chapter 6).

These examples demonstrate that it is a legal fiction that the influence of an NSAG simply disappears with the end of a NIAC. This challenges a common assumption among legal scholars that NSAGs simply cease to exist with the end of a NIAC, with no one left to assume responsibility. The general argument holds that an NSAG either wins and becomes the new government or state to which (state) responsibility can be attributed under international law, or loses with its complete elimination as a result, thus leaving its responsibility without practical relevance.[166]

164 Dudai (n 2). Dudai further discusses the example of the ANC in South Africa, which offered some limited post-conflict reparations. However, note that the question whether the conflict in the country should be classified as an armed conflict had been the focus of extensive legal debate. See Neil Boister, 'The Ius in Bello in South Africa: A Postscript?' (1991) 24 Comparative and International Law Journal of Southern Africa 72.

165 'Comunicado a La Opinión Pública Del Colectivo Nacional de Desmovilizados AUC' (21 March 2019) <https://www.justiciaypazcolombia.com/comunicado-a-la-opinion-publica-del-colectivo-nacional-de-desmovilizados-auc/>; 'Desmovilizados de Las AUC Contarán Su Verdad a La Comisión de La Verdad' *Análisis Urban* (23 March 2019). As part of the working group *Narrativas de Excombatientes,* various ex-members of guerrilla groups (such as the FARC-EP, Popular Liberation Army (EPL), ELN and M-19) as well as of the AUC, among others, convened monthly between February and November 2019 to contribute to the work of the Truth Commission of Colombia, which led to the adoption of the *Declaración por la vida, la Paz y la Reconciliación* signed on 15 November 2019 [on file with the author].

166 'Fourth Report on State Responsibility, by Mr Roberto Ago, Special Rapporteur' Yearbook of the International Law Commission (1972) Vol II UN Doc A/CN.4/264 and Add.1 para 154; Éric David, *Principes de Droit Des Conflits Armés* (3rd edn, Bruylant 2002) 643; Zegveld (n 100) 152; ILA Committee on Non-State Actors (n 10) 9; Veronika Bílková, 'Establishing Direct Responsibility of Armed Opposition Groups

Two preliminary observations can be drawn from the discussion. First, certain persons or entities, which are somehow linked to a defunct NSAG, could, at least in certain circumstances, still contribute to providing redress in a post-conflict situation. This can possibly be framed as being on behalf of the group. Second, this implies that victims of an NSAG may still have an avenue to seek redress for a group's violations after the conflict has ended.

These observations find further support in the practice of the truth commissions for El Salvador and Guatemala. Both called on the respective NSAGs' former command structures to provide reparations on behalf of the group. The Commission on the Truth for El Salvador held that the *Frente Farabundo Martí para la Liberación Nacional* (FMLN) must provide "moral and material compensation [...] where it is found to have been responsible" and stressed the need for guarantees of non-repetition by the group, now operating as a political entity, to prevent similar abuses in the future. Notably, the Commission's recommendations were submitted to both the state and the former commanders of the FMLN.[167] However, there appears to have been little support within the FMLN, which had successfully transitioned into a legally recognised political party, for the Commission's recommendations regarding redress.[168] In another instance, the Guatemalan Commission for Historical Clarification recommended the assistance of the "former Guatemalan National Revolutionary Unity" (URNG) in the search for those who were disappeared during the conflict.[169] Furthermore, it recommended, with the primary aim of restoring dignity to the victims, that the "ex-Command" of the group publicly and solemnly ask for forgiveness and assume responsibility for the harmful acts committed by the "ex-guerrillas".[170] Like the FMLN, the URNG registered as a political party in the aftermath of the NIAC.[171] After the publication of the Commission's report, the former leader of the URNG apologised in the name of the group: "[w]ith profound pain and humbleness we ask for forgiveness from the memory of the victims, their families and communities for any kind of excesses".[172]

for Violations of International Humanitarian Law?' in Noemi Gal-Or, Cedric Ryngaert and Math Noortmann (eds), *Responsibilities of the Non-State Actor in Armed Conflict and the Market Place* (Brill Nijhof 2015) 282.

167 Commission on the Truth for El Salvador (n 104) 175, 185, 188; Veronique Dudouet, Katrin Planta and Hans J Giessmann, 'The Political Transformation of Armed and Banned Groups' (Berghof Foundation and UNDP 2016) 11.

168 Alexander Segovia, 'The Reparations Proposals of the Truth Commissions in El Salvador and Haiti' in Pablo de Greiff (ed), *The Handbook of Reparations* (Oxford University Press 2006) 159–160.

169 Guatemalan Commission for Historical Clarification, 'Memory of Silence: Conclusions and Recommendations' (1999) 52.

170 Ibid. 49.

171 Michael E Allison, 'The Guatemalan National Revolutionary Unit: The Long Collapse' (2016) 23 Democratization 1042; Dudouet, Planta and Giessmann (n 167) 17, 33.

172 'Guatemala Rebel Apology' *The Associated Press* (14 March 1999); 'Guatemala Rebels Apologize for Abuses During Civil War' *The Miami Herald* (14 March 1999).

It is evident that the feasibility of such post-conflict reparations will be dependent on the circumstances of a given case and, hence, will not be applicable to all NSAGs. In some cases, reparations by a defunct NSAG may simply remain out of reach. A case in point is the example of the LTTE in Sri Lanka. The group was completely eliminated in the aftermath of the conflict, with no military and political structures remaining.[173] Engaging in a reparations process may also clash with the narrative of former fighters and the remaining political wing of an NSAG about their violent struggle. Victims may not accept reparations when these actors fail to acknowledge responsibility and continue to justify their past actions as legitimate. At the same time, reparations can be a way for a defunct group to reshape its image or facilitate its reintegration into society.[174]

REPRESENTATIVE AUTHORITY OF FORMER MEMBERS, A SUCCESSOR ENTITY OR OTHER ACTORS

Although the observations made in the previous section have important implications for the delivery of post-conflict reparations by defunct NSAGs, they result in a challenging exercise when seeking to translate these complex socio-political realities into international legal terms. Under international law, the concept of legal personality takes a central place, since it allows to determine the participants within the international legal system. Despite its importance, the concept is characterised by a lack of consensus on its precise meaning and on how actors can acquire it. This has led some scholars to propose ways to rethink the concept and has prompted others to propose discarding it altogether.[175] The concept of international legal personality is not considered useful when seeking to grasp the complex realities discussed above. Although the premise of the analysis is that certain persons or entities somehow linked to an NSAG could play a role in post-conflict reparations on behalf of the group (at least in certain situations), the objective is not to argue that such actors should have defined duties in international law, or that they should even be recognised as legal subjects. Instead, the aim is to develop the contours of a conceptual approach, which allows us to take account of such factual realities and complexities and, most importantly, to better understand the role that NSAGs could still play in post-conflict reparations by way of other actors. In doing so, the analysis finds its basis in the law, but also crosses its boundaries.

173 Dudai (n 2) 807–808; Mastorodimos (n 106) 134; 'Death of the Tiger' *The New Yorker* (9 January 2011).

174 Reparations, Responsibility & Victimhood in Transitional Societies (n 37) 37; Moffett (n 37) 217–218.

175 Rosalyn Higgins, *Problems and Process: International Law and How We Use It* (Clarendon Press 1994) 49–50.

Starting point In their work on the international responsibility of NSAGs, legal scholars Heffes and Frenkel suggest that stakeholders "assess on a case-by-case basis the feasibility of having the former organs of a NSAG providing for reparatory measures".[176] The potential of their proposal was illustrated by the example of a former NSAG leader who was still able to provide a public apology to victims, despite his NSAG having dissolved at the conclusion of a NIAC.[177] Their proposal is apt for analysis and expansion, as it is in line with the observations drawn in the previous section of this study. In attempting to build on this suggestion, at least two initial questions arise: first, 'what criteria, features or factors determine which persons could take up such a representative post-conflict role?' and, second, 'is such a role restricted to former members, or could other persons or entities fulfil a similar function?'[178]

Insights from official or public apologies In seeking to answer these questions, the existing literature on official or public apologies is particularly instructive. The primary reason is that such apologies are carried out on behalf of a larger collectivity, such as a state or other organised entity. As such, they differ from interpersonal apologies. One of the central questions addressed by scholars seeks to ask *who* is to deliver such an apology, and the larger process that accompanies the selection of an apparently legitimate 'apologiser'. As a result, this body of work can tell us more about who can take on a representative role when dealing with past wrongs and on what basis this person is determined. While contributions which have tackled this who-question typically deal with official apologies by states regarding historical injustices, the question appears to be understudied with regard to NSAGs.[179]

The existing literature on official apologies by states remains useful to the extent that certain analogies can be made when reducing states and NSAGs to a common core feature: namely, their collective nature. Moreover, an empirical study of apologies carried out by NSAGs will provide deeper insights. Several practical examples are considered, which are complemented by an enquiry into the role of the FARC-EP in post-conflict reparations in Chapter 6.

The notion of an official apology has been defined in several ways, with scholars tending to take a narrow or broader approach to its scope. Murphy adopts a narrow definition that involves "an apology offered by an official representative of a state (or some state agency) for past actions committed by a state or under state sanction".[180] Even more restricted, Teitel speaks of the 'transitional apology' as being deliverable

176 Heffes and Frenkel (n 100) 71.
177 Ibid.
178 Similarly, Kleffner (n 11) 265.
179 Notable exceptions are UNGA (n 12) and the research project titled 'Apologies, Abuses & Dealing with the Past' (Queen's University Belfast) <https://apologies-abuses-past.org.uk>.
180 Michael Murphy, 'Apology, Recognition, and Reconciliation' (2011) 12 Human Rights Review 47, 49.

only by the head of state, which embodies representative functions, among others.[181] In contrast, Thompson defines such an apology in a broader sense as "an official apology given by a representative of a state, corporation, or other organized group to victims, or descendants of victims, for injustices committed by the group's officials or members".[182] The term 'other organized group' could easily include an NSAG. The 2019 report on apologies by the UN Special Rapporteur on the promotion of truth, justice, reparation and guarantees of non-recurrence offers a more explicit reference to such groups. The Rapporteur defines the concept of public apologies as involving a "truthful admission of individual, organizational or collective responsibility".[183] It acknowledges that "representatives of non-State armed groups or the political movements with which they are affiliated" can carry out such apologies for past harms.[184]

While much of the literature on official apologies is focused on the state, the latter two definitions indicate that NSAGs can also effectuate such symbolic actions concerning their collective responsibility for past wrongful conduct. An additional common element can be identified across the definitions, namely that of *representation*. This is evident from the very nature of an official apology, which necessitates a representative to deliver the action on behalf of the group that, as a non-human entity, cannot act by itself. In this sense, such apologies are dependent on representation. Accordingly, the notion of representation also forms the central element in the discussion on post-conflict reparations carried out on behalf, or rather in representation, of a dissolved NSAG.

Research has shown that who apologises matters, as the status of the speaker will necessarily affect the effectiveness of the apology.[185] A necessary basic condition is that the apologiser is actually recognised as representing the collectivity and, hence, as having the authority to speak on its behalf.[186] Consequently, apologies given by someone without the capacity or authority to represent the entity will suffer. In other words, the speaker relies on his or her authority and status to render the apology legitimate.[187] This translates itself into a notion of *representative authority*.[188] This is not only the case for

181 Ruti Teitel, 'The Transitional Apology' in Elazar Barkan and Alexander Karn (eds), *Taking Wrongs Seriously: Apologies and Reconciliation* (Stanford University Press 2006).

182 Janna Thompson, 'Apology, Justice and Respect: A Critical Defense of Political Apology' in Mark Gibney and others (eds), *The Age of Apology: Facing Up to the Past* (University of Pennsylvania 2008) 31.

183 UNGA (n 12) 4.

184 Ibid.

185 Danielle Celermajer, *The Sins of the Nations and the Ritual of Apologies* (Cambridge University Press 2009) 252; ICTJ, 'More Than Words: Apologies as a Form of Reparation' (2015) 13.

186 Sanderijn Cels, 'Saying Sorry: Ethical Leadership and the Act of Public Apology' (2017) 28 The Leadership Quarterly 759, 260.

187 Celermajer (n 185) 256; Mihaela Mihai, 'Apology' (*The Internet Encyclopaedia of Philosophy*) <https://iep.utm.edu/apology/>.

apologies given by states, but also those offered by NSAGs. One of the main findings of the aforementioned UN Special Rapporteur's report on apologies underscores that the person selected to deliver an apology must have the necessary leadership and credibility to effectively represent those who inflicted the harms. Hence, the individual should have the authority to speak on behalf of the responsible NSAG. Otherwise, the apology's delivery, perceived sincerity and effectiveness risk being undermined.[189]

To ensure the effectiveness of an apology, it is generally desired that the preparatory process should incorporate the extensive involvement of both the victims and the wrongdoers, or their representatives. It is important that the victims, or at least their representatives, have a central say in who should deliver the apology and that they, accordingly, recognise the authority of the apologiser.[190] Consultations with the NSAG's own constituency are also necessary in order to avoid subsequent backlash.[191] This would ideally involve a process in which an agreement is reached as to how and under which circumstances the apology will be presented, including clarification of the identity of the speaker.[192] Although an NSAG no longer legally exists in a post-conflict context, a consultation process with former members could still potentially take place. As the previous example regarding the AUC indicates, former members may continue to organise themselves in associations or foundations that allow them to maintain, to an extent, their social and political bases, and to represent their common interests after the conflict has ended. Other examples can be found in the Colombian context. An example is *La Fundación Aulas de Paz*, which was initiated within a proposal presented by a group of demobilised AUC members before the Chamber of Justice and Peace as part of their re-socialisation process. It initially emerged as an initiative of symbolic reparations and as a commitment to non-repetition. Subsequently, the foundation appears to have been engaged in reconciliation and peacebuilding work.[193]

188 Hanna F Pitkin, *The Concept of Representation* (University of California Press 1972) 42–43.

189 UNGA (n 12) 15, 17, 20.

190 Carlton Waterhouse, 'The Good, the Bad, and the Ugly: Moral Agency and the Role of Victims in Reparations Programs' (2009) 31 University of Pennsylvania Journal of International Economic Law 257, 259, 267–270; UNGA (n 46) para 77; ICTJ (n 185) 17; UNGA (n 12) 5, 15–17, 20; Reparations, Responsibility & Victimhood in Transitional Societies (n 37) 37–38.

191 UNGA (n 12) 15, 19–20.

192 Thompson (n 182) 41–43.

193 *Case against Iván Roberto Duque Gaviria and Others* Superior Tribunal of Bogotá (Colombia) Justice and Peace Chamber (11 August 2017) 563–572; 'De La Violencia Paramilitar a Las Aulas de Paz' *Buena Gente Periódico* (21 July 2019). Another example is *La Fundación Semillas de Paz* created by demobilised fighters of the AUC-linked *Bloque Libertadores del Sur*, which was, however, closed due to security concerns. FUCE PAZ (*Fundación Colombiana de Ex Combatientes y*

Victim representatives indicated in the *El Mozote* case, before the Inter-American Court of Human Rights, that the acknowledgement of responsibility by El Salvador had to be made by the president, in his capacity as head of state, and in the presence of senior officials for it to have true meaning for the victims.[194] This illustrates that the choice of representative is important as it also reflects the degree of recognition and respect the victims are being accorded. As such, the choice of representative may profoundly determine the perceived legitimacy and symbolic weight of the action.[195] By analogy with apologies delivered by states, the most natural link between an NSAG and a public apology would be reflected by apologies made by a former leader, commander-in-chief or any other official who occupied the highest position or rank in the group. It makes the apology official, endows it with formality and solemnity, and signals the full backing of the (defunct) group.[196] For example, Xanana Gusmão, then President of Timor-Leste, apologised before the Commission for Reception, Truth and Reconciliation in his capacity as the former leader of the resistance army the Armed Forces for the National Liberation of East Timor (FALINTIL) for killings and other violence directed at rival groups and civilians.[197] Another example is when the defunct FARC-EP's commander-in-chief, Rodrigo Londoño, asked for forgiveness and acknowledged the group's collective responsibility in the framework of Colombian's Truth Commission in 2020.[198] It could also be envisioned that a commander of an NSAG's substructure, such as a front, that had a particular link to the violation or the territory in which it occurred, could be in a better position to carry out the apology on behalf of the group.[199]

Conclusions With respect to the first question regarding what criteria, features or factors determine which persons could provide post-conflict reparations on behalf of a dissolved NSAG, the analysis has made it clear that a key criterion is the person's authority to represent and act on behalf of the

Promotores de Paz) is the FARC-EP's first legal organisation of ex-FARC-EP fighters created for the purpose of promoting their reintegration. 'Fundación de Desmovilizados En Nariño Fue Cerrada Por Inseguridad' *W Radio* (23 July 2007); 'Last Year They Were Enemies. Now FARC Guerrillas and Civilians Are Trying to Pick up the Pieces Together' *De Correspondent* (15 June 2017).

194 *Case of the Massacres of el Mozote and Nearby Places v El Salvador* IACtHR (Judgment Merits, Reparations and Costs) Series C No 252 (25 October 2012) para 354.

195 Murphy (n 180) 50.

196 ICTJ (n 185) 13.

197 Gene Christy, 'Armed Groups and Diplomacy: East Timor's FRETILIN Guerrillas' in Jeffrey H Norwitz (ed), *Armed Groups: Studies in National Security, Counterterrorism and Counterinsurgency* (US Naval War College 2008) 44; ICTJ (n 185) 16; UNGA (n 12) 14.

198 Truth Commission of Colombia, 'Los Impactantes Crímenes de las Antiguas FARC-EP Relatados ante la Comisión de la Verdad' (19 May 2022). See further Chapter 6.

199 Murphy (n 180) 50; ICTJ (n 185) 14–15, 18.

defunct group, as opposed to acting in a merely personal capacity. In other words, a person's representative authority, *vis-à-vis* the group itself, functions as a criterion of capacity. It has also become clear that the determination of such authority is not necessarily objective. Depending on the context, it could require a participatory process in which a central voice is given to the victims as beneficiaries of the reparatory action. On the other hand, involvement of the constituency of the NSAG is also necessary to ensure support and avoid any subsequent backlash that could diminish the effectiveness of the measure.

Besides the need to engage both of these key groups of actors, representative authority could also be preliminarily evaluated by carrying out a case-specific assessment which could take account of certain *actor features* and *contextual factors*. This possibility is informed by the fact that NSAGs and post-conflict contexts can differ significantly from one another. Actor features refer to the features of the scrutinised NSAG (e.g. its organisational structure), as well as the features of the person taking the representative role (e.g. their past role in the group and current one). When dealing with, for instance, a political-military NSAG in which the two wings are not merged, the question may arise whether someone from the military or political side of the group should deliver the apology: the question being, 'who would bear the necessary authority to represent the group as a whole?' In the Northern Ireland context, neither the President, nor the Vice-President of Sinn Féin, the political wing of the IRA, had an IRA background. This could have put their authority to deliver a collective apology into question. Such questions may be less pertinent regarding NSAGs that merge the political and the military. The status of Nelson Mandela as the leader of both the political and military wings of the ANC was, for instance, never in doubt when he responded to the findings of the Skyweyiya Commission, which documented the abuses by the ANC against its own members.[200] Contextual factors relate to the prevailing external circumstances that may impact a person's authority, such as the provisions in a peace agreement and the broader post-conflict context in which the actions are set to take place.

The second question that requires answering, is whether such a representative role would be restricted to former members of the group, such as a former group leader, as suggested by Heffes and Frenkel, or whether other persons, or even entities, could fulfil a similar function. There is no specific reason to exclude other persons or entities, which are somehow linked to an NSAG, from taking a similar representative role. The most natural link would indeed lie with members of the former military leadership of the group. Nevertheless, former mid-level commanders, members of a still existing political wing or of a civil society organisation consisting of ex-fighters, or even ex-foot soldiers or third persons empowered to represent the defunct group, could have a representative function depending on the particularities of the case.[201] The same can

200 Dudai (n 2) 796; UNGA (n 12) 15.
201 Moffett (n 37) 213–214.

be argued regarding a political party or movement into which an NSAG collectively transforms as part of a broader peace process.[202] As will be demonstrated in Chapter 6, such successor entities can form a vehicle for NSAGs to provide post-conflict reparations on that NSAG's behalf. Finally, it is plausible that the military activities of an NSAG could become dormant, resulting in the threshold criteria of a NIAC no longer being satisfied. In such cases, the group could still be called upon as a non-state actor.

A final question that arises from the discussion is for which forms of post-conflict reparations this approach can be useful. The approach would appear to be most appropriately applicable to symbolic forms of redress, such as: a public apology on behalf of the group; the recognition of collective responsibility; an official declaration that restores the dignity and reputation of the victim; commemorations and tributes; as well as the provision of guarantees of non-repetition. It could also be envisioned that representatives of a defunct NSAG could play a role in material forms of reparations, such as restitution and monetary compensation. A successor entity with representative authority could, for instance, provide compensation on behalf of its predecessor, or play a role in the restitution of property and assets taken over the course of the conflict.

RELEVANCE FOR INTERNATIONAL LAW

Contrary to the previous two approaches, the representative authority approach is less relevant from a strict international legal perspective. The aim has not been to argue that actors holding representative authority should be held internationally responsible on behalf of a defunct NSAG. Instead, it presents a conceptual approach that allows for the grasping of actual realities, which are relevant for reparations purposes, but which remain out of reach due to the restrictions inherent in the existing tools of international law. The representative authority approach allows us to better understand the role which defunct groups could still play in post-conflict reparations. Transitional justice measures or strategies could be adjusted in recognition of this understanding, to provide space for actions involving what remains of a defunct-NSAG and its representatives.[203] Contrary to common assumptions of international legal scholarship, the discussion has suggested that, at least in some cases, there is still an identifiable actor that could be called upon to make certain forms of reparations on behalf of an NSAG after the conflict has ended. Although this actor may not be held legally responsible, it can still play a valuable role in providing redress. Nevertheless, this may much depend on the willingness of the concerned actor, how a conflict has ended and the post-conflict context. If there is some kind of agreement between the parties at the end of the conflict, it could be a first instrument for putting the responsibility

202 Dudouet, Planta and Giessmann (n 167) 7; Íñigo Álvarez (n 9) 202.
203 Dudai (n 2) 808.

of the NSAG into practice.[204] This could involve carving out a space for former commanders/leaders, or a successor entity, to take an active role in the reparations process. It could even be agreed that such an entity takes responsibility for the legal consequences of the wrongful acts committed by its predecessor, even if there is no such rule in present international law.

4.6 Conclusions

This chapter has examined how a duty of NSAGs to provide reparation for internationally wrongful acts could be operationalised under international law from a *de lege ferenda* perspective. Overall, a multifaceted proposal that seeks to respond to the particularities presented by NSAGs has been put forward. The analysis has revealed that some of the main rules and principles concerning reparation within the law of state responsibility could be transposed into this NSAGs' framework by analogy, without too many modifications. It has been deemed possible to apply the principle of full reparation to NSAGs. The same holds for the five main forms of reparations, namely restitution, compensation, rehabilitation, satisfaction and guarantees of non-repetition, which are equally applicable within the context of NSAGs. Accordingly, the examination has found that a duty of reparation for NSAGs can be conceptualised in a comparable way to the duty placed on states under international law.

The key distinction arises in the practical implementation and specific application of these abstract rules and principles when dealing with NSAGs. A proposal has been made to take an actor-specific approach to the concrete application of an NSAG's duty to make reparation. This approach allows to take the diverse organisational capabilities of NSAGs into account. The rationale behind this proposal stems from the necessity to establish a realistic normative framework within international law. This framework should reasonably ensure that the obligations imposed on an NSAG are effective and not mere legal fictions. Subsequently, the responsibility of the territorial state may come into play as part of the proposed cascading regime of responsibility for reparation. The state's subsidiary responsibility would apply to the extent that the NSAG lacks the capacity or willingness to fulfil its own duty to provide reparation. Consequently, this cascading regime has the potential to result in a division of responsibility between the NSAG and the state. Especially in weak and resource scarce countries, the international community should play a crucial role in providing additional support. The argument underlying this regime is based on the premise that reparations cannot depend solely on the responsible NSAG. Altogether, this multifaceted proposal allows for holding all types of NSAGs to the various forms of reparations, with a view to delivering full reparation to victims of armed conflict, with possible substitution by the state and support of the international community.

204 Mastorodimos (n 106) 134.

A future domestic or international forum could apply this proposed scheme when adjudicating or addressing reparations claims aimed at NSAGs, whether through judicial or administrative processes. Additionally, it can serve as a valuable resource for extra-judicial initiatives, such as truth commissions and peace negotiations, which seek to address the question of reparation in relation to NSAGs. The analysis in this chapter has also stimulated the reader to think beyond the concept of compelling NSAGs to provide reparations. This has involved exploring the potential of engagement with NSAGs on the issue of reparations through voluntary or non-coercive mechanisms during and at the end of an armed conflict. When an NSAG ceases to exist, it may result in reparations claims against this entity becoming unfeasible. Nonetheless, the cascading regime of responsibility for reparation would provide for a final safety net for the victims, by ensuring that reparations are still granted by the state based on its subsidiary responsibility. In addition, the discussion has shown that the provision of post-conflict reparations by a legally defunct group should not be simply disregarded. Instead, different approaches have been presented that illustrate possible ways in which such reparations could still be provided in a post-conflict setting. In doing so, they inject new insights into the scholarly debate on this challenging issue.

Part 3

Insights from the operationalisation of reparations by non-state armed groups in Colombia

Chapter 5

Reparations by the AUC under the Justice and Peace Law

5.1 Introduction

This chapter examines the transitional justice process in Colombia regulated by the Justice and Peace Law of 2005 through the largely uncharted lens of the duty of NSAGs, as collective entities, to make reparation.[1] Although the Justice and Peace Law has been extensively scrutinised over the years, it has commonly been analysed from other perspectives, such as victims' rights and state responsibility.[2] The Justice and Peace process deals with both the individual and collective demobilisation of NSAGs.[3] Given the scope of the chapter, the analysis only concerns itself with the collective demobilisations of the paramilitary groups that are linked to the United Self-Defence Forces of Colombia (*Autodefensas Unidas de Colombia* or AUC).[4] Paramilitary groups played a violent role in the NIAC in Colombia through the perpetration of massacres, killings, enforced disappearances, torture and massive forced displacements, among other

1 Law No 975 of 2005 (Justice and Peace Law). The following contributions consider the issue: Luke Moffett, 'Beyond Attribution: Responsibility of Armed Non-State Actors for Reparations in Northern Ireland, Colombia and Uganda' in Noemi Gal-Or, Cedric Ryngaert and Math Noortmann (eds), *Responsibilities of the Non-State Actor in Armed Conflict and the Market Place* (Brill Nijhof 2015); Laura Íñigo Álvarez, *Towards a Regime of Responsibility of Armed Groups in International Law* (Intersentia 2020) 179–180.

2 See, e.g., Jemima García-Godos and Knut Andreas O Lid, 'Transitional Justice and Victims' Rights before the End of a Conflict: The Unusual Case of Colombia' (2010) 42 Journal of Latin American Studies 487; Francesca Capone, 'From the Justice and Peace Law to the Revised Peace Agreement between the Colombian Government and the FARC: Will Victims' Rights Be Satisfied at Last?' (2017) 77 Heidelberg Journal of International Law 125.

3 Arts 1–2, 9–11 Justice and Peace Law.

4 Within the framework of the Justice and Peace Law, several FARC-EP and ELN members demobilised individually, whereas AUC-linked groups collectively submitted to the process. The term demobilisation refers to the individual or collective act of disarming and leaving an NSAG as part of a government-led process. Art 9 Justice and Peace Law.

DOI: 10.4324/9781003401292-9

serious violations.[5] The paramilitary phenomenon went beyond a simple counter-insurgency strategy; it encompassed a complex set of economic and political interests involving a network of actors linked to the state's security forces, drug-trafficking, as well as political and business sectors.[6] Since this study specifically focuses on NSAGs that operate independently from states, the analysis makes an abstraction of legal questions relating to the shared responsibility between the Colombian state and paramilitary groups. However, this should not be understood as a rejection or denial of the state's responsibility.[7] Indeed, the process itself has been criticised for neglecting efforts to determine state responsibility in relation to the crimes under scrutiny.[8]

The Justice and Peace process was previously touched upon in Chapter 2. That discussion identified this process as a significant instance of state practice. More specifically, it was indicated that the Colombian Constitutional Court recognised the 'solidarity civil responsibility' of NSAGs which submitted themselves to the criminal justice process, regulated by the Justice and Peace Law. Even though criminal responsibility for the crimes remains individual, civil responsibility emanates from the criminal conduct that involves serious violations of IHL and IHRL. This allows victims to seek monetary compensation from the criminally convicted NSAG members, in the first instance, and, thereafter, from the specific NSAG to which the perpetrator belonged by virtue of the principle of solidarity.[9] These initial findings indicate that this case may hold valuable information on how a duty to repair for NSAGs could be legally operationalised and enforced through a judicial process.

This chapter therefore conducts a more thorough examination of the Justice and Peace process, informed by fieldwork conducted in Colombia. This examination involves enquiring into the underlying rationales, nature and modalities of this legal responsibility of the NSAGs. It also probes whether these groups

5 Centro Nacional de Memoria Histórica, 'Basta Ya! Colombia: Memories of War and Dignity' (2016) 40–43; Truth Commission of Colombia, 'Informe Final: Hasta La Guerra Tiene Límites' (2022) 984–1007.

6 Amnesty International, 'The Paramilitaries in Medellín: Demobilization or Legalization?' (2005) 4–6, 8–10; Truth Commission of Colombia, 'Informe Final: Hallazgos y Recomendaciones' (2022) 180.

7 See *Case of the "Mapiripán Massacre" v Colombia* IACtHR (Judgment Merits, Reparations and Costs) Series C No 134 (15 September 2005); *Case of the Ituango Massacres v Colombia* IACtHR (Judgment Preliminary Objections, Merits, Reparations and Costs) Series C No 148 (1 July 2006); Amnesty International (n 6) 11; ICTJ, 'From Principles to Practice: Challenges of Implementing Reparations for Massive Violations in Colombia' (2015) 15; Truth Commission of Colombia (n 6) 284, 290.

8 Lisa J Laplante and Kimberly Theidon, 'Transitional Justice in Times of Conflict: Colombia's Ley de Justicia y Paz' (2006) 28 Michigan Journal of International Law 49, 90–91.

9 *Judgment C-370/06* Constitutional Court of Colombia (18 May 2006) para 6.2.4.4.

are not only engaged in monetary compensation, but also in other forms of reparations. To this end, the examination in this chapter follows the approach taken by the Justice and Peace Law and analyses it from the perspective of NSAGs' duty to repair. The main purpose of the analysis is to distil those aspects of the Justice and Peace process that can inform the legal debate as to how a possible duty of NSAGs to provide reparation could be operationalised under international law. Any insights that can be drawn from this examination will be compared and placed in the context of the findings concerning international law identified in the previous parts of this book. Some of these case-based insights may be tentative, in the sense that they display one possible approach to reparations *vis-à-vis* NSAGs that may not necessarily be feasible or adequate with respect to other situations or groups.

5.2 An overview of the Justice and Peace Law

Law No. 975 of 2005, known as the Justice and Peace Law, introduced transitional justice in Colombia. The Justice and Peace Law provides for a legal framework that, for the first time, recognised and enforced victims' rights to truth, justice and reparation, which was in stark contrast with previous peace processes in Colombia.[10] Unusually, the process was initiated in the midst of the armed conflict, and lacked any clear political transition.[11] The Law was adopted as part of the collective demobilisation processes of the AUC-linked paramilitary groups. Instead of treating transitional justice and demobilisation, disarmament and reintegration (DDR) as independent processes, they were directly linked within a single legal framework.[12] The Justice and Peace Law has faced significant criticism since its adoption in 2005, including for its apparent concealed attempts to grant impunity and to institutionalise the paramilitary project.[13] Despite the challenges and criticism it has faced, the Justice

10 Arts 1, 4–8 Justice and Peace Law; Ana María Gutiérrez Urresty, 'Las Amnistías e Indultos, Un Hábito Social En Colombia' in Camila de Gamboa Tapias (ed), *Justicia Transicional: Teoría y Praxis* (Editorial Universidad del Rosario 2006); Laplante and Theidon (n 8) 59–61.

11 Rodrigo Uprimny Yepes and others, *Justicia Transicional Sin Transición? Verdad, Justicia y Reparación Para Colombia* (Dejusticia 2006); Eduardo Pizarro and León Valencia, *Ley de Justicia y Paz* (Grupo Editorial Norma 2009) 35–40.

12 Laplante and Theidon (n 8) 51–52.

13 Felipe Gómez Isa, 'Challenges for Transitional Justice in Contexts of Non-Transition: The Colombian Case' in Amanda Lyons (ed), *Contested Transitions: Dilemmas of Transitional Justice in Colombia and Comparative Experience* (ICTJ 2010) 150–152. For an extensive discussion of the criticisms voiced against the Justice and Peace Law, see Laplante and Theidon (n 8); Felipe Gómez Isa, 'Justicia, Verdad y Reparación En El Proceso de Desmovilización Paramilitar En Colombia' in Felipe Gómez Isa (ed), *Colombia en Su Laberinto: Una Mirada al Conflicto* (Libros de la Catarata 2008).

and Peace Law marks a milestone in the search for justice and accountability in Colombia.[14]

Shortly after the presidential election of Uribe in August 2002, the unified command of the AUC announced its intention to negotiate the terms of demobilisation. In accordance with the precondition set by the Colombian government for such talks, the AUC declared a unilateral ceasefire on the first of December 2002.[15] The government sought to accommodate the negotiation process by adjusting the existing legal framework under Law No. 418 of 1997, which regulated individual and collective demobilisation processes, by adopting Law No. 782 of 2002 and, later, by regulating Decree No. 128 of 2003. Law No. 782 gave a "legal mandate" to initiate the negotiation process with the AUC-linked paramilitary groups, as so-called 'organised armed groups at the margins of the law'.[16] Moreover, Article 13 of Decree No. 128 provided for legal benefits in terms of pardons and amnesties to the paramilitaries, with the exclusion of persons who were being investigated for or who had been convicted of serious crimes.[17] However, these legal instruments were criticised for consolidating impunity and neglecting victims' rights to truth, justice and reparation.[18] Along with not being required to identify illegally obtained assets, none of the paramilitaries who obtained legal benefits were required to provide reparations to their victims.[19]

Under mounting pressure, the government presented various bills before Congress that sought to bring a balance between the demands of peace and justice. This eventually resulted in the adoption of the Justice and Peace Law in 2005.[20] The process regulated by the Law has been subsequently modified, resulting in a complex legal and institutional framework. It is only of a residual nature, meaning that it complements and does not supersede the preceding laws that regulate the demobilisation efforts. Consequently, only those who were excluded from the existing amnesty scheme, under Law No. 782 and Decree No. 128, would fall under the special criminal justice process regulated by the Justice and Peace Law.[21]

14 Jemima García-Godos, 'Colombia: Accountability and DDR in the Pursuit of Peace?' in Chandra Lekha Sriram and others (eds), *Transitional Justice and Peacebuilding on the Ground: Victims and Ex-combatants* (Routledge 2013) 220.

15 Baltasar Garzón (coord.), 'Diagnóstico de Justicia y Paz En El Marco de Justicia Transicional En Colombia' (OEA and Mapp-OEA 2011) 16.

16 See Section 5.4 for a discussion of this concept. García-Godos (n 14) 222.

17 Art 50 Law No 418 of 1997 as modified by Art 19 Law No 782 of 2002; Art 21 Decree No 128 of 2003; IACHR, 'Report on the Demobilization Process in Colombia' OEA/Ser.L/V/II.120 Doc 60 (13 December 2004) para 62.

18 UNCHR, 'Report of the United Nations High Commissioner for Human Rights on the Human Rights Situation in Colombia' (17 February 2004) UN Doc E/CN.4/2004/13 Annex III para 8; García-Godos and Lid (n 2).

19 Amnesty International (n 6) 13, 20–21; Laplante and Theidon (n 8) 65.

20 Rodrigo Uprimny and Maria Paula Saffon, 'Uses and Abuses of Transitional Justice Discourse in Colombia' (PRIO 2007) 9–10.

21 Art 62 Justice and Peace Law; Comisión Colombiana de Juristas, 'Anotaciones Sobre Ley de Justicia y Paz' (2007) 14.

In 2010, a complementary transitional justice scheme was introduced under Law No. 1424 which modified the original treatment offered to low-level offenders not covered by the Justice and Peace Law. This scheme involved engaging them in a truth-seeking process in exchange for judicial benefits.[22] According to a governmental report of 2017, only 6,7% of the 58.161 demobilised persons registered between 2002 and 2016 were to be dealt with under the Justice and Peace Law.[23] This is an alarming number given their involvement in serious crimes and the impact on victims' rights.

The Justice and Peace Law regulates a system of special criminal proceedings as part of Colombia's ordinary justice system. These proceedings deal with the investigation, prosecution and sanctioning of individuals (so-called *postulados*), who have committed or participated in serious crimes during and on the occasion of their membership in an NSAG which has subjected itself to the collective demobilisation process.[24] These crimes involve conduct which amounts to serious violations of IHL and IHRL.[25] The reform introduced by Law No. 1592 in 2012 provided for the prioritisation of cases and made it possible to prosecute crimes together, grouped into patterns of macro-criminality. This allowed to better respond to the distinct nature of the systematic violations committed by the paramilitary organisations and the resulting reparations claims of victims, which necessitated a different set of legal tools than those typical for common crime.[26]

The Law seeks to strike a balance between the demands for peace and justice. NSAGs are encouraged to participate through the granting of judicial benefits, in the form of alternative sanctions, to their members. These benefits, however, are conditioned on the NSAG member's contributions to truth, justice and reparations for victims. Such sanctions involve the

22 Silke Pfeiffer, 'Transitional Justice for Rank-and-File Combatants in Colombia: Insights from Law No. 1424' (NOREF 2015).

23 Contraloría General de la República, 'Análisis Sobre Los Resultados y Costos de La Ley de Justicia y Paz' (2017) 7; Truth Commission of Colombia (n 6) 450.

24 Arts 1–2, 9 Justice and Peace Law; Arts 1(1), 2(1) Decree No 3391 of 2006; Comisión Colombiana de Juristas (n 21) 444; Kai Ambos, *Procedimiento de La Ley de Justicia y Paz (Ley 975 de 2005) y Derecho Penal Internacional* (GTZ GmbH 2010) 21–26.

25 See Law No 599 of 2000, Título II; *Case against Fredy Rendón Herrera* Superior Tribunal of Bogotá (Colombia) Justice and Peace Chamber (16 December 2011) 412; *Case against Manuel De Jesús Pirabán and Others* Superior Tribunal of Bogotá (Colombia) Justice and Peace Chamber (25 July 2016) para 5.5.2.2; *Case against Iván Roberto Duque Gaviria and Others* Superior Tribunal of Bogotá (Colombia) Justice and Peace Chamber (11 August 2017) para 6.4.1.

26 IACHR, 'Country Report Colombia: Truth, Justice and Reparation' OEA/Ser.L/V/II. Doc 49/13 (31 December 2013) paras 41, 358–359; María Camila Moreno, 'Uncovering Colombia's Systems of Macro-Criminality' *openDemocracy* (12 August 2014).

suspension of the ordinary criminal sanction, which is replaced by a significantly reduced prison sentence of five to eight years.[27]

One of the salient features of the Justice and Peace Law is the recognition of victims' right to reparation.[28] From the opposite perspective, convicted individuals who benefit from this legal framework have a duty to make reparation on the basis of their criminal responsibility.[29] In line with the UN Basic Principles and Guidelines, this involves a right and corresponding duty in respect of the five main forms of reparations including through actions such as the handing over of illegally obtained goods or a public recognition of responsibility.[30] Although the Justice and Peace Law does not expressly base its approach to reparations on international law, the case law of the Justice and Peace Chambers extensively refers to international legal instruments, such as the UN Basic Principles and Guidelines.[31]

Reparations are based on the individual criminal responsibility of the demobilised person and are judicially determined. As a result, victims can only claim reparations at the end of the criminal proceedings during a reparations hearing (the so-called *incidente de reparación*).[32] This hearing cannot be held without or separated from the criminal proceedings. Thus, the procedure is first and foremost a criminal process, with the principal interest being the exercise of criminal justice.[33] The scheme has resulted in significant challenges for victims who are seeking reparations. As a result, additional efforts were made to establish an individual administrative reparations programme in 2008 as a first step and, later, a comprehensive policy under the so-called Victims' Law of 2011 to deal with reparations in a more efficient manner. All in all, the implementation of the judicial path to reparations has experienced considerable criticism.[34] A 2017 report of the Office of

27 Arts 3, 29 Justice and Peace Law; Arts 1(2), 2(2) Decree No 3391 of 2006.
28 Art 4 Justice and Peace Law.
29 Arts 37 para 38.3, 42(1) Justice and Peace Law.
30 Arts 8, 44, 46–48 Justice and Peace Law; Art 16 Decree No. 3391 of 2006; UNGA, Basic Principles and Guidelines on the Right to a Remedy and Reparation for Victims of Gross Violations of International Human Rights Law and Serious Violations of International Humanitarian Law adopted by UNGA Res 60/147 on 16 December 2005 (21 March 2006) UN Doc A/RES/60/147 (UN Basic Principles and Guidelines) principles 18–23.
31 See, e.g., *Case against Edgar Ignacio Fierro Flores and Others* Superior Tribunal of Barranquilla (Colombia) Justice and Peace Chamber (18 December 2018) 1304–1305; *Case against Iván Roberto Duque Gaviria and Others* Superior Tribunal of Bogotá (Colombia) Justice and Peace Chamber (19 December 2018) 3835, 6852; *Case against Germán Antonio Pineda López* Superior Tribunal of Medellín (Colombia) Justice and Peace Chamber (25 January 2019) 491–492.
32 Arts 23, 45 Justice and Peace Law.
33 Claudia López Díaz (coord.), 'Daño y Reparación Judicial En El Ámbito de La Ley de Justicia y Paz' (GTZ 2010) 15.
34 García-Godos (n 14) 226; Camilo Andrés Hernández Barreto, 'Justicia Transicional Para Víctimas En Colombia. Más Allá Del Posconflicto' (2014) 83 Cien Días Vistos por CINEP/PPP 15, 17; Capone (n 2) 140; Nelson Camilo Sanchez and Adriana Rudling, 'Reparations in Colombia: Where To?' (Queen's University Belfast 2019)

the Comptroller revealed that, by the time of the completion of the report, only 6.4% of the compensation measures ordered had been paid through the proceeds of assets handed over by the *postulados*.[35]

5.3 The *raison d'être* of the Justice and Peace Law

The Justice and Peace process aims to establish individual criminal responsibility for crimes under the consideration of the special criminal proceedings. However, the system's underlying *raison d'être* is not found in its commitment to deal with crimes perpetrated in an individual and isolated manner. It emanates instead from the need to deal with the investigation and prosecution of, and the matter of judicial benefits for, persons linked to so-called 'armed groups at the margins of the law' which have committed themselves to collective demobilisation under the Justice and Peace Law framework. The access to the judicial benefits is explicitly conditioned, from the perspective of the subject, on the person's membership within the NSAG that is participating in the collective demobilisation process and, from a causal point of view, on the punishable actions committed during and on the occasion of that person's membership within such a group. Accordingly, the Justice and Peace Law's *raison d'être* is to be found in the relation that exists between the crimes themselves and the activity of the NSAG. For this reason, crimes committed by paramilitaries that are unrelated to the activities of the respective group do not fall within the scope of the Justice and Peace Law. They are to be dealt with in the ordinary justice system.[36] This consideration is also reflected in the definition of 'victim' under the Justice and Peace Law, which is a person that individually or collectively suffered harm as a result of the criminal actions "carried out by organised armed groups at the margins of the law".[37]

This was also underscored by the Supreme Court of Justice in response to the first judgment against Wilson Salazar Carrascal, *alias* El Loro, which was eventually struck down. The Court held that the objective of the Law is to attend to massive and systematic violations perpetrated within the context of NSAGs' activity, and not to crimes perpetrated in an individual capacity. Therefore, it is necessary to uncover the larger collective context in which a violation takes place.[38] This requires an exploration of, among other issues, the

29, 48; '15 Años de Justicia y Paz: Avances En Reparación y Deudas En Justicia' *El Colombiano* (4 January 2020).

35 Contraloría General de la República (n 23) 29. See also Wilson Alejandro Martínez Sánchez, 'La Extinción de Dominio En El Posconflicto Colombiano: Lecciones Aprendidas de Justicia y Paz' (Ministerio de Justicia y del Derecho – Colombia and UNODC 2016).

36 Arts 1, 2, 10, 20 Justice and Peace Law; *Judgment C-370/06* (n 9) para 6.2.4.4.4.-6.2.4.4.7.

37 Art 5 Justice and Peace Law [own translation].

38 Arts 7, 15, 56 Justice and Peace Law.

underlying motives of the organisation, its chain of command and its power structures, "with a view to establishing both the responsibility of the illegal armed group and that of the demobilised".[39] This process involves examining the phenomena of macro-criminality and necessitates a contextualisation of the case within the broader activities of the NIAC, while simultaneously identifying the broader patterns of violence and the other actors involved.[40] Indeed, the reform of Law No. 1592 in 2012 further sharpened the collective focus by introducing the concept of so-called 'patterns of macro-criminality' to guide the criminal investigations. Within this framework, the crime of conspiracy to commit serious crimes (*concierto para delinquir agravado*) constitutes the foundation to consider other imputed crimes carried out within the context of an NSAG's activities.[41] Hence, the so-called *delito base* of the Justice and Peace Law provides the necessary basis to legally establish the causal relation, as previously mentioned.[42]

5.4 Scope of application

5.4.1 Organised armed groups at the margins of the law

The Justice and Peace Law aims to facilitate peace processes and the individual and collective demobilisation of members of so-called "organised armed groups at the margins of the law" (*grupos armados (organizados) al margen de la ley*).[43] Under Colombian national law, this concept refers to:

> a guerrilla or self-defence group, or a significant and integral part of these [groups] such as blocks, fronts or other modalities of those same organisations.[44]

39 *Appeals Judgment No 31539* Supreme Court of Justice of Colombia (Criminal Cassation Chamber) (31 July 2009) para 1.1 [own translation].

40 Catalina Díaz Gómez and Camilo Ernesto Bernal Sarmiento, 'El Diseno Institucional de Reparaciones En La Ley de Justicia Y Paz: Una Evaluación Preliminary' in Catalina Díaz Gómez, Nelson Camilo Sánchez and Rodrigo Uprimny Yepes (eds), *Reparar en Colombia: Los Dilemas en Contextos de Conflicto, Pobreza y Exclusión* (ICTJ and Dejusticia 2009) 596–604.

41 Ambos (n 24) 131. *Concierto para delinquir agravado* presents itself when various persons come together with the objective to commit serious crimes such as genocide, forced displacement of persons, torture and enforced disappearances, among other crimes. 'Concierto Para Delinquir Simple En El Marco de La Ley 975' (*Observatorio Legislativo*, 2007); Marco Sassòli, 'Taking Armed Groups Seriously: Ways to Improve Their Compliance with International Humanitarian Law' (2010) 1 Journal of International Humanitarian Legal Studies 5, 43.

42 *Appeals Judgment No 31539* (n 39) paras 1.1–1.7; Comisión Colombiana de Juristas, 'La Justicia Se Acerca a Las Víctimas: La Corte Suprema de Justicia Anuló La Primera Sentencia de La Ley 975 En El Caso Del Paramilitar Alias "El Loro"' (2009) Boletín No 38: Serie sobre los Derechos de las Víctimas y la Aplicación de la Ley 975.

43 Arts 9–11 Justice and Peace Law [own translation].

44 Art 1 Justice and Peace Law [own translation].

Moreover, in conformity with the requirements of IHL, such groups are described as those that, "under the direction of a responsible command, exercise such control over a part of the territory that allows them to realise sustained and concerted military operations".[45] The definition draws directly from the threshold criteria included in Article 1(1) of Additional Protocol II applicable to NIACs, but adds a further restrictive condition that relates to the nature of the NSAG. Namely, the actor should be a guerrilla or self-defence group.[46] Accordingly, the Justice and Peace Law provides for a single legal framework under which ideologically different NSAGs are to be treated equally.[47] On the other hand, criminal organisations or simple bands engaged in common crimes are excluded. The scope of application is directed to armed organisations that have challenged the stability of the country and national peace, therefore requiring special criminal treatment, different from that applied to common crimes in ordinary times.[48] Law No. 782 modified the original definition by no longer requiring that the government explicitly recognise an NSAG's political character as a condition for peace talks.[49] Consequently, the legal framework was adjusted to accommodate the process to the paramilitaries, whose characteristics sowed doubts about whether they could be granted the status of political agents.[50]

The notion of organised armed group at the margins of the law does not only encompass the armed organisation itself, but also its substructures, such as blocks or fronts. In the words of the Constitutional Court, these are "specific armed groups that realise their criminal activities in a determinate zone of the national territory".[51] Thus, the Justice and Peace Law deals not only with an NSAG that is recognised as a party to a NIAC, but also with its substructures that fulfil the Additional Protocol II criteria and are, hence, NSAGs in themselves. This appears to accommodate decentralised NSAGs.

45 Art 8(1) Law No 418 of 1997; Art 3 Law No 782 of 2002 [own translation].
46 Andrea Forer (coord.), *Manual de Procedimiento Para Ley de Justicia y Paz* (Editorial Milla Ltda 2009) 119–120.
47 García-Godos and Lid (n 2) 504.
48 López Díaz (n 33) 14.
49 Art 8 Law No 418 of 1997 as modified by Art 3 Law No 782 of 2002; Laplante and Theidon (n 8) 61. It is generally agreed that the (political) motives of an NSAG are irrelevant when assessing the requirements listed within IHL. Marco Sassòli, *International Humanitarian Law: Rules, Controversies, and Solutions to Problems Arising in Warfare* (Edward Elgar Publishing Limited 2019) para 6.38.
50 Manuel Fernando Quiche Ramírez, *Los Estándares de La Corte Internacional y La Ley de Justicia y Paz* (Editorial Universidad del Rosario 2009) 308; Christine Evans, *The Right to Reparation in International Law for Victims of Armed Conflict* (Cambridge University Press 2012) 208; Centro Nacional de Memoria Histórica (n 5) 243, 248, 250.
51 *Judgment C-370/06* (n 9) para 6.2.4.4.4 [own translation].

5.4.2 The AUC under the Justice and Peace Law

The various paramilitary groups which eventually made up the AUC were initially not formally connected to each other. They operated on an autonomous basis across several parts of the country. This changed with the creation of the AUC in 1997. In an effort to co-ordinate their actions nationally and reinforce their common interests, Carlos Castaño, who was the leader of one of the most powerful paramilitary groups in Colombia, brought together several disparate paramilitary groups within the AUC, as an umbrella organisation, with the support of territorial elites and drug traffickers.[52] The group defined itself as a national counter-subversive organisation in arms and, politically, as a civil resistance movement, which sought to represent and defend national rights and interests neglected by the state and affected by guerrilla violence.[53] By 2003, the AUC had approximately 13,500 members, who were organised in a series of blocks that operated through fronts, with control and influence in several government departments and municipalities.[54]

The AUC portrayed its organisation as an armed contra-insurgency force, with a hierarchical pyramid structure and a responsible national command, the *Estado Mayor Conjunto*, as well as an internal disciplinary statute and a solid political and ideological formation.[55] Correspondingly, the AUC has been understood and identified as a single party to the NIAC, albeit a party characterised by its complex relations with the state.[56] However, it is commonly agreed that, contrary to its initial aim, the AUC never managed to fully unify and consolidate its structures at the national level. It lacked well-defined rules that regulated the structure of the paramilitary groups, their mechanisms of internal control and their methods of operation. Moreover, these groups were heterogeneous in nature. Some were analogous to private armies in the service of drug trafficking, whereas others were driven by a stronger counter-insurgency

52 Francisco Gutiérrez Sanín, 'Telling the Difference: Guerrillas and Paramilitaries in the Colombian War' (2008) 36 Politics & Society 3, 14.

53 *Case against Manuel De Jesús Pirabán and Others* Superior Tribunal of Bogotá (n 25) para 556.

54 Amnesty International (n 6) 10; International Crisis Group, 'Colombia's New Armed Groups' (2007) 3–5; Felipe Gómez Isa, 'Paramilitary Demobilisation in Colombia: Between Peace and Justice' (FRIDE 2008) 12; IACHR (n 26) para 47; Ana Arjona, *Rebelocracy: Social Order in the Colombian Civil War* (Cambridge University Press 2016) 99.

55 *Case against Manuel De Jesús Pirabán and Others* (n 25) para 556.

56 See, e.g., Human Rights Watch, 'War Without Quarter: Colombia and International Humanitarian Law' (1998); Arturo Carrillo-Suárez, 'Hors De Logique: Contemporary Issues in International Humanitarian Law as Applied to Internal Armed Conflict' (1999) 15 American University of International Law Review 1, 112; US Department of State, 'Country Report on Human Rights Practices 2002 – Colombia' (2003); Felicity Szesnat and Annie R Bird, 'Colombia' in Elizabeth Wilmshurst (ed), *International Law and the Classification of Conflicts* (Oxford University Press 2012).

motivation. Certain groups were also more disciplined than others. It has been suggested that far from being a centralised NSAG, the AUC should instead be viewed as a national confederation of paramilitary structures, which was characterised by its decentralised nature that provided for great autonomy in respect of its constituent paramilitary blocks.[57]

The AUC's narrative, and particularly the nature of its organisational structure, have been challenged in light of information which surfaced within the context of Justice and Peace Law cases against paramilitary members.[58] In a judgment of 2017, the Justice and Peace Chamber reflected critically on the AUC's official narrative by carrying out a review of the preceding 44 judgments. Various arguments casting doubt over the AUC narrative were raised.[59] Based on several findings, it was, for instance, questioned whether there was a responsible AUC command at the national level in accordance with the understanding of this concept in ICL and IHL. On the basis of the analysis, the Chamber proposed that the AUC should not be identified as a federal criminal organisation with a responsible national command, but rather as a temporary and unstable alliance of various owners of regional private armies and drug traffickers. These actors came together to benefit from the opportunities arising from a peace process, which, in principle, offered them a flexible and convenient legal framework to demobilise, hand in their weapons and return to civil life.[60] Similar considerations were formulated in an interview with a Justice and Peace Magistrate:

> [W]e are realising more and more that it was not the great United Self-Defence Forces of Colombia, no, it did not exist, they consisted of blocks independent from one and other […] they were confederated each one with their own commanders and if they needed to join forces for convenience to do an operation, they did, but even so between the same fronts or blocks there were always wars […] they were more independent, more autonomous, there was not the same degree of hierarchy that characterised the FARC-EP, for this reason we cannot speak of the group of Self-Defence Forces of Colombia, but rather of the *Bloque Norte, Bloque Central Bolívar, Bloque Vencedores de Arauca* and those blocks because there was no dependence of one on the other like in the FARC-EP.[61]

57 Sanín (n 52) 17, 28; Arjona (n 54) 98–100.

58 Centro Nacional de Memoria Histórica, 'Paramilitarismo: Balance de La Contribución Del CNMH al Esclarecimiento Histórico' (2018) 64–65.

59 '"Las Auc Fueron Una Alianza Criminal de Ejércitos Privados"' *VerdadAbierta* (10 June 2017).

60 *Case against Indalecio José Sánchez Jaramillio* Superior Tribunal of Bogotá (Colombia) Justice and Peace Chamber (23 May 2017) 109–142.

61 Interview No 3 (Colombia, April 2019).

Thus, the AUC seems to have never managed to fully consolidate at the national level. It remained a conglomerate of units, which responded to their own commanders and maintained their own distinct internal structures.[62] Although the top commanders would unite when shared interests arose, the group had no centralised and hierarchical command structure comparable to that which characterised the FARC-EP. The paramilitary leaders came together, for example, to demobilise collectively, but in practice this was not done in a united manner at the level of the AUC. Instead, the paramilitary blocks and their commanders negotiated their respective demobilisations in several parallel talks with the Colombian government.[63] This process stands in stark contrast with the FARC-EP peace negotiations, in which the group took part as a single and unified entity.

In terms of IHL, an NSAG that operates in a decentralised manner and consists of various sub-groups is not necessarily excluded from meeting the IHL requirement of organisation and, thus, from being identified as a single party to a NIAC.[64] The legal implication, when such a group is found to be a single party, is that IHL would regulate all those who are part of this united force. Research has indicated that international law requires more than a *de facto* relationship between sub-groups for such an entity to be identified as a singular party to a conflict. Instead, it appears essential that at least some form of centralised leadership be exercised.[65] Rodenhäuser proposes that a party's leadership should exercise both a degree of operational co-ordination, which refers to the ability to co-ordinate military activities and distribute logistics, as well as strategic authority to determine the overall military objectives and the sub-groups' internal rules.[66] From this perspective, it can be questioned whether the AUC could be understood as a single organised group which is party to the conflict. This would imply that a separate examination should be carried out *vis-à-vis* the application of IHL to each group allied under the AUC banner.

The way the AUC is dealt with in the Justice and Peace process appears to respond to the particularities of its decentralised nature. The criminal proceedings before the Justice and Peace Chambers, for example, are commonly held against members of a particular AUC-linked paramilitary block or front, which is recognised as constituting an individual, organised NSAG pursuant to Common Article 3 and Additional Protocol II, instead of the AUC as such.[67]

62 Arjona (n 54) 91.
63 *Case against Indalecio José Sánchez Jaramillio* (n 60) 136–137, 139; Interview No 3 (Colombia, April 2019).
64 Sandesh Sivakumaran, *The Law of Non-International Armed Conflict* (Oxford University Press 2012) 173.
65 Ibid. 175–176; Katharine Fortin, *The Accountability of Armed Groups under Human Rights Law* (Oxford University Press 2017) 133–134.
66 Tilman Rodenhäuser, *Organizing Rebellion: Non-State Armed Groups under International Humanitarian Law, Human Rights Law, and International Criminal Law* (Oxford University Press 2018) 75–85.
67 See, e.g., *Case against José Rubén Peña Tobón and Others* Superior Tribunal of Bogotá (Colombia) Justice and Peace Chamber (1 December 2011) paras 1–2; *Case*

5.4.3 Concluding insights on non-state armed groups as responsible actors

Several initial insights can be derived from the approach of the Justice and Peace process that have broader relevance to the operationalisation of the duty of NSAGs to provide reparation under international law. The approach suggests that the organisational structure of an NSAG could direct the way its responsibility and resulting duty to make reparation could be attributed and operationalised. This observation constitutes a novel finding that, thus far, has not been explored. The Justice and Peace process deals with organised armed groups at the margins of the law, which are NSAGs, as such, or a significant and integral part of these groups, such as blocks or fronts, which satisfy the additional requirements set by Additional Protocol II. This would appear to accommodate NSAGs that operate in a decentralised manner and are made up of several sub-groups, which are themselves recognised as organised NSAGs. Indeed, the criminal proceedings in Colombia have commonly been brought against the members of specific AUC-linked paramilitary blocks or fronts as distinct actors. Consequently, and as will be extensively discussed in Section 5.5, monetary compensation can not only be claimed from the convicted member but also from the paramilitary block or front to which the person belonged instead of the AUC as such. The civil responsibility of a paramilitary block or front is based on the nexus of causality that exists between the structure's illegal activity (being the context in which the crimes were perpetrated) and the harm that it caused. It follows from this, for example, that the assets handed over by a specific paramilitary block cannot be used to provide reparations to all the victims of the AUC, but only to those of that particular paramilitary block. Thus, the NSAG's organisational structure has direct implications for the way the civil responsibility of the collectivity is operationalised. In addition, the Justice and Peace Law is concerned with NSAGs that satisfy the higher requirements of Article 1 Additional Protocol II, which involves the condition of territorial control. This converges with one of the international legal tendencies identified in Chapter 2, which emphasised the possible international responsibility of NSAGs which exercise control over part of a territory.

5.5 Monetary compensation

5.5.1 The collective duty to hand over illegally obtained goods

In cases of collective demobilisation, the Justice and Peace Law imposes a duty to hand over all goods, which were *illegally obtained* over the course of the NIAC, as a condition of eligibility and to have access to the judicial benefits.[68] The Fund for the Reparation of the Victims (Reparations Fund) administers

against Salvatore Mancuso Gómez Superior Tribunal of Bogotá (Colombia) Justice and Peace Chamber (31 October 2014) paras 699–700. Jan Römer, *Killing in a Gray Area between Humanitarian Law and Human Rights* (Springer 2010) 19–20.

68 Art 10.2 Justice and Peace Law.

and liquidates these goods in order to carry out judicially ordered compensation measures.[69] Hence, there is a direct co-relation between the duty to hand over the illegally obtained goods, as a condition for access to the judicial benefits, and the compensation measures.[70] Besides these goods, the convicted members, or the NSAGs themselves by virtue of the principle of solidarity, may be obligated by judicial order to hand over *legally obtained goods* to fully satisfy their duty to provide compensation (see the following section).[71]

The duty to hand over all illegally obtained goods can be understood as resulting in obligations for both the members and the NSAGs themselves. As stated in Article 54(2) of the Justice and Peace Law, the Reparations Fund is made up of the goods or assets handed in by "the persons or illegally organised armed groups" that fall within the purview of the Law.[72] Moreover, the goods handed over by any member of an NSAG in accordance with Article 10.2 of the Justice and Peace Law, which sets this eligibility condition in the case of collective demobilisation, are "to be understood as being carried out in the name of the respective group".[73] In other words, they are considered as collective goods or rather goods that the group illegally obtained in the framework of its criminal activities during the NIAC. As further discussed in Section 5.5.4, these goods are the first to be affected for compensation purposes. Ultimately, the totality of the illegal goods collected, which may have been handed over both individually and collectively, are destined to compensate those victims who are recognised as having suffered harm due to activities of an NSAG, where specific demobilised members of that NSAG have been held criminally responsible for the activities. This approach fits with the logic that the objective of the law is not to affect the goods in an individual manner, but rather at the level of the organisation.[74]

69 Arts 54–55 Justice and Peace Law.

70 Art 45.1 Justice and Peace Law identifies the delivery of the illegally obtained goods to the state for the provision of reparations to the victims as an action of integral reparation.

71 *Judgment C-370/06* (n 9) para 6.2.4.1.18.

72 [own translation] Art 18(1) Decree No 3391 of 2006; Fondo para la Reparación de las Víctimas – Unidad para la Atención y la Reparación Integral a las Víctimas, 'Informe Ejecutivo (Fecha de Corte de La Información Reportada: 30 de Septiembre de 2016)' (2016) 2.

73 Art 14 para Decree No 3391 of 2006 [own translation].

74 For example, the judgment rendered against members of the *Bloque Centauros* and *Bloque Héroes del Llano y del Guaviare* lists a number of goods that were handed over during the collective demobilisation of both blocks in April 2006. In addition, some *postulados* individually delivered various goods intended for reparations, whereas others declared that they did not possess any goods that could be used to that end. When evaluating the eligibility condition in Art 10.2 Justice and Peace Law, the court confirmed that the *postulados* handed over the illegally obtained goods in both an individual and collective manner in the framework of their demobilisation and over the course of the Justice and Peace process to contribute to reparations. Hence, the eligibility condition was deemed satisfied. *Case against Manuel De Jesús Pirabán and Others* (n 25) 27–34, 53–54. For another example, see

The illegal goods can be considered as belonging to a specific NSAG for the purposes of the Justice and Peace Law, when they were acquired during and on the occasion of the group's activities over the course of the NIAC. However, the actual management of these assets by the AUC-linked paramilitary structures was more complex in practice. Paramilitary leaders and mid-ranking figures accumulated significant assets and property over the course of the conflict. Sanín explains that the driving logic was, "the higher you are in the hierarchical ladder, the more territory and rents you have access to".[75] Accordingly, these goods and assets did not necessarily go to the organisation itself. This is in sharp contrast to the way the FARC-EP managed the assets it acquired over the course of its activities. These goods were considered as collective property of the movement, and keeping them for personal benefit was considered stealing from the movement.[76]

The duty to hand over all illegally obtained goods is a condition for individual NSAG members to gain access to the judicial benefits. This implies that those who fail to comply with this obligation should lose the afforded benefits.[77] This should, in principle, have resulted in a significant incentive to act in accordance with the requirements. In addition, it should have contributed to the process of effectively dismantling paramilitary structures by targeting their considerable wealth.[78] However, the surrender of assets quickly became one of the main challenges confronting the Justice and Peace process.[79] As reported, "the former paramilitary chiefs are reluctant to surrender assets and resort to grey areas of the law or legal tricks, corruption of officials and violent acts of intimidation, all of which dampen expectations and instil fear in victims who resort to litigation to get their property returned to them".[80] Consequently, the major share of compensation orders have been financed through public money, rather than by the paramilitaries.[81] While few assets were actually seized, others significantly decreased in their value due to mismanagement. Other assets found their way to poor conditions or remote areas.[82] All in all, the duty appears to

Case against Iván Roberto Duque Gaviria and Others (n 25) 44–48. Interview No 3 (Colombia, April 2019).

75 Sanín (n 52) 16.

76 Art 13 FARC-EP Statute (as adopted at the Ninth National Guerrilla Conference) (2007); Arts 3(l), 4(3) Reglamento de Régimen Disciplinario de las FARC-EP (as adopted at the Ninth National Guerrilla Conference) (2007); Sanín (n 52) 13–16.

77 An explicit exclusion ground was only provided in 2012 with the passing of Law No 1592. See Arts 5 and 8 Law No 1592 that introduce new Arts 11A(3) and 11D respectively to the Justice and Peace Law; Art 34(3) Decree No 3011 of 2013. Compare to Art 12 Decree No 3391 of 2006.

78 Gómez Isa (n 54) 12.

79 Martínez Sánchez (n 35) 35–36.

80 IACHR (n 26) 141.

81 Fondo para la Reparación de las Víctimas – Unidad para la Atención y la Reparación Integral a las Víctimas (n 72) 7–8; Martínez Sánchez (n 35) 43; Contraloría General de la República (n 23) 29.

82 Sanchez and Rudling (n 34) 48, 59.

have remained largely ineffective in practice, despite its strict legal character. In addition, the Justice and Peace experience exposes the significant challenges that come along with attempts to recover and seize assets from NSAGs.

5.5.2 Ruling C-370/06: introducing a cascading responsibility scheme

With the introduction of the Justice and Peace Law, a debate unravelled on various aspects relating to the question of responsibility for reparations.[83] Eventually, the Constitutional Court was seized on the question and put forward an interesting cascading responsibility scheme in its landmark ruling C-370 of 2006. This ruling was significant in recognising the civil responsibility of the NSAGs to which the *postulados* belonged.[84]

The Constitutional Court made its first pronouncements regarding this responsibility scheme when it determined whether convicted persons should provide reparations, not only through their illegally obtained assets, but also through their *legally attained resources*. The Court questioned whether it would be justified, within transitional justice processes, to drift away from a core general principle of law that 'those who are responsible for causing harm or damage are obligated to repairing it' by shifting this duty from the perpetrator to the state. Here also played the consideration that the prospect of having one's personal assets completely depleted, in the face of repairing mass victimisation, could present itself as a disincentive for NSAG members to submit themselves to the peace process.[85] Rather than yielding to this argument, the Court identified its several weaknesses and concluded that the provisions of the Justice and Peace Law, which confined the source of reparations only to illegally obtained assets, were unconstitutional.[86]

As for the first concern, the Court held that there was no constitutional reason which would allow an exception to the aforementioned principle of law regarding reparation for wrongful acts. It explained that compensation provided through the perpetrator's personal assets is considered a necessary condition to both guarantee the rights of victims and promote the fight against impunity. The complete exemption of the responsible person's duty to repair would result in a sort of blanket amnesty for civil responsibility. In this light,

83 Nelson Camilo Sánchez, '¿Perder Es Ganar Un Poco? Avances y Frustraciones de La Discusión Del Estatuto de Víctimas En Colombia' in Catalina Díaz Gómez, Nelson Camilo Sánchez and Rodrigo Uprimny Yepes (eds), *Reparar en Colombia: Los Dilemas en Contextos de Conflicto, Pobreza y Exclusión* (ICTJ and Dejusticia 2009) 647–748; Sanchez and Rudling (n 34) 6.

84 See *Judgment C-370/06* (n 9) para 6.2.4.

85 Julian Guerrero Orozco and Mariana Goetz, 'Reparations for Victims in Colombia: Colombia's Law on Justice and Peace' in Mariana Goetz and Alan Stephens (eds), *Reparations for Victims of Genocide, War Crimes and Crimes against Humanity* (Martinus Nijhoff Publishers 2009) 446.

86 *Judgment C-370/06* (n 9) paras 6.2.4.1.7–6.2.4.1.11.

the Court considered it justified that such persons should answer the duty to provide reparation with their personal assets, while setting the possibility of a decent livelihood as a proportional limit. On this basis, the Constitutional Court confirmed that the *postulados* are the actors who bear the primary responsibility to provide reparation with their entire patrimony to the victims who experienced harm due to their criminal actions.[87]

The Constitutional Court went a step further, by holding that it is not only those who were held criminally responsible that should provide compensation, but also the NSAGs to which they belonged. The Court explicitly recognised the solidarity civil responsibility held by NSAGs, which it based on the legal principle regarding reparation for wrongful conduct linked to the underlying rationale of the Justice and Peace Law.[88] This civil responsibility of the NSAG is subsidiary to the primary responsibility of the convicted member: meaning that it is triggered when the legally obtained assets of the convicted NSAG member are not sufficient to cover the compensation order.[89] Accordingly, the civil responsibility of the NSAG forms the second step in the responsibility scheme.[90]

The Constitutional Court was left to decide on the precise role of the Colombian state in the question of reparations for victims of NSAGs. While some argued that public resources should not be used, others asserted that the state, and not the perpetrators, should take the principal role in ensuring reparations in a transitional justice system seeking to deal with serious violations that have resulted in an immense universe of victims.[91] The Court held that responsibility could not be entirely shifted to the state, as such a shift would, in practice, result in placing the reparative burden upon Colombian citizens.[92] Instead, the Court held that the state only takes a residual role in safeguarding victims' rights. Concretely, this means that the state assumes a subsidiary responsibility, only where the convicted person, or the NSAG to which he or she belonged, fail to fulfil their obligations.[93] The Victims' Law makes clear that it does not imply any recognition of the state's direct responsibility for the wrongful conduct.[94] Instead, the duty to provide residual reparations is based on the state's duty to guarantee human rights, in conformity with international and constitutional law.[95] The complete negation of

87 Ibid. paras 6.2.4.1.11–6.2.4.1.16.

88 *Concepto No 2362* Council of State of Colombia (Sala de Consulta y Servicio Civil) (20 March 2018) Section 3 of Part II.

89 *Judgment C-370/06* (n 9) para 6.2.4.4.

90 Nelson Camilo Sánchez León and Clara Sandoval-Villalba, 'Go Big or Go Home? Lessons Learned from the Colombian Victims' Reparation System' in Carla Ferstman and Mariana Goetz (eds), *Reparations for Victims of Genocide, War Crimes and Crimes against Humanity* (Brill 2020) 551.

91 Sánchez (n 83) 648.

92 *Judgment C-370/06* (n 9) para 6.2.4.1.13.

93 Ibid. paras 6.2.4.1.12–13, 6.2.4.4.11.

94 Art 10 Law No 1448 of 2011 (Victims' Law).

95 *Judgment C-160/16* Constitutional Court of Colombia (6 April 2016). See also Art 6 (1) Justice and Peace Law; ICTJ (n 7) 25–26.

state responsibility is, however, problematic in cases where paramilitaries may have operated with the support or acquiescence of the Colombian state. Yet, from the perspective of the responsibility of non-state actors, it forms an important recognition that reparations cannot be solely dependent on the responsible individual and NSAG. Instead, the state should play an important role in safeguarding victims' right to reparation.

The resulting cascading scheme of responsibility falls partly in line with the UN Basic Principles and Guidelines, which hold that persons or other entities should provide reparations to victims for which they have been found liable, with the state taking a subsidiary role. The Colombian scheme does, however, not foresee an obligation, on the part of the responsible actor, to compensate the state where the state has already provided reparations to the victim. The role of the state has been strengthened by way of the administrative programme under the Victims' Law of 2011 that seeks to guarantee the right to reparation when the actors responsible for the harm are unable or unwilling to meet their resulting obligations.[96] The scheme legally implies that victims have rights in respect of three actors for the harm they have experienced because of paramilitary violence. However, these rights can only be exercised in a gradual manner, following the hierarchy of responsibility outlined above.[97]

5.5.2.1 Solidarity civil responsibility of non-state armed groups

As discussed in Section 5.3, the Justice and Peace Law concerns itself with the relation that exists between the criminal activity of the demobilised individuals and their membership within a specific NSAG in whose service or activities their crimes were carried out. This generates a so-called nexus of causality between the activity of this group and the harm that has been inflicted by it.[98] In ruling C-370/06, the Constitutional Court recognised the solidarity civil responsibility of NSAGs based on this nexus,[99] and used this reasoning to justify the extension of civil responsibility beyond the convicted individual. It noted that, although criminal liability remains individual in nature, the civil responsibility which derives from the criminal act allows for an element of solidarity: not only between those held criminally responsible, but also with regard to all identified members of the NSAG under consideration.[100]

Furthermore, the Constitutional Court coupled the enjoyment of judicial benefits to the question of responsibility. It argued that, if judicial benefits are granted to an NSAG which has made a commitment to collectively demobilise, or rather to its members due to their membership in this group, this necessitates

96 UN Basic Principles and Guidelines principles 15–17.
97 Laplante and Theidon (n 8) 105.
98 This nexus of causality is also expressly referred to in Art 42(2) Justice and Peace Law, which deals with anonymous harm (see Section 5.5.3).
99 *Concepto No 2362* (n 88) Section 3 of Part II.
100 *Judgment C-370/06* (n 9) para 6.2.4.4.7.

a corresponding civil responsibility on the condition that: 1) the real, concrete and specific harm is established; 2) the harm's causal relationship to the activity of the NSAG is demonstrated; and, 3) the membership of the demobilised persons within that group has been judicially determined.[101] The Court further held that limiting the right of victims to reparation, to the extent that the convicted person has sufficient resources to cover the compensation order, would disproportionately impair this right. An interpretation to the contrary would be manifestly unconstitutional in a context in which the demobilisation of NSAGs is incentivised by the granting of judicial benefits. Accordingly, an important justification for extending a subsidiary responsibility to NSAGs can be found in this necessity to safeguard victims' right to reparation.[102]

The civil responsibility of the NSAGs is legally construed based on the principle of solidarity. This results in holding all judicially determined members of the NSAG, to which the convicted member belonged, jointly and severally liable to repair the damages caused by the wrongful act.[103] The Colombian legal tradition is no stranger to solidarity in civil liability or its extension to persons other than those held criminally responsible. According to this tradition, the damages caused must be repaired by those held criminally responsible, jointly and severally, and by those who are obligated to respond pursuant to a substantive law.[104] The Justice and Peace Law, as modified in accordance with the constitutionally sound interpretation given by the Constitutional Court, thus provides the legal basis for such an exceptional responsibility in the case of NSAGs.[105] By extending the responsibility of solidarity beyond those members that were held criminally responsible, the Law adopts a form of vicarious liability.[106]

When addressing the responsibility of the NSAGs, the Court explicitly clarified that these groups are to be understood as paramilitary blocks or fronts.[107] This is also stated in implementing Decree No. 3391 of 2006, which holds that, in this case, the organised armed groups at the margins of the law are "understood as the respective block or front".[108] Thus, instead of holding the AUC civilly responsible, the AUC-linked paramilitary blocks and fronts, which

101 Art 15(2) Decree No 3391 of 2006; *Judgment C-370/06* (n 9) para 6.2.4.4.10.

102 *Judgment C-370/06* (n 9) paras 6.2.4.4.10–6.2.4.4.12.

103 Ibid. paras 6.2.4.4.7, 6.2.4.4.12; Gómez Isa, 'Justicia, Verdad y Reparación En El Proceso de Desmovilización Paramilitar En Colombia' (n 13) 133; López Díaz (n 33) 251; Republic of Colombia, 'Justice and Peace Law: An Experience of Truth, Justice and Reparation' Review Conference of the Rome Statute RC/ST/PJ/M.1 (1 June 2010) 7.

104 Art 96 Law No 599 of 2000.

105 *Judgment C-370/06* (n 9) paras 6.2.4.4.8–6.2.4.4.9; López Díaz (n 33) 254.

106 Laplante and Theidon (n 8) 105; Shane Darcy, *Collective Responsibility and Accountability under International Law* (Brill 2007) xix.

107 *Judgment C-370/06* (n 9) paras 6.2.4.4.7, 6.2.4.4.11.

108 Art 15 Decree No 3391 of 2006 [own translation].

satisfy the criteria set by Article 1 Additional Protocol II, are deemed to hold solidarity civil responsibility as separate NSAGs.

Certain paramilitary structures did not participate in the collective demobilisations.[109] This could have complicated the extent to which the AUC, as such, could have been held responsible as one could have argued that the collectivity did not subscribe to the process. However, this question does not arise in practice, as responsibility is considered at the sublevels of the AUC: namely, the individual AUC-linked paramilitary blocks and fronts.[110]

In many of the judgements rendered in the Justice and Peace process, magistrates have had to rely on the civil responsibility of solidarity.[111] This suggests that it has been unfeasible, in practice, to place the obligation to provide compensation solely on the convicted perpetrator in a situation of mass victimisation. This is true even when considering the fact that some paramilitary leaders accumulated significant wealth over the course of the armed conflict.[112]

Overall, the concept of the civil responsibility of NSAGs, operationalised on the basis of the principle of solidarity, provides for an interesting approach to dealing, within the confines of a criminal justice procedure, with the harmful consequences of crimes perpetrated within the context of an NSAG's activities. Furthermore, it circumvents the challenges that could have arisen when seeking to enforce responsibility directly against an NSAG and not by way of its constituent members. For instance, the group itself would have ceased to legally exist with its collective disarmament and demobilisation. From the perspective of the victims, it provides for an additional layer which safeguards, at least theoretically, their right to compensation.

5.5.3 Anonymous harm

The reparations hearing is the moment, during the criminal procedure, in which the appropriate measures to redress harms suffered by victims can be claimed

109 *Case against Iván Roberto Duque Gaviria* Superior Tribunal of Bogotá (Colombia) Justice and Peace Chamber (11 June 2010) 4–5; Garzón (n 15) 18.

110 Interview No 3 (Colombia, April 2019).

111 See, for instance, *Case against Edwar Cobos Téllez and Uber Enrique Banquéz M (Mampuján case)* Superior Tribunal of Bogotá (Colombia) Justice and Peace Chamber (29 June 2010) 205; *Case against Orlando Villa Zapata and Others* Superior Tribunal of Bogotá (Colombia) Justice and Peace Chamber (24 February 2015) 1046; *Case against Edilberto de Jesús Cañas Chavarriaga and others* Superior Tribunal of Medellín (Colombia) Justice and Peace Chamber (24 September 2015) para 833; *Appeals Judgment No 45463* Supreme Court of Justice of Colombia (Criminal Cassation Chamber) (25 November 2015) 124; *Case against Iván Roberto Duque Gaviria and Others* (n 25) 1913; *Case against Edgar Ignacio Fierro Flores and Others* (n 31) 1753–1754; *Case against Iván Roberto Duque Gaviria and Others* (n 31) 6924.

112 *Judgment C-370/06* (n 9) para 6.2.4.1.14; Human Rights Watch, 'Smoke and Mirrors: Colombia's Demobilization of Paramilitary Groups' (2005) 13–22.

and the distinct forms to achieve integral reparation are to be determined.[113] However, in cases in which it is not possible to identify the person who caused the harm, so-called anonymous harm results. To combat anonymous harm, Article 42(2) of the Justice and Peace Law allows for the possibility of holding an exceptional reparations hearing. This provides victims with the possibility to still claim reparations when the harm and the nexus of causality with the activities of an NSAG (which benefits from the Law) can be proven.[114] In such cases, the court either orders compensation directly or by way of referral by the Unit of the Public Prosecutor through the Reparations Fund, which consists of the goods handed over by demobilised members and NSAGs, among other contributors (see further Section 5.5.4).[115]

According to Article 5(3) Justice and Peace Law, the status of victim is acquired regardless of whether the author of the harmful conduct was identified, apprehended or convicted.[116] Accordingly, victims are not required to identify a specific individual perpetrator when registering with the Office of the Public Prosecutor, instead they can limit themselves to identifying the NSAG to which the perpetrator belonged.[117] This addresses a specific hurdle inherent in criminal proceedings since, in principle, a concrete crime must be linked to an identifiable author or participant. Otherwise, the harmful act remains outside of the criminal process. The Constitutional Court has held that anonymous harm cannot remain unaddressed. Where the necessary conditions are satisfied, the victim can still rely on the mechanisms provided in the Justice and Peace Law.[118] This alternate route to reparations should not be underestimated in terms of its importance, as the impossibility of individualising the offender is not exceptional in the Colombian case.[119] Moreover, direct perpetrators might have died or not submitted themselves to the Justice and Peace process.[120] This is a significant advancement for victims in terms of the exercise of their right to reparation.

The Supreme Court of Justice listed the specific conditions that must be met in order to open the reparations hearing on the basis of Article 42(2) Justice and Peace Law, while clarifying that the status of victim of the armed conflict is not sufficient in itself. The specific conditions are as follows:

113 Art 23 Justice and Peace Law; Gabriel Arias Hernández, 'Representación Judicial de Las Víctimas En Justicia y Paz' (Defensoría del Pueblo – Colombia 2009) 137.

114 *Judgment C-370/06* (n 9) para 6.2.4.4.10.

115 Art 18 Decree No 3391 of 2006; Hernández (n 113) 139–141.

116 Ibid. 139, 141.

117 Fiscalía General de la Nación (Colombia), 'Formato Registro de Hechos Atribuibles a Grupos Armados Organizados al Margen de La Ley' (Version 02 of 2018); García-Godos (n 14) 226.

118 Art 15 Decree No 3391 of 2006; *Judgment C-370/06* (n 9) paras 6.2.4.4.10–6.2.4.4.11.

119 Gómez Isa, 'Justicia, Verdad y Reparación En El Proceso de Desmovilización Paramilitar En Colombia' (n 13) 134; López Díaz (n 33) 171.

120 Interview No 1 (Colombia, February 2019); Interview No 3 (Colombia, April 2019).

1 The identification or individualisation of the NSAG (block or front);
2 The establishment of the causal relation between the harm and the activity of the group (conspiracy among its members);
3 The group has demobilised and the members have submitted themselves to the Justice and Peace Law; and,
4 The Office of the Public Prosecutor has exhausted all possible ways to identify the individual perpetrator or is able to state that this was not possible.[121]

The conditions reaffirm that the Justice and Peace process occupies itself with macro-criminality rather than ordinary and individual crime.[122] If the conditions are met, the NSAG collectively satisfies the payment of the ordered compensation through the Reparations Fund.[123] However, to the knowledge of an experienced Justice and Peace Magistrate, it has never been impossible, in practice, to attribute a criminal act to one of the individual *postulados* on the basis of the chain of command that existed within the group. As a result, this person is obligated to respond for the harm caused by the criminal act.[124]

Besides the judicial path to claim reparations, victims can also rely on the administrative programme established under the Victims' Law of 2011. In accordance with Article 3 of this Law, victims are considered as persons that have individually or collectively suffered harm due to actions that constitute infractions of IHL or grave and manifest violations of IHRL which occurred on the occasion of the NIAC. This broad conceptualisation does not require the victim to identify the author of the harmful act. However, it is indispensable to prove the link between the harmful act and the armed conflict.

5.5.4 Fund for the Reparation of the Victims: order of affection

The Justice and Peace Law created the Fund for the Reparation of the Victims, which is in charge of implementing the judicial decisions concerning monetary compensation. It has been managed since the passing of the Victims' Law by the Victims' Unit.[125] The Reparations Fund consists of assets and goods that come

121 *Appeals Judgment No 28769* Supreme Court of Justice of Colombia (Criminal Cassation Chamber) (11 December 2007); *Appeals Judgment No 29240* Supreme Court of Justice of Colombia (Criminal Cassation Chamber) (21 April 2008); *Appeals Judgment No 29642* Supreme Court of Justice of Colombia (Criminal Cassation Chamber) (23 May 2008); *Appeals Judgment No 31320* Supreme Court of Justice of Colombia (Criminal Cassation Chamber) (21 March 2009); García-Godos and Lid (n 2) 510.
122 Interview No 3 (Colombia, April 2019).
123 López Díaz (n 33) 172, 332.
124 Interview No 3 (Colombia, April 2019). However, the following publication of 2011 mentions that more than 500 victims filed a petition based on Art 42(2) Justice and Peace Law. All were rejected because of, i.a., the impossibility of determining a causal nexus between the act and the demobilised NSAG. Garzón (n 15) 74–76.
125 Art 168(8) Victims' Law. See also implementing Decree No 4802 of 2011.

from several sources. Besides the resources coming from the national budget and donations, the primary source is the illegal goods handed over in accordance with Article 10.2 of the Justice and Peace Law (see Section 5.5.1). This includes goods that were linked to relevant criminal investigations and were consequently seized.[126] Moreover, legally obtained goods may find their way into the Fund when judicially ordered to secure the full satisfaction of compensation measures. Such an order is directed against criminally convicted NSAG members or even against other members of the same block or front on the basis of its solidarity civil responsibility (see Section 5.5.2).[127]

The Victims' Unit has to take into account an order of affection with regard to the goods and assets that are in the Fund when implementing the compensation orders. In accordance with the cascading responsibility scheme, the Constitutional Court held that the perpetrators of the crimes are the first actors obligated to repair and, joining them in subsidy and by virtue of the principle of solidarity, the specific group to which the perpetrators belonged. As such, before resorting to the national budget, the perpetrators and the respective block or front should be called upon to respond with their own legally obtained goods or assets. The state only takes a residual role when the preceding resources are insufficient.[128] This process is implemented in the following manner:

1 The first stage in the order of affection concerns the *illegally obtained goods and assets of the respective block or front that collectively demobilised*. From the liquidation of these goods, the compensation ordered against the convicted members will be paid. The same goes for cases of anonymous harm.
2 When these illegal resources do not suffice to cover the amount of the ordered compensation, the further payment will be carried out using the *legal goods or assets*, which were the object of precautionary measures or were handed in by the *convicted demobilised members*.
3 When the legal resources of the persons held criminally responsible are not sufficient, the payment will be carried out using *the legal assets of the other members* of the block or front to which the convicted members belonged. This block or front must have been judicially declared as bearing a *civil responsibility of solidarity*. Hence, they also must respond to the reparatory obligation that resulted from the criminal conviction.
4 As a last resort, the national budget may be allocated with a limit set in Article 10 of the Victims' Law.[129]

126 Art 54 Justice and Peace Law. See also Art 177 Victims' Law, for an overview of the additional resources that are included in the Fund.
127 Art 18 Decree No 3391 of 2006; *Judgment C-370/06* (n 9) para 6.2.4.1.
128 Ibid. para 6.2.4.4.11; *Judgment C-575/06* Constitutional Court of Colombia (25 July 2006).
129 Art 18 Decree No 3391 of 2006.

The overview indicates that the totality of the assets and goods handed over, both individually and collectively, are destined to compensate victims. These victims have been recognised as having suffered harm due to the activities of a particular NSAG for which certain demobilised members have been held criminally responsible. Put differently, the goods of block or front A cannot be used to repair the victims of block or front B. A contrary approach would break the nexus of causality between the illegal activity of the group and the harm that it caused, which fundamentally underpins its civil responsibility. Accordingly, it would constitute an unconstitutional and illegal action. Furthermore, it would disproportionately impair the rights of the victims of group A, given that they would be left unprotected in the face of scarce resources.[130]

5.5.5 Concluding insights for non-state armed groups under international law

5.5.5.1 Operationalising the obligation to provide monetary compensation

The Justice and Peace process provides for a concrete example of how NSAGs could contribute to monetary compensation, and how their relating obligations could be operationalised in a judicial process. It also sheds light on some of the opportunities and challenges that may accompany such an effort. From this perspective, it can serve as a tentative proposal for broader, international application.

The examination has shown that the forfeiture of an NSAG's illegal assets can be tied to its members' access to certain judicial benefits granted by the state. This demonstrates the potential of offering incentives to NSAGs in return for access to their assets, which can subsequently go to the funding of reparations. Indeed, the case has indicated that these illegal assets can be used directly to provide compensation to victims of the NSAG. At the same time, the forfeiture of assets can contribute to the dismantling of the NSAG as its resources dwindle. Despite the apparent potential of the approach, the Justice and Peace experience has also exposed the significant challenges that may come along with such an endeavour. The discussion has, furthermore, indicated the need for effective enforcement mechanisms for situations where an NSAG fails to surrender its assets.

Furthermore, the NSAG holds an obligation to provide monetary compensation with its legally obtained assets, which occurs where one of its members has been convicted in relation to the activities of the group. This innovative approach to responsibility is referred to as the solidarity civil responsibility of the NSAG. It entails that all judicially determined members of the specific NSAG are jointly and severally liable to compensate damages caused by the wrongful act. Thus, the group is, in essence, held responsible by way of its

130 *Concepto No 2362* (n 88).

constituent members. This represents an interesting approach, as it avoids some of the practical and legal difficulties which could conceivably arise when bringing reparations proceedings directly against an NSAG. One such difficulty could be the legal, and even *de facto,* extinction of the group. As demonstrated in this study, an NSAG ceases to legally exist post-NIAC. The Colombian approach, thus, offers something of a response in such circumstances, whereby the responsibility of an NSAG could still be invoked for reparations purposes, but implemented at the level of its members. This supplements the discussion on post-conflict reparations in Chapter 4.

The civil responsibility of the NSAGs is based on the general principle of domestic law, which requires those causing harm to repair it. As discussed in Chapter 2, this principle has also a firm basis in international law at least with respect to states. This special form of NSAGs' civil responsibility specifically arises from the nexus of causality that exists between the activity of the specific group, as the context in which the crimes were carried out, and the harm that it caused. It illustrates that the NSAG is the broader system that facilitated the perpetration of the crimes by its members. Importantly, the Justice and Peace process strongly indicates that this system should not be left unaddressed.

5.5.5.2 Rearranged cascading regime of responsibility for monetary compensation

The Justice and Peace Law did not establish an accountability mechanism to primarily or exclusively deal with the responsibility of NSAGs as such. Instead, it is centred on the individual responsibility of the members of NSAGs, while the responsibility of these groups takes a subsidiary position. The resulting responsibility scheme, which is applicable to monetary compensation awards, partly overlaps with the proposal for the 'cascading regime of responsibility for reparation' as set out in Chapter 4. At the same time, the Colombian approach provides new insights.

Both approaches depart from the same argument, namely that the actor responsible for harms should bear the principal duty to provide reparation. In the Justice and Peace process, this actor is the *postulado*. Both approaches are also equally informed by a strong acknowledgment that reparations for gross violations cannot solely depend on non-state actors. In doing so, both support the argument that there is a need to safeguard effective reparation through subsidiary responsibility mechanisms. In the Justice and Peace system, this entails the subsidiary responsibility of the NSAG and the subsequent residual responsibility of the territorial state. More generally, this responsibility scheme underscores the importance of the final safety net to be provided by the territorial state based on its duty to guarantee human rights. Thus, the state is required to play an active role in safeguarding the satisfaction of victims' right to reparation. This requirement generally follows from Article 6 Justice and Peace Law, which provides that the state has a duty to guarantee victims' access to effective resources for repairing the harm inflicted. This assertion is further strengthened by the residual role assigned to the state regarding monetary compensation, in accordance with the Constitutional Court's landmark ruling C-370. A further, clear indication of the pivotal role that the state should play in dealing with mass victimisation is the existence of the administrative reparations programme, first established by Decree No. 1290 of 2008, and later replaced by the Victims' Law of 2011. This administrative programme seeks to deal with victims' rights in a more ambitious and comprehensive manner, being established against the backdrop of the inefficiencies and challenges that the Justice and Peace process faced regarding reparations.[131] However, the administrative path does not involve the acceptance or recognition of state responsibility for harm caused.[132]

Although some of the core considerations overlap with those presented in Chapter 4, the two responsibility schemes depart from different perspectives. The scheme developed in Chapter 4 is conducted from the perspective of the international responsibility of the NSAG, whereas the Justice and Peace scheme starts from the criminal responsibility of the individual member. The concurrent existence of both schemes can be compared to the system of responsibility under international law in which state responsibility does not exclude the individual criminal responsibility of state agents and their resulting duty of reparation under, for example, the reparations regime of the International Criminal Court. In this sense, both schemes can be understood from the different perspectives from which they start, the violations they address and the purposes they serve.

In the Colombia case, a somewhat rearranged cascading regime of responsibility emerges that is, however, based on similar arguments. It provides new insights into the role that the responsibility of an NSAG could take in relation to that of its members and the state. In addition, it concretises some of the reasons why it might be advantageous to hold an NSAG to a duty of reparation. The overall justification lies in the need to better safeguard the right of victims to reparation. This safeguard is particularly necessary when the convicted member is indigent, but also when the identity of the perpetrator remains unknown or when the perpetrator has died. Such concerns are certainly not uncommon in situations of armed conflict.

5.5.5.3 Special criminal proceedings as a forum for reparations

The Justice and Peace case indicates that criminal litigation can constitute a judicial forum in which reparations can be claimed from an NSAG. The condition is that the criminally convicted individual was a member of the group and was acting in that capacity when committing the relevant crime. At the same time, the discussion has shown some of the limitations of a criminal justice forum. The question of reparation is, in principle, dependent on the

131 Sanchez and Rudling (n 34) 29, 31–37.

132 Preamble and Arts 2, 3, 5, 12 Decree No 1290 of 2008; Arts 9–10 Victims' Law.

establishment of the criminal responsibility of a group's individual members. As a result, reparation can only be dealt with in the final stages of the lengthy criminal procedure. In addition, the case illustrates some of the challenges judicial reparations claims may face when concerning gross and systematic violations committed during situations of armed conflict. There are significant limits in concentrating all efforts on a criminal justice procedure, which aims to provide both criminal and reparative justice in contexts of mass perpetration and victimization. In the Colombian example, the administrative reparations programme established by the Victims' Law responded to the need for a more expeditious and comprehensive policy to deal with mass reparations. Similar issues are likely to develop in analogous mass violation contexts.

5.6 Other forms of reparations

5.6.1 Satisfaction

Satisfaction constitutes another form of redress that has been ordered pursuant to the Justice and Peace Law.[133] It is broadly defined as including actions that seek to re-establish the dignity of victims and spread the truth about what happened.[134] Satisfaction measures have regularly been ordered against the criminally convicted members of NSAGs. Even so, in some cases, ordered measures appear to have also reflected the collective responsibility of the NSAG to which the individual perpetrator(s) belonged. Such measures include the following: apology and recognition of responsibility, the building of a monument, and the rebuilding of a health centre.

5.6.1.1 Apology and recognition of responsibility

Convicted paramilitary members have been required to publicly apologise and recognise their individual responsibility for the crimes they committed.[135] Although the Justice and Peace Law seeks to deal with system criminality, it does not expressly foresee measures which would require a former member to provide a public apology, or recognition of collective responsibility, on behalf of the NSAG.[136] Nevertheless, in at least one case of 2019, against a former member of the *Bloque Suroeste Antioqueño*, the *postulado* was ordered to publicly recognise the responsibility of the block for its involvement in acts of sexual and gender-based violence.[137] Furthermore, according to a Justice and Peace Magistrate, an apology by a *postulado* may reflect

133 Arts 44, 48 Justice and Peace Law.
134 Art 8(5) Justice and Peace Law.
135 See, e.g., *Case against Fredy Rendón Herrera* (n 25) 387; *Case against Ramiro Banoy Murillo and Others* Superior Tribunal of Medellín (Colombia) Justice and Peace Chamber (28 June 2018) 2386.
136 See Arts 44, 48 Justice and Peace Law.
137 *Case against Germán Antonio Pineda López* (n 31) 717–718, 757.

both the person's individual responsibility as well as the responsibility of the block or front within the activities of which they committed the crimes. This would depend on the role that the *postulado* had in the concerned NSAG:

> if he is a commander he will carry it out personally and on behalf of the block, if he is a low-level member he will carry it out individually because he did not have command, he did not organise anything, he fulfilled his orders and – let us say – that he caused harm at an individual level.[138]

This explanation tentatively suggests that particularly high-level members could possibly bear a certain degree of authority to represent the group in such symbolic measures of satisfaction.[139]

5.6.1.2 The building of a monument

The former commanders of the AUC-linked *Bloque Montes de María* and the *Frente Canal del Dique* both proposed, during a reparations hearing before the Justice and Peace Chamber, to build a monument in commemoration of victims, as a form of symbolic reparations for the harm caused by a paramilitary attack against the community of Mampuján in 2000.[140] Besides financing the construction of the monument, they were, quite exceptionally, allowed to actively engage in the construction of the monument upon the request of the victims. This resulted in a co-ordinated process, led by the Victims' Unit, which allowed the community to determine the design of the monument and the location, among other details.[141] While the symbolic measure was realised in the perpetrators' personal capacities, it was, according to a Justice and Peace Magistrate, also carried out in the name of the group, given the perpetrators' representative position as former commanders.[142] This example adds to the discussion of the previous section.

5.6.1.3 The rebuilding of a health centre

In a case against several demobilised members of the *Bloque Vencedores de Arauca* of the AUC, it was determined that the paramilitary group violated IHL

138 Interview No 3 (Colombia, April 2019).

139 See, for example, '"Hoy Queremos Decir: Nunca Más": Ex "Paras" Del Bloque Central Bolívar' *VerdadAbierta* (29 January 2015).

140 CITpax, 'Relatoría Del Primer Incidente de Reparación Integral a Las Víctimas En El Marco Del Proceso de Justicia y Paz Contra Alias "Diego Vecino" y Alias "Juancho Dique"' (2010) 9.

141 *Mampuján case* (n 111) para 360; *Appeals Judgment No 34547* Supreme Court of Justice of Colombia (Criminal Cassation Chamber) (27 April 2011) 340; CITpax, 'Sexto Informe' (2013) 83; 'Romper El Círculo Del Odio En Los Montes de María' *El Espectador* (21 March 2018); Interview No 5 (Colombia, February 2019).

142 Interview No 3 (Colombia, April 2019).

by converting a health centre into a command post that served as a place for acts of torture and sexual violence, among other abuses.[143] As part of the measures of satisfaction, the court ordered the reconstruction of the health centre to provide satisfaction to the victims and the affected community.[144] Although such measures are not uncommon in Justice and Peace judgments,[145] it was unusual that the reconstruction was ordered directly from "the members of the demobilised *Bloque Vencedores de Arauca*".[146] Thus, the members of the group were collectively called upon to carry out the measure. It appears that the court sought to tackle the harmful impact left by the collective perpetration by the NSAG. As clarified by a Magistrate who was involved in this specific case, the measure did not actually require the demobilised members to rebuild the health centre with their own hands. Instead, the liquidated goods they had handed over to the Reparations Fund would be allocated to this end. The Victims' Unit, which administers the Fund, was required to co-ordinate the completion of the measure along with the relevant state institutions.[147] It is unclear to what extent the group was in fact capable of financing this measure, besides the ordered compensation.[148]

The explicit involvement of the entire NSAG in this type of reparatory measure has not escaped criticism and appears to not have been included in subsequent judgements. One Justice and Peace Magistrate expressed the concern that a similar approach could lead to the perpetuation of the perception that paramilitary groups are social actors or agents of change. During the conflict, paramilitaries were, in some cases, not considered as an armed enemy by local communities, but rather as agents that would build and repair roads, schools and infrastructure in the place of the state. Where victims explicitly request that a court orders a specific NSAG to rebuild, this could imply that this image of the NSAG as a state-like service provider has not been broken. Moreover, it could lead to confusion on the part of communities about which actor is generating welfare. The Magistrate contended that one of the lessons learnt is that such measures can only be carried out by the state, and that the transitional jurisdiction should ensure that the NSAG does not continue to mutate into the role of the state.[149]

Contrary to this position, one could argue that this is exactly the role of a court: to ensure that its judgment or order clearly indicates that the given measure of reparations has been imposed as a form of redress for the harm

143 *Case against José Rubén Peña Tobón and Others* (n 67) paras 70, 292.

144 Ibid. paras 360, 376, 384.

145 Other examples include the reconstruction of cultural or sport centres, churches and schools. For an example, see *Case against Iván Roberto Duque Gaviria and Others* (n 31) 6873, 6875–6876, 6888.

146 *Case against José Rubén Peña Tobón and Others* (n 67) 104, 408 [emphasis added] [own translation].

147 Interview No 3 (Colombia, April 2019).

148 'Incumplen Promesas a Las Víctimas de Arauca' *VerdadAbierta* (28 September 2013).

149 Interview No 1 (Colombia, February 2019).

caused by wrongful conduct, rather than as an action out of good will or as a favour towards the community. A fitting example is displayed in the case against Fredy Rendón Herrera, which involved the illegal enlistment of child soldiers. The court noted that, during the hearing, several of the minors indicated that they continued to see the *postulado* as a sort of father figure, to whom they were grateful for many of the things he had done for them. Moreover, several minors retained feelings of obedience and subordination to the former commander. In consideration of the Paris Principles, it was held that the first guarantee of non-repetition should consist in breaking or preventing the reproduction of these hierarchical structures beyond the armed conflict, and ensuring that the victims would not continue to identify their former commander as a superior or a benefactor.[150] The court held that the necessity to break with these former structures does not mean that the participation of the perpetrator is not necessary, rather that the facts should be evaluated on a case-by-case and request-by-request basis, while always ensuring that the state retains the direction over the reparations measure. These observations were considered when evaluating the proposal made by the *postulado* and the victim representatives, that the *postulado* would assume the responsibility of paying for the construction of various monuments in public spaces, as a measure of symbolic reparations. This proposal was eventually rejected. With respect to a possible public apology, the participation of the former commander was considered as being important to achieve the objective of redress, but this process had to be directed by the state.[151]

5.6.2 Guarantees of non-repetition

For an NSAG to have access to the judicial benefits under the Justice and Peace Law, the group must have demobilised and dismantled.[152] Demobilisation entails collectively handing over weapons and abandoning the NSAG.[153] Besides constituting a condition of eligibility, demobilisation is also recognised as a guarantee of non-repetition, which can be understood as being provided by the NSAG concerned.[154] In other words, each group has provided a guarantee that it will refrain from perpetrating violations into the future, by disarming and dismantling its structures. Gómez Isa argues that the effective dismantlement of the paramilitary phenomenon is absolutely essential for the establishment of guarantees of non-repetition.[155] However, the Justice and Peace process did not succeed in preventing the emergence

150 UNICEF, 'The Paris Principles: Principles and Guidelines on Children Associated with Armed Forces or Armed Groups' (2007).
151 *Case against Fredy Rendón Herrera* (n 25) 383–387.
152 Art 10(1) Justice and Peace Law.
153 Art 9 Justice and Peace Law.
154 Art 8(6) Justice and Peace Law.
155 Gómez Isa, 'Justicia, Verdad y Reparación En El Proceso de Desmovilización Paramilitar En Colombia' (n 13) 139.

of successor groups after the demobilisation of the paramilitaries.[156] It appears from the Justice and Peace judgments that this measure, guaranteed at the level of the group, was not sufficient. Individual *postulados* have been requested by victim representatives, and subsequently ordered by magistrates, to provide personal guarantees that they will no longer engage in harmful conduct.[157] Justice and Peace Magistrates have observed, in this regard, that the norm of non-repetition involves both the personal commitment of the *postulado* and that of the group to which the person belonged.[158] This suggests that such personal and collective guarantees could reinforce one another.

5.6.3 Concluding insights on engagement in satisfaction and guarantees of non-repetition

The operationalisation of the reparations forms encompassing satisfaction and guarantees of non-repetition, as applied within the Justice and Peace process, allows for several conclusions relevant to international law. The analysis has tentatively suggested that former high-level members of an NSAG, such as commanders, could potentially bear a degree of authority to represent the group in satisfaction measures. These preliminary observations are instructive for the discussion in Chapter 4, which considered the potential role that former members with representative authority could take in post-conflict reparations. In addition, the analysis has shed light on some of the challenges that may arise when engaging NSAGs in reparations, such as perpetuations of the image of such groups as state-like social actors or their hierarchical structures. The discussion has further indicated that an NSAG can provide a guarantee of non-repetition. Such measures could be granted by an NSAG prior to the judicial proceedings as part of a group's collective demobilisation process. Moreover, it has been suggested that such collective guarantees, and the personal guarantees provided by individual members, can fulfil a complementary function.

5.7 Conclusions

The analysis has revealed an insightful case of state practice for international law. More specifically, the approach taken in the transitional justice process

156 International Crisis Group, 'Colombia: Peace at Last?' (2012) 21–23; UNHRC, 'Report of the United Nations High Commissioner for Human Rights on the Situation of Human Rights in Colombia' (31 January 2012) UN Doc A/HRC/19/21/Add.3 9; Human Rights Watch, 'World Report: Colombia' (2018); Truth Commission of Colombia (n 6) 272–273.

157 See, for instance, *Case against Salvatore Mancuso Gómez* (n 67) 802; *Case against Manuel De Jesús Pirabán and Others* (n 25) paras 2028, 2876, 2885; *Case against Iván Roberto Duque Gaviria and Others* (n 25) 1866, 1893.

158 Interview No 2 (Skype Interview, March 2019); Interview No 3 (Colombia, April 2019).

adds to the discussion on how a possible duty of NSAGs to provide reparation could be legally operationalised under international law. It confirms some of the international legal tendencies and arguments which have been discussed in the preceding two parts of this book, while, at the same time, presenting new insights that invite further reflection. However, as was previously noted, the insights that can be drawn from the case for international law are tentative in the sense that they are based on one possible example of how NSAGs' duty of reparation could be conceptualised and enforced through a judicial process. Moreover, the approach may not be appropriate for every situation or group. The Justice and Peace process places, for instance, a clear obligation on the NSAGs to contribute to monetary compensation. Yet, this may not be feasible in other cases that deal with groups that have little to no resources.

Broadly speaking, the Justice and Peace process provides insights into what kind of forms of reparations could be required from NSAGs, and into some of the underlying reasons or advantages of extending such mechanisms to these groups and how they could be applied. The discussion has shown that at least monetary compensation and guarantees of non-repetition, which are commonly ordered from states under international law, could also be sought from NSAGs. In terms of satisfaction, the analysis is too preliminary to draw a similar conclusion. Yet, some more tentative insights can be identified. The process sheds further light on the relationships that could exist between the responsibility of an NSAG and that of individual NSAG's members and the territorial state. In addition, the Justice and Peace process confirms some of the tendencies in international law regarding the characteristics of NSAGs that could possibly be held responsible, while also stimulating further reflection on how the organisational structure of an NSAG and the question of reparation could interrelate. Lastly, criminal justice proceedings represent a somewhat surprising setting in which NSAGs' duty to repair is addressed, which is instructive for the overall question of forum.

Chapter 6

Reparations by the FARC-EP under the Comprehensive System for Truth, Justice, Reparation and Non-Repetition

6.1 Introduction

In 2012, the Colombian government and the Revolutionary Armed Forces of Colombia - People's Army (*Fuerzas Armadas Revolucionarias de Colombia – Ejército del Pueblo* or FARC-EP) initiated peace negotiations to end one of the longest-running NIACs in the Western Hemisphere. The negotiation process with Colombia's largest and longest-standing guerrilla group resulted in the adoption of the Final Agreement to End the Armed Conflict and Build a Stable and Lasting Peace (Final Peace Agreement or FPA), in November 2016.[1] The signing of the FPA constitutes an undoubted milestone in the country's history, which witnessed the signatory parties commit to ending the war, satisfying victims' rights and guaranteeing non-repetition. In the FPA, the parties agreed to establish a comprehensive transitional justice system, the so-called Comprehensive System for Truth, Justice, Reparation and Non-Repetition (Comprehensive System). Within this framework, the FARC-EP committed itself, based on international law, to contribute to reparations for the victims of the armed conflict. The Comprehensive System seeks to address the immense scale of victimisation that Colombian society has suffered due to armed violence. According to the final report of Colombia's Truth Commission, 450,664 persons lost their lives due to the conflict between 1985 and 2018, 121,768 persons were forcibly disappeared between 1985 and 2016, 50,770 persons were kidnapped and taken hostage between 1990 and 2018, and around 8 million were displaced, among other grave abuses.[2] Although the conflict with the FARC-EP is now

1 Acuerdo Final para la Terminación del Conflicto y la Construcción de una Paz Estable y Duradera (Government of Colombia – FARC-EP) (24 November 2016) (Final Peace Agreement or FPA).

2 Truth Commission of Colombia, 'Informe Final: Hallazgos y Recomendaciones' (2022). See also Centro Nacional de Memoria Histórica, 'Basta Ya! Colombia: Memories of War and Dignity' (2016); Centro Nacional de Memoria Histórica, 'Subjetos Victimizados y Daños Causados' (2018); Unidad para la Atención y Reparación Integral a las Víctimas, 'Registro Único de Víctimas (RUV)' <www.unidadvictimas.gov.co/es/registro-unico-de-victimas-ruv/37394>.

DOI: 10.4324/9781003401292-10

over, armed violence with other actors, such as the National Liberation Army (ELN), persists in the country.

The present chapter examines how the responsibility of the FARC-EP and, particularly, its duty of reparation for violations of international law are conceptualised and implemented within the framework of the FPA. The main purpose of this examination is to draw insights that can inform the broader discussion on how such a duty could be operationalised within a future regime of responsibility for NSAGs under international law. Accordingly, the insights extracted from this case are considered with respect to the international legal findings from the previous two parts of this book. Parallels and differences are also drawn with the Justice and Peace Law process, discussed in the preceding chapter. An in-depth examination of this case is a significant addition to this discussion. As indicated in Chapter 2, the FARC-EP case constitutes a recent and prominent instance of state practice, which recognises a duty to repair for an NSAG as a matter of international law. Additionally, the continuing implementation process offers the opportunity to obtain insights into the way an NSAG can be engaged in a reparations process, including related challenges and opportunities. At the same time, the case is characterised by its own particularities, which may not be present in other contexts. This may limit the extent to which certain insights can be generalised or transferred to other cases. Nevertheless, this does not take away the fact that the FARC-EP case can significantly add to our understanding of the role that NSAGs can play in the provision of reparations. In terms of method, the chapter first examines the approach taken to the FARC-EP's duty of reparation within the transitional justice process, before reflecting on its broader significance for international law. The research carried out for this chapter draws in part from fieldwork conducted in Colombia. The examination is structured around the following themes: the FARC-EP's responsibility and duty to provide reparation; the FARC-EP as a responsible actor, before and after the end of the armed conflict; and the engagement of the FARC-EP in the reparations component of the Comprehensive System.

6.2 Comprehensive transitional justice system with a reparations component

A broad legal framework based on domestic and international legal standards guided the peace negotiations between the Colombian government and the FARC-EP.[3] The resulting FPA consists of several interconnected sub-agreements that seek to contribute, in sum, to the satisfaction of victims' rights to truth,

3 These included, i.a., the Colombian Constitution, the principles of international law, IHRL, IHL, the ICC Statute, and the decisions of the Inter-American Court of Human Rights. FPA 1–2; Fabio Andrés Díaz Pabón, 'Transitional Justice and the "Colombian Peace Process"' in Fabio Andrés Díaz Pabón (ed), *Truth, Justice and Reconciliation in Colombia* (Routledge 2018) 5.

justice and reparation, amongst other objectives.[4] The sub-Agreement on the Victims of the Conflict aims to address, in a comprehensive manner, the harms suffered by those affected by the armed conflict.[5] The related negotiations, and the later implementation process, were guided by the Declaration of Principles.[6] This set of agreed principles reflected the parties' commitment to the victims, and ensured that the satisfaction of their rights to truth, justice, reparation and non-repetition would be at the centre of any final agreement.[7] With these principles as a backbone, the parties agreed to establish a transitional justice system to deal with the legacies of the conflict: the Comprehensive System for Truth, Justice, Reparation and Non-Repetition.

The Comprehensive System is marked by several particularities, which are important to bear in mind over the course of the analysis. First of all, it is the product of a negotiated peace deal, which did not involve the defeat of the, albeit significantly weakened, FARC-EP.[8] Consequently, both parties, and not only the FARC-EP, submitted themselves to the terms. Moreover, the Comprehensive System is part of a larger peace agreement that seeks to bring an end to the conflict and to establish a stable peace. As a result, the transitional justice system had to be devised in such a way that it allowed the process to strike a delicate balance between redressing and re-vindicating the rights of the victims, whilst also carving out space for the FARC-EP to transform into a political movement or party. In addition, the Colombian state did not experience a complete breakdown because of the armed conflict. It has been capable of establishing an institutionally and legally complex transitional justice system, which may not be feasible for other states emerging from conflict. As a final note, it is not the first time that a peace agreement has recognised the direct responsibility of an NSAG and its commitment to provide reparations.[9] However, the process is marked by an unprecedented engagement on the part of the FARC-EP, as an NSAG, alongside the Colombian state in both the design of the Comprehensive System and its implementation.[10] The group's participation in the Comprehensive System was made dependent upon its disarmament.[11]

Contrary to the Justice and Peace Law, the FPA provides for a new and comprehensive system of transitional justice. The Comprehensive System

4 FPA 2, 7–9. See also General Agreement for the Termination of the Conflict and the Construction of a Stable and Lasting Peace (Government of Colombia – FARC-EP) (26 August 2012).

5 FPA 124.

6 These principles are complemented by the transversal principles included in the sub-agreement dealing with implementation and verification. FPA 193–195.

7 FPA 124–126.

8 FPA 143.

9 See Chapter 2.

10 Francesca Capone, 'From the Justice and Peace Law to the Revised Peace Agreement between the Colombian Government and the FARC: Will Victims' Rights Be Satisfied at Last?' (2017) 77 Heidelberg Journal of International Law 125, 159–160.

11 FPA 151.

combines a judicial mechanism for the investigation and sanctioning of serious violations of international law (the Special Jurisdiction for Peace), with various extra-judicial mechanisms and measures that contribute to the clarification of the truth, the search for the disappeared, reparations for victims and non-repetition.[12] These measures and mechanisms seek to contribute to several common objectives, including the satisfaction of victims' rights and accountability through the establishment of responsibilities.[13] Moreover, they are interconnected by relations of conditionality and incentives. This allows responsible actors to obtain judicial benefits under the System's criminal justice component, so-called 'special treatment'.[14]

The Comprehensive System includes a reparations component as one of its main pillars, which seeks to provide integral or comprehensive reparation.[15] Indeed, since the beginning of the peace talks, it was agreed that providing redress to victims would be at the centre of any agreement.[16] The reparations component is largely based on two premises: first, all those who directly or indirectly participated in the armed conflict must contribute to repairing the damages caused and, second, the FPA offers the opportunity to strengthen and adjust the existing administrative reparations programme under the Victims' Law of 2011.[17] The component fulfils a distinct and essential role within the Comprehensive System in that it focuses most directly and explicitly on the victims and the harms they have endured.[18]

In accordance with the progressive jurisprudence of the Inter-American Court of Human Rights, the Comprehensive System seeks to guarantee integral or comprehensive reparation. The same approach has been consistently followed in both the Justice and Peace Law and the Victims' Law.[19] Understanding reparations from an integral perspective seeks to grasp the full complexity of the harms from armed violence.[20] It involves going beyond a sole focus on

12 FPA 127, 129–130.
13 Art 1 Legislative Act No 01 of 2017; FPA 128–129.
14 Such benefits basically encompass more lenient sentences that do not necessarily involve effective deprivation of liberty and depart from a restorative approach to justice. FPA 130, 146.
15 FPA 129–130.
16 General Agreement for the Termination of the Conflict and the Construction of a Stable and Lasting Peace (n 4); FPA 8, 127. This is also reaffirmed in the Declaration of Principles.
17 Law No 1448 of 2011 (Victims' Law); FPA 129–130; Nelson Camilo Sanchez and Adriana Rudling, 'Reparations in Colombia: Where To?' (Queen's University Belfast 2019) 64.
18 Lisa Magarrell, 'Reparations in Theory and Practice' (ICTJ 2007) 2.
19 Art 23 of Law No 975 of 2005 (Justice and Peace Law); Art 25 Victims' Law; Art 18 Legislative Act No 01 of 2017; Arts 7, 39 Law No 1957 of 2019; FPA 129–130.
20 *Judgment T-130/16* Constitutional Court of Colombia (14 March 2016) para 2.5.3.2; Dina Donoso, 'Inter-American Court of Human Rights' Reparation Judgments: Strengths and Challenges for a Comprehensive Approach' (2009) 49 Revista IIDH 29, 29.

monetary compensation, by including other forms of reparations, in their individual and collective, as well as material and symbolic dimensions, which seek to re-establish, to the extent possible, the *status quo ante*.[21] Accordingly, the FPA includes the five main forms of reparations, as described in the UN Basic Principles and Guidelines. These should be coherently applied in combination with each other and with the other initiatives of the Comprehensive System aimed at truth, justice and non-repetition.[22]

6.3 Responsibility and reparation

6.3.1 Recognition of the FARC-EP's responsibility and duty to contribute to reparation

During the peace negotiations, the Colombian state understood that, as guarantor of the safety and well-being of all the inhabitants of its territory, it had a subsidiary responsibility to make reparation to the victims of all parties to the armed conflict. At the same time, it demanded that the FARC-EP, being responsible for causing serious harm to the civilian population, contribute to providing reparations.[23] The government considered the issue of reparation as being governed, both domestically and internationally, by the principle that all parties responsible for damages are obliged to repair them.[24] Thus, the practice

21 Carlos Martín Beristain, *Diálogos Sobre La Reparación: Qué Reparar En Los Casos de Violaciones de Derechos Humanos* (IIDH 2010) 123; Thomas M Antkowiak, 'An Emerging Mandate for International Courts: Victim-Centered Remedies and Restorative Justice' (2011) 47 Stanford Journal of International Law 279; Jo Pasqualacci, *The Practice and Procedure of the Inter-American Court of Human Rights* (Cambridge University Press 2013) 191; Capone (n 10) 132–133.

22 UNGA, Basic Principles and Guidelines on the Right to a Remedy and Reparation for Victims of Gross Violations of International Human Rights Law and Serious Violations of International Humanitarian Law adopted by UNGA Res 60/147 on 16 December 2005 (21 March 2006) UN Doc A/RES/60/147 (UN Basic Principles and Guidelines) principles 18–23; Arts 11–12 Victims' Law; Art 1 Legislative Act No 01 of 2017; *Judgment C-715/12* Constitutional Court of Colombia (13 September 2012) para 4.3; FPA 130; Carlos Martín Beristain, *Diálogos Sobre La Reparación: Experiencias En El Sistema Interamericano de Derechos Humanos*, vol 2 (IIDH 2008) 14–15.

23 Institute for Integrated Transitions, 'The Colombian Peace Talks: Practical Lessons for Negotiators Worldwide' (2018) 19; Mark Freeman and Iván Orozco, *Negotiating Transitional Justice: Firsthand Lessons from Colombia and Beyond* (Cambridge University Press 2020) 153–154; César Rojas-Orozco, *International Law and Transition to Peace in Colombia: Assessing Jus Post Bellum in Practice* (Brill Nijhof 2021) 110.

24 Freeman and Orozco (n 23) 155; Elizabeth Salmón and Juan-Pablo Pérez-León-Acevedo, 'Reparation for Victims of Serious Violations of International Humanitarian Law: New Developments' (2022) 104 International Review of the Red Cross 1315, 1325.

by the Colombian government of holding the FARC-EP to a duty of reparation can be understood as arising from the belief that a rule of law requires it.[25]

From the side of the FARC-EP, it appears that the NSAG insisted on a collective, rather than an individual, approach to responsibility.[26] In the interviews conducted with several former FARC-EP members and representatives of its successor political party in 2019, the respondents generally explained the notion of collective responsibility by relating it to the collective nature of the armed hostilities and the characteristics of the group's organisational structure.[27] In the words of a representative of the successor political party:

> why collective responsibility? because we are talking about an organisation, that is to say, the FARC-EP always acted as an armed rebel organisation, as an organisation that always claimed the right to rebellion. Thus, its action has to be seen from that perspective, in terms of an organisation that acquired the characteristics of an army [...] it is important to take into account that it is an organisation in which its members did not act freely, in fact the FARC-EP had an internal regulation and a manual related to the civilian population.[28]

Ultimately, under the Comprehensive System, all those who participated in the armed conflict are required to contribute to reparations, through their recognition of responsibility for the damages caused and the duty to provide concrete actions of symbolic and material reparations.[29] With respect to the FARC-EP, responsibility involves, not only a duty of reparation for its individual members, but also for the NSAG as such.[30] This suggests that both forms of responsibility can be understood as fulfilling a complementary function within the transitional justice system.

The duty of the FARC-EP to provide reparation finds its basis in the group's perpetration of serious violations of IHRL and breaches of IHL committed

25 *North Sea Continental Shelf (Federal Republic of Germany v Netherlands)* ICJ (Judgment) [1969] ICJ Rep 3 para 77; *Case Concerning the Military and Paramilitary Activities in and against Nicaragua (Nicaragua v United States of America)* ICJ (Merits Judgment) [1986] ICJ Rep 14 para 207.

26 Marina Aksenova, 'Achieving Justice Through Restorative Means in Colombia: New Developments in Implementing the Peace Deal' (*EJIL: Talk!*, 3 May 2017); Freeman and Orozco (n 23) 138–139; Interview No 5 (Colombia, February 2019).

27 Interview No 8 (Colombia, February 2019); Interview No 9 (Colombia, April 2019); Group Interview No 11 (Colombia, March 2019); Interview No 13 (Colombia, March 2019); Interview No 17 (Colombia, March 2019).

28 Interview No 9 (Colombia, April 2019).

29 Art 1 Legislative Act No 01 of 2017; FPA 127–128, 178–186; Sanchez and Rudling (n 17) 64.

30 Art 39 Law No 1957 of 2019; *Judgment C-071/18* Constitutional Court of Colombia (4 July 2018) para 126; FPA 144, 146, 178; Salmón and Pérez-León-Acevedo (n 24) 1323–1324.

during the armed conflict.[31] This is in accordance with the breach-based understanding of responsibility in international law. It further indicates that the FARC-EP is considered as having been able to violate human rights law. Consequently, victims are entitled to reparations and the NSAG is obligated to repair. Although the FPA does not specify what wrongful conduct would amount to such serious infringements, they include at least within the framework of the Special Jurisdiction for Peace genocide, crimes against humanity, serious war crimes, and kidnapping or other severe deprivation of physical liberty, among others.[32] On the other hand, the concept of serious violations/breaches can be compared to the broad approach taken in the UN Basic Principles and Guidelines, which deals with gross and serious violations of IHRL and IHL.

The FPA suggests that the FARC-EP can, as an NSAG, make valuable contributions to the integral reparation of victims, through symbolic and material reparations.[33] The reparative actions carried out by the FARC-EP, as the actor responsible for the wrongful conduct, are nevertheless complemented by the administrative reparations programme regulated by the Victims' Law. The latter forms one of the key ingredients of the reparations component of the Comprehensive System.[34] As is the case under the Justice and Peace process, this complementary system involves a subsidiary undertaking on the part of the state. It does not constitute an acknowledgment of state responsibility for the violations suffered by the victims.[35] The scheme indicates that the provision of redress is not solely dependent on the FARC-EP. Instead, it emphasises the subsidiary role of the state in guaranteeing the right to reparation of victims of the group.[36]

Further insights into the FARC-EP's responsibility under the FPA are provided by the Council of State, the highest Court in Colombia for acts or omissions committed by the state. The Court addressed this form of responsibility in a case dealing with state responsibility for a kidnapping carried out by the group. In this case, the Court recalled that the negotiating parties recognised their respective responsibilities with regard to the victims of the conflict as one of the guiding principles of the FPA's sub-agreement on victims.[37] The Court held that the FPA, in other words, recognises the FARC-EP as a collectivity or

31 Art 1 Legislative Act No 01 of 2017; *Judgment No 00463* Council of State of Colombia (7 May 2018) Section 6 and specifically para 6.4.5; FPA 127–128.

32 Art 42 Law No 1957 of 2019; FPA 145 para 9, 151 para 40.

33 Art 39 Law No 1957 of 2019; FPA 178–180, 186.

34 *Judgment C-071/18* (n 30) paras 121–123, 126–127; FPA 184–185; Sanchez and Rudling (n 17) 64.

35 Art 9 Victims' Law; ICTJ, 'From Principles to Practice: Challenges of Implementing Reparations for Massive Violations in Colombia' (2015) 25; Sanchez and Rudling (n 17) 31.

36 Art 18 Legislative Act No 01 of 2017; Arts 1, 28 Law No 1957 of 2019; Freeman and Orozco (n 23) 153–154; Rojas-Orozco (n 23) 110.

37 *Judgment No 00463* (n 31) para 6.3.1; FPA 124.

organisation that transcends the individuality of its constituent members. Consequently, the Court considered that responsibility could not only be attributed to these individuals, through the Special Jurisdiction for Peace, but also to the FARC-EP, as a collective subject that acted as 'an organised apparatus of irregular power' during the conflict.[38] This is the case when the violent actions, perpetrated by members of the organisation, were carried out pursuant to plans set by its commanders or leaders, in the furtherance of their common objectives through an armed struggle.[39] Thus, the Court recognises the complementarity that exists between individual and collective responsibility within the context of NSAGs. The Court further held that such collective responsibility finds its normative basis in IHRL and IHL, instead of criminal law. Accordingly, the declaration of civil or administrative responsibility is not followed by the imposition of a sanction, but rather results in a duty to repair that is not punitive in character. This entails that the death of an individual member, which would cause a criminal action to halt, does not impede holding the organisation, within which the harmful act was consented to, planned or executed, responsible. Hence, the collectivity continues to bear the duty to repair the victims.[40] Significantly, this conception of responsibility, as set out by the Court, is similar to that of states under international law in terms of its character and relationship to individual criminal responsibility.

However, the FPA neither creates a mechanism that is mandated to legally determine the responsibility of the FARC-EP, nor does it provide for a legal framework that regulates such an exercise. Although the Truth Commission is tasked with uncovering and contributing to the recognition of the collective responsibility of the FARC-EP, it lacks the capacity to demand reparations from the group, or to receive corresponding legal claims from victims.[41] In response, the Council of State urged the government to create the legal instruments, administrative and/or judicial, which would allow victims to obtain reparations from the FARC-EP, where it is responsible for serious violations of IHRL and IHL. The Court contemporaneously recalled the state's underlying duty to combat impunity.[42] However, no steps seem to have been taken to that end.

38 This concept has been used to tackle system criminality in national and international criminal law with the objective of holding the indirect perpetrator responsible for the organisational wrongdoing. Hence, it holds on to the principle of personal culpability as one of its cornerstones. It broadly involves understanding NSAGs as independent organisations based on hierarchical relationships that operate outside of the law. See further Kai Ambos, 'The Fujimori Judgment' (2011) 9 Journal of International Criminal Justice 137; Claus Roxin, 'Crimes as Part of Organized Power Structures' (2011) 9 Journal of International Criminal Justice 193.

39 *Judgment No 00463* (n 31) para 6.3.7–6.3.8, see also para 6.3.11.

40 Ibid. paras 6.3.10–6.3.11.

41 FPA 131, 134.

42 *Judgment No 00463* (n 31) paras 6.1, 6.3.14, 6.4.

It appears that the implementation of the FARC-EP's commitments to reparations, made in the FPA, rest on good faith and reciprocity between the parties to the agreement.[43] This is reinforced by the obligation of the ex-guerrilla commanders, now members of the directive organs of the successor political party, to guarantee the proper execution and stability of the FPA.[44] The implementation of the FPA is verified by a political, rather than a judicial, mechanism, composed of representatives of the government and the FARC-EP, and, subsequently, its successor political party.[45] The condition-based access of the group's individual members to judicial benefits, granted by the Special Jurisdiction for Peace, could arguably function as an additional incentive to carry out its collective commitments.[46] Moreover, the status of the FPA, as a special agreement under Common Article 3, may remain relevant to compliance, as it may raise the reputation costs of noncompliance and encourage the parties to take their obligations more seriously.[47]

An exception to this scheme is the obligation of the FARC-EP to surrender its assets to be used for material reparations.[48] This obligation is strict in its nature, with clear legal consequences. According to Decree No. 903 of 2017, the formal delivery of the FARC-EP's inventory of assets to the government is understood as marking the end of the group's disarmament, which was a condition for the FARC-EP to gain access to the Comprehensive System, and the termination of all the activities and conduct related to the conflict.[49] Non-declared assets do not have repercussions for the FARC-EP itself, which ceased to exist. Instead, individual members who failed to declare such assets could lose their judicial benefits and could be redirected to the ordinary justice system.[50] Thus, by enforcing the collective obligation of the FARC-EP at the level of the individual members, the approach gives teeth to this obligation and counters the group's subsequent lack of legal existence.

43 FPA 196.
44 FPA 77.
45 See the sub-agreement dealing with implementation, verification and public endorsement of the FPA.
46 The regime of conditionality requires that FARC-EP members contribute to providing truth, reparations and guarantees of non-repetition, as a condition to have and maintain access to any form of special treatment. Art 20(iii) and para 1, and Art 39 Law No 1957 of 2019; FPA 130, 146.
47 FPA 277–278; Christine Bell, 'Peace Agreements: Their Nature and Legal Status' (2006) 100 American Society of International Law 373, 384, 386–387; Marcela Giraldo Muñoz and Jose Serralvo, 'International Humanitarian Law in Colombia: Going a Step Beyond' (2019) 101 International Review of the Red Cross 1117, 1135.
48 FPA 186.
49 Art 2 Decree No 903 of 2017; Art 20 Law No 1957 of 2019; FPA 151.
50 Art 5 Legislative Act No 01 of 2017; Art 20(iii) and para 1 Law No 1957 of 2019; *Judgment C-071/18* (n 30) para 127; CINEP/PPP-CERAC, 'Informe De Verificación Del Primer Año De Implementación Del Acuerdo Final De Paz En Colombia' (2018) 9; Sanchez and Rudling (n 17) 64.

6.3.2 Concluding insights on non-state armed groups' international responsibility and their duty to repair

The analysis has demonstrated that the collective responsibility of the FARC-EP, as one of the main participants in the armed conflict, forms a central aspect of the transitional justice process. This indicates that it was important for the transition to address the responsibility of the NSAG as such, which could not simply be reduced to its constituent members. Put differently, it was not sufficient to only address the responsibility of these individuals. Instead, both the FARC-EP and its members bear a resulting duty to provide reparation as distinct subjects. In this sense, their respective responsibility can be understood as fulfilling a complementary function. A further form of complementarity can be found between the individual criminal responsibility of the members, to be determined by the Special Jurisdiction for Peace, and the responsibility of the FARC-EP, which is not punitive in character. The scheme provides support for the conclusions presented in Chapter 3 on what the character of a possible international responsibility of NSAGs should be. In addition, the examination has shown that the obligations of the NSAG and its members can interrelate. This provides new insights into the possible relationships that could exist between the respective responsibilities of both actors. For instance, the obligation of the FARC-EP to hand over its assets as a contribution to reparations is enforced at the level of the members when the NSAG has already ceased to exist. As will be discussed in Section 6.5.4, the fulfilment of this collective obligation is also one of the factors that underpin the individual members' exemption from their personal obligation to provide monetary compensation.

The FARC-EP case provides support for the argument made in the second part of this study, that the possible international responsibility of NSAGs and, particularly, their resulting duty to provide reparation could be conceptualised analogously to that of states. Indeed, the FARC-EP's duty of reparation finds its basis in internationally wrongful acts, which give rise to the responsibility of the group. Both the way responsibility arises and the character of the responsibility itself are comparable to that of states. Significantly, the Colombian state considered that the fundamental principle of international law, regarding the obligation to make reparation for wrongful acts, applies to the FARC-EP. As discussed in Chapter 2, this constitutes the only instance of such state practice, identified in this study, which supports extending this principle to NSAGs.

Finally, the scope of the FARC-EP's duty of reparation does not extend to delivering full reparation to the victims. Instead, the group's duty can be understood as one of contribution. It adds to the efforts of the other reparations measures and mechanisms within the Comprehensive System. More specifically, the Colombian state takes a subsidiary role in this System by way of an administrative reparations programme. In doing so, the case supports the argument from Chapter 4 that reparations cannot depend solely on an NSAG, even if the NSAG is highly organised and wealthy, as was the case with the

FARC-EP. Instead, as argued in that chapter, the territorial state should retain a role in subsidy, as guarantor of victims' right to reparation. As such, the FARC-EP case lends support for a cascading regime of responsibility for reparation.

6.4 Understanding the FARC-EP as a responsible actor

6.4.1 During and before the end of the armed conflict

This section seeks to provide a deeper understanding of the FARC-EP as an actor bearing responsibility for repairing the harms it caused. The focus here is on the FARC-EP when it was still in existence as an NSAG, thus before the end of the armed conflict. This examination involves tracing how the FARC-EP's origins and nature have shaped the group's self-image and its role as a responsible actor in the reparations process. Additionally, the organisational structure and characteristics of the FARC-EP offer further insights into how the group is perceived as a unified, responsible actor and was able to participate in this process accordingly. Building further on this discussion, the role of the defunct FARC-EP as a responsible actor in post-conflict reparations is examined in the following section (Section 6.4.2).

Although the exact birth and origins of the FARC-EP remain subject to debate, they are commonly traced back to communist and peasant self-defence groups established in the context of the civil conflict known as *La Violencia*.[51] Such actors, influenced by communist ideology, formed agrarian movements referred to as 'independent republics'. These republics were based on economic self-management and military self-defence. They constituted enclaves in rural Colombia, where the peasant population, which had taken up arms, was beyond the control of the state.[52] According to the FARC-EP's official version of its history, the group finds its origin in 1964, when the Colombian army launched a large military offensive against the peasant republic of Marquetalia, located in the south of Tolima.[53] Survivors of this attack regrouped as the *Bloque Sur*, which involved the transformation of the self-defence force into an

51 Juan Guillermo Ferro Medina and Graciela Uribe Ramón, *El Orden de La Guerra. Las FARC-EP Entre La Organisación y La Política* (Pontificia Universidad Javeriana 2002) 25; Centro Nacional de Memoria Histórica, 'Basta Ya! Colombia: Memories of War and Dignity' (n 2) 123. For an extensive discussion of the history of the FARC-EP, see Mario Aguilera Peña, *Guerrilla y Población Civil: Trayectoria de Las FARC 1949–2013* (3rd edn, CNMH 2014); Alfredo Molano, 'Fragmentos de La Historia Del Conflicto Armado (1920–2010)' in Comisión Histórica del Conflicto y sus Víctimas (ed), *Contribución al Entendimiento del Conflicto Armado en Colombia* (2015).

52 Molano (n 51).

53 Fabio Andrés Díaz Pabón, 'Conflict and Peace in the Making: Colombia from 1948–2010' in Fabio Andrés Díaz Pabón (ed), *Truth, Justice and Reconciliation in Colombia: Transitioning from Violence* (Routledge 2018) 18–19.

offensive force fighting for political change.[54] Two years later, the group officially organised itself as the FARC and, in 1982, eventually as the FARC-EP.[55] Even though the FARC-EP began its formal operations in 1966, the group considers the attack on Marquetalia as bearing greater symbolic meaning in terms of its development into a revolutionary guerrilla movement.[56] The group found willing recruits amongst the peasant communities displaced due to the civil war of a decade earlier, and hence it also emerged from their economic and political grievances.[57] The historical origins of the FARC-EP shaped the group's self-image and the resulting justification for its rebellion. The group was particularly cognisant of the original state aggression it faced. In this sense, the FARC-EP carried a collective memory, in which its members were portrayed as peasant victims of abusive state power.[58]

Although the FARC-EP was a relatively weak NSAG at its outset, it transformed into the largest and most powerful guerrilla group in Colombia, partly due to its gradual involvement in the illicit drug trade in the early 1980s.[59] The estimated number of FARC-EP fighters ranged between 17.000 and 22.000, prior to the government's offensive in the early 2000s.[60] To give a more recent estimate, as part of the 2016 FPA, 14.086 members submitted themselves to the reincorporation process by May 2023.[61] The FARC-EP developed into a political-military organisation that sought to seize power and transform the state.[62] Over the course of the armed conflict, the FARC-EP perpetrated multiple serious violations of international law against the civilian population, including killings, kidnappings, the recruitment and use of minors, and forced displacement. These abuses left a devastating impact on Colombian society.[63]

54 Marco Palacios, *Entre La Legitimidad y La Violencia: Colombia 1875–1994* (2nd edn, Editorial Norma 2003) 264–265.

55 Norman Offstein, 'An Historical Review and Analysis of Colombian Guerrilla Movements: FARC, ELN and EPL' (2003) 1(52) Revista Desarrollo y Sociedad 99, 103; Eduardo Pizarro Leongómez, *Una Democracia Asediada: Balance y Perspectivas Del Conflicto Armado En Colombia* (Grupo Editorial Norma 2004) 86–88.

56 Ferro Medina and Uribe Ramón (n 51) 34.

57 Ibid. 29, 36; Francisco Gutiérrez Sanín, 'Telling the Difference: Guerrillas and Paramilitaries in the Colombian War' (2008) 36 Politics & Society 3, 12–13; Aguilera Peña (n 51) 17.

58 International Crisis Group, 'Colombia: Peace at Last?' (2012) 13; Aguilera Peña (n 51) 20, 31, 44.

59 See further Susan Virginia Norman, 'Narcotization as Security Dilemma: The FARC and Drug Trade in Colombia' (2018) 41 Studies in Conflict & Terrorism 638.

60 Sanín (n 57) 12.

61 Colombian Agency for Reincorporation and Normalization (ARN), 'ARN En Cifras' (May 2023) <www.reincorporacion.gov.co/es/agencia/Paginas/ARN-en-cifras.aspx>.

62 Arts 1–2 FARC-EP Statute (as adopted at the Ninth National Guerrilla Conference) (2007).

63 Human Rights Watch, 'War Without Quarter: Colombia and International Humanitarian Law' (1998) 138–165; Amnesty International, 'Leave Us in Peace: Targeting Civilians in Colombia's Internal Armed Conflict' (2008); Truth Commission of Colombia, 'Informe Final: Hasta La Guerra Tiene Límites' (2022) 925–943.

Under Colombian national law, the FARC-EP constitutes an 'organised armed group at the margins of the law', which is a concept used when regulating the demobilisation and submission to transitional justice of NSAGs. In Chapter 5, it was explained that such groups are defined, in conformity with Article 1 Additional Protocol II, as those that "under the direction of a responsible command, exercise such control over a part of the territory that allows them to realise sustained and concerted military operations".[64]

Indeed, the FARC-EP was an army-like NSAG that engaged in guerrilla warfare. The group was characterised by its highly centralised organisational structure, with a vertical line of command, strict hierarchies and internal rules. There was also a high degree of unity and cohesion among its members. The structure and climate within the group fostered a strong collective identity.[65] The FARC-EP's organisational structure consisted of political organs, organs of direction (political-military) and military organs. The FARC-EP did not separate the military from the political leadership, which formed an integrated whole.[66] The high-level commanders of the Central High Command and its Secretariat can be considered as belonging to the leadership of the group, with the commander-in-chief as superior leader. Other important military structures were the blocks (*bloques*), which joined and co-ordinated several fronts (*frentes*) as regional forces.[67] The group exercised significant control over large areas of the country and implemented a state-like structure where the state was absent.[68] Although the FARC-EP operated over vast territory, its organisational structure allowed the central command to keep tight control over its units and strategy.[69]

Accordingly, the FARC-EP was generally deemed to be bound by Additional Protocol II, after its ratification by the government in 1995, in addition to Common Article 3 and customary IHL.[70] Although IHL applied without question to the FARC-EP, the group did not always accept the application of these

64 Art 3 Law No 782 of 2002 [own translation]; Art 5 Legislative Act No 1 of 2017; Art 63 Law No 1957 of 2019; FPA 148.

65 Ferro Medina and Uribe Ramón (n 51) 163; Ana Arjona, *Rebelocracy: Social Order in the Colombian Civil War* (Cambridge University Press 2016) 97–98; ICRC, 'The Roots of Restraint in War' (2018) 24, 38–43.

66 Arts 1, 10 FARC-EP Statute.

67 Ferro Medina and Uribe Ramón (n 51) 41–55.

68 Arturo Carrillo-Suárez, 'Hors De Logique: Contemporary Issues in International Humanitarian Law as Applied to Internal Armed Conflict' (1999) 15 American University of International Law Review 1, 94–95; IACHR, 'Third Report on the Human Rights Situation in Colombia' OEA/SER.L/II.102 Doc 9 rev 1 (26 February 1999) para 29; René Provost, 'FARC Justice: Rebel Rule of Law' (2018) 8 UC Irvine Law Review 227.

69 Human Rights Watch (n 63).

70 Carrillo-Suárez (n 68) 90, 97; IACHR (n 68) ch IV para 20; Human Rights Watch, 'Colombia: Beyond Negotiation International Humanitarian Law and Its Application to the Conduct of FARC-EP' (2001) Vol 13 No 3B 3; Felicity Szesnat and Annie R Bird, 'Colombia' in Elizabeth Wilmshurst (ed), *International Law and the Classification of Conflicts* (Oxford University Press 2012) 227.

norms. The FARC-EP argued that it had not expressly agreed with them and that they represented "elite interests".[71] However, the group still insisted that their military might and territorial control should raise them to the level of belligerents, thereby suggesting that IHL applicable to international armed conflicts might apply.[72] Nonetheless, a more favourable attitude towards IHL is observable over time, particularly when negotiating for peace talks in 2016.[73]

The highly organised nature of the FARC-EP arguably provided the group with the capacity to provide certain reparations measures as part of the peace process and prior to the end of the NIAC. It is probable that some of the organisational factors that characterised the FARC-EP, such as the leadership's authority and the group's internal cohesion and discipline, provided the conditions for the leadership to engage in, for example, actions of public apology and acknowledgement of collective responsibility on behalf of the group. It may have equally facilitated the collective engagement of the FARC-EP's members in the search for the disappeared as an early measure of redress.[74] Moreover, the FARC-EP's considerable wealth is to be redistributed for the purpose of material reparations. The implementation of this accountability measure clearly corresponds to the group's organisational capacity in respect of redress. These reparations measures are further discussed in Section 6.5.

The FARC-EP case indicates that, at least in some instances, it is feasible to engage on the question of reparation with a politically motivated NSAG whose struggle is based on grievances. In Chapter 4, it was suggested that such groups might be hesitant to take part in these efforts, as it could be understood as betraying or undermining their efforts or cause. Indeed, similar concerns are reflected in the present case. The final terms of the FPA reflect a significant departure from the original attitude of the FARC-EP, which involved, among others, the group's initial opposition to the mention of transitional justice, its self-portrayal as a victim rather than perpetrator, and its placement of the primary responsibility for the conflict on the Colombian state.[75] In this sense, the final agreement, and the FARC-EP's willingness to engage on reparations, can be better understood as the result of a larger process. The FARC-EP's political motivations to participate in the democratic arena may have constituted a

71 Human Rights Watch (n 70) 6–7.

72 Carrillo-Suárez (n 68) 57–60.

73 Hyeran Jo, 'International Humanitarian Law on the Periphery: Case of Non-State Armed Actors' (2020) 11 Journal of International Humanitarian Legal Studies 97, 105–106; Ezequiel Heffes, 'From Words to Deeds: A Research Study of Armed Non-State Actors' Practice and Interpretation of International Humanitarian and Human Rights Norms. Case Study: FARC-EP' (2021) 12–15.

74 Compare to Ron Dudai, 'Closing the Gap: Symbolic Reparations and Armed Groups' (2011) 93 International Review of the Red Cross 783, 797.

75 International Crisis Group, 'Left in the Cold? The ELN and Colombia's Peace Talks' (2013) 21–22; Freeman and Orozco (n 23) 105, 123, 138–139; 'Kidnappings in Colombia: FARC Leaders Acknowledge Full Responsibility' *JusticeInfo.net* (7 May 2021). See also Jo (n 73) 105–106.

notable incentive to engage in the reparations process as a means to gain political support.[76]

6.4.2 Post armed conflict

Even though the FARC-EP constituted an identifiable legal entity during the armed conflict, it legally ceased to exist with the end of the conflict, due to the group's temporary international legal personality. This fact challenges whether the FARC-EP, as such, can carry out its commitments to reparations in a post-conflict setting. It also raises the question as to which person or entity one could call upon when these commitments are not being complied with. In this section, an analysis is made as to how this issue is dealt with within the scope of the FPA. In terms of timeline, the signing of the FPA in November 2016 marked the start of the FARC-EP's disarmament process that resulted in the end of the FARC-EP as an armed actor in August 2017. The following month, the FARC-EP officially transitioned into the political party *Comunes*, initially named *Fuerza Alternativa Revolucionaria del Común* or FARC.[77] The party is hereinafter referred to as *Comunes*.

6.4.2.1 Political transformation of the FARC-EP

The transformation of the FARC-EP, from an NSAG into a new political party, forms a central aspect of the FPA.[78] During the Tenth, and last, National Guerrilla Conference, which was held in September 2016, it was collectively decided that the group would leave its armed struggle behind and convert into a legal political party.[79] There was a clear, collective commitment of the group's constituency to the FPA, and to their political transformation. As a result, a successor entity with legal personality under national law emerged: namely the political party *Comunes* headed by the group's former commander-in-chief.[80]

76 Reparations, Responsibility & Victimhood in Transitional Societies, 'Engaging Non-State Armed Groups on Reparations' (Queen's University Belfast 2022) 13–14.

77 Art 2 Decree No 903 of 2017; Art 1 Legislative Act No 3 of 2017; FPA 67, 69; FARC-EP, 'Segunda y Definitiva Entrega de Información Del Listado de Bienes y Valores de Economía de Guerra de Las FARC-EP' (15 August 2017); Marco Sassòli, *International Humanitarian Law: Rules, Controversies, and Solutions to Problems Arising in Warfare* (Edward Elgar Publishing Limited 2019) para 6.59; Liliana Zambrano Quintero, 'La Reincorporación Colectiva de Las FARC-EP: Una Apuesta Estratégica En Un Entorno Adverso' (2019) 121 Revista CIDOB d'Afers Internacionals 45, 46, 51.

78 See sub-Agreement on the End of the Conflict that specifically deals with the FARC-EP's political reincorporation.

79 Ferro Medina and Uribe Ramón (n 51) 43; Liliana Zambrano Quintero, 'Desarmar La Política Para Fortalecer La Democracia' (University of Deusto 2018) 158.

80 Art 1 Legislative Act No 3 of 2017; FPA 69–70; 'Esta Es La Dirección Del Nuevo Partido Político de Las Farc' *El Espectador* (3 September 2017).

Besides constituting a direct result of the FPA, the successive nature of the party is also apparent from, i.a., the initial decision to keep the same acronym and a similar name as a way of retaining a link with the group's past.[81] In addition to referencing the FARC-EP's founders, the political party's Statute also provides that former FARC-EP members who decide to be part of the political party are so-called militants and are required to observe, comply and defend what was agreed upon in the FPA.[82]

The degree of organisational continuity that exists between both actors can be better understood when considering it from the perspective of the broader reintegration process in which the FARC-EP engaged. A different approach was taken to DDR, which is traditionally designed as an individual process that seeks to dismantle the collectivity in its entirety. The government agreed to a collective reincorporation process, which allowed for maintaining some of the group's cohesive elements, and facilitated the formulation of a collective political identity.[83] The FARC-EP wanted a disarmament process that would not create the perception that it had been military defeated, since it had voluntarily decided to hand in its weapons and to transition into a legal entity.[84] By tying in the group's political transformation with the members' collective social and economic reincorporation, the FARC-EP strategically sought to maintain its initial cohesion and unity. This would constitute one of the group's main strengths during the transformation process.[85]

Along with this, a change in the usual DDR terminology was advocated by the FARC-EP. This terminological change emphasised that the group's disarmament only involved dismantling its military structures. The group continues to exist as a political organisation, seeking to attain its objectives by legal and non-violent means.[86] According to this interpretation, the NSAG did not 'disarm' as such, but 'laid down its weapons' to continue the fight with democratic and non-violent means. The group did not 'demobilise'; only the military structures were dismantled, while the collectivity remained intact. For example, according to a former FARC-EP member,

> we continue the same party [Clandestine Colombian Communist Party], but legally. With the same level of organisation and everything, the only thing that has changed is the way to call it. At least before, the basic unit

81 Arts 1–2 Estatutos del Partido Comunes (2021) (Comunes Statute); Zambrano Quintero (n 77) 60.

82 Arts 5, 8, 13(15) Comunes Statute.

83 'The Integrated DDR Standards' (UN DDR Resource Centre, 2006); Veronique Dudouet, Katrin Planta and Hans J Giessmann, 'The Political Transformation of Armed and Banned Groups' (Berghof Foundation and UNDP 2016) 22–23.

84 Institute for Integrated Transitions (n 23) 21.

85 Zambrano Quintero (n 77) 46–47; Interview No 5 (Colombia, February 2019).

86 Zambrano Quintero (n 77) 47.

> that is called a *comuna* [basic unit of the political party], was not called *comuna* but [political] cell. It was the cell of the party, now it's the *comuna*, and it's the same but we changed the name.[87]

Finally, instead of individually 'reintegrating' into society, the FARC-EP 'reincorporated' itself collectively into civilian life and the political system.[88] Accordingly, one of the objectives of the reincorporation process was to maintain a collective sense of organisation.[89] In the words of a former FARC-EP member:

> We are not ex-combatants, we are ex-guerrillas because the fight continues, with words, with mobilisation, with the organisation of the masses. We continue in combat, no longer with arms, but with the word in a moderate manner.[90]

The discussion clearly shows that the FARC-EP did not consider the reincorporation process as bringing an end to the collectivity, which rather continues to exist in a different form.

To undergo the collective reincorporation process, it was agreed that FARC-EP members would reside in various territorial areas for training and reincorporation, so-called ETCR, which were scattered around the country.[91] Although not obligatory, approximately 3,500 reincorporating members decided to reside in these areas in 2019.[92] When deciding to be a member of the political party, *Comunes*, the person becomes, as a militant, part of a so-called *comuna*, which is the basic unit of the political party.[93] By integrating them directly into the party's organisational structure, it appears that an attempt was made to keep the collectivity intact.[94] In this regard, a former fighter argued that "[t]here is no other [political] party that has communities all over the country."[95]

87 Interview No 10 (Colombia, March 2019).
88 Zambrano Quintero (n 77) 46; Interview No 10 (Colombia, March 2019); Interview No 13 (Colombia, March 2019).
89 Fundación Ideas para la Paz, 'Trayectorias y Dinámicas Territoriales de Las Disidencias de Las FARC' (2018) 37; Renate Segura and Sabrina Stein, 'The Colombian Peace Process with the FARC: A Mapping of Vulnerabilities' (Conflict Prevention and Peace Forum 2018) 22; Zambrano Quintero (n 77) 56.
90 Group Interview No 11 (Colombia, March 2019).
91 Art 3 Decree No 1274 of 2017; Decree No 2026 of 2017; FPA 62.
92 Fundación Ideas para la Paz, 'La Reincorporación de Los Excombatientes de Las FARC' (2019); UNSC, 'UN Verification Mission in Colombia – Report of the Secretary-General' (27 June 2019) UN Doc S/2019/530 5.
93 Arts 8, 15 Comunes Statute.
94 The same holds for those militants who reside outside of these territorial areas. Zambrano Quintero (n 77) 47.
95 Interview No 17 (Colombia, March 2019).

6.4.2.2 Representative authority of the political party and former high-level commanders

The FPA neither regulates the manner in which the FARC-EP responds before the Comprehensive System with regard to its reparation obligations once it ceased to exist, nor does it clarify the successive role of the political party within the scheme.[96] Nonetheless, an analysis of several post-conflict reparations delivered on behalf of the defunct FARC-EP suggests that the political party had, at that time, at least the *de facto* authority, as successor entity, to represent the group in the implementation of the FPA. It appears, in particular, that former high-level commanders, who were then part of the political leadership, had such representative authority and, thus, not just any former member. The central role of these persons in the post-conflict phase follows more generally from the FPA. The latter provides that former guerrilla commanders, who are members of the directive organs of the new political party that emerged from the transition of the FARC-EP to legality, are obligated to ensure the proper implementation and stability of the FPA.[97]

An interesting example is the reconciliation process that has taken place between the FARC-EP and the victims of the bombing of Bogotá's El Nogal club, which was carried out by the group in 2003. It is of interest since it was initiated when the NSAG still existed and continued after its disarmament and political transformation. The efforts of one of the victims, Bertha Lucía Fries, in searching for the truth about the attack, provided her with the opportunity to hold private meetings with members of the FARC-EP leadership during the 2016 peace negotiations. This resulted in the adoption of an unprecedented Agreement on Truth, Forgiveness and Reconciliation, between the Secretariat of the FARC-EP and Bertha Lucía Fries, as victim representative, in March 2017.[98] In this seven-point agreement, the FARC-EP committed itself to engage in the Comprehensive System, with the purpose of contributing to the clarification of the truth about this attack and the provision of certain symbolic reparations, among other commitments.[99] For example, in February 2018, the group engaged in a public act of forgiveness and acknowledgement of responsibility. The act was carried out by a former member of the Secretariat, who, at that time, belonged to the political leadership of the newly established party. It was

96 However, the political party does succeed more clearly in some of the other obligations or roles of the defunct FARC-EP within the framework of the FPA. See, e. g., Art 141 Law No 1957 of 2019 [adds "o sus sucesoras"] and FPA 173 with regard to the Special Jurisdiction for Peace, and FPA 47 and 195 concerning ex-FARC-EP representatives in some of the key mechanisms established by the FPA.

97 FPA 77. More broadly, the FPA indicates that the entire Colombian society has a role to play in the implementation of the FPA, which includes the movement that emerged from the FARC-EP's political transition. FPA 196.

98 The FARC-EP was still an NSAG at that time.

99 Acuerdo sobre la Verdad, el Perdón y la Reconciliación con Víctimas del Atentado al Club El Nogal de Bogotá (FARC-EP – Bertha Lucía Fries) (2017).

explicitly carried out in the name of the defunct FARC-EP, as illustrated by the following passage: "the former commanders and ex-combatants of the FARC-EP, we accept the responsibilities for this unjustifiable act, convinced that this reparatory action will pave the way that will permit reconciliation".[100] Bertha Lucía Fries explains that she understands such actions on two levels: first, as collective actions, which are in accordance with what is described in the FPA as 'early acts of acknowledgement of collective responsibility', carried out by the high-level leadership on behalf of the FARC-EP collectivity (see further Section 6.5); and, second, as personal actions, with regard to those individuals who carry out the measures.[101]

There are other examples that confirm these observations. In September 2017, a former FARC-EP leader, who was then a member of the successor political party, asked for forgiveness for the harms caused by the extinct FARC-EP in the department of Antioquia.[102] In April 2019, the party asked, in a communiqué, for forgiveness from the persons who suffered during the conflict, due to the actions of the FARC-EP, and guaranteed that it would comply with the commitments to reparations included in the FPA.[103] During an event held in June 2019, a party member, who was formerly with the Central High Command, stated the following, "I take advantage of this moment to [...] apologise for the victimising actions that we have been able to carry out as an organisation."[104] A further example relates to the FARC-EP's commitment to the search and recovery of the disappeared in the FPA, which led the political party to co-ordinate, under the direction of a former high-ranking commander, collective efforts by former members to that end.[105] These efforts have resulted in the collection and delivery of information concerning a considerable number of cases.[106] Finally, in 2020, former members of the FARC-EP Secretariat, who were then members of the successor political party, publicly apologised for the kidnappings carried out by the extinct NSAG.[107]

100 Own translation, see *Judgment No 00451* Council of State of Colombia (16 August 2018) para 3.5.1; 'FARC Piden Perdón Por El Atentado Contra El Club El Nogal En Bogotá' *El País* (13 February 2018).
101 Interview No 20 (Skype Interview, May 2019).
102 'Granada Perdona, Pero No Olvida' *VerdadAbierta* (26 September 2017).
103 'FARC Pidió Perdón a Las Víctimas Del Conflicto Armado' *El Espectador* (10 April 2019).
104 'El Pedido de Perdón Del Excomandante de Las Farc "Solis Almeida" En Valledupar' *El Espectador* (13 June 2019) [own translation].
105 FPA 142, 179.
106 'Video: FARC Anuncia Que Entregará Información De 182 Cuerpos De Desaparecidos' *El Espectador* (28 September 2018); 'La Comisión de Farc Que Busca a Los Desaparecidos' *El Espectador* (12 March 2019). See further Section 6.5.3.3.
107 Anna Myriam Roccatello, 'What Does a Heart-Felt Apology From FARC Mean for Colombia?' (ICTJ 2020); 'Colombian Ex-FARC Rebels "Ashamed" of Kidnappings' *BBC* (15 September 2020).

However, the unity of the reincorporation of FARC-EP members under the banner of the new political party has experienced pressure. The instances of dissidence by those members who rejected the peace process or who rearmed has led to the emergence of FARC-EP dissident groups.[108] This development may have the potential to challenge the extent to which *Comunes*, as successor entity, retains the authority to act on behalf of the FARC-EP.[109] In 2019, for example, a dissident group which had rearmed, and which included some former FARC-EP leaders, announced the rebirth of the FARC-EP as a guerrilla group.[110] However, from both a domestic and international legal perspective, these dissident groups are generally not considered as constituting a direct continuation of the FARC-EP. Instead, they are evaluated as new actors falling within the law enforcement or armed conflict frameworks.[111] Another challenge results from internal disagreements and divisions within the political party, which led some to revoke their memberships. For instance, in 2019, a group of former FARC-EP members, many of them mid-level commanders, united themselves into a separate organisation. The latter was said to represent more than 2,000 ex-fighters, who did not feel represented by the party. Besides reincorporating separately, the group sought to be represented in the mechanisms created by the FPA and to advance reparations for their part in the violations of the conflict. This shows some of the challenges which the group has faced in maintaining the collective life and organisation that they had in arms. It also illustrates challenges facing the government in dealing with several counterparts in the FPA's implementation process.[112]

6.4.2.3 Nature of the successor entity's responsibility

The discussion has revealed that there have been three simultaneous processes at play. These processes have, on the one hand, brought an end to the legal and practical existence of the FARC-EP as an NSAG and, on the other hand,

108 International Crisis Group, 'Colombia's Armed Groups Battle for the Spoils of Peace' (2017) 3–6; Truth Commission of Colombia (n 63) 976.

109 Javier Cárdenas and others, 'Perceptions of FARC Dissident Groups in Colombia: Implications for Future Peace' (2022) 10; Jerónimo Ríos and others, 'The Political Discourse of Comunes Regarding FARC-EP Dissidents in Colombia' (2023) Critical Studies on Security 1, 5, 17–20.

110 'Los Mensajes de Iván Márquez al Volver a Liderar Una Guerrilla' *La Silla Vacia* (29 August 2019); 'Colombian Transition Gets Confusing with a Disarmed FARC and an Armed One' *JusticeInfo.net* (9 September 2019).

111 ICRC, 'Estos Son Los Grupos Que Hacen Parte Del Conflicto Armado En Colombia' (24 September 2018); Juan Pappier and Kyle Johnson, 'Does the FARC Still Exist? Challenges in Assessing Colombia's "Post Conflict" Under International Humanitarian Law' (*EJIL: Talk!*, 22 October 2020). See Art 63 Law No 1957 of 2019 for how they are dealt with under the Comprehensive System.

112 'La Reincorporación Ya Tiene Otra Cara Distinta a Farc' *La Silla Vacia Sur* (16 December 2019); 'La Farc Se Fragmenta' *La Semana* (26 January 2020); International Crisis Group, 'A Fight by Other Means: Keeping the Peace with Colombia's FARC' (2021) 19–21.

allowed the defunct group to continue carrying out its commitments to reparations in a post-conflict setting. Following the international legal process, the FARC-EP ceased to legally exist with the end of the armed conflict. This was accompanied by a DDR process, which facilitated the disarmament of the group, but did not lead to its complete dismantlement. The political transformation process allowed the group to retain some of the positive cohesive elements of the collectivity. This enabled it to successfully transform into a legal political party, which is, itself, characterised by a certain organisational continuity with the defunct FARC-EP. As a result, a successor entity, with legal personality under national law, emerged. In other words, a new identifiable subject was constituted. The analysis suggests that this new entity has been a vehicle for the defunct group to remain an influential post-conflict actor. In particular, it has allowed the group to collectively participate in the Comprehensive System.

From this observation, the question arises as to whether the political party assumes the defunct FARC-EP's legal duty to repair, as recognised in the FPA, or, even more broadly, the responsibility for the legal consequences of the violations committed by the NSAG during the armed conflict. Under international law, there is no rule which holds that a non-state successor of an NSAG would succeed in the responsibility of its predecessor. Oddly, the FPA does not explicitly address this important issue. At best, it holds that former commanders, who now belong to the *Comunes* political leadership, should ensure the proper implementation and stability of the FPA.[113] The Council of State held, in its interpretation of the FPA, that the political transformation of the FARC-EP does not result in the attribution of responsibility to the state for the organisation's wrongful acts, which is in accordance with the international legal standards on the matter.[114] At the same time, the Court argued that it also does not legally disconnect the organisation from its past actions and violations, given that the FPA, under no circumstance, seeks to grant impunity. Although the Council clearly held that the FARC-EP's responsibility does not simply disappear, it concluded by calling upon the state to regulate this lacuna left by the FPA.[115]

Following the lack of any express conferral of legal responsibility upon the successor political party in the FPA or any other related instrument, it seems that the negotiating parties did not intend for such a transposition. As a result, such responsibility would remain with the FARC-EP, which no longer legally exists, and the former members who subscribed to the FPA. Instead, it could be argued that *Comunes* bears at least a moral and political responsibility to ensure, to the extent possible, the correct and full implementation of the FPA in light of its successive nature.

113 FPA 77.
114 See Chapter 3 Section 3.2.
115 *Judgment No 00463* (n 31) paras 6.4.2–6.4.4.

6.4.3 Concluding insights on non-state armed groups as responsible actors

Similar to the Justice and Peace process, the case provides support for the tendency in international law to emphasise the possible international responsibility of NSAGs that hold control over parts of the territory during an armed conflict.[116] In contrast to the approach taken towards the responsibility of the AUC, the duty of reparation has been attributed to the FARC-EP as such and not to its substructures, such as blocks or fronts. This approach follows the centralised organisational structure that characterised the FARC-EP as an NSAG. A concrete example of this difference can be found in the way the assets of both actors are dealt with for the purposes of reparations. The legal frameworks regulating the respective processes reflect the organisational differences between them. Each AUC-linked paramilitary group was required to hand over its assets, which would then be used to provide reparations to their respective victims. Differently, the FARC-EP is to deliver its collective assets as a unified entity (see Section 6.5.4). This further adds to the observation made in Chapter 5 that the organisational structure of an NSAG could play a role in the operationalisation of a duty to repair for NSAGs.

With respect to the discussion of an actor-specific approach (see Chapter 4), the question was raised concerning which indicia might be applicable when evaluating the organisational capacity of an NSAG to provide reparations. The FARC-EP can be understood as a more traditional NSAG, which is characterised by maximalist features. It sets a high standard in terms of its level of organisation and wealth. As a result, the organisational capacity of the group to engage in reparations can be considered as being high. The examination has suggested that factors, such as the authority that the leadership enjoyed, the group's internal cohesion, the disciplined nature of the armed force, and its wealth, could have facilitated its ability to provide redress. Consequently, some of the elements of the FARC-EP case may be difficult to transfer to other NSAGs, when they enjoy a low degree of organisation and/or limited resources. This reinforces the argument, voiced in Chapters 3 and 4, for an actor-specific approach to deal with inevitable differences between cases.

Regarding engagement with a responsible NSAG on the issue of reparations, a contextual approach is important given the heterogeneous nature of NSAGs operating around the world. As discussed in Chapter 4, such an approach can involve taking account of case-specific conflict dynamics and group features relating to, for example, an NSAG's organisational structure, grievances or ideology. For instance, the FARC-EP was characterised by a strong collective identity and conscience, which is reflected in its submission to the transitional justice system as a collectivity. The discussion suggests that this stems from how the NSAG operated during the conflict, specifically as a well-organised armed force with a high level of unity and cohesion (see also Section 6.3.1).

116 See Chapter 2.

Regarding NSAGs that are politically motivated or based on grievances, the FARC-EP case has exposed some of the tensions that such groups might experience when seeking to participate in a reparations process. At the same time, it has shown that political groups can have the willingness to contribute to repairing the harms caused. This, in turn, may be a means for NSAGs' to pursue their own set of goals.

The FARC-EP case is particularly interesting when seeking to obtain a better understanding of the roles a successor entity and the former members of an NSAG could take in the provision of post-conflict reparations on behalf of a defunct group. It also outlines some of the related challenges that could arise. The analysis has made use of the notion of representative authority, which was developed in Chapter 4. This assessment has involved taking account of certain contextual factors, such as the nature of the conflict's settlement, the political and justice provisions of the agreement, and the post-war context including instances of dissidence. Actor features were also considered, including the former and current roles of ex-members and the relationship between the NSAG and its successor entity. The analysis has shown how the proposed notion can be used as a conceptual lens to study a concrete case. In the examination, the successor political party has been identified as a vehicle for the extinct NSAG to carry out its collective commitments to reparations. In this framework, former high-ranking commanders, who are now part of the political leadership, appear to have taken an important role. However, the examination has also identified challenges to the successor entity's capacity to represent or act on behalf of the extinct group. This suggests that the representative authority of an entity is not static, but rather susceptible to the changing realities in a volatile post-conflict context.

Overall, the analysis has indicated that an NSAG could continue to take part in a reparations process after it ceases to exist, by way of other entities that are somehow linked to it. However, it seems beneficial to expressly stipulate the nature, legal or otherwise, of the successor entity's responsibility within the agreement or other instrument that regulates the issue of reparation to avoid any uncertainty once the NSAG no longer exists. In respect of the successor entity *Comunes*, the FPA neglects to provide more clarity on the nature of its responsibility *vis-à-vis* the reparation obligations of the defunct FARC-EP. The analysis has suggested that its nature is political and moral, rather than legal. As a result, the case does not provide support for the suggestion, made in Chapter 3, that a successor entity could inherit the legal responsibility of its predecessor, when there is a certain element of organisational continuity.[117] Instead, the analysis has displayed some of the challenges that could come along with such an exercise, such as the fragmentation of a successor entity.

117 Even though the discussion in Chapter 3 is made regarding governments of national reconciliation, the argumentation could also be applied more broadly to political transformation processes.

6.5 Engagement of the FARC-EP in the comprehensive reparations measures for peacebuilding

6.5.1 Introductory remarks

This section conducts a closer examination of some of the FARC-EP's obligations to contribute to symbolic and material reparations within the context of the reparations component of the Comprehensive System. The reparations component is made up of several groups of comprehensive or integral reparations measures for peacebuilding.[118] The following analysis focuses on the reparations measures that most expressly involve the FARC-EP as a collective responsible actor, namely the early acts of acknowledgement of collective responsibility; the concrete actions of contribution to reparations; and, the FARC-EP's contribution to material reparations through its collective goods and assets.

Although the reparation obligations of the FARC-EP situate themselves primarily within the reparations component, the FPA recognises that the group's participation in the other components of the Comprehensive System and their respective mechanisms can also contribute to reparations. For instance, the FARC-EP's engagement in the truth-seeking process led by the Truth Commission is understood as advancing the right to truth and, at the same time, contributing to reparations.[119] Although the right of victims to guarantees of non-repetition is recognised as an aspect of the reparations component, such guarantees, in themselves, also constitute one of the main separate components of the Comprehensive System.[120] This component fulfils an overarching function, insofar as it is the result of: first, the coordinated implementation of the different measures and mechanisms of the Comprehensive System, as well as the other parts of the FPA; and, second, the implementation of the additional measures of non-repetition included in the sub-agreement dealing with the end of the conflict.[121] Accordingly, the FARC-EP can be broadly understood as contributing to non-repetition by participating in the peace process itself. Moreover, the reincorporation of the FARC-EP into civilian life is recognised as a concrete commitment of the group to non-repetition.[122]

6.5.2 Early acts of acknowledgement of collective responsibility

At the end of 2015, a FARC-EP delegation, headed by a member of the Secretariat, travelled to Bojayá, in the department of Chocó, to ask forgiveness from

118 See FPA 178–186.

119 FPA 131–132, 136, 138; UN Basic Principles and Guidelines principle 22.

120 FPA 129–130. See also UN Basic Principles and Guidelines principle 23, which recognises guarantees of non-repetition as a form of reparations.

121 FPA 125, 128, 130, 186–188.

122 FPA 8, 68; Freeman and Orozco (n 23) 140.

the victims of a 2002 massacre, which left 79 dead and over 100 injured.[123] This constitutes an example of an act carried out pursuant to the first group of reparations measures. These measures include the early acts of acknowledgement of collective responsibility for harm caused and acts of public apology offered by the FARC-EP as an expression of the group's willingness to contribute to a definite *Nunca Más*.[124] These acts can be identified as measures of both satisfaction and guarantees of non-repetition, which are carried out on behalf of the FARC-EP as a collectivity.[125] Although the FPA leaves room for similar acts to be carried out by individuals, the emphasis is placed on the collective form of these symbolic acts. The early acts may further include manifestations of commitments to contribute, with concrete actions, to integral reparations for the victims (see Section 6.5.3), coexistence, non-repetition, and the peacebuilding process in general.[126] Even if the aspect of acknowledgement has been identified as a key concern for victims, it has also been argued that the engagement of the FARC-EP in reparations cannot be limited to such public acts.[127] Otherwise, they may very well lose their potential for redress and reconciliation.[128]

The early acts of acknowledgement were to be carried out in the early stages of the peace process, both before and shortly after the signing of the FPA. They were designed to constitute the opening phase of the larger process and, therefore, to form the initial step in the recognition and dignification of the victims.[129] As such, they mark a symbolic turning point.[130] It was believed that such acts could create a

123 Rosa Emilia Salamanca González and Ricardo Mendoza, 'Imagining Peace and Building Paths to Inclusive Reconciliation in Colombia' (2016) Accord Insight 23, 24; 'Las FARC Piden Perdón En Bojayá Por Su Peor Masacre' *El País* (9 December 2015). Note that the sub-Agreement on the Victims of the Conflict was already concluded in 2015.

124 The aspect of acknowledgement of collective responsibility also forms a component of the national plans of collective reparations, which are part of a specific group of comprehensive reparations measures. More specifically, the acknowledgement of the responsibility of the state, the FARC-EP, the paramilitaries and any other group, organisation or institution that has caused harm during the conflict are to be fostered within the framework of these plans. See FPA 181.

125 UN Basic Principles and Guidelines principles 22(e), 23; Camila de Gamboa Tapias and Fabio Andrés Díaz Pabón, 'The Transitional Justice Framework Agreed Between the Colombian Government and the FARC-EP' in Fabio Andrés Díaz Pabón (ed), *Truth, Justice and Reconciliation in Colombia* (Routledge 2018) 81 n 13.

126 FPA 178.

127 'Las FARC Piden Perdón En Bojayá Por Su Peor Masacre' (n 123); '"No Queremos Perdón de Las Farc Para Llorar, Sino Para Dignificar": Líder de Víctimas de La Chinita' *El Espectador* (30 September 2016); 'Three Years On, Colombians Still Await FARC Public Remorse' *JusticeInfo.net* (1 October 2019).

128 Kroc Institute for International Peace Studies, 'Segundo Informe Sobre El Estado Efectivo De Implementación Del Acuerdo De Paz En Colombia: Diciembre 2016 – Mayo 2018' (2018) 211; UNGA, 'Report of the Special Rapporteur on the Promotion of Truth, Justice, Reparation and Guarantees of Non-Recurrence' (12 July 2019) UN Doc A/74/147 17–19.

129 Freeman and Orozco (n 23) 152.

130 ICTJ, 'More Than Words: Apologies as a Form of Reparation' (2015) 4; UNGA (n 128) 13.

favourable context for the building of peace, by reflecting the commitments of the parties to the process and the satisfaction of victims' rights.[131] As explained by a former governmental official involved in the peace negotiations, it created an opportunity for the FARC-EP to do this as a group.[132]

In terms of requirements, the collective acts had to be formal, public and solemn. Governmental actors and others, such as the *Conferencia Episcopal Colombiana*, coordinated the acts in dialogue with victims' and human rights organisations, among other groups.[133] The coordinators had to ensure that the acts met the expectations of the victims and communities, avoided re-victimisation and empowered the victims.[134] For example, the relatives of the state legislators from Cali, who were kidnapped and killed by the FARC-EP, met privately with the group on three occasions to plan the ceremony held in late 2016.[135] The Truth Commission eventually took charge of coordinating these acts.[136] The process appears to have shown a clear concern for the centrality of the victims, while seeking to render the acts effective and meaningful.[137] Some of the early acts apparently emerged at the initiative of the victims and/or the FARC-EP itself.[138]

6.5.3 Concrete actions of contribution to reparations

6.5.3.1 General framework

The concrete actions of contribution to reparations constitute another group of reparations measures in which the FARC-EP is directly engaged. The group

131 FPA 178.

132 Interview No 5 (Colombia, February 2019).

133 CINEP/PPP-CERAC, 'Cuarto Informe de Verificación de La Implementación Del Acuerdo Final de Paz En Colombia' (2018) 209.

134 FPA 178; Kroc Institute for International Peace Studies, 'Informe Sobre El Estado Efectivo de Implementación Del Acuerdo de Paz En Colombia' (2017) 63; Kroc Institute for International Peace Studies (n 128) 210.

135 'FARC Pidieron Perdón a Familiares de Los Diputados de Valle del Cauca' *VerdadAbierta* (11 September 2016); 'Three Years On, Colombians Still Await FARC Public Remorse' (n 127).

136 Kroc Institute for International Peace Studies (n 128) 211; Kroc Institute for International Peace Studies, 'Estado Efectivo de Implementación Del Acuerdo de Paz de Colombia 2 Años de Implementación: Informe 3 (Diciembre 2016 – Diciembre 2018)' (2019) 141. See also Truth Commission of Colombia, 'Lineamientos Metodológicos: Escuchar, Reconocer, y Comprender Para Transformar' (2019) 15–18.

137 Luke Moffett and others, 'Alternative Sanctions Before The Special Jurisdiction For Peace: Reflections on International Law and Transitional Justice' (Queen's University Belfast 2019) para 127.

138 Kroc Institute for International Peace Studies (n 128) 210; 'Las FARC Piden Perdón En Bojayá Por Su Peor Masacre' (n 123). See also Section 6.4.2.2 on the reconciliation process between the FARC-EP and the victims of the El Nogal bombing.

commits itself, during the process of reincorporation into civilian life, and as part of this process, to realise actions that contribute to repairing harms caused by the group. The actions do not pretend to be sufficient by themselves but are rather devised as useful contributions to reparations. These concrete actions can include infrastructure-rebuilding work in the most affected areas; programmes to clear areas of anti-personnel mines and other explosive devices; programmes to substitute illicit crops; efforts to contribute to the search, localisation, identification and recuperation of persons who have died or disappeared in the context and on the occasion of the conflict; and, programmes of reparation of environmental damage.[139]

As such, these actions involve a form of collective reparations to be granted by the FARC-EP. Individual members are incentivised to participate in these type of actions, as the Special Jurisdiction for Peace may take their participation into account as a contribution to reparations, with a view to granting special treatment to the person concerned.[140] Such actions can be recognised as so-called anticipated works, actions and activities with reparative-restorative content (TOAR), which can ultimately lead to sanction reduction in the event of a criminal conviction. In this manner, perpetrators can begin providing reparations in anticipation of any potential proceedings before the Special Jurisdiction for Peace.[141] Within this context, it appears that the successor political party has taken a role in managing and systematising the activities realised by former members.[142] Research suggests that the ex-FARC-EP has placed emphasis on the symbolic and voluntary nature of carrying out anticipated TOAR for several purposes, reflecting their intentions to demonstrate compliance with the FPA, transform how victims and society perceive them, and establish their legitimacy to partake in politics and reincorporate into civilian life.[143]

Actions relating to, for instance, mine clearance and the search for the disappeared have the potential to greatly benefit from the engagement of the

139 FPA 179.

140 FPA 178.

141 Arts 139, 141 Law No 1957 of 2019; FPA 172–174; Special Jurisdiction for Peace, 'Lineamientos En Materia de Sanción Propia y Trabajos, Obras y Actividades Con Contenido Reparador – Restaurador' (2020); Clara Sandoval Villalba and others, 'TOAR Anticipados y Sanciones Propias: Reflexión Informada para la Jurisdicción Especial para la Paz' (Dejusticia 2021) 13–17; Special Jurisdiction for Peace, 'Guía Básica Sobre Medidas Reparadoras o Restaurativas y Su Seguimiento Por Parte de la Secretaría Ejecutiva de la JEP' (2021) 3–5; 'Reparación de Antiguas Farc a Sus Víctimas Empieza a Tener Ladrillos y Cemento' *El Espectador* (3 August 2022).

142 CINEP/PPP-CERAC, 'Quinto Informe de Verificación de La Implementación Del Acuerdo Final de Paz En Colombia' (2019) 169; CINEP/PPP-CERAC, 'Sexto Informe de Verificación de La Implementación Del Acuerdo Final de Paz En Colombia' (2019) 204; Interview No 8 (Colombia, February 2019).

143 Beatriz E Mayans-Hermida, Barbora Hola and Catrien Bijleveld, 'Between Impunity and Justice? Exploring Stakeholders' Perceptions of Colombia's Special Sanctions (Sanciones Propias) for International Crimes' (2023) International Journal of Transitional Justice 1, 8.

FARC-EP, considering the intimate knowledge it holds regarding its own activities during the conflict. The group's profound knowledge of the regions and local communities in which it was active, especially where these areas were remote and marked by a general lack of state presence, could also assist in facilitating some of the other actions.[144] The FARC-EP has engaged in several concrete actions of contribution to reparations, such as infrastructure-rebuilding work, including the paving of roads and maintenance of public works in the communities which surround some of the former ETCR.[145] Since the FARC-EP is in charge of actively carrying out the concrete actions, it may stimulate a sense of agency and ownership over the process of dealing with the past. It may also encourage a better understanding of the harms the group caused over the course of the conflict, and may stimulate active engagement to right the wrongs.[146]

The concrete actions undertaken by the FARC-EP are expressly linked to the group's reincorporation process. This interrelation is notable, given that DDR processes are traditionally security-driven rather than being intertwined with transitional justice.[147] The combined approach to redress and DDR may be beneficial for the provision of reparations. It allows for the delivery of reparations early in the transition, when the context may be more conducive to their constructive reception. Providing reparations in a timely manner could maximise their reparative impact.[148] This differs from the approach taken under the Justice and Peace Law, which made reparations dependent upon a lengthy judicial process. The requirement for members of NSAGs to provide reparations as part of a DDR process is not unprecedented. However, the Colombian approach stands out, since it does not only focus on engaging these individuals, but also on engaging the FARC-EP as a collective entity.[149] Such an approach corresponds to the collective nature of the reincorporation process.

144 'Will Colombia's FARC Be Allowed to Clear Mines to Repair Their Victims?' *JusticeInfo.net* (2 March 2020); Interview No 3 (Colombia, April 2019).

145 Kroc Institute for International Peace Studies (n 128) 211. Such actions also came up in several interviews with former FARC-EP members and representatives of the political party conducted in 2019.

146 Jennifer Larson Sawin and Howard Zehr, 'The Ideas of Engagement and Empowerment' in Gerry Johnstone and Daniel W Van Ness (eds), *Handbook of Restorative Justice* (Willan Publishing 2007) 45.

147 Annyssa Bellal, 'Non-State Armed Groups in Transitional Justice Processes: Adapting to New Realities of Conflict' in Roger Duthie and Paul Seils (eds), *Justice Mosaics: How Context Shapes Transitional Justice in Fractured Societies* (ICTJ 2017) 247.

148 Emanuela-Chiara Gillard, 'Reparation for Violations of International Humanitarian Law' (2003) 85 International Review of the Red Cross 529, 530; Brandon Hamber, 'The Dilemma of Reparations: In Search of a Process-Driven Approach' in Koen de Feyter and others (eds), *Out of the Ashes: Reparations for Victims of Gross and Systematic Human Rights Violations* (Intersentia 2005) 146–147.

149 Dudai (n 74) 792.

6.5.3.2 Humanitarian demining

A first concrete action that is examined more closely is the active engagement of the FARC-EP in humanitarian demining, as a contribution to reparations. Under the FPA, mine action is a cross-cutting issue as it touches upon several of the agreement's components. It is recognised as a vehicle for providing reparations and for the socio-economic reincorporation of former fighters, as well as an important measure for rural development.[150] Involving demobilised fighters in mine action is not an uncommon practice. It acknowledges their potential to contribute to the peacebuilding process.[151]

During the peace negotiations, the FARC-EP and the Colombian government jointly participated in several humanitarian measures as part of a confidence-building process. This involved humanitarian demining, as well as the search for the disappeared. These actors concluded a specific humanitarian agreement on the matter in 2015, with the purposes of advancing the building of confidence, contributing to the improvement of the security conditions for inhabitants of the targeted zones, and providing guarantees of non-repetition to communities through mine action.[152] While the agreement does not explicitly identify the mine clearance activities as a measure that contributes to reparations, it does involve some notable aspects that can be deemed relevant to that end. In itself, it constitutes a form of positive engagement of the FARC-EP. The group's engagement can be understood as being implicitly based on the recognition of its responsibility to have unlawfully handled such devices during the conflict.[153] By committing to demining, the group gets the opportunity to face its past and to contribute to rectifying it. In this sense, the group is not just considered as having contributed to the problem, but is, instead, also part of the solution.[154] Importantly, the action had to be carried out in a continuous dialogue with the affected communities, acknowledging in this way their key role in matching the action with victims' needs. In addition, the decontaminated land had to be formally handed over to the communities and the national and local authorities, which of itself may constitute an important symbolic measure.[155] Lastly, the FARC-EP provided guarantees of non-repetition to

150 FPA 67, 75, 106, 179.

151 Dahlia Simangan and Rebecca Gidley, 'Exploring the Link Between Mine Action and Transitional Justice in Cambodia' (2019) 31 Global Change, Peace & Security 221, 241.

152 Colombian government and FARC-EP, 'Comunicado Conjunto: Acuerdo Sobre Limpieza y Descontaminación Del Territorio de La Presencia de Minas Antipersonal (MAP), Artefactos Explosivos Improvisados (AEI) y Municiones Sin Explotar (MUSE) o Restos Explosivos de Guerra (REG) En General' (7 March 2015) 1.

153 Nicolás Carrillo-Santarelli, 'Colombian Government and FARC Armed Group Reach a Mine Clearance Agreement' (*Armed Groups and International Law*, 11 March 2015); Sanchez and Rudling (n 17) 65.

154 Simangan and Gidley (n 151) 239.

155 Colombian government and FARC-EP (n 152) 2.

the communities by committing to maintain the areas in a clean and decontaminated state.[156] At a later stage, *Humanicemos DH* was established. This civil organisation consists of former FARC-EP fighters involved in humanitarian demining. The organisation was established as an initiative to facilitate their collective economic and social reincorporation. In addition, their activities have been characterised as serving a reparatory goal.[157] In the words of an ex-FARC-EP member involved in the programme, "the vision is that as we were part of the conflict, we help make up for the pain that we caused during it".[158]

Humanitarian demining has the potential to contribute to collective reparations. This could be achieved in several ways. Mine action could, for instance, form a commitment to non-repetition, with a strong preventative component.[159] It could also be identified as a form of restitution, where it provides the conditions for the return of displaced persons to their place of residence, for restoration of employment, or for return of property.[160] Moreover, the delivery of information on the location of mines, or the acknowledgement of the facts and acceptance of responsibility for the damages caused by them, could provide measures of satisfaction.[161] A former FARC-EP member, part of *Humanicemos DH*, explained their work as a contribution to reparations in the following words:

> by restoring people's peace of mind, because where there are explosive devices there is anxiety as people cannot move freely within the territory. Already when we leave the areas completely clear of the suspected presence of mines, it will be possible to cultivate and the farmer will be able to return [...] To repair is to say: "I made a mistake, I am going to do this to repair".[162]

Nonetheless, the FPA does not clarify how the concrete actions involving humanitarian demining attain their reparative value.[163] The engagement of the responsible actor is not sufficient in itself. Instead, it appears vital that the action is directed at acknowledging and remedying the harms caused by the use of mines during the conflict, and that it is part of a broader participatory process, run in consultation with affected communities.[164] The following explanation, provided by an official of the Special Jurisdiction for Peace, gives further

156 Ibid. 3.
157 Kroc Institute for International Peace Studies (n 134) 53–54; Kroc Institute for International Peace Studies (n 128) 111; 'Will Colombia's FARC Be Allowed to Clear Mines to Repair Their Victims?' (n 144).
158 Interview No 12 (Phone Interview, March 2019).
159 CINEP/PPP-CERAC (n 50) 131.
160 UARIV, '"El Desminado Es Una Garantía de No Repetición Para Las Víctimas y Favorece Su Reparación"' (4 April 2018).
161 UN Basic Principles and Guidelines principles 19, 22(b)(e), 23.
162 Interview No 12 (Phone Interview, March 2019). See also 'Will Colombia's FARC Be Allowed to Clear Mines to Repair Their Victims?' (n 144).
163 Kroc Institute for International Peace Studies (n 128) 130.
164 Moffett and others (n 137) para 159.

insights into how the respective standards of humanitarian demining and reparations processes differ from one another, but also how mine action could contribute to providing reparations:

> [I]n the case of humanitarian demining, for example [...] it is not about how many meters were cleared, how many meters are free from the suspected presence of anti-personnel mines, but what is the impact of demining on the lives of the communities where the mine action was realised, how the land is being re-used, whether schools are being re-opened and whether teachers are working or not [...] whether or not places for cultural activities are activated. The most traditional standard of a demining process is the amount of meters that have been cleared, which is completely different from a rights-based approach that implies the participation of victims, the valorisation of that process.[165]

It appears necessary to have a set of guidelines or criteria, which allow for determinations as to how mine action could attain its reparative value and, subsequently, how demining operations could be designed in accordance with these observations. In 2020, the Special Jurisdiction for Peace published guidelines outlining the requirements that actions, such as demining involving former FARC-EP members, must meet to qualify as part of its sanctions regime. One such requirement is that a given action must have a reparative-restorative character, which is evaluated according to certain parameters.[166] As further discussed in Section 6.5.3.4, these parameters provide more clarity on what could determine the reparative value of humanitarian demining, as a concrete action of contribution to reparations.

6.5.3.3 Search for the disappeared

The second concrete action as a contribution to reparations that is considered more closely is the involvement of the FARC-EP in the search, localisation, identification and recuperation of persons who have died or who disappeared in the context and on the occasion of the armed conflict. This is in accordance with the UN Basic Principles and Guidelines, which identifies such actions as measures of satisfaction.[167] The FPA conceptualises 'disappearances' in a broader manner than traditional IHRL, by including actions carried out by the FARC-EP as a non-state actor.[168] According to Dempster, state and non-state

165 Interview No 6 (Colombia, April 2019).

166 Special Jurisdiction for Peace, 'Lineamientos En Materia de Sanción Propia y Trabajos, Obras y Actividades Con Contenido Reparador – Restaurador' (n 141) 10.

167 UN Basic Principles and Guidelines principle 22(c).

168 Art 2 International Convention for the Protection of All Persons from Enforced Disappearance (2006) 2716 UNTS 3; UNCHR, 'Report Submitted by Mr Manfred Nowak, Independent Expert Charged with Examining the Existing International

disappearances are connected by both their impact on those who are left behind and the imperative to meet their needs within a transitional justice context.[169]

In respect of the search for the disappeared, there exists an overlap between the reparations, truth and criminal justice components of the Comprehensive System. In addition to being recognised as a reparations measure, these efforts are led by the Special Unit for the Search for Persons Deemed as Missing and can be taken into consideration by the Special Jurisdiction for Peace for the purpose of granting special treatment to participating individuals. In the context of the truth component, the FARC-EP undertakes to provide the Special Unit with all the relevant information at its disposal. This is understood to contribute to the satisfaction of victims' rights to truth and reparation.[170] The FPA also takes note of the immediate humanitarian measures relating to the search for the disappeared, which were jointly undertaken by the Colombian government and the FARC-EP, as part of a confidence-building process during the peace negotiations.[171] The ICRC and the National Institute of Legal Medicine accompanied these efforts carried out by the FARC-EP.[172] The successor political party seems to have taken part in the subsequent delivery of information collected in this context to the Special Unit.[173]

Within this framework, the FARC-EP established, in 2016, the National Committee for the Search of Disappeared Persons, to advance its efforts to collect information on disappearances from its members, as a reparations measure for the victims.[174] These efforts were coordinated at the national level, but also benefitted, at the local level, from the work of small teams of former fighters in every ETCR.[175] The first results collected by the group provided information on the location of 33 disappeared persons.[176] In 2017, the successor political party started participating in a special process to collect humanitarian information, which included the engagement of, i.a., victims' organisations, the ICRC and the Ministry of Defence. The process involved the participation of

Criminal and Human Rights Framework for the Protection of Persons from Enforced or Involuntary Disappearances, Pursuant to Paragraph 11 of Commission Resolution 2001/46' (8 January 2002) UN Doc. E/CN.4/2002/71 31.

169 Lauren Dempster, 'The Republican Movement, "Disappearing" and Framing the Past in Northern Ireland' (2016) 10 International Journal of Transitional Justice 250, 254.

170 Decree No 589 of 2017; FPA 139, 142, 178–179.

171 FPA 126, 143. These activities find their basis in Colombian government and FARC-EP, 'Comunicado Conjunto No. 62' (17 October 2015).

172 CINEP/PPP-CERAC, 'Segundo Informe de Verificación de La Implementación Del Acuerdo Final de Paz En Colombia' (2018) 137–138, 140; Kroc Institute for International Peace Studies (n 128) 194–195.

173 CINEP/PPP-CERAC, 'Sexto Informe' (n 142) 192–193; ICMP, 'Mapeo De Organizaciones De Familiares De Personas Desaparecidas Y De Otras Organizaciones De La Sociedad Civil: Colombia' (2020) 77–78.

174 CINEP/PPP-CERAC, 'Sexto Informe' (n 142) 191; ICMP (n 173) 26.

175 ICMP (n 173) 75.

176 'La Comisión de Farc Que Busca a Los Desaparecidos' (n 106).

more than 70 delegates of the party, who focused on collecting information from ex-fighters within the ETCRs. In 2019, the political party formally delivered information on 276 cases to the Special Unit as a result of the process.[177] This constitutes a concrete example of how a coordinated approach, led by the successor entity, had the potential to maximise the ability of former FARC-EP members to collectively crowd-source information on the disappeared as a contribution to reparations.[178]

6.5.3.4 Some challenges

Although the concrete actions of contribution to reparations form an innovative way of engaging an NSAG in reparations, some challenges can be identified. First, affected communities may not experience the concrete actions, such as the repairing of infrastructure affected by the conflict, as reparations. Instead, they may consider these actions as, for example, measures to which they are entitled as citizens and for which the Colombian government bears the primary responsibility. Consequently, there is a need to appropriately match the actions with the harms that they aim to address. In this context, a participatory process involving victims is required, which could involve providing the victims a central role in the identification of the harms and resulting needs, the design of the measures and the implementation process.[179] Such a process should additionally include the acknowledgement of the wrong and responsibility, which serve as important elements to distinguish reparations from development or assistance measures.[180]

A second fundamental challenge relates to the question concerning 'what determines the reparatory value or character of the concrete actions carried out by the FARC-EP?' The FPA does not provide the necessary information to answer this question. However, the issue is deemed of significant importance, since it clarifies how concrete actions are to be designed and carried out, with the view of fulfilling their reparatory goal. Moreover, it is otherwise conceivable that former fighters might gain the impression that they are actively contributing to reparations through actions that, in practice, do not attain that function. Indeed, some interviews carried out with former FARC-EP members

177 ICMP (n 173) 78–79; 'La Farc Da La Cara a Los Desaparecidos, Pero Les Falta Mucho' *La Silla Vacía* (20 August 2019); 'Las FARC Entregan Información De 276 Desaparecidos' *El País* (22 August 2019).

178 Moffett and others (n 137) para 132.

179 UNOHCHR, 'Rule-of-Law Tools for Post-Conflict States: Reparation Programmes' (2008) 15–16; Mijke de Waardt and Sanne Weber, 'Beyond Victims' Mere Presence: An Empirical Analysis of Victim Participation in Transitional Justice in Colombia' (2019) 11 Journal of Human Rights Practice 209.

180 Luke Moffett, 'Beyond Attribution: Responsibility of Armed Non-State Actors for Reparations in Northern Ireland, Colombia and Uganda' in Noemi Gal-Or, Cedric Ryngaert and Math Noortmann (eds), *Responsibilities of the Non-State Actor in Armed Conflict and the Market Place* (Brill Nijhof 2015) 325.

in 2019 revealed a more literal understanding of the notion of reparations. For example, one former member explained that, "when a community needs that a road which is in a bad shape is fixed, we go. The communities see that we are working and this is a form of reparation".[181] Similarly, another member argued that their productive projects could be considered as being reparative in nature, since they bring economic prosperity to the communities surrounding the ETCRs.[182] Explanations provided by members of the higher levels of the political party were more related to the legal notion of reparations in transitional justice processes. They indicated, for example, that the actions should re-establish a right of victims and that the action itself should be accompanied by a participatory process with the victims.[183]

Care must be taken not to stretch the concept of reparations to fit any type of action that seems to have some sort of positive impact in terms of development. This could risk robbing the concept of its specificity and significance. Minimum requirements that could, for instance, help assess whether a concrete action has a reparatory character might include: the acknowledgement of responsibility for the wrong and the harm caused; the establishment of a direct relation between the action and the harm that resulted from the violation of a right; and, the inclusion and effective participation of the victims in the process.[184] Indeed, in 2020, the Special Jurisdiction for Peace published guidelines that include a non-exhaustive list of parameters to evaluate the reparative-restorative character of such type of concrete actions within the justice component of the Comprehensive System. Specifically, the actions must guarantee the effective participation of the victims; must attend to the damages caused; cannot infringe upon the rights of the victims; must contribute to the reconstruction of social ties or to a transformation of society that allows for actors to overcome the effects of the conflict; and, must contribute to the reintegration of the appearing party.[185] While the final two elements more clearly relate to the concept of restorative justice, they generally indicate the elements through which the concrete actions could attain their reparative value or character.

6.5.4 Collective goods and assets for material reparations

During the peace negotiations, the question of how the FARC-EP was going to repair the victims with its own assets was of a highly contentious nature. It was imperative for the government that the NSAG would contribute to reparations, not only symbolically or through their labour, but also by using their wealth.

181 Group Interview No 11 (Colombia, March 2019).
182 Interview No 17 (Colombia, March 2019).
183 Interview No 8 (Colombia, February 2019); Interview No 9 (Colombia, April 2019).
184 Fundación Ideas para la Paz – FIP and others, 'Comunicado Sobre La Reincorporación de Las FARC' (9 November 2017).
185 Special Jurisdiction for Peace, 'Lineamientos En Materia de Sanción Propia y Trabajos, Obras y Actividades Con Contenido Reparador – Restaurador' (n 141) 10.

Calculations for the FARC-EP's annual earnings for 2015–2016, before it disarmed, have been estimated at $580 million.[186] In 2014, the FARC-EP was ranked as the third richest NSAG.[187] Eventually, in the aftermath of the negative plebiscite *vis-à-vis* the original FPA, the measure found its way into the revised version of the agreement, as one of the main and most important additions to the reparations component of the Comprehensive System.[188] Considering the significant wealth that the FARC-EP acquired over the course of the NIAC, it certainly represents one of the central accountability measures in respect of the group in the FPA. It can also be understood as a symbolic commitment of the FARC-EP to share in the significant costs of reparations borne by the state to all victims.[189]

As stated in the FPA, "the FARC-EP as insurgent organisation that acted in the framework of rebellion" has to contribute to material reparations.[190] To this end, the FARC-EP was required to hand over an inventory of all types of goods and assets that it acquired over the course of the armed conflict and, subsequently, to deliver them to the state.[191] Correspondingly, they are considered as "collective goods of the members of the FARC-EP" or so-called "resources for war".[192] As a result, "[t]he ex-combatants of the FARC-EP bear a collective obligation to hand over the goods for reparations", which are to be placed in a newly created Fund for Victims.[193] In cases of non-compliance, FARC-EP members may lose their judicial benefits and may be redirected to the ordinary justice system. That said, although the FARC-EP had agreed to hand over $291 million in assets, the group only delivered $12.9 million by the end of 2020, citing lack of state action and threats to former fighter, among other reasons.[194] In 2022–2023, around $4.3 million in

186 'The FARC's Riches: List of Assets Fails to Reveal Guerrillas' Total Wealth' *InSight Crime* (29 August 2017).

187 'Farc Es El Tercer Grupo Terrorista Más Rico del Mundo: Forbes Israel' *El Tiempo* (12 November 2014).

188 The original agreement between the Colombian government and the FARC-EP was rejected in a plebiscite vote held in October 2016. A revised version of the agreement was adopted the following month. Capone (n 10) 127–128, 156; de Gamboa Tapias and Díaz Pabón (n 125) 72–73; Freeman and Orozco (n 23) 155; 'Colombian Government and FARC Reach New Peace Deal' *The Guardian* (13 November 2016).

189 Kroc Institute for International Peace Studies (n 136) 152; Moffett and others (n 137) para 125; UNHRC, 'Report of the Special Rapporteur on the Promotion of Truth, Justice, Reparation and Guarantees of Non-Recurrence' (11 July 2019) UN Doc A/HRC/42/45 para 92.

190 Art 39 Law No 1957 of 2019; FPA 186 [own translation].

191 Art 1 Decree No 205 of 2020. The Constitutional Court held that these assets can only be used for material reparations and not to finance the group's reincorporation programmes. See *Judgment C-071/18* (n 30) para 138.

192 Arts 1–2 Decree No 903 of 2017 [own translation]; FPA 186 [own translation].

193 Art 3 Decree No 903 of 2017; *Judgment C-071/18* (n 30); *Judgment C-080/18* Constitutional Court of Colombia (15 August 2018) para 4.1.7.4 [own translation].

194 'Colombia's FARC Delivers a Fraction of Pledged Peace Deal Assets by Deadline' *Reuters* (31 December 2020).

FARC-EP's collective assets were used to compensate more than 2300 individual victims of the group. FARC-EP assets were also allocated to collective reparations for groups of victims, around $1.6 million in cash and $3.4 million in kind.[195]

Partly because of this collective obligation, individual members of the FARC-EP are exempted from their obligation to provide monetary compensation. Instead, the Colombian state oversees the provision of compensation through the administrative reparations programme regulated by the Victims' Law. Although this limitation partially reduces members' individual responsibility and the right of victims to integral reparation, the Constitutional Court held that these restrictions are not contrary to the Constitution. In its reasoning, the Court made two initial observations. First, the balance of all the components of the Comprehensive System seeks to provide an integrated response to the victims. Consequently, the System has to be evaluated in its entirety, with a view to determine whether the response of the state is consistent and proportionate to the harm suffered. Second, the traditional model of individual reparations is not tenable in situations of massive and systematic violations, and should instead be adjusted to the particularities of this context. Taking these observations into account, the Court held that the restriction does not result in a complete exemption of responsibility *vis-à-vis* the victimiser. This was concluded on the basis of the following three elements: 1) the measure is preceded by the handing over of the assets of the FARC-EP, to be used for reparations; 2) the legal limitation only extends to the personal assets of the members, while hidden collective assets can still be judicially pursued to provide reparations; 3) it only relates to the monetary component of reparations, whereas members' contributions to the other (non-compensatory) components will need to be applied with more rigour.[196] Interestingly, the assets of the FARC-EP, and the correlating obligations of the group, take a central place in the reasoning of the Court. The decision suggests that the respective responsibilities of the group and its constituent members, in terms of their duty to repair, can interrelate. However, the scheme does not imply that the members can hide behind the collectivity, since they still need to contribute to the other forms of reparations.

6.5.5 Concluding insights on non-state armed group's engagement regarding reparations

The inclusion of the FARC-EP's commitments to reparations within the FPA constitutes the result of the peace negotiations between the Colombian government and that group. It constitutes a concrete example of the first form of

195 UNSC, 'UN Verification Mission in Colombia – Report of the Secretary-General' (24 March 2023) UN Doc S/2023/222 para 99.

196 *Judgment C-674/17* Constitutional Court of Colombia (14 November 2017) paras 5.5.1.9–5.5.1.10; *Judgment C-080/18* (n 193) para 4.1.7.4; Comisión Colombiana de Juristas, 'Colombia: Jurisdicción Especial Para La Paz, Análisis a Un Año y Medio de Su Entrada En Funcionamento' (2019) 40.

engagement with an NSAG on reparations as discussed in Section 4.5.1 of Chapter 4. The extent of the FARC-EP's engagement is unprecedented. The group was not only involved in the design of the reparations measures and mechanisms that form part of the Comprehensive System, but also played an active role in the transitional justice process, first as an NSAG and, later, as a successor political party. Within the context of the peace process, the adopted approach did not only consider legal standards, but also political considerations and societal demands as part of the broader transition. In such a framework, reparations may not only seek to restore the situation that existed before, insofar as possible in cases of gross or systematic violations, but they may also aim to support other initiatives like community reintegration of demobilised fighters.

A comprehensive transitional justice system constitutes the forum in which the FARC-EP is to provide reparations. The case has provided for a different perspective on the question of forum than that offered in the context of the Justice and Peace Law, which regulates a system of special criminal proceedings as the forum for reparations. On the contrary, the FARC-EP carries out its obligations through extra-judicial measures part of the transitional justice system's reparations component. By making reparations not dependent upon a lengthy judicial process, the opportunity was created to provide reparations early in the process. The analysis has indicated that certain reparations, such as symbolic measures or guarantees of non-repetition, could already be provided by an NSAG during peace negotiations and the demobilisation process. At the same time, the case has provided for an interesting example of how an NSAG can support the work of other transitional justice mechanisms, such as a body charged with the search for the disappeared, as a contribution to reparations.

The FARC-EP is required to contribute to the integral reparation of victims through symbolic and material reparations. In this regard, the examination has shown that an emphasis is placed on the provision of collective reparations. This approach appears to be more apt in terms of dealing with a significant number of victims, than the traditional approach favouring individualised reparations. When linking the discussion back to the five reparations forms included in the UN Basic Principles and Guidelines, the engagement of the FARC-EP centres itself primarily on the forms of satisfaction, guarantees of non-repetition and restitution. Additionally, the assets handed over by the group have been used to provide compensation and collective reparations. The central function assigned to these collective assets in the reparations scheme corresponds to the considerable wealth the FARC-EP acquired over the course of the conflict. A similar approach may not apply easily to every NSAG. The FARC-EP takes a central role in symbolic reparations, by carrying out acts acknowledging its responsibility and through public apologies. Both bear significant value in the peace process and within the transitional justice system more specifically. This shows the potential of NSAGs to provide symbolic reparations.

The FARC-EP case indicates that an NSAG could contribute to some of the main forms of reparations, which are normally required from states under international law. At the same time, it provides new insights into how the specific capabilities of an NSAG can be taken into account when designing reparations measures. The collective efforts of a group, including its members' knowledge and abilities in particular areas, can be geared towards reparations. This is apparent in the FPA's concept of concrete actions of contribution to reparations, such as those involving humanitarian demining or the search for the disappeared, which can capitalise on the knowledge of former fighters and their collective efforts to gather relevant information. These actions also fulfil other functions by seeking to contribute to the reincorporation of the ex-fighters who are taking part. However, while exploring new approaches, it is essential to uphold the core principles underlining the concept of reparation to avoid diluting its distinctiveness and significance.

6.6 Conclusions

The examination in this chapter has unpacked the duty of the FARC-EP to provide reparation for violations of international law, to be carried out in the framework of a comprehensive transitional justice system. It has shed light on how this duty has been conceptualised and implemented in practice. Overall, the analysis has unveiled an unprecedented case, in which an NSAG has been actively engaged in a reparations process for wrongs committed during armed conflict. Over the course of the chapter, specific insights have been drawn from the case that hold broader relevance for the discussion on how a possible duty of NSAGs to repair could be operationalised in international law. These findings have been presented pursuant to three overarching themes, these being NSAGs' international responsibility and resulting duty to repair; NSAGs as responsible actors; and, NSAG's engagement *vis-à-vis* reparations.

These chapter's findings are complemented with some concluding points regarding the case's broader significance for international law and policy. The FARC-EP case constitutes a recent and unprecedented instance of state practice and *opinio juris*, which recognises an NSAG's international responsibility and its resulting duty of reparation, as a distinct subject. Thus, the case can be viewed as contributing to the possible formation of a norm of customary international law on the matter. In this regard, some of the international rules and principles that are traditionally applicable to states are followed. For instance, the NSAG's responsibility finds its basis in internationally wrongful acts and is not punitive in character. The group is also required to provide certain forms of reparations that are normally requested from states under international law. Overall, the case challenges international lawyers' traditional understanding of reparation, as being limited to the realm of states.

Despite the similarities to concepts from the law of state responsibility, the case has also provided new insights into how the application of a reparation duty *vis-à-vis* NSAGs could accommodate their distinct nature in comparison to states. These insights also shed light on some potential challenges and opportunities in respect of the relationship between reparation and such actors. In addition, the case has demonstrated that it can be feasible to engage on reparations with an NSAG. This suggests that states' concerns over conferring some type of legitimacy on NSAGs can be overcome, while a politically motivated NSAG can be willing to contribute to reparations. This could arguably have been facilitated through both actors choosing to place redress for victims at the centre of the peace negotiations from the very beginning.[197] In addition, the case has shown that, in some instances, NSAGs can have the capacity to provide or at least make contributions towards reparations.

The innovative Comprehensive System has received significant attention and support from the international community. This adds to its potential to serve as an example of practice for processes elsewhere. More specifically, it provides for an example of how an NSAG could be engaged as a responsible actor in a diverse set of reparations measures, following international legal standards. It may encourage greater attention by states and international actors to a possible role for NSAGs in reparations. Therefore, the case is also significant from a policy perspective.

Chapters 5 and 6 both deal with reparations from NSAGs in Colombia. However, the examination has revealed two transitional justice processes that approach the operationalisation of NSAGs' duty of reparation in a somewhat different manner. Over the course of the analysis, differences and similarities have been drawn between these processes that involve NSAGs that significantly differ in terms of their nature and organisational structures. For example, the responsibility of the AUC-linked paramilitary groups is addressed as part of a criminal justice process, whereas the FARC-EP is required to contribute to reparations within a comprehensive transitional justice system. The FARC-EP case complements the discussion of the Justice and Peace Law, by providing insights into how an NSAG could contribute to other forms of reparations beyond monetary compensation. In both cases, however, the Colombian state takes a subsidiary role in guaranteeing the right of victims to reparation. It shows that reparations cannot be solely dependent upon an NSAG. These examples indicate that both cases complement one another, by generating a greater understanding as to how a reparation duty of NSAGs could be conceptualised and put into practice under international law. In doing so, they enrich the international legal debate on these questions.

197 Freeman and Orozco (n 23) 105–106.

Conclusion

This book contributes to the academic debate on the role of NSAGs in reparations. The overall aim of this study is to bring clarity to whether and how NSAGs might be required under international law to provide reparations for their wrongful acts committed during situations of NIAC. The focus of this study is of substantial practical importance considering that NSAGs are one of the main participants in today's landscape of armed conflict and cause significant harm within war-torn societies worldwide. Although it appears logical to argue, from a legal perspective, that reparations need to be made by the actor responsible for causing damage or harm, the study shows that this issue is both delicate and complex when NSAGs are the wrongdoer. Within this framework, the objectives of this book have been to determine:

1 whether NSAGs possess international legal personality as distinct, collective entities;
2 whether these actors have a duty to provide reparation for wrongful acts in contemporary international law; and,
3 how such a duty of NSAGs to provide reparation could be operationalised under international law.

In this concluding part, the main research findings of the study are summarised, several areas for further research are identified, and some final remarks are formulated.

C.1 The duty of non-state armed groups to provide reparation at an incipient stage in international law

In the first part of this book, the current international legal framework governing a possible duty of NSAGs to provide reparation was examined. Under international law, the duty of reparation is one of the legal consequences which arises when an entity is held responsible for its internationally wrongful acts. When dealing with the responsibility of an NSAG as such, it is first necessary to determine whether such a collective entity has international legal personality,

DOI: 10.4324/9781003401292-11

distinct from its individual members. The concept of international legal personality allows for the identification of entities that have an independent legal existence in international law, as bearers of certain rights and obligations. The analysis in Chapter 1 demonstrates that an NSAG has a distinct, but limited, legal personality under international law. More specifically, such an entity holds certain international obligations under the primary rules of IHL and possibly IHRL over the course of the NIAC which it is a party to. Thus, violations of these primary obligations under international law committed by an NSAG could potentially result in the entity's international responsibility.

Chapter 1 determines that IHL imposes international obligations on the parties to a NIAC. The analysis finds that being a collective entity, which holds a certain degree of organisation, constitutes one of the fundamental requirements to qualify as a party to a NIAC. Consequently, this encompasses an NSAG and the armed forces of a state. In addition, the argument is made that one of the main functions of the organisation requirement, which is used to determine the existence of a NIAC, is to establish whether a group has attained a sufficient level of organisation to be treated as a legal entity distinct from its members. This entity should be capable of fulfilling and ensuring compliance with IHL obligations. The analysis further shows that the direct application of IHL to NSAGs finds broad support in the ICRC commentaries, international practice, legal literature, and the different theories which have been put forward to explain how IHL may bind NSAGs as non-signatories to IHL treaty law.

While the limited legal personality of NSAGs under IHL is generally not deemed controversial, Chapter 1 identifies the direct application of international human rights obligations to such entities as a continuing topic of discussion. However, the concept is increasingly gaining support in international practice and scholarship. This study recognises that a valid argument can be made to, at a minimum, extend the human rights framework to an NSAG engaged in a NIAC and having control over territory and persons. This extension is warranted when such control leads to a situation where a state is incapable of guaranteeing the human rights of persons living within that territory and fulfilling its due diligence obligations within those areas. When it comes to subjecting an NSAG to human rights obligations, the study argues that such a group should have a certain level of organisation to identify it as a legal entity that can be distinguished from its individual members. This should also provide the NSAG with the reasonable capacity to implement these obligations. The indicative factors developed to evaluate the organisation requirement under IHL could inform such an analogous assessment in respect of IHRL, considering that it relates to the same type of entity. However, certain human rights norms, depending on their nature and scope, might require a higher or distinct form of NSAGs' organisation to ensure such normative capacity.

Based on the conclusion that an NSAG, as a collective legal entity, bears certain primary obligations under international law, such an entity would logically incur legal responsibility when it violates these norms. Accordingly, the latter would give rise to a duty of reparation where the NSAG breaches any of its obligations. This concept finds its expression in the maxim '*ubi responsabilitas, ibi jus*', which, as explained by Pellet, holds: "where, in a normative system, the violation of rules results in foreseeable consequences, there can be no doubt that the system can be qualified as a 'legal' one".[1] In this sense, the question of responsibility can be considered as touching on the very essence of the international legal system. Moreover, it would, at least theoretically, contribute to its effectiveness.[2] Furthermore, this would be in accordance with the fundamental principle of international law that any wrongful act requires reparation. Nonetheless, based on an analysis of treaty and customary international law as well as international practice, Chapter 2 did not identify an established secondary norm or a uniform set of rules and principles that specify the new legal relations which would arise from the commission of an internationally wrongful act by an NSAG. The international legal system also does not provide for a forum with the mandate to examine possible claims arising from such wrongful acts. Although some mechanisms have dealt with the international responsibility of NSAGs, including the issue of reparation, a uniform legal framework underlying such efforts is lacking. In addition, these mechanisms have generally not provided victims with an avenue to claim reparations from the NSAGs concerned. This situation leads to the existence of a problematic responsibility gap in current international law. The latter is evident, theoretically, in the asymmetry between the primary and secondary rules applicable to NSAGs and, practically, in the *de facto* impunity for violations that are not covered by the existing international regimes of state responsibility and individual criminal responsibility. All things considered, Chapter 2 concludes that the international responsibility of NSAGs remains controversial. However, it can be said that the greatest potential for development lies in the IHL regime, in which it is generally accepted that NSAGs enjoy limited international legal personality. In contrast, the discussion on the application of IHRL to NSAGs continues to mainly centre on the primary rules of this body of law. Moreover, Chapter 3 found little support, in present ICL, for the collective criminal responsibility of NSAGs, as a way of holding such groups to account and possibly to impose a duty of reparation.

Within this framework, Chapter 2 determines that a possible duty of NSAGs to provide reparation is marked by uncertainty in international law. No sound legal basis for such a duty was found in current treaty or customary law. Moreover, other than the FARC-EP case in Colombia, no express support was

1 Alain Pellet, 'The Definition of Responsibility in International Law' in James Crawford, Alain Pellet and Simon Olleson (eds), *The Law of International Responsibility* (Oxford University Press 2010) 4.

2 Annyssa Bellal, 'Establishing the Direct Responsibility of Non-State Armed Groups for Violations of International Norms: Issues of Attribution' in Noemi Gal-Or, Cedric Ryngaert and Math Noortmann (eds), *Responsibility of the Non-State Actor in Armed Conflict and the Market Place* (Brill Nijhof 2015) 304.

found for the idea of applying the fundamental principle of law, concerning reparation for wrongful acts, to NSAGs under international law. At present, a possible duty of reparation for NSAGs finds its most authoritative basis in principle 15 of the UN Basic Principles and Guidelines, which were adopted by the UN General Assembly without a vote. This pivotal soft law instrument, which concerns reparations in international law, tentatively recognises an emerging concept of the international responsibility of NSAGs with a correlating duty to make reparation for, at least, serious violations of IHL. Despite its authoritative character, it has not generated the necessary state practice to lift this soft legal norm into the domain of hard law. This conclusion notwithstanding, some limited instances of state practice, which recognise such a duty for NSAGs in international law, are identified. The most prominent present case is the transitional justice process in Colombia, which concerns the responsibility of the FARC-EP. Besides contemporary state practice, this study finds historical precedent, within the somewhat antiquated laws of belligerency and insurgency, which concerns NSAGs that held effective control over territory. In these examples, the analysis shows that circumstance made it legally and practically sensible for states to engage directly with an NSAG on responsibility matters during an ongoing conflict. These circumstances arose when the NSAG had international legal personality and the NSAG's wrongful conduct occurred beyond the control of the parent state. With a view to current international law, the analysis suggests that this historical precedent is particularly significant when it comes to making determinations of possible responsibility for, at least, those NSAGs with exclusive territorial control that satisfy the higher threshold of Additional Protocol II. Further recognition that NSAGs should provide reparations for violations of international law is found in several instances of UN practice and, in a more limited manner, in the reports of some truth commissions. Overall, the examination in Chapter 2 concludes that this body of practice remains minimal. Nonetheless, the study still identifies it as contributing to the initial foundations of a possible duty of reparation. In addition, the research finds increasing support for such a duty among international experts and legal scholars who have the capacity to bring this discussion forward.

Taking these findings into consideration, the book concludes that the duty of NSAGs to provide reparation presents itself, primarily, as a matter of *lex ferenda*. At present, international law lacks an established secondary norm that provides a sound legal basis for such a duty. Moreover, there is a clear need for further clarification of the possible rules and principles which could regulate the new legal relationship that would arise from the commission of an internationally wrongful act by an NSAG, in terms of its obligation to provide reparation for harm caused. In addition to its primary status as *lex ferenda*, the duty of an NSAG to provide reparation, at the same time, finds itself at an incipient stage in international law. This conclusion recognises the existence of at least some legal precedent and recognition that such entities should provide reparations when breaching their primary obligations under IHL, and possibly IHRL, during situations of NIAC.

Over the course of the study, several reasons emerged for imposing a duty to repair on NSAGs. They complement and further concretise the discussion on the necessity of such a duty presented in the introduction to this book. First of all, the analysis indicates that reparations for wrongful acts are understood as facilitating compliance with the law during armed conflict. Additionally, reparation has been identified as an important justice and accountability measure for victims that should not be neglected in the face of the fight against impunity. Thus, the possibility of claiming reparations from NSAGs, based on international law, could fulfil an important function from both a compliance and accountability perspective. This is especially important considering that NSAGs are party to most present-day armed conflicts. Furthermore, the Colombian case indicates that the circumstances of armed conflict can make it difficult for victims to identify the specific person who committed an abuse. In contrast, it may be easier to pinpoint the NSAG to which this person belonged. In addition, an individual perpetrator may have died, or may not have submitted themselves to a given justice process. Even if the person can be identified, it could still be beneficial to pursue the assets of a well-financed NSAG. The case law of the International Criminal Court and Colombia's Justice and Peace Chambers, respectively, have indicated that an NSAG's member may be indigent or not capable of providing adequate reparations to all victims. In response, the Justice and Peace process in Colombia shows how the subsidiary responsibility of the NSAG, to which the convicted person belonged, could provide a potential means of safeguarding, at least to a greater extent, victims' right to reparation. Lastly, the FARC-EP case demonstrates how the collective effort of an NSAG has the potential to maximise its contribution to reparations. This is, for instance, illustrated by the NSAG's engagement in the search for the disappeared as a form of satisfaction.

C.2 A multifaceted proposal for operationalising a duty of non-state armed groups to provide reparation under international law

In moving beyond the current state of affairs in international law, a multifaceted proposal, suggesting how a possible duty of NSAGs to repair could be operationalised under international law, is presented in the second part of the book. This proposal draws from a *de lege ferenda* analysis of a broad reference framework, with a basis in both international law and practice.

As a starting point, Chapter 3 argues that the possible legal responsibility of NSAGs requires a new and separate regime in international law that is akin in character to that of state responsibility. This conclusion results from the limitations of the existing regimes of state responsibility and individual criminal responsibility, due to their inability to address the violations committed by

NSAGs in a satisfactory manner. This proposal finds further support in both international practice and legal scholarship. The argument is put forward that the international responsibility of NSAGs can be conceptualised in a similar manner to state responsibility and as being *sui generis* in character, rather than assimilating it to notions of domestic law. The *sui generis* character additionally reflects that the rules and principles governing the responsibility of NSAGs should give appropriate weight to the particularities of these entities, especially in comparison to states. This differs from taking a copy-paste approach to existing standards in the law of state responsibility. Moreover, the analysis suggests that the responsibility of NSAGs can be understood as complementary to the individual criminal responsibility of group members, by analogy with the responsibility of states and their agents.

This conclusion is significant for two reasons. It clarifies what character a future regime of NSAGs' responsibility could take in international law. In addition, it presents the methodological framework for exploring how the rules and principles comprising this regime could be operationalised under international law. Correspondingly, Chapter 4 proceeds by using the reparation standards from the law of state responsibility as a blueprint to examine their analogical application to NSAGs. This examination also considered international legal approaches to and debates on reparations provided by international organisations and individuals. Within the framework of this analysis, it proved essential to first grasp the distinct attributes that characterise NSAGs, especially in comparison to states, as well as those specifically relevant to the issue of reparation. First, the analysis finds that considerable differences can exist in the organisational capacity of NSAGs to provide reparations. This is found to be true between different NSAGs, and between NSAGS and states. As a result, the study argues that there is a need for abstract legal rules which can be applied generally. They should, at the same time, provide the necessary flexibility to effectively respond to such disparities, to ensure that the regulatory framework is realistic in practice. Second, there is a need to devise a mechanism that guarantees, to the greatest extent possible, the provision of redress to victims where an NSAG has limited or no capacity or is simply unwilling to grant reparations. The same holds for situations in which a group ceases to legally exist or when it is, for instance, no longer possible to identify the original group that is internationally responsible due to changing conflict dynamics. On this basis, the research finds that reparations cannot be solely dependent upon an NSAG. This argument is also reflected in certain international legal instruments and practice. Moreover, it manifests in legal scholarship and, similarly, in the reparations practices concerning other non-state actors. The preliminary suggestions for addressing these two main concerns are further developed based on current international law and practice. Ultimately, they form the basis of the book's multifaceted proposal as to how NSAGs' duty to provide reparation could be operationalised as part of a future regime of international responsibility.

Chapter 4 shows that a duty of NSAGs to provide reparation for internationally wrongful acts can be conceptualised in a manner similar to that of states under international law. Although an NSAG may face difficulties when making reparations, the study argues that this does not provide for a sufficient justification to exclude a responsible group from the well-established principle of full reparation. The research also demonstrates that it is possible to apply the five main forms of reparations listed in the UN Basic Principles and Guidelines to NSAGs. These include restitution, compensation, rehabilitation, satisfaction and guarantees of non-repetition. Thus, some of the main reparation rules and principles governing the international responsibility of states can be transposed to NSAGs without too many modifications. To exemplify, one such modification is the restriction which prevents a responsible entity from relying on internal law as justification for a failure to provide full reparation. The notion of internal law used in this principle can be reinterpreted as referring to the internal regulations of a transgressing NSAG.

In contrast to the law of state responsibility, Chapter 4 proposes embracing an actor-specific approach to the application of the reparation duty of a specific NSAG. This approach introduces flexibility into the abstract rules and principles governing such a duty, which allows responding to the particularities of a given case. In more specific terms, the approach does not entail that the responsible entity would dictate the quantum or quality of redress. The duty of reparation itself is still framed by the nature of the violation and the harm done, while paying little attention to the entity responsible for the wrongdoing. However, the approach entails that when applying this duty to an NSAG, a case-specific assessment is made of that group's level of organisation and resources. These elements are understood as important indicators of the group's organisational capacity to actually comply with the imposed duty of reparation. Ultimately, this assessment aims to determine the concrete scope of the group's duty regarding the forms of reparations it is required to grant, and the extent to which it will be engaged in the provision of the reparations measures. Hence, it results in a differentiated approach that responds to disparities in the organisational capacities of NSAGs. Moreover, it seeks to ensure that the reparation obligations imposed on a given NSAG are feasible in practice. Although the approach deviates from the law of state responsibility, it finds support in the legal regulation of NSAGs under the primary rules of international law. Similarly, considerations of capacity, feasibility and context take an important role.

The study proposes that, to the extent that an NSAG lacks the required capacity to comply with its duty of reparation, a cascading regime of responsibility for reparation should apply. This proposal draws from approaches taken in practice, some international law instruments and legal scholarship. Under this mechanism, the territorial state has a subsidiary responsibility to provide the required reparations for the wrongful acts of the NSAG, insofar as the group lacks capacity. Depending on the case at hand, this could generate a division of responsibility between the NSAG and the state, for instance when a group is able to contribute to but not fully provide the required reparations. In addition, the study suggests that the international community could take on a supplementary role, particularly in weak and resource scarce countries. The same subsidiary mechanism would be triggered when a responsible NSAG is unwilling to provide reparations. The main objective is to guarantee, to the greatest extent possible, the required redress for victims. The study's multifaceted proposal – composed of the actor-specific approach and the cascading regime – allows for the targeting of all types of NSAGs, not only those that resemble states or hold control over territory. This proposal is not just theoretical in nature, but also forms a framework that can be applied in practice, for example, in the work of truth commissions or in peace negotiations with NSAGs.

Chapter 4 also clarifies the question of at what point in time an NSAG might be called upon to provide reparations. Within this context, the study argues that it should be possible to invoke the international responsibility of an NSAG both during and after an armed conflict. Over the course of a conflict, it appears sensible to argue that an NSAG holds the duty to provide reparation for its own wrongful conduct. This follows from its existence as a distinct entity that has (limited) international legal personality. The actor-specific approach could certainly be applied. However, political and practical challenges could still complicate the provision of reparations by these entities. Concerning the provision of reparations by NSAGs during and at the end of an armed conflict, the study pays particular attention to exploring the possibility of engaging with NSAGs on reparations through voluntary mechanisms. In doing so, the notion of engagement is extended from its original purpose of enhancing compliance by NSAGs with their primary obligations under IHL, to the sphere of secondary norms, particularly reparations. The idea of engagement involves the establishment of meaningful contact with a group to facilitate exchanges on the question of reparation, with the overall aim of promoting its delivery. The study proposes that engagement can serve two distinct purposes: to make an NSAG voluntarily comply with its *lex ferenda* duty to repair or to involve a group in reparations regardless of any question of legal responsibility. The discussion contributes to scholarly debate and invites further reflection, including on the motives or behaviours that could be drivers for an NSAG to engage on reparations. The FARC-EP case forms a concrete example of the first form of engagement and concerns the involvement of a politically-motivated group in both the design and implementation of reparations measures and mechanisms.

In the aftermath of an armed conflict, the provision of reparations by an NSAG becomes more complicated if the group no longer exists as an entity in international law. However, the study's proposal entails that victims could still invoke the subsidiary responsibility of the state, based on the cascading regime of responsibility for reparation. This would provide a response to the vacuum left. In addition, the research suggests that the provision of post-conflict reparations by a legally defunct group should not be dismissed merely due to this legal challenge. Chapter 4 analyses how this could occur by way of three illustrative approaches. In doing so, the book explores an important issue which has remained largely unaddressed in present legal scholarship. The first approach focuses on the possibility of recovering assets for reparations purposes from former members and third parties, who were enriched by the activities of the NSAG. The second approach draws from the *Omagh bombing* case heard at the High Court of Justice of Northern Ireland. The case suggests that reparations could be claimed from a legally extinct NSAG that still factually exists, by way of representative proceedings against members of the group as an unincorporated association. The study argues that this could provide a tentative proposal for the enforcement of reparations at the domestic level. The final approach conceptualises a notion of representative authority of former members, a successor entity, or other actors, who could potentially provide reparations on behalf of a defunct group. Two additional points can be added to this discussion. First, Chapter 3 suggested that an NSAG which transforms into a political party at the end of an armed conflict could, at a minimum, inherit the legal consequences of the wrongful conduct of its predecessor. Hence, there would be a successor entity that could be called upon for reparations. However, Chapter 6, concerning the FARC-EP, revealed some of the challenges that may come along with such an approach in practice, such as the fragmentation of the successor party. Moreover, little support exists in state practice for the proposal. Second, Chapter 5 provided another example of how the temporary legal existence of an NSAG could be countered by holding the group responsible by way of its constituent members.

C.3 Concluding insights from reparations by non-state armed groups in Colombia

In the final part of the book, an in-depth analysis is carried out of the duty of NSAGs to provide reparation for wrongful conduct within the context of two transitional justice processes in Colombia: the Justice and Peace Law process and the Comprehensive System for Truth, Justice, Reparation and Non-Repetition. Although both processes were considered in the previous parts of the study, a comprehensive analysis was reserved for Chapter 5 and Chapter 6. The study reveals two insightful reparations processes that contribute, in an important manner, to the broader discussion on how a possible duty of NSAGs to repair could be conceptualised and put into practice under international law. Overall, the reparations processes in Colombia provide support for some of the main arguments formulated earlier in the study and deepen them by contextualising the discussion. At the same time, new and different perspectives are revealed, which invite further reflection. The Colombian case generally challenges the traditional view that reparations for victims of armed conflict are mainly a matter of state provision. Instead, the analysis encourages understanding NSAGs not only as perpetrators, but also as responsible actors that need to contribute to reparations in response to their wrongful conduct.

Part 3 identifies insights from reparations by NSAGs in Colombia that inform the international legal discussion on how their duty of reparation could be operationalised. It is important to recall in this regard that the purpose of the analysis was not to make normative claims on this basis. Still, some of these insights allow for more generalised conclusions that can be extended to other contexts. For example, the case affirms that reparations should not be made exclusively dependent on NSAGs, even if a group has considerable organisational capacity and resources. The emphasis is placed on the role of the state in guaranteeing reparations for victims. The case also demonstrates the significant role that an NSAG could take in the provision of symbolic reparations. This form of reparation could be provided early on in a justice process and contribute to creating a more favourable context for peacebuilding. Hence, this form of redress should not be overlooked when dealing with NSAGs, especially considering that they generally require less organisational capacity and can take an important role in a reparations process for victims.

At the same time, other findings are more tentative in nature. They constitute possible lessons or approaches that could inform discussions but are not necessarily feasible or adequate in respect of every NSAG or situation. For instance, while the emphasis in Colombia was placed on the contribution of the NSAGs to reparations by way of their wealth, such an approach may not be feasible regarding other groups that are poorly financed. Another example concerns the possibility of engaging a defunct NSAG in post-conflict reparations by way of a successor political party. This will depend on the contextual realities of a given case and the nature or motives of the concerned actor. Additionally, the research considered reparations by NSAGs within a specific situation, namely a sophisticated state-led transitional justice process as part of a negotiated settlement. As a legitimacy-seeking NSAG, the FARC-EP also showed, as a collective actor, willingness to provide reparations to the victims. Other contexts may be dictated by other realities, such as a complete collapse of the state, the defeat and elimination of the NSAG concerned, or the lack of political will. Thus, the extent to which a similar approach could be reproduced in another case is contingent on the specific context at hand. Overall, these examples underscore the need to take an actor- and context-specific approach to reparations by NSAGs due to inevitable differences between situations.

The study shows that the Colombian case is of considerable interest to the discussion on reparations by NSAGs under international law. This is the case, in the first instance, due to the minimal practice which exists on the matter. Moreover, both the Justice and Peace process and the Comprehensive System constitute notable instances of state practice, which recognise NSAGs' duties to provide reparation for violations of international law. Significantly, in the latter process, the government expressly considers the issue of reparation to be governed both domestically and internationally by the principle that all parties responsible for damages are obligated to repair them, including the FARC-EP.[3]

3 Mark Freeman and Iván Orozco, *Negotiating Transitional Justice: Firsthand Lessons from Colombia and Beyond* (Cambridge University Press 2020) 155.

Thus, the processes can add to the possible development of a relating norm of customary international law. Furthermore, the two transitional justice processes take, in some respects, different approaches to the operationalisation of the concerned NSAGs' duty to repair. The NSAGs themselves are also organisationally distinct. These differences enriched the analysis and the insights which can be drawn from it.

Despite the prominent place of NSAGs in Colombia's reparations processes, a different discourse, or even the absence of any discussions, can be noted in other contexts. As mentioned above, the duty of NSAGs to contribute to reparation is understood in Colombia as required by the law. However, as this study concludes, this is not a universally accepted view. Accordingly, the question of reparations by NSAGs may not be considered relevant in other contexts. Other factors may also play a role, including the lack of an NSAG's willingness to provide reparations and a state's refusal to directly engage with an NSAG so as not to confer legitimacy. From this perspective, it was, for example, considered unrealistic to expect that ISIS and the Iraqi government, respectively, would accept a direct role for the group in granting reparations to victims in Iraq. Nevertheless, other approaches to securing reparations from NSAGs could still be pursued in contexts where a counterterrorism-focused framework prevails and positive engagement might not be possible, such as the tracing and recovery of assets for the financing of reparations or restitution.[4] That said, it is wrong to assume that the FARC-EP was not considered a pariah in Colombian society and by the international community during several decades of brutal war. The peace agreement and the group's commitment to reparations were the culmination of a larger process within a transitional justice approach. Moreover, Colombia is not a stand-alone case. In Yemen, for example, UN experts and civil society have called on the *de facto* authority – the Ansar Allah (Houthi) armed group – to ensure reparations based on international law.[5]

The Colombian case sheds light on the importance of addressing the collective responsibility of NSAGs and their resulting duty of reparation. The study indicates that the NSAGs could not simply be reduced to their individual members when dealing with the collective violence perpetrated during the armed conflict. The analysis also reveals concrete advantages of or reasons for calling upon an NSAG to contribute to reparations in cases where there is, for instance, anonymous harm, insolvency on the part of group members, or the presence of a wealthy NSAG. In such circumstances, the responsibility of an

4 Clara Sandoval and Miriam Puttick, 'Reparations for the Victims of Conflict in Iraq: Lessons Learned for Comparative Practice' (Ceasefire Centre for Civilian Rights and Minority Rights Group International 2017) 24.

5 UNHRC, 'Report of the Detailed Findings of the Group of Eminent International and Regional Experts on Yemen' (3 September 2019) UN Doc A/HRC/42/CRP.1 paras 868, 930(f); Mwatana for Human Rights and Lowenstein International Human Rights Clinic Yale Law School, 'Returned to Zero: The Case for Reparations to Civilians in Yemen' (2022) 24–25, 138–143.

NSAG could also form a subsidiary mechanism to guarantee, at least to a greater extent, the satisfaction of victims' right to reparation for wrongs committed within the context of that entity. On a more fundamental level, the responsibility of NSAGs in the Colombian case fulfils an important accountability function that fits within the larger picture of the fight against impunity.

The analysis demonstrates that the potential concerns of states regarding the possibility of conferring some form of legitimacy on an NSAG, which may be even greater when it comes to reparation if seen as a measure reserved for states, are certainly not insurmountable.[6] From the perspective of NSAGs, the study shows that at least some groups may be willing to contribute to reparations and may have the organisational capacity to do so. Otherwise, it could still prove possible, depending on the specific circumstances, to, at a minimum, locate and seize the assets of an NSAG for reparations purposes.

The Colombian case deals with the responsibility of NSAGs that satisfy the application requirements of Additional Protocol II, which includes the requirement to exercise control over a part of a territory. As such, the case reinforces the tendency in international law to emphasise the possible international responsibility of NSAGs when they exercise territorial control during the course of an armed conflict.

Although the study deals with the responsibility of two NSAGs that were bound by the same primary rules of international law, they are, at the same time, marked by their distinct organisational structures. The FARC-EP was characterised by its centralised structure, whereas the AUC-linked paramilitary groups operated in a decentralised manner. Chapter 5 questions whether the AUC can be identified as a single NSAG which satisfied the IHL requirement of organisation. Regardless of this question, the approach taken in the Justice and Peace process allows for the separate treatment of the reparative duty of the different paramilitary blocks, as sub-structures of the AUC, which are themselves organised NSAGs. Simultaneously, the process maintains a recognition of the various groups' relation to the AUC. As a result, the concern regarding the AUC's actual status as a single entity did not present itself directly. Instead, the Justice and Peace approach appears to have accommodated a decentralised organisation. In contrast, Chapter 6 shows that the FARC-EP was called upon to contribute to reparations as a unified entity, which converges with the group's centralised organisational structure. Following from this discussion, the study suggests that the organisational structure of an NSAG could direct the way in which responsibility and the resulting duty of reparation could be attributed and operationalised. This novel finding warrants further examination.

The book shows that the responsibility of the NSAGs addressed in both the Justice and Peace process and the Comprehensive System is conceptualised in an analogous manner to the responsibility of states under international law. This is

6 Ron Dudai, 'Closing the Gap: Symbolic Reparations and Armed Groups' (2011) 93 International Review of the Red Cross 783, 793.

evident from the non-punitive character of the approach, and that it results in a duty to make reparation for the damages arising from wrongful conduct. Moreover, both processes appear to have followed the approach of the UN Basic Principles and Guidelines, regarding the five main forms of reparations, and which are normally requested from responsible states. Accordingly, they provide concrete examples of how NSAGs have been required to provide restitution, compensation, satisfaction and guarantees of non-repetition in a similar manner to states. Although the role of NSAGs in rehabilitation was not at issue, assets seized from a group could still be used to finance such services. The analysis of each process provides further insights into how some of these reparations forms could be operationalised in practice. For instance, the Justice and Peace process serves as a tentative proposal for how an NSAG could contribute to monetary compensation within a judicial process, while the FARC-EP case indicates the potential of NSAGs to provide collective and symbolic reparations. Nevertheless, other NSAGs operating in different contexts may not hold the organisational capacity to provide all, or some, of these forms of reparations. This reinforces the study's argument in favour of an actor-specific approach to their application. Overall, the case studies concretely illustrate how some of the international rules and principles governing reparation in respect of responsible states could be applied by analogy to NSAGs.

At the same time, the analysis stimulates reflection beyond a state-centric approach to reparations. Chapter 6 suggests that, when circumstances permit, reparations measures could take into account the potential for redress of an NSAG's collective efforts, abilities, and knowledge in certain areas. This is apparent in the concrete actions of contribution to reparations which include, among other measures, the engagement of the group in the search for the disappeared as a form of satisfaction. This approach could also involve requiring other measures from NSAGs beyond those that are non-exhaustively listed in the UN Basic Principles and Guidelines. Such measures could include humanitarian demining or infrastructure-rebuilding work performed with a reparatory goal in mind. Yet, the discussion stresses the importance of maintaining the legal concept of reparation in such cases. This concept should not be extended to every action that promotes some form of development.

Additionally, Part 3 demonstrates that the engagement of an NSAG in reparations is not necessarily without challenges. These may result from, for instance, the potential perpetuation of certain conflict and actor dynamics, the political nature of an NSAG, or the unwillingness of a group and its members to comply with their obligations. At the same time, the analysis suggests that the access of members of an NSAG to judicial benefits could be used as an incentive for the NSAG itself to comply with its obligations in respect of redress.

Both transitional justice processes deal, for a large part, with the duty of NSAGs to provide reparation in a post-conflict setting. This underscores the need for further legal research on the provision of post-conflict reparations by such entities. The book provides deeper insights into some of the aspects that are of relevance to this discussion, such as the use of tort law figures to construe and enforce the collective responsibility of a defunct NSAG, and the role of persons or entities with representative authority in post-conflict reparations. Regarding this last aspect, the analysis of the FARC-EP case is particularly insightful and offers a greater understanding as to how a successor entity, in the form of a political party that includes former high-level members, could provide reparations on behalf of an extinct NSAG.

The Colombian case strongly confirms that reparations cannot be reliant on NSAGs alone. Although the analysis illustrates that an NSAG can make important contributions to reparations, the case indicates that the territorial state should still guarantee the subsidiary satisfaction of victims' right to reparation when a group is unwilling or unable to do so. Consequently, both processes corroborate this book's proposal for a cascading regime of responsibility for reparation. The different perspective taken by the Justice and Peace Law adds to this discussion by showing that the responsibility of an NSAG could itself form an important subsidiary mechanism in such a scheme. In addition, the case study provides further insights into the possible relationships which could exist between the respective responsibilities of an NSAG and its individual members in terms of complementarity and interrelation.

Regarding the forum in which reparations by NSAGs could be provided, the analysis of the Colombian case provides two distinct examples. On the one hand, the examination of the Justice and Peace process offers insights into how judicial reparations could be claimed from an NSAG within the context of criminal justice proceedings and related challenges. On the other hand, the FARC-EP case is an example of how an NSAG could deliver predominantly collective, instead of individualised, reparations earlier on in a process through extra-judicial measures and mechanisms which are part of a comprehensive transitional justice system. However, in this process, the discussion notes that victims are not given the possibility to exercise their right to obtain reparation from the NSAG before a mandated body. Finally, the study suggests that certain forms of reparations, such as symbolic reparations and guarantees of non-repetition, could already be provided during peace negotiations or the demobilisation process of an NSAG.

C.4 Final remarks

Accountability and the fight against impunity are high on the international agenda. Moreover, concerns for the victims of armed conflict are increasingly being heard. Nonetheless, there is a general reluctance to address the responsibility of NSAGs for conflict-related violations as opposed to that of individual members of NSAGs under international criminal law. Despite the prevalence of NIACs, the question concerning NSAGs' duty to make reparation for the harmful consequences of their wrongful acts remains marked by controversy in the international legal system. The ambivalent attitude of states constitutes one of the principal obstacles for establishing a regime of responsibility of NSAGs in current international law, which could potentially include a duty of reparation. The potential of conferring any measure of legitimacy or recognition constitutes one of the main concerns in this regard. Given the controversial character of NSAGs, such concerns will most likely continue to restrict any attempt to establish a responsibility regime in respect of NSAGs.

Nonetheless, the recent transitional justice process with the FARC-EP in Colombia has certain potential to shift such perspectives. The process has attracted considerable attention and support of the international community and has even been hailed as an example for future processes in other contexts. The book shows that a crucial aspect of this process is the collective role of the FARC-EP in the reparations scheme as a responsible actor. This prominent case of state practice could encourage other states and international actors to pay greater attention to the role of NSAGs in reparations in their respective conflict resolution and transitional justice policies. This case debunks assumptions of reparations by NSAGs as simply unrealistic or unwanted, while informing policymakers about the concrete ways in which an NSAG could contribute to a reparations process in other situations based on international law standards. Importantly, it shows that the responsibility of NSAGs is not about extending legitimacy or recognition, but rather about taking NSAGs seriously as wrongdoers. In addition, the research identifies some recent examples of UN practice which go in this direction, and which could leave a further mark on states' views and practice due to their authoritative character. Such policy shifts would ultimately inform states' approaches to peace negotiations and the design and implementation of reparations strategies.

That said, it appears too optimistic to argue that such efforts have the potential to elicit international legal developments through the practice of states in the near future. Instead, there might be more merit in recognising that the issue has the potential to become one of the new frontiers in legal and transitional justice scholarship, international practice and human rights advocacy.[7] This could open the door to an exercise concerned with the progressive development of international law, which would be oriented towards developing this new type of responsibility for NSAGs. Such an exercise could take the form of an initiative geared at drafting legal rules and soft law principles which could benefit from a broad participatory process involving key stakeholders.

7 Elizabeth Salmón and Juan-Pablo Pérez-León-Acevedo, 'Reparation for Victims of Serious Violations of International Humanitarian Law: New Developments' (2022) 104 International Review of the Red Cross 1315, 1317.

Annex 1 List of Interviews

Interviewee	*Reference*
Justice and Peace Magistrate	Interview No 1 (Colombia, February 2019).
Former Justice and Peace Magistrate	Interview No 2 (Skype Interview, March 2019).
Justice and Peace Magistrate	Interview No 3 (Colombia, April 2019).
Reparations expert of the National Center for Historical Memory	Interview No 4 (Colombia, February 2019).
Former Director of the Unit for the Attention and Integral Reparation to the Victims	Interview No 5 (Colombia, February 2019).
Official of the Special Jurisdiction for Peace	Interview No 6 (Colombia, April 2019).
Official of the Agency for Reincorporation and Normalization	Interview No 7 (Colombia, March 2019).
Advisor of the political party *Comunes* (formerly FARC)	Interview No 8 (Colombia, February 2019).
Delegate of the CSIVI-*Comunes* (formerly FARC)	Interview No 9 (Colombia, April 2019).
Former FARC-EP member	Interview No 10 (Colombia, March 2019).
Two former FARC-EP members	Group Interview No 11 (Colombia, March 2019).
Former FARC-EP member	Interview No 12 (Phone Interview, March 2019).
Former FARC-EP member	Interview No 13 (Colombia, March 2019).
Two former FARC-EP members	Group Interview No 14 (Colombia, March 2019).
Former FARC-EP member	Interview No 15 (Colombia, March 2019).
Former FARC-EP member	Interview No 16 (Colombia, March 2019).
Former FARC-EP member	Interview No 17 (Colombia, March 2019).
Head of a victims' organisation	Interview No 18 (Colombia, March 2019).
Head of a victims' organisation	Interview No 19 (Colombia, March 2019).
Victim representative, Bertha Lucía Fries	Interview No 20 (Skype Interview, May 2019).
In-house NGO lawyer	Interview No 21 (Colombia, February 2019).
NGO researcher	Interview No 22 (Colombia, March 2019).
UN Official	Interview No 23 (Colombia, February 2019).

Index

Note: Page numbers followed by 'n' refer to notes.

accountability 11, 51, 55, 65, 112, 203, 254, 263; framework 4, 14; of NSAGs 64
actor-specific approach 143–149, 175, 232, 256, 257, 262
Additional Protocol II to the Geneva Conventions 27–33, 35, 36, 38, 39, 41, 43, 56, 57, 78, 111, 119, 147, 187, 190, 191, 223, 253, 261
Additional Protocol I to the Geneva Conventions: article 91 of 58
ad hoc international obligations 75
administrative reparations programme 97, 151, 184, 204, 205, 214, 217, 220, 246
African National Congress (ANC) 137, 153, 173
Ago, Roberto 57, 73, 75, 99, 111, 112n22
Agreement on Accountability and Reconciliation 83
Agreement on Truth, Forgiveness and Reconciliation 228
Ahlborn, Christiane 115n39
Alien Tort Claims Act (ATCA) 80–81
American Civil War 71, 77
analogical reasoning 116
Appeals Chamber of the Sierra Leone Special Court 30
armed conflicts 1, 221–225, 261, 263; during and after 154–175; internal 34; international 1, 59, 71, 224; post 225–231; regulating 67–69
Armed Forces for the National Liberation of East Timor (FALINTIL) 172
armed non-State actors (ANSAs) 93, 94
armed violence 1, 2, 9, 17, 28, 115, 211, 212, 214
Article 1(1) of Additional Protocol II 31–32, 38, 57, 187
Article 1 Additional Protocol II 223
Article 5(3) Justice and Peace Law 199
Article 6 Justice and Peace Law 203
Art 8(1) ICC Statute 118n51
Article 9 ARS 110
Article 9.2 of the Agreement 84
Article 10 ARS 110–114
Article 10 of the Victims' Law 201
Article 10.2 of the Justice and Peace Law 192, 201
Article 13 of Decree No. 128 182
Article 25 of the Rome Statute 129
Articles 31 and 34 of the ARS and ARIO 147
Articles 34–36 VCLT 35
Article 32 ARS 149
Article 37(3) ARS 152
Article 42(2) Justice and Peace Law 199
Article 42(2) of the Justice and Peace Law 199
Article 54(2) of the Justice and Peace Law 192
Article 58 ARS 133
Articles on the Responsibility of International Organizations (ARIO) 54, 139, 140
Articles on the Responsibly of States for Internationally Wrongful Acts (ARS) 53, 57, 58, 77, 133, 148
Arusha Peace and Reconciliation Agreement 85
Autodefensas Unidas de Colombia (AUC) 166, 171, 182, 197, 198, 206, 232, 261; under the Justice and Peace Law 188–191

Bassiouni, M Cherif 87, 87n182
Belfast Agreement 1998 165

Belfast Guidelines on Reparations in Post-Conflict Societies 101
Bellal, Annyssa 7, 66, 67, 156
belligerency: laws of insurgency and 70–79, 103; recognition of 32, 33
Bílkova, Veronika 68
Blázquez Rodríguez, Paloma 8, 62

Capone, Francesca 5
Carrascal, Wilson Salazar 185
case-by-case assessments 47
Cassese, Antonio 35
Castaño, Carlos 188
Chicago Principles on Post-Conflict Justice 99
civil resistance movement 188
civil society organisation 173
Clapham, Andrew 26, 49
Colectivo Nacional de Desmovilizados AUC 166
collective criminality 119
collective criminal responsibility 122–131, 252
collective demobilisation process 182, 183, 185, 192
collective political identity 226
collective reincorporation process 226, 227
collective responsibility 10, 17, 49, 56, 65, 82, 94, 95, 122, 123, 132, 170, 172, 174, 205, 216, 218, 220, 224, 229, 234–236, 260, 263
Colombian Constitutional Court 180
Colombian legal tradition 197
Colombian national law 186, 223
Colombian Truth Commission 98, 211
Commission of Inquiry on Libya 45, 95
Committee on the Elimination of Discrimination against Women 45
Common Article 3 27–33, 35–38, 41, 43, 57, 78, 80, 111, 115, 144, 147, 190, 219, 223; of the First Geneva Convention 79; of the Geneva Conventions 31, 81
Common Article 3(1)(d) 36
complementary transitional justice scheme 183
Comprehensive Agreement on Human Rights 83
Comprehensive System 211–217, 219, 220, 228, 231, 234, 242, 244–247, 249, 258, 259, 261
comprehensive transitional justice system 211–215, 247, 248, 263
Comunes 225, 227, 230, 231, 233
Conferencia Episcopal Colombiana 236
Convention on the Prevention and Punishment of the Crime of Genocide 133
counter-terrorism legislation 159
'crimes of obedience' 119
criminal liability 61, 139, 196
criminal litigation 204
criminal responsibility of group members 117–121
customary international law 34, 80, 90, 91
customary law theory 34

Daboné, Zakaria 7, 103
Dam-de Jong, Daniëlla 86n175
D'Aspremont, Jean 25
Deed for the Protection of Children 158
Deed of Commitment 152, 158
de facto governance 42
degree of organisational continuity 226
"degree of realism" 39
de lege ferenda perspective 16, 103, 117, 156, 175
demobilisation, disarmament and reintegration (DDR) 181, 231, 238
Democratic Republic of Congo 154
Dempster, Lauren 241
Doe v Islamic Salvation Front 81
domestic jurisdictions 79–86
domestic law 79, 82, 138, 164
domestic legal systems 53
Dudai, Ron 7, 87, 137, 146, 151, 152, 156, 165

El Mozote case 172
Estado Mayor Conjunto 188
ETCRs 227, 238, 242–244

federal class-action civil lawsuit 130
federal criminal organisation 189
Ferstman 143
Final Peace Agreement (FPA) 16, 85, 213
Forces Patriotiques pour la Libération du Congo (FPLC) 63
Fortin, Katharine 36, 41, 73
Francioni, Francesco 86
Frenkel, Brian 103, 169, 173
Frente Farabundo Martí para la Liberación Nacional (FMLN) 167
Fries, Bertha Lucía 228, 229
Fuerzas Armadas Revolucionarias de Colombia – Ejército del Pueblo (FARC-EP) 16, 150, 212, 215–219, 248, 264; engagement of 234–248; political transformation of 225–227; as responsible actor 221–233
Fund for the Reparation of the Victims 191

Geneva Conventions 27, 37; Additional Protocol II to the 27–33, 35, 36, 38, 39, 41, 43, 56, 57, 78, 111, 119, 147, 187, 190, 191, 223, 253, 261; Additional Protocol I to the 58; Common Article 3 of the 31, 81
Goldstone Commission 95n221
Gómez Isa, Felipe 208
Green, Fergus 26
Guatemalan Commission for Historical Clarification 98, 167
Gusmão, Xanana 172

Hamilton, V Lee 119
health centre 206–208
Heffes, Ezequiel 103, 169, 173
High Contracting Parties 28
Humanicemos DH 240
humanitarian demining 239–241
human rights: law 2, 40–42, 44–48, 142, 217; obligations 43; regime 40
Human Rights Council 64

ICRC Commentary to Common Article 3 2020 30, 56
ILA Committee on Non-State Actors 100, 101
ILC Articles on the Responsibility of States 108–114
ILC Commentary to Article 14(3) 77
ILC Commentary to Article 34 ARS 149
ILC Special Rapporteur Ago 111
illegal armed groups 154
Independent International Commission of Inquiry on the Syrian Arab Republic 96
individual administrative reparations programme 184
individual criminal responsibility 117–130, 134; collective criminal responsibility of non-state armed groups 122–130; criminal responsibility of group members 117–121; new *sui generis* regime 130–134
individual demobilisation processes 182
Íñigo Álvarez, Laura 7
Institute of International Law 73
insurgency, general legal frameworks of 70–71
insurrectional movement 57, 78, 110
Inter-American Commission on Human Rights 30, 64
Inter-American Court of Human Rights 2, 214
internal armed conflicts 34
international armed conflicts 1, 59, 71, 224
International Commission of Inquiry on Darfur 34, 95, 104, 129, 134, 150
International Commission of Inquiry on Libya 95
International Committee of the Red Cross (ICRC) 1, 57, 242
international community 34
International Court of Justice 24–25, 39, 133, 147
international crimes 34
international criminal court 2, 54, 61, 62, 122, 127–129, 139, 140, 204; and tribunals 124–130
international criminal jurisdiction 127
international criminal justice 121
international criminal law (ICL) 10, 52, 61–63, 121, 124–126, 129–131, 189, 252, 263
international criminal norms 129
International Criminal Tribunal for Rwanda (ICTR) 117
International Criminal Tribunal for the former Yugoslavia (ICTY) 28, 126
international criminal tribunals 126–127
international expert documents 99–101
international humanitarian law (IHL) 3, 16, 27–44, 48, 49, 55–60, 64, 65, 82, 84, 86, 87, 95–97, 114, 121, 122, 129, 144, 155, 156, 158, 180, 189, 190, 200, 216, 218, 251, 253, 254
international human rights law (IHRL) 16, 40–49, 60–61, 64, 65, 82, 84, 86, 87, 89, 95–97, 114, 121, 129, 144, 180, 200, 216, 218, 251, 252, 254
international law 1–4, 6, 7, 11–16, 22, 23, 28, 33, 34, 39, 49, 55–57, 79, 117, 138, 145, 152, 166, 168, 231, 250–254, 256; fundamental principle of 52–55; non-state armed groups under 202–205; obligations 54; regulating armed conflict 67–69; relevance for 174–175; reparation under 254–258; violations 80, 84
International Law Association (ILA) Declaration of International Law Principles on Reparation for Victims of Armed Conflict 100
International Law Commission (ILC) 53, 57, 77
international legal analysis 16
international legal developments 55
international legal framework 49, 138
international legal order 23

international legal personality 22–26, 28, 34, 37–40, 49, 168, 251
international legal scholarship 174
international legal system 2, 4, 14, 22, 49, 54, 58, 123, 252, 263
International Military Tribunal (IMT) 125–126
international obligation 53
international responsibility 11
international trust fund 142
inter-state mechanisms 2
Irish Republican Army (IRA) 137, 153
Islamic Salvation Front (FIS) 81
Islamic Salvation Front II 81

Jo, Hyeran 9n50
Justice and Peace Law 5, 16, 17, 79, 82, 179–185, 203, 208–210, 212, 213, 217, 232, 238, 247, 249, 254, 258, 259, 261–263; AUC under 188–191; *raison d'être* of 185–186

Kelman, Herbert C 119
Klabbers, Jan 24, 25
Kleffner, Jann K 35, 67, 115, 119, 146, 152
Klinghoffer v S.N.C. Achille Lauro case 80

La Fundación Aulas de Paz 171
Lauterpacht, Hersch 26, 133
La Violencia 221
law of belligerency 71–73
law of insurgency 73–76
law of international responsibility 147
law of state responsibility 108, 109, 114–117, 131, 134, 135, 139, 144, 255, 256
Lawther, Cheryl 7
legal reasoning 114
legal responsibility framework 68
legislative jurisdiction theory 35, 36
Linder v Portocarrero case 79
Lomé Peace Agreement 83
Lord's Resistance Army (LRA) 83

mass victimisation 136
Mastorodimos, Konstantinos 6
material reparations, collective goods and assets for 244–246
McCarthy, Connor 62
McEvoy, Kieran 7, 156
Mégret, Frédéric 145
'modest and cautious' approach 88
modus operandi 9
Moffett, Luke 5, 7, 8, 87, 137, 146, 164
Mohamad v Palestinian Authority and Palestinian Liberation Organization of 2012 81
monetary compensation 150, 202–203; anonymous harm 198–200; C-370/06 194–198; collective duty 191–194; Fund for the Reparation of the Victims 200–202; non-state armed groups under international law 202–205; responsibility for 203–204
Monitoring and Reporting Mechanism (MRM) 65
Moro Islamic Liberation Front (MILF) 84

Nairobi Declaration on Women's and Girl's Right to a Remedy and Reparation 100
National Committee for the Search of Disappeared Persons 242
National Institute of Legal Medicine 242
national judicial system 79
National Liberation Army (ELN) 150
national reconciliation governments 113
National Transitional Council 95
New People's Army (NPA) 159
new *sui generis* regime 130–134
Nicaraguan civil war 79
NMRD 34
Nollkaemper, Andre 118
non-international armed conflict (NIAC) 1, 9, 13, 15, 17, 27–34, 36, 37, 39, 41, 43, 48, 49, 155, 187, 200, 224, 251
non-state actors 22, 99, 100n251; international legal personality of 22–26
non-state armed groups (NSAGs) 1–11, 13–17, 21, 27–40, 50–51, 63–67, 83–86, 93, 96, 107, 155, 203–206, 210, 220, 229, 232, 233, 243, 247, 249–258; actor-specific approach 143–147; during and after armed conflict 154–175; collective criminal responsibility 122–130; in current international law 76–79; as duty bearers 42–44; engagement regarding reparations 246–248; forms of reparations 149–154; individual criminal responsibility 117–130; international humanitarian law 27–40; international human rights law 40–48; under international law 202–205; international legal personality of non-state actors 22–26; international responsibility for 52–69, 130–134, 220–221; law of state responsibility 108–117; new *sui*

generis regime of international responsibility 130–134; principle of full reparation 147–149; recognition 69–101; regime of responsibility for reparation 138–143; reparations 71–79, 135–138, 258–263; as responsible actors 165–168, 191, 232–233; solidarity civil responsibility of 196–198
Nuremberg International Military Tribunal (IMT) 124
Nuremberg model 126

Omagh bombing case 163, 164, 258
Order 15 Rule 12 of the Rules of the Supreme Court 163
organisational competence 38
organised armed groups 186–187

Palestinian Liberation Organization (PLO) 80
'patterns of macro-criminality' 186
Pellet, Alain 252
Permanent Court of International Justice 138, 147
political-military organisation 222
post armed conflict 225–231
post-conflict reparations 155, 160, 161, 168, 174, 176, 257, 262; actors with representative authority 165–175; asset tracing and recovery for reparations purposes 161–162; representation order in civil proceedings 162–165
principle of full reparation 147–149
public international law 22

Real Irish Republican Army (Real IRA) 82
rehabilitation programmes 151–152, 161
Rendón Herrera, Fredy 208
Reparation for Injuries Suffered in the Service of the United Nations 24
reparations 12–13; comprehensive transitional justice system with 212–215; contribution to 236–244; forms of 149–154; fund 162; guarantees of non-repetition 208–209; under international law 254–258; non-repetition, satisfaction and guarantees of 209; by non-state armed groups in Colombia 258–263; regime of responsibility for 138–143; responsibility and 215–221; satisfaction 205–208
Reparations Fund 199, 200, 207
"resources for war" 245
responsibility 10–11
Revolutionary Armed Forces of Colombia – People's Army *see Fuerzas Armadas Revolucionarias de Colombia – Ejército del Pueblo* (FARC-EP)
revolutionary guerrilla movement 222
Rodenhäuser, Tilman 28, 46n149, 190
Roht-Arriaza, Naomi 148
Rome Statute of the International Criminal Court 117, 133
Ronzitti, Natalino 86
Rousseau, Charles 74n114, 75
rule of law 51, 67, 68, 100, 216
Rwanda 126–127

Sassòli, Marco 38, 40, 48
Schmalenbach, Kirsten 21, 86
Sierra Leone Truth and Reconciliation Commission 98, 151
Sinn Féin 173
Sivakumaran, Sandesh 38
Skyweyiya Commission 173
socio-political realities 161
solidarity civil responsibility 82, 180, 195, 196–198
Spanish Civil War 74
Special Jurisdiction for Peace 237, 241, 244
state armed groups 83–86
state practice 79–86
Statute of the International Criminal Court 127
'subject of international law' 22
sui generis rules 116
Syrian Democratic Forces 150
system criminality 118, 119

Taylor, Charles 162
term paramilitary group 9
theory of legislative jurisdiction 37
Thompson, Janna 170
TOAR 237
Tomuschat, Christian 152
Torture Victims Protection Act (TVPA) 80
traditional international law 14
traditional modes of liability 120
traditional public international law 22
'transitional apology' 170
transitional justice 174; approach 260; mechanisms 247; process 209, 244, 247, 253, 260, 262, 264; system 213, 232, 247
Trial Chamber of the ICTY 130
Trindade, Cançado 53
Trust Fund 63, 140

Trust Fund for Victims 140
Truth Commission 99, 166, 172, 211, 218, 234, 236
truth commissions 97–99

UN Assistance Mission in Afghanistan (UNAMA) 92
UN Basic Principles and Guidelines on the Right to a Remedy and Reparation 2, 12, 54, 84, 86–91, 99, 102, 103, 141, 148, 184, 196, 215, 217, 241, 247, 253, 256, 262
UN Commission on Human Rights 92
UN Group of Eminent International and Regional Experts on Yemen 31
UN High Commissioner for Human Rights on the Occupied Palestinian Territories 45
UN Human Rights Council 93, 150
UN human rights machinery 63
UN Office of the High Commissioner for Human Rights (UNOHCHR) 92
UN practice 91–97
UN Security Council 8n45, 64, 65, 92, 95
US Alien Tort Statute 130

van Boven, Theo 87, 90
Velásquez Rodríguez v. Honduras 2
Victims' Law of 2011 184, 196, 214
Vienna Convention on the Law of Treaties (VCLT) 35

War Reparations Fund 162
Whiteman, Marjorie M 72

Yugoslavia 126–127

Zegveld, Liesbeth 5, 35, 36, 146